Learning to Be Old

PRAISE FOR PREVIOUS EDITIONS

"One of [the book's] strengths is its weaving of themes from different fields and disciplines. . . . Another is in presentation—it is informative, lively, and well researched."—*Journal of Women & Aging*

"The major contribution may be her analysis of the potential negative effects of women's family roles and her suspicion that grandmothers are being exploited. This book . . . raises a number of important questions." —*Journal of Marriage and Family*

"In her excellent book, *Learning to Be Old*, Margaret Cruikshank compares the aged to a 'colonized people,' suggesting that ageism goes beyond de-humanization into actual scapegoating of the old."—*The New York Times*

"This text is such a gem that it is tempting to quote from it non-stop." —*Canadian Women's Studies*

"*Learning to Be Old* is a nice text for both the graduate and undergraduate levels, either in courses on the sociology of aging or in women's studies courses to provide a feminist perspective on aging."—*The Gerontologist*

"Compressing a significant amount of important information on issues of race, gender, social class, economics, and ethnicity, Cruikshank has created a readable book on the general theme of gerontology. The current research, theories, and practices outlined by Cruikshank will give readers of all ages insights into 'learning to be old.' An extensive bibliography is provided for further study. Essential."—*CHOICE*

"Sheds light on a particular bias inherent in studying this country's bur-geoning aging population and asks why unlike gender, race, and sexual orientation—identities that have been reinterpreted as socially constructed phenomena—aging is still seen through physically constructed lenses." —*Tucson Weekly*

"A valuable book on aging. Scholarly and well-documented."—*The Senior Times*

Learning to Be Old

Gender, Culture, and Aging

Third Edition

Margaret Cruikshank

ROWMAN & LITTLEFIELD PUBLISHERS, INC.
Lanham • Boulder • New York • Toronto • Plymouth, UK

Published by Rowman & Littlefield Publishers, Inc.
A wholly owned subsidiary of The Rowman & Littlefield Publishing Group, Inc.
4501 Forbes Boulevard, Suite 200, Lanham, Maryland 20706
www.rowman.com

10 Thornbury Road, Plymouth PL6 7PP, United Kingdom

British Library Cataloguing in Publication Information Available

Library of Congress Cataloging-in-Publication Data
Cruikshank, Margaret.
   Learning to be old : gender, culture, and aging / Margaret Cruikshank. — 3rd
ed.
      p. ; cm.
   Includes bibliographical references and index.
   ISBN 978-1-4422-1364-7 (cloth : alk. paper) — ISBN 978-1-4422-1365-4 (pbk. :
alk. paper) — ISBN 978-1-4422-1366-1 (electronic)
   I. Title.
   [DNLM: 1. Aging—psychology—United States. 2. Aged—United States.
3. Aging—physiology—United States. 4. Sex Factors—United States. 5. Social
Values—United States. 6. Socioeconomic Factors—United States. WT 145]

   305.26—dc23
                                                                    2012043505

∞™ The paper used in this publication meets the minimum requirements of
American National Standard for Information Sciences—Permanence of Paper
for Printed Library Materials, ANSI/NISO Z39.48-1992.

Printed in the United States of America

For Donna

Contents

Preface

Perhaps, with full life-spans the norm, people may need to learn how to be aged as they once had to learn to be adult.

—Ronald Blythe, *The View in Winter*

Two ideas run through this book. The first is that aging in North America is shaped more by culture than biology, more by beliefs, customs, and traditions than by bodily changes. In other words, it is socially constructed. The second is that awareness of social constructions and resistance to them is crucial for women's comfortable aging.

Nevertheless, our aging bodies matter greatly. No matter how clearly we understand the complex and interconnecting forces of social aging, we age in our individual bodies.

Sometimes chronological age holds great significance and sometimes it does not.

Accepting this fact is an important part of learning to be old. Equally important is a willingness to imagine what aging would be like if we could free ourselves, even partially, from negative beliefs about it and if social policy favored healthy aging.[1]

My title has two meanings. First, aging in contemporary North America is so multidimensional that studying it is worthwhile, even necessary, for those who wish to do it consciously and without fear. Second, "learning to be old" means unlearning much of what we think is true. The misconceptions about aging—that decline and loss are its central features, for example—will have less power to limit our experience if we can examine them critically. Entering the third (or fourth) stage of life with no preparation or forethought would perhaps not be dangerous in a society organized for the well-being of its oldest members. In our market economy, however, mindless aging leaves us vulnerable to many forms of exploitation. This is especially true for women.

Learning to Be Old falls somewhere in the large space between practical guides to aging and theoretical work. I have attempted to bring together matters usually treated separately: health, politics, the humanities, feminist gerontology, and cultural analysis. At the same time, I have not taken up except in passing some topics important to women's aging such as housing, transportation, Medicare, and nursing homes.

My motive for writing this book is the belief that neither women's studies nor gerontology has come to grips with the fact that "old" means "women." *Learning to Be Old* is but one response to the remarkable and unremarkable longevity of women.

Women's aging is like the Chinese ideogram that means both danger and opportunity.

I agree with British philosopher Helen Small: "One of the problems with and for old age is that, while there has been too little serious thinking about it over the years, there have been quite enough pronouncements" (*The Long Life*, 265). *Learning to Be Old* modestly offers serious thinking about late life.

As in the second edition, the phrase "the elderly" is no longer used because it suggests a uniform group, counter to the book's assumption that elderly persons are extremely diverse.

In the third edition, the last two chapters are reorganized: humanistic gerontology and critical gerontology are now in chapter 9, with a new title, "Countercultural Gerontology." New material has been added on Alzheimer's disease, the brain, mind-body connections, narrative gerontology, and the feminist concept of intersectionality. Research published since 2010 has been summarized throughout.

Earlier, I referred to "natural aging" as if that were a self-evident contrast to drugged aging, irrational fear of an aging population, or acceptance of the paradigm of loss for old age. Now it seems that whatever appears natural about aging may also be socially constructed. To age naturally, would I not have to avoid not only Botox but moisturizing creams, vitamins, immune system boosters such as cranberry or blueberry juice, and physical therapy, and are not these aids emblems of a particular time and culture? If our grandparents at fifty were encumbered by the stiffness and joint pain that some do not today experience until their seventies or eighties, whose aging is more natural?

Geropsychiatrist Gene Cohen wrote that "with age can come a new feeling of inner freedom, self-confidence, and liberation from social constraints that allows for novel or bold behavior" ("Creativity," 195). This may be especially true for women.

Acknowledgments

For their work on the third edition I thank Sarah Stanton and her assistant, Jin Yu, and Jehanne Schweitzer.

Gerontologist friends whose work informs my own include Mary O'Brien Tyrrell, Elizabeth Johns, and Pamela Gravagne.

I thank the Collegeville Institute for Ecumenical and Cultural Research, St. John's University, for the opportunity to be a short-term scholar. Carla Durand of the Institute was particularly helpful, as was the staff of Alcuin Library at St. John's.

I am grateful as well to the interlibrary loan staff and reference librarians of Fogler Library, University of Maine, especially Nancy Lewis. I thank the University of Maine Center on Aging for its excellent conferences and for naming me a faculty associate.

Particular friends in their nineties, Mary Lou Hill of Minneapolis, Betsy Presley of Duluth, and Hannelore Eck of Kalamazoo inspire me. A friend nearly ninety, Ruth Moss, of Sorrento, Maine, doyenne of the Democratic Party of Hancock County Maine, impresses me by her energy. The late Norma Canner of Boston, my summer neighbor, modeled vibrant aging for me. The late Jane Emery encouraged my writing for many years.

I owe the greatest thanks to my partner, Donna Murphy.

Margaret Cruikshank
Corea, Maine

Introduction

In this book I propose alternatives to the ways aging is usually understood in both popular culture and mainstream gerontology. Although my chief concern is women's aging, I try to place it in a broad context, considering issues that may also affect men. Because of age denial, it is hard to see how common beliefs limit our perceptions of the aging process. Customarily we think of aging as something that happens in our individual bodies—slowly, imperceptibly, inevitably. Learning to be old means fully experiencing the physical, bodily changes that accompany aging while at the same time recognizing that those changes occur in a particular social setting, influenced by our ethnicity, class, and gender, and by the political and economic climate. It is also shaped by developments such as the burgeoning population of elders. Our condition in old age is largely determined by forces over which we have no control, although it is also partly determined by heredity and by our earlier life choices and habits.

I believe that the survival of large numbers of old women is a desirable demographic change. It may help to balance the bland and homogenizing tendencies of globalization, for example. Instead of fearing that a tidal wave of elders will engulf our society, I note that declining fertility makes population aging possible. Usually this decline is associated with improvements in women's lives and is therefore deemed beneficial. From a woman's perspective, aging may have unforeseen dimensions. But the potential created by longevity will not be realized until conventional views of aging are set aside.

The vigor with which feminists have challenged notions of biological determinism leaves us in an awkward position with aging because this process happens in/to our bodies. The spin of social construction offers non-deterministic ways to view aging, but for nearly everyone, aging means some bodily decline. For many of our mothers and grandmothers, a common interpretation of aging was, "We fall apart and there's nothing to be done about it." For many today this attitude still holds true. An alternative is to say, yes, some loss is likely—but what else defines my aging? *Learning to Be Old* attempts to answer this question.

To the extent that we are conditioned to view aging through these paradigms, we must "learn" to be old. It is not just a natural process like breathing but something we are initiated into, and we learn to be old partly in response to the ways we are treated. The other meaning of "learning to be old," however, is acquiring the knowledge that aging is a creation of this time and place, more cultural than biological, determined by social institutions, or, more optimistically, a set of life experiences we can consciously shape, once we see how others are attempting to shape them for us. Thus learning to be old requires that we both observe how aging is socially constructed and find ways to resist being molded to its dictates. As Margaret Gullette writes, the single concept "aging" "covers and confuses socially produced diseases (caused by pollution, poverty, and hazardous work) that take years to show themselves . . . [and] when all the external forces are accounted for, little may remain to constitute biological age processes" ("Age, Aging," 10).

Philosopher Helen Small believes that "evolutionary theory removes any basis in nature for claiming that old age has a purpose, or is part of a design for our lives" (271). Thus the meaning of late life comes from ourselves. Surrendering the idea of an over-arching purpose for old age is not easy.

A popular idea, for example, "successful aging," is now circulating in the media and among gerontologists—for example, in the report of a ten-year aging study by the MacArthur Foundation, edited by John W. Rowe and Robert L. Kahn and titled *Successful Aging*. The authors challenge the disease model of aging and offer many insights into late-life potential. When "success" is proposed as an aging model, however, a business and competitive standard is used to measure a complex human process, and a white, male, middle-class professional outlook is taken for granted. While business success can be measured by profits, aging well has no such definitive marker. Athletes succeed by winning competitions, a framework unsuitable for aging. "Successful aging" overlooks the very important role class plays in determining not only how healthy we are in old age but even whether we get to be old. The phrase is prescriptive. Our physical health may be rated good or bad, but it is intertwined with our psychological health and depends on factors that may be elusive, changing, or knowable only by intuition. Research in a positivist spirit will not grasp them. A poor and sick old woman ages unsuccessfully by material yardsticks, but suppose she raises two grandchildren and helps out a neighbor who is older and sicker than she is. Does this constitute "success"?

Another problem with "successful aging" and its counterpart, "productive aging," is its implication that aging depends mostly on our own efforts. Throughout their book, for example, Rowe and Kahn state that we are responsible for our aging. Even for affluent and powerful men, this is manifestly untrue. This belief about aging is a cultural artifact, a small stone bearing the inscription "rugged individualism." That is, successful aging "seriously underestimates the extent to which human beings are social and political agents, presenting them as unrealistically isolated masters of their own destinies" (Jolanki, 263).

The success model overlooks the elements of luck and mystery in aging. Recommendations for social engagement in late life overlook barriers such as poor health, heavy caregiving responsibilities, and the ways choice is limited by inequalities in class and gender (Rozanova, Keating, and Eales, 26–32). Moreover, care work itself should be considered a form of social engagement (Netting, 244).

Although personal responsibility undeniably plays some role, being white and middle class are powerful predictors of the late-life health and well-being of Americans. No amount of individual effort or sturdy self-reliance can gain for working-class people or people of color the advantages enjoyed by the white middle class, especially by men. Working-class people and people of color can obviously make healthy choices that narrow somewhat the gap between themselves and the more favored old. But the often substantial differences in aging created by ethnicity, class, and gender are covered up by the falsely universalizing phrase "successful aging." It masks both a wish to "continue mid-life indefinitely" and the white, middle-class, Western values of researchers, causing them to emphasize productivity, effectiveness, and independence (Tornstam, 3; 22). So many purveyors of "anti-aging" remedies tout their products that "successful aging" is itself a commodity (Hadler, 2).

A study of successful aging discourse from the *Globe & Mail* in Toronto found three themes: (1) successful aging is a personal choice; (2) individuals are responsible for unsuccessful aging; and (3) successful aging is accomplished by staying engaged (Rozanova, 217).[1] Consumerism and consumption of products aid successful aging, and a "morally-laden message" identifies the ideal citizen as one who remains youthful as long as possible (218; 220). These assumptions "embody the neo-liberal principles of minimizing public support and maximizing individual effort" (220). Thus the innocuous-sounding "successful aging" furthers a political agenda.

Moreover, the phrase may reflect a hidden contempt for weakness in Western culture (Tornstam, 12). "Women, who are least likely to define productivity and who would benefit most profoundly from a re-imagining of old age, will be particularly vulnerable to the effects of a work-related standard, especially if it becomes a social expectation" (Holstein, "Women," 364). In other words, "productive" aging not only sees late life through a lens of economic usefulness but also suggests social conformity (Estes, Biggs, and Phillipson, 70). Old citizens are too diverse in their ethnicity, their income, their interests, and their degree of physical health to be fit into the narrow mold of "productive" aging.

When "successful aging" means such things as creative adaptation to loss of function or to the death of a spouse, "successful aging" is clearly desirable, but this model misses much of the context in which we age. It cannot tell us if the aging lobby in Washington is strong or weak or if supermarket food is laced with sugar and salt. It cannot tell us the prevalence of elder abuse or gauge the impact of media stereotypes, and it cannot guarantee that when journalists write about proposals to "privatize" Social Security, the probable harmful effects on women and people of color will be carefully weighed. The concept of "successful aging" is popular with gerontologists because of its positive connotations, but it is simplistic and its promise of mastery is false.

"Aging comfortably" is preferable to "successful aging" because it emphasizes ease rather than external measurement and because we can judge for ourselves whether or not we are comfortable. While "successful aging" implies that failure is possible, "comfortable aging" has a more neutral and non-judgmental opposite. "Comfortable aging" also carries a faint hint of emancipatory hedonism, for which we have little time in youth and middle age and too little permission at any age. I would broaden "hedonism" to include the pleasures of breathing deeply and being still.

Another aging model uses an analogy: The old are like a colonized people. The term "ageism" denotes negative attitudes and unjust treatment, but the dehumanization of older adults is more profound than "ageism" indicates. Seeing old women as a colonized people risks trivializing victims of colonial domination in other countries, for in important respects the analogy does not work. Forced labor, common to colonization, is not demanded of old women, and they are not deprived of political rights. They are not beaten or jailed for being old, although the dependent among them may suffer physical and psychological abuse. Old women share with colonized people the following characteristics, however: They are thought less intelligent than the dominant group. They are judged solely by appearance. They are encouraged to imitate the dominant group. They are figures of fun. They are scapegoated. They may internalize messages of their inferiority, and their movements may be controlled. In late old age they may be confined to very small spaces.

Because old women are seen as old bodies, physical appearance encompasses their whole being. Just as dark-skinned people under colonization are viewed only as manifestations of color, the old are equated with declining bodies. In both cases, physical difference from the dominant group is the key to lesser status. By a process called "internal colonization," one group dominates another within the same country, causing a wide range of inequalities and "dis-ease" for the subordinate group.[2] The educational needs of the old are neglected; for example, most doctors have little preparation for treating them competently, and psychoactive drugs are overprescribed for them (Green, 138).

Furthermore, the colonized are manipulated by the colonizers, who see them as incapable of managing themselves and in fact benefiting from being managed (139). Old women may respond to systematic devaluation by becoming docile or taking on a "colonized personality" (Franz Fanon's phrase). The old may demonstrate their oppression, that is, by "obsessive self-concern, passivity, clowning, fear of aging, and failure to identify themselves as old" (Green, 141). According to this interpretation, such traits, usually thought of as aspects of individual personality, reflect powerlessness. If friends and family of older adults understood internal colonization, they might have more patience with parents and grandparents who seem self-absorbed, docile, or afraid of aging. Instead of reacting with amusement to elders' disavowal of the label "old," they would see why it appears so undesirable.

Old women are not confined to certain parts of the country or neighborhoods as South African blacks used to be. The most obvious way their movements are controlled is by confinement in nursing homes, where many are given an average of eight medications a day. This amounts to massive social control of the institutionalized old, under the guise of medical need. Less obvious physical control takes two forms: encouraging the old who are not institutionalized to see sickness as their natural condition and overmedicating them. Whenever drug-induced slowing down or confusion are mistaken for normal aging, or medication causes a fall that results in an injury, the drug industry's role in colonizing old women is apparent. Sometimes families discourage an elderly parent from continuing an activity, traveling, or initiating a sexual relationship when no danger is involved—a subtle form of physical and psychological control.

When an old woman becomes "the Other," fundamentally different from others, those in the dominant group create emotional distance from her by exaggerating difference and overlooking shared characteristics. An old woman is an alien creature, costly and crabby, and her life stage is seen as disconnected from youth and midlife rather than as an outgrowth of them. At seventy, Baba Copper wrote that she felt socially segregated, "as if I had a disease that might be catching" (80). A white person who "others" a black will not herself become black, but a thirty-year-old who "others" someone over seventy-five may well live to join the minority that now seems so distant. Conscious aging requires that we become aware of being seen as "other" and resist impositions of difference.

The view that old women are a colonized people seems to account for more aspects of aging than are covered by "successful aging" or "productive aging," but it tends to see old people as a monolithic group, captured by biology as if they were specimens in amber. When old people are defined by a total category, a "false homogeneity" is imposed on them (Hazan, 81). Decline is their characteristic mark. They are the group that gerontologists and social workers want to help. The category is meaningful to the extent that people who get Social Security and Medicare share something in common and face certain forms of prejudice and discrimination, but "old," in and of itself, is merely a site on the life span. If a person over seventy lived alone on an island, age would not be very relevant. No social cues would evoke it. Just as the concept of race is deeply entwined with ideas of racial superiority, the term "old" carries connotations of dependency and loss. It tells who is less powerful, compared to others, and less respected. In fact, "being old, in and of itself, confers a loss of power" (Calasanti, "Theorizing Feminist Gerontology," 474).

If "old" is a fluid and changing identity, one that comes from outside of us rather than from within, then arranging people by years accumulated seems highly arbitrary, especially given the great diversity among people over sixty-five. It is not the changes in our bodies that define "old"; it is the meanings given to those changes. If our culture interprets the changes as shameful decrepitude, we can resist being pinned down by the category "old" by interpreting them as challenges instead. When "old" seems to be a woman's whole identity, however, her ability to act on her own behalf and to resist ageist stereotypes is lost sight of.

The inexactitude of "the old" is revealed when another life stage is used for comparison. Childhood is only eighteen years but it has distinct periods of infant, toddler, schoolchild, pre-adolescent, and adolescent. Someone in her early sixties may not wish to be grouped with everyone from sixty to one hundred. "Young old," the designation gerontologists use, is an oxymoron, but at least it acknowledges differences between seventy and ninety.

Some have suggested seeing aging as part of the life course rather than as a unique time. This emphasis has the advantage of finding roots of old-age problems or conditions in earlier decades—for example, the problem of low-paying jobs leading to inadequate Social Security later on—and it stresses the continuities of aging. But a life course interpretation may de-emphasize the role prejudice plays in aging in our society. Just as some whites like to say that skin color doesn't matter and blacks reply that whites have the privilege of not seeing what difference it makes, saying that "old" is a stage in human development obscures the fact that youth is favored, while age is not.

The challenge, then, is to see the politics of aging and personal/ individual aging simultaneously. From this perspective, the injustice of late-life poverty is exposed but the subjective experience of poverty is acknowledged to vary. The poverty of a group comprised equally of old black women and white, for example, was found to be "a mold both strong and loose" (Black and Rubinstein, 20). Social inequality character- izes American aging, but the emotional and spiritual growth possible in late life deserves equal attention. One study of older Jewish women found that their chief regrets about advancing age were diminishing vision and declining mobility, but these concerns were balanced by perceived gains: The women considered themselves more calm and mellow, enjoyed hav- ing fewer obligations, respected their past accomplishments, and felt they had grown emotionally and psychologically (Furman, 97–102).

In an autobiographical and anecdotal book on aging, Paul Tournier tells of a Swiss doctor assigned to several old and severely ill patients in a psychiatric hospital who used exercise, games, group therapy, and the telling of life stories to bring about "unexpected revival of the personal- ity" (38). These same four activities would be extremely beneficial for elders outside of institutions, too. Why group therapy?—admittedly a middle-class activity. The speed, fragmentation, and noise of American life take a toll on minds and bodies; thus old women and men might benefit from sessions in which recovery is a theme. Perhaps an important purpose of late life is to recover from the harried pace of earlier times. A person who tries to make healthy choices about diet, exercise, medication, relationships, and activities cannot very easily tune out the materialism of our society, its addictive cravings for bigger and more. To be old and psy- chologically healthy in a society marked by destructive impulses requires great equilibrium and balance. In supportive groups, older women could perhaps come to regard moving slowly not as humiliation but as a chance to tap into the life force that is unnaturally suppressed by speed and frag- mentation. As for life stories, elders who take time to reflect on their own stories and share them with others participate in an ancient ritual of most other cultures across time.

Aging is a process socially constructed as a problem. Public discussion of aging in America is narrowly focused on politics and economics, while a wide range of other relevant topics is ignored. Old women and men are seen in a utilitarian light of cost rather than potential. Who can they become is an unasked question. Can they be socially useful in ways that do not exploit them? In marking the International Year of Older Persons (1999), Kofi Annan said that "a society for all ages is one that does not caricature older persons as patients and pensioners. Instead it seeks a balance between supporting dependency and investing in lifelong development" (P5).

Learning to be old may be the last emotional and spiritual challenge we can agree to take on. While aging is shrouded in denial or shame, it will be seen simply as defeat. For many Americans, inability to think about being old, to plan for late life psychologically and not just financially, or to look squarely at its many complexities precludes conscious aging. Stoic resignation or despair may be their only reaction to bodily decline. The promise of other ways to age is exhilarating, though, if we can imagine late life as the time when we are most fully ourselves, a time to strengthen our survivor fiber. After all, "humans are biologically programmed to remain intact" (C. Fry, 513). Women, especially, may flourish in old age if we can "break out of the confines of youthful adaptations" (LaBouvie-Vief, "Women's Creativity," 163–64). In the following chapters, I suggest some ways of accomplishing this shift.

1

❦

Cultural Myths
and Aging

Learning to be old means knowing that the way you age depends on where you live. In the mountains of Peru, you may be expected to do hard physical labor in your eighties. In Japan, your children may house you from a sense of filial duty but wish you could live alone. As an elderly woman in the Chagga tribe of Mt. Kilimanjaro, you have the right to pick a grandchild to live with you and help with daily chores, a custom practiced by some Navajo in the Southwest. In many societies, your tasks of childcare and food preparation fully integrate you into your group. Infirmity may lower your status, for "nowhere is decrepitude valued" (Nydegger, 76), but if you live in Vatican City and wear a red hat, your power will draw attention away from your infirmities.

The commonplace that the old are devalued in North America and venerated in other societies is oversimplified. In non-industrial societies, treatment of elders depends on wealth, gender, political role, and religious function (Foner, 390–95). Professed attitudes of regard for them do not necessarily reflect actual treatment, and respect for a few powerful old people can be mistaken for respect for the old in general (Nydegger, 74–75). Nevertheless, high status for elders in many cultures past and present sharply contrasts with the relatively low status of the old in America today. Among the Nama people, a pastoral group in South Africa, for example, elders have high status for their medicinal lore, willingness to make loans from their pensions, and knowledge of cultural traditions. Their advice is sought by the young on social and political matters and they are consulted about land claims, both current and past (Oakley, 49–59).[1]

A key to mindful aging is the ability to think critically about the culturally determined place one is assigned, so that discriminatory attitudes and questionable assumptions can be challenged, quietly within ourselves if not in spoken words. When we receive a chirpy letter from AARP at fifty or later when a Medicare card arrives, no insert tells us that long-held cultural myths strongly influence the ways we age.

SELF-RELIANCE

One of the most obvious and pervasive American myths is self-reliance, expressed by the phrase "rugged individualism." Is this myth useful for old age, or should it be discarded or at least reconsidered? The people best able to embody the extreme individualism of American culture are the young and strong. The middle-aged can do fairly well, but old people are bound to fail if this is a measure for judging them. To be sure, some old women and men have the physical and psychic energy to be as self-reliant and autonomous as anyone else. More often, to be old (at least, to be over eighty) means needing some help; it means acknowledging that total independence is no longer possible. In America, this recognition often brings anguish and humiliation. In other cultures, where interconnectedness is lifelong and often necessary for survival, old-age dependency is not so radically different from dependency during other life stages.

The cultural myth of self-reliance suggests pushing against barriers and obstacles, dogged perseverance, and left-brain logic. It connotes competition, action, and freedom in separation. Self-reliance appears to be a male model, for women are often depicted as being in relation to others, whether by choice or conventional expectation. Women, like the poor, disabled people, or members of minority groups, may also lack the control over their life circumstances that is often a precondition for self-reliance, a value better suited to Anglo America than to the culturally diverse population reflected in the most recent census. Despite these inherent limitations, self-reliance is commonly urged upon old citizens as if they were a monolithic group.

Emerson's essay "Self-Reliance" (1841) is a classic text on this American virtue, but for Emerson the phrase does not suggest the ability to take care of oneself without depending on others. The focus of the essay is independent thinking. Emerson expresses the Transcendental faith in the individual's inner light. He praises non-conformity.

Those over sixty-five who scorn senior centers, saying that they do not want to be around "all those old people," may unconsciously be avoiding the unpleasant truth that some people cannot *be* totally autonomous as they age. Elders who stay away from senior centers avoid seeing signs of dependence in age: canes, wheelchairs, walkers. Self-imposed isolation from others who are old allows one to preserve the fiction that one will never lose autonomy and thereby join a devalued group. The fact that people at senior centers have banded together for a common purpose, however, suggests the limits of late-life individualism.

A curious pattern in gerontological research is that when questioned about their health in relation to their age, subjects tend to express a gloomy view of the health of the old in general, but consider themselves lucky exceptions to the decline they think characteristic of their life stage. This pattern clearly illustrates the cultural emphasis on individualism. Caught in its grip, many old people are unable to imagine large numbers of their peers as favored as they are. By viewing themselves as *not like* all of the others, healthy elders stress separation from their group. Distancing strategies, a form of denial, may also be a reasonable response to ageism, a way of resisting oppressive expectations of sickness or decrepitude. Such attitudes, of course, work against group solidarity among old women and men. Seeing oneself as an exception, a "queen bee" of aging, limits awareness of the large social and cultural factors that shape the category "old."

If I emphasize that I differ from the "typical" old who are deteriorating, I try to dodge the scorn often heaped on them. Unlike dependent old persons, whom I perceive as weak, I stand as a strong individual. And the more I claim difference, the better I feel about myself. Like light-skinned blacks who pass for white and thus escape the stigma borne by the dark-skinned, the old who deny they are like the other old try to be taken for someone they are not. They assume that dependency and self-reliance are complete opposites.

Many old women and men cling fiercely to their right to drive because they well know that anyone too old to drive is indisputably old. Loss of the ability to drive is an informal rite of passage to the next life stage, in which autonomy, self-reliance, and freedom from interference are all threatened. What does this important transition mean for the psychological well-being and social life of the old? Is it more traumatic for men than for women? Drivers control their own schedule and their movements. When a man or woman stops driving and must then ask others for rides, he or she is in a subordinate position, one created not by age itself but by location in America.

Fifty-four percent of our communities have no publicly funded senior transportation and the rest have limited systems (Freund). The lack of good public transportation in most places, especially rural America, helps to keep an elderly person at home. The belief that he or she shouldn't ask others for help becomes another reason to stay there (Nelson, 89). "Surviving without driving" is such a challenge, in fact, that a transportation expert has recommended a national education campaign to persuade elders that if they stop driving, they are still worthy persons (Freund), a proposal that vividly illustrates the power of the self-reliance myth to lower self-esteem among those who can no longer follow its dictates.

The primacy of the automobile is understood to be a threat to the environment, but it is also a factor in colonizing people who no longer drive, a group that is predominantly female. When lack of transportation leads to loss of mobility, which in turn contributes to physical decline, the problem is rooted in social status. If old citizens really had the political clout that politicians and the media like to attribute to them, every community would have transportation for them, and the system would be seen not as a special favor to an interest group but as a necessity like paved streets. The obstacles to such a system are not only cost but the myth of self-reliance. It casts normal physical change as a stigmatizing deficit.

The ultimate failure, according to self-reliance, is confinement in a nursing home. "I'd rather die than go there" is a commonly heard statement from people who have passed seventy-five. Their understandable fear comes not only from threatened self-reliance, of course, but from oppressive conditions in some nursing homes. Psychologist Ellen Langer has shown how the dependency fostered by nursing homes can be reversed when residents make many ordinary daily-life choices. Mindfulness exercises and activities that encourage independence can reverse memory loss and actually lengthen lives (81–89). Israeli researchers who listened closely to nursing home residents found "variability and potential for adaptation" among them, challenging the stereotype that old people in that setting are "homogeneous and passive" (Gamliel and Hazan, 367).

The Eden Alternative nursing home model was developed by William Thomas to decrease the boredom and loneliness of life there. Nursing home reformers believe that people there suffer more from these emotional conditions than from their medical conditions (Power, 14). Among Eden Alternative strategies are caregiving teams who share in decision making, visits by pets and children, and an emphasis on freedom of movement (Deaton et al., 196). More recently, Thomas created the Greenhouse Project. The prototype in Tupelo, Mississippi, designed by Richard McCarty, features eight to ten residents in private rooms with a common kitchen. The emphasis is on sunlight and accessible outdoor space. The focus is on relationships rather than medical needs. Many nursing homes in the United States are converting to the Greenhouse Project.

The bad image of nursing homes results from widespread abuses and unnecessary regimentation, but irrational fear of them impedes creative thought about their possibilities. Major problems of nursing homes are low pay and extremely high worker turnover, as much as 100 percent a year in some homes. Many aides are recent immigrants. A sensible nursing home plan would be to offer English as a Second Language classes to workers, who would be encouraged to practice their skills by talking to residents and writing down some of their stories. Workers would then have an incentive to pay attention to the individuality of residents and to keep their jobs at least until completing their classes. Moving into a nursing home looms as a hateful eventuality partly because of our cultural myth of individualism. Conditioned to link old age with dependency and dependency with nursing homes, we prefer not to think about aging.

Rosalie Kane notes that the number of nursing homes is declining and urges consumers to be aware that they are not the automatic recourse for adults who need long-term care (Rosalie Kane, 10).

In fact, home- and-community based services should be the first choice and institutions a last resort, even as efforts continue to improve institutions (Kane and Kane, 131).

Shame, depression, or a sense of unworthiness may result from trying to conform to a cultural ideal of individualism. Each loss of function is humiliating. For many old women and men, having to ask for help is regarded as a weakness. "I don't want to be a burden to anyone," one of the most frequently heard statements from the old, has a hidden subtext: "I will cling to my independence as long and as fiercely as I can, and you can count on me not to ask for help until I absolutely need it." This attitude is expected of old people; someone who said she looked forward to being helped would lose face. In noting the need for interdependence in late life, Seattle doctor Christopher Bailey assails the "fig-leaf of phony self-reliance" (letter in *New York Times*, Health Times, April 3, 2012, D4). "The claim 'I can do it myself' reverberates throughout the lifecycle, perhaps becoming a dominant note in individualist competitive cultures" (Ruddick, 59). Rural old women especially value self-reliance; their "worldviews strongly condition the extent to which they accept nontraditional sources of assistance" (Kivett, 361). Naming needs discloses that the flame of self-reliance is sputtering. Another possibility is that a woman may fend off efforts to place her in a nursing home, saying she wants to live "independently," even though she is both "heavily dependent on and heavily discounting her daughter's financial and emotional support" (Nelson, 87). In such a case it is hard to disentangle strong social pressure to be self-reliant from the expression of an individual's wishes.

In the introduction to his cultural history of American aging, *The Journey of Life*, Thomas R. Cole discusses "our culture's intractable hostility to physical decline and mental decay, imposed with particular vengeance on older women. Their shame and revulsion also reflects the scientific management of aging" (xxiv). People are known through their bodies, and therefore, as Sally Gadow says, "repudiation of the body as a failed object, or worse, as an enemy, jeopardizes that connection of persons and their world" ("Frailty and Strength," 45). A massive shift in consciousness would have to occur before old American women who are frail could love their bodies or women not yet frail could see old bodies in decline as simply old and not ugly. Jacqueline Hayden's life-size nude photographs of old women and men are startling because they disrupt our culturally sanctioned notions of beauty. Whose body merits representation?[2]

An individual's desire to be self-reliant when increasingly frail becomes especially poignant when early signs of dementia appear. "Early" is imprecise and easily contested, as I discovered when the niece of a woman I had befriended wanted to move her to the Jewish Home for the Aged in San Francisco. My friend, Frieda Walter, clearly suffered from mild dementia, but she was able to walk by herself every day to the neighborhood senior center. She told me that when she couldn't remember what day it was she called the childcare center next door. To me these were signs that she could still look after herself. When the niece took Frieda to the home and asked her to fill out an application, she refused. The niece interpreted this as a sign of dementia; to me it seemed the rational choice of someone not ready to surrender her freedom. Frieda's social worker was appalled that she had not seen a doctor in four years, even though she was eighty-six. But her disengagement from medicalized aging could also be seen as a calculation that she had more to lose than to gain by seeing a doctor. The social worker assumed Frieda was incapable of choosing wisely. At the home, Frieda was immediately put on drugs. Soon her ankles were badly swollen, and she broke her wrist in a fall. Placement in the dementia ward ensured her rapid mental deterioration. Drugged dependency was forced upon her. Population aging, especially the coming large increase in the number of women over eighty-five, ensures that some version of Frieda's story will be repeated often.[3]

Although people of any age are vulnerable to disease, disability, loss of friends, and lack of respect based on some arbitrary characteristic, elders are especially vulnerable to these and other conditions. Holding up self-reliance as a cross-generational ideal is singularly inappropriate. Too great an emphasis on self-reliance "reinforces the norm of living in single family units, the belief that the old should look after themselves, and the belief that their problems are their own and of no concern to the rest of us" (Tronto, 273).

Such attitudes of course may characterize white middle-class life far more accurately than for example the lives of American Indians, many of whom are accustomed to interdependence and reciprocity throughout their lives; consequently, among them, "dependency and need in old age are judged less harshly" (John, Blanchard, and Hennessy, 309). The same may be true of Latinos accustomed to letting adult children take over responsibility for them. The notion of individual autonomy familiar in white, middle-class life is also out of place among Chinese Americans in the case of hospitals' policy of informed consent because families are expected to make decisions for their elders, sometimes deciding not to tell a parent that she is terminally ill (Yeo, 77). Similarly, among Korean Americans, conveying a fatal diagnosis seems disrespectful.

A deeper understanding of late-life frailty and dependence would not seriously challenge a mainstream cultural value as deeply entrenched as self-reliance, but it might take away some of the shame now associated with the end of complete autonomy. Dependency comes in many forms, some of which do not entail powerlessness, and dependency must be distinguished from incompetence (M. Baltes, 11), an insight that mitigates age shame. Frailty after all is only one dimension of a person, is not the same as withering away, and is a more or less apt description depending on circumstances. Most important, frailty can coexist with strengths. Someone who walks with great difficulty may have a strong voice, a strong will, or strong self-esteem.[4]

The intertwining of frailty and strength was brought home to me in a dramatic way several years ago when I heard Sir Georg Solti conduct the San Francisco Symphony during one of his last U.S. appearances. The stage door opened and out walked a very old, frail man who moved slowly and stiffly. I watched nervously, wondering if he would make it to the podium. As soon as he raised his baton, though, he became a powerful figure. The orchestra played beyond its usual capacity. At the end of the concert, as the musicians clapped loudly for Solti, the audience shared in the intensity of the moment. Then the conductor left the podium, once more a frail old man, walking with very small steps. The musicians and the audience intuitively knew that frailty made mastery more triumphant.

"Frailty is dialectical," writes Sally Gadow, "containing within itself its apparent opposite, new life and strength." She cites Florida Scott-Maxwell's description of "fierce energy" possible through frailty, when the life force appears in full strength as it cannot at times of "busy engagement with the world" ("Frailty and Strength," 146). The idea that the life force does not depend on physical energy is arresting. It implies that frailty is relative and contingent rather than a fixed quality. Moreover, in Gadow's view, frailty is "essential to the making of a self" (146)—a viewpoint better suited to late life than "successful aging" or "productive aging." Moreover, the term "frailty" is used by caregivers to justify categorizing patients (Bytheway, *Unmasking*, 138).

Late in her life, painter and writer Mary Meigs expressed frustration in her journal at controlling, insensitive treatment by caregivers. After one said sharply to her, "Look at me!" she felt resentful. "The old person becomes a person who can be disciplined. Lesson—you must learn to have the dignity of someone who can't be disciplined" (*Beyond Recall*, 104). In other words, a person who resists being controlled.[5]

Images that romanticize individualism appear to counter ageist stereotypes in that they depict old people as able and honorable, but such images perpetuate the myth of self-reliance as preeminently worthy. This is true of "Alice Bell," a powerful story at the end of Pat Barker's *Union Street*. The eccentric old woman in the story is heroically self-reliant, fights off attempts to subdue her into dependency, starves herself to pay for her funeral, and finally kills herself. Her suicide is portrayed as a noble expression of her idiosyncratic self. Similarly, in May Sarton's novel *As We Are Now*, the suicide of Caro Spencer that also kills others in her nursing home represents a triumph of individualism over an oppressive, dehumanizing environment. Self-reliance is a transcendent virtue even in a violent and murderous form.

Feminist philosopher Margaret Urban Walker writes that "the recruitment of women to the paradigm of individuality visits on them a cultural life pattern that renders later life . . . a space not literally but by social definition empty" (*Moral Contexts*, 197).

Learning to be old is hard when it means being able to accept dependency with grace. For women, especially, whose struggle to become whole human beings often requires a great degree of self-sufficiency, at least in white, middle-class life, letting go of triumphant individualism must be painful and shaming. But the willingness to ask for help and the acknowledgment that one is not wholly self-sufficient are signs of emancipation from socially constructed aging. Autonomy is incompatible with many of the facts of old age, and held up as an ideal, leads inevitably to disappointment (Moody, "Age," 418).

In their study *Life beyond 85 Years: The Aura of Survivorship*, Colleen Johnson and Barbara Barer found that their subjects "reconstituted" themselves as they increasingly needed help from others and that their adaptations were highly individualized (192). Even when their disabilities increased, they maintained their equilibrium (219). Compared to a group of seventy- to eighty-four-year-olds, the people over eighty-five accepted dependency more easily and gave up control over some aspects of their lives, changes that usually did not undermine their sense of well-being (224). Perhaps these findings show that the people in the study outgrew the cultural norm of self-reliance. Were they exceptional? Is it futile to expect individualism to lose its central place in our system of values even when we are no longer able to exemplify it?

The need to be self-reliant may not press as heavily on women as on men because women are expected to relate to others and see to their needs. On the other hand, since most men who reach late life have a spouse to help them and most women do not, women have more opportunity to display self-reliance. Traditional female socialization might be advantageous in old age if it prepares women to accept dependence. In practice, it seems not to work this way. The cultural exhortation to stand on one's own two feet is stronger than the social message that caring for others and being cared for are equally admirable. At the same time, a male-identified woman whose life has been shaped by her autonomy may have a harder time when old than a woman who has lived out a subordinate role.

Social historian Stephanie Coontz points out that the pioneer families who settled the West saw themselves as self-reliant but in fact were subsidized by the federal government, for example by military campaigns that took land from Indians and appropriated half of Mexico. She believes that "depending on support beyond the family has been the rule rather than the exception in American history" (214). And as feminist theorist Josephine Donovan notes, the "vision of the independent, autonomous individual (male) ignores the network of supporting persons (usually female) who enable his autonomy" by food, clothes, shelter, and nurture (15). Seen from these perspectives, old people who can no longer be self-reliant are like other Americans, in need of a web of support. Realistically, the very old "cannot maintain a façade of independence and self-reliance" (Holstein, Parks, and Waymack, 14). Without a framework of interconnectedness and a critique of rugged individualism, however, old women and men are more likely to see themselves as failures when their self-reliance slips away. Old-age policies that assume independence is necessary ignore or devalue women's lifelong connections with others (Rodeheaver, 745). They ignore something else: our individual choices occur in a "global system that influences the way we age far more than most of the steps we take as individuals" (Fishman, 69).

Nevertheless, the dominant American cultural virtue of self-reliance has been "glorified, intensified, and championed as a leading value upon which we should base all social policies" (Olson, *Not-So-Golden*, 245). This bodes ill for the aging of baby boomers, who will be healthier than their parents but will still be subject to aging policies based on a myth unhelpful to them in late old age. The fundamental problem lying ahead for them, as for their parents, is that for old persons, self-esteem is very closely linked to the cultural value of independence, that is, autonomy and self-reliance, but many in late life will need "help and support in order to survive" (M. Clark and Anderson, 290).

At the same time that self-reliance is overvalued as an ideal for the old to embody, many suffer from learned helplessness. "Older people often end up in a Catch-22, caught between a social ethic of independence on the one hand, and a service ethic which constructs them as dependent on the other" (Robertson, 82). They or their families think they should give up an activity or avoid trying something new because of age. "Mind sets about old age confirm a sense of incompetence" (Langer, *Mindfulness*, 87). When a doctor questioned a middle-aged nurse about her mother, she replied tartly, "Why don't you ask her; she's right here." Several experiences of this kind condition an old woman to be silent. In other situations, well-intentioned protectiveness can undermine autonomy in older persons, especially among those who are institutionalized.

SELF-REINVENTION

An American cultural myth that fits the aging process better than self-reliance is the belief that we can reinvent ourselves. Originally subjects of a king, white Americans remade themselves into rebels. When life in the East became too confining, some went West. And when they arrived, nobody cared about the status, occupation, or wealth of their families. We mobile Americans know instinctively that if things don't work out where we are, we can go elsewhere, if we can afford to. Hard times decrease mobility but can also drive people out of their places. "Americans have always had second acts. They have been immigrants beginning anew. They have left behind families and scrawled 'Gone to Texas' on the walls of their houses. Second and third marriages are routine. And even in the most conventional lives, retirees leave familiar worlds behind for the Florida sun" (Applebome, 1). Cutting loose has always been the prerogative of the young, but today millions of Americans over sixty-five are settling in towns and regions far from where they raised families. And a surprising number are going home again, after having tried Florida, Arizona, and California.

Since Gold Rush days and especially since the end of the Second World War, California has been the quintessential American place for reinventing the self. Judy Garland left Grand Rapids, Minnesota, for Hollywood. Young people who worked as waiters and clerks in the Midwest found similar jobs after moving to California but called themselves writers and artists. Women and men who led closeted lives in other places came to California for the freedom to be openly gay. Particularly since the 1960s, California has been the place to go after divorce. The high cost of living in California has dissuaded some retirees from moving there but the climate remains a draw for others.

Today the myth of reinventing the self plays out in the immigrant communities. Parents of community college students from China, Vietnam, and the Philippines, for example, typically work long hours in low-paying jobs, but the older brothers and sisters of these students often work in professions. Political upheavals in Central America in the 1980s resulted in the displacement of many Latino families whose members include aged parents, newcomers to California. Also in the 1980s, many Russian

Jews relocated to San Francisco and Los Angeles. Some elders who settled in suburbia are moving back to the city, a trend that may revitalize some American cities.

The more interesting aspect of reinventing the self is not the geographical move but the interior one. When the old come to a new place, they may choose to develop facets of themselves that found no expression earlier. New activities, new friends, and a new community all contribute to a sense of possibility. This is truer of course of the white middle class than of those who "age in place" because they have no other choice. People who have endured years of uncongenial work may take renewed pleasure in life. Some people stop going to church or find religion for the first time. Although colleges and universities have not been welcoming places for older students, many have found taking college classes the occasion for reinventing selves. Simply discovering that they have the ability to do college work can be exhilarating. Some of the ablest re-entry students are working-class women for whom higher education was unattainable at eighteen.

The American myth of reinventing the self has traditionally been a male myth, one sometimes involving deception or a criminal past. In Willa Cather's story "Paul's Case," the reinvention myth is beautifully rendered. Paul escapes a smothering bourgeois family, crass teachers, and a dull job for the aesthetic pleasures of New York. Although reinvention ends tragically in this instance, it is portrayed in such psychologically satisfying and enlarging terms that its possibility seems not completely denied by Paul's death.[6]

The prospect of reinventing the self in old age has special relevance for women, who may not have been able earlier to express their full individuality. Family responsibilities, work pressures, constraints imposed by sexism, and the expectation that they juggle many things at once without complaint all hamper women's self-development. For healthy women, life after seventy may present unanticipated opportunities. Sometimes they are more willing to risk social disapproval for their choices. For those conditioned to meet all demands made of them, the simple act of saying no is freeing. The death of a husband may be the occasion for unexpected change. Redefinition of self is almost inevitable for married heterosexual women because many are widows by age sixty-five. More black women than white are widowed by then. Perhaps an older woman reinvents herself when she marries a man younger than herself, a good strategy for preserving companionship in late life, but not yet a common one.[7] A current example of self-reinvention is the Buranova Babushkas, widows from a poor village 600 miles east of Moscow who created a singing group and now tour widely in Russia. Their repertoire includes rock music and Beatles' songs.

"Some of us who are old," writes Carolyn Heilbrun, "suspect that a transformation of the self may require an abandonment of all that our consumer society identifies as woman's nature" (4). Deference, compliance, and attentiveness to men are examples.

A woman who has never expressed anger may find, late in life, that she has much to be angry about. Families have trouble dealing with this shift in a parent or grandparent. Too often, an old woman's anger, particularly if it is uncharacteristic, signals to her family that she should be given drugs to calm her down. Another way to view the unexpected anger is as a sign of growth or newly discovered power.[8] If old women don't stifle anger, they appear intractable. In a story by Mary Wilkins Freeman, "A Village Singer" (1891), Candace Whitcomb is dismissed from her position of honor, lead soprano in the church choir, because she is old and her voice is fading. She erupts with anger and plots revenge. As she argues forcefully with her minister, the only way he can cope with her is to order her to pray with him. She refuses, defying his authority to silence her. For a woman of her time and place, that was an act of extreme rebellion. Even when the anger of the old seems justified by losses and humiliations, those around them may resist letting the anger play out.

At seventy-nine, Jeannette Picard was told she was too old to become one of the first women ordained as Episcopal priests. She and her sister priests dramatically reinvented themselves from laywomen to authority figures. Imogene Cunningham conceived of her late-life development as "a process of constant refocusing of the self" (M. Mitchell, 17). A Minneapolis woman, Nina Draxten, cast off the role of retired professor when she was eighty to become an actor, first in commercials and later in the movie *Far North*. Jon Hendricks tells of a concert clarinetist who turned his instrument into a lamp when he retired, explaining that he wanted new challenges ("Creativity," 105).

Sometimes adaptations are as meaningful as reinventions. De Beauvoir describes Renoir in his sixties, unable to hold a paintbrush in his paralyzed hand, continuing to paint until he was seventy-eight by having a brush taped to his wrist (313). People over eighty-five in the study cited earlier were found to "reinvent a self-concept that [takes] their survivorship into account" (Johnson and Barer, 163). Accepting help is not traumatic for them, for example. Some who had been very engaged socially now "cherish peaceful solitude" and do not feel lonely (156).

Lately gerontologists have suggested that "self" is really "selves" and that they require social interaction to call them forth (Hendricks, "Practical Consciousness," 200; Ray, *Beyond Nostalgia*, 22). Baba Copper describes her aging as a "familiar process to which I bring an ever-expanding self," (91), suggesting that the "self" in "reinvention of the self" evolves. The conflict that old women may experience between their inner self and who they appear to be may ease if they value their aging faces and their ag-ing selves (Meyers, 32), a difficult feat, perhaps, for younger women to imagine. Seen from these perspectives, reinvention is more a process than an event, interpersonal as well as intrapersonal. In contrast to some of its past guises, in late life the reinvention myth is anti-heroic and rooted in the ordinary.

Social class, a source for many assumptions about the world, exerts a powerful influence on self-concept. "Far from being simply a mosaic of occupational, educational, and financial resources, social class wields considerable sway over all aspects" of our lives, including what we per-ceive as meaningful and how we age (Hendricks, "Practical Conscious-ness," 203–4). Moreover, the great variation observed among old women and men, usually assumed to reflect individual personalities, may be explained by "a lifetime's experience of social class" (207). Class privilege facilitates creative late-life reinventions, but these take place in people of all classes. Consider, for example, the poor women of Argentina whose sons and husbands disappeared. Unable to protest in the usual ways, they gathered in small groups in their communities to make *arpilleras*, small drawings or weavings that told what happened and commemorated their family members. Through their ingenuity they were not silenced.

Reinventing the self may also be thought of as a strategy for maintain-ing self-respect. Usually I will be respected if I am seen as exerting power or influence on others or as controlling my own life. If I can drive, climb stairs, use a computer, carry bags of groceries, handle tools, arrange for services I need, and refuse whatever does not suit me, I exercise mastery over my environment without having to think about it. Others tacitly acknowledge my competence by not interfering. What happens when I can no longer drive, manage stairs, and so on? My self-respect must rest on some other set of competencies. How can I feel worthy without the independence that previously marked my life? Will I respect myself when I hear "poor thing!" in the voices of those who speak to me? How can I feel able when my sphere of movement shrinks? Perhaps if I know others like me, who have a sense of irony and a healthy self-regard, I can more easily base my self-worth on some inner qualities and thus avoid the shame that seems to accompany waning physical capacity. If I am no longer one who lives completely independently, who exerts her will in hundreds of small ways, can I become a woman who accepts this change with detachment? Will I have a context for understanding it that leaves me dignity? Can I simultaneously admit that I miss my former activities and see them as not so important now? If I project a sense of power when I can no longer move about freely, will others treat me as competent? If they see me only as diminished, can I parallel that partial truth with other truths about myself?

It is easy to admire the eighty-year-old woman who jogs or the eighty-year-old man who plays tennis. Our admiration reflects dominant cultural values. The ultimate countercultural stance is forcefully to declare one's worth in the face of irreversible physical decline. To do so requires setting aside the belief that aging is a falling from grace.[9] Avoiding the numbing effect of age denial and challenging cultural values can sharpen my awareness of aging's relativity. Others may see me as a pitiable wreck, but I know that in another society I would have meaningful tasks to undertake, my opinion would be sought, and no one would be embarrassed by my appearance.

The current popularity of "anti-aging" products and claims makes clear the appeal of self-reinvention as a cultural myth. A desire to prolong human life is not mere narcissism, but a worthy aspiration based on love, both of the natural world and of other people (Meilaender, 43). Anti-aging medicine has been described, however, as "an aggregate of distractions for the overly hopeful, not a revolution in human health (Rose, 121). And as noted biogerontologist Leonard Hayflick observes, the phrase "anti-aging medicine" is an oxymoron, because it is impossible to be against a fundamental property of matter (6).[10] Anti-aging medicine is really "geriatric medicine in disguise" rather than research on aging *per se*; age-associated diseases must be distinguished from the aging process itself (3–4). Far from being beneficial, in fact, "anti-aging medicine is actually harmful" (Holstein, Parks, and Waymack, xvi).

Nevertheless, fear of physical aging creates a market for books and products promising intervention against aging, and even those who understand the difference between aging and disease may be susceptible to unproven claims.

CONCLUSION

It may be that those best suited to sustaining self-esteem are old women and men characterized by the same sturdy individualism that earlier in the chapter was judged a poor value to carry into old age. Perhaps instead of outgrowing this value, we need only transmute it. When we are too slow for competition, too buffeted by life to look down on others as weak or inept, and too appreciative of our friends' regard to overvalue material possessions, our individualism can soften. We can then see exaggerated forms of it as thwarting our development. If needing much help from others does not fill us with shame, we may readily accept Emerson's view of self-reliance as freeing our minds of common opinions, especially when these common opinions devalue ourselves.

Trying to live up to the contemporary American myth of self-reliance, on the other hand, may undermine our psychological health in late life. Seeing its limits and resisting it may free us from shame when we are no longer totally self-sufficient, when the value of interdependence comes into sharper focus. No greater challenge faces women growing old in America than the preservation of self-worth in a culture of extreme individualism.

2

❧

Fear of an
Aging Population

Another cultural myth, of more recent origin than those described in the preceding chapter, is that an aging population threatens the non-old. In the United States and other industrialized nations, population aging is a major trend. Here older people make up 13 percent of the population, while the figures for other countries are slightly higher—15 percent in Germany, for example, and 16 percent in Japan. In some North American communities, population aging is marked. On Cape Cod, for example, 25 percent of the residents are over sixty-five, according to an Associated Press story (January 7, 2008), and in a few towns on the east coast of Vancouver Island, 60 percent are over sixty-five. The fastest growing segment of the population used to be people over eighty-five and is now those aged sixty-five to sixty-nine.

Improved longevity is the most obvious reason for the growing numbers of older people, but an important and often overlooked reason is the decline in the fertility rate. The same factors that cause increased life expectancy, "education, income, good health care, sanitation, and nutrition" lead to decreased fertility (Carstensen, *Long Bright Future*, 34). Worldwide, women today have only half as many children as they had in 1972 (Longman, 31). The *combination* of these two trends from opposite ends of the life course is needed to make older people as numerous as they now are in Western nations. The number of Chinese over sixty is increasing by six million a year, and by 2025 China's elderly population may reach 290 million, or nearly the whole of the U.S. population (*Boston Globe*, January 2, 2007).

25

Increased longevity has been defined as a menace by conservative commentators. Using appeals to emotion rather than evidence, they have constructed population aging as a fearful development. A few gerontologists have challenged their assumptions and refuted their claims, but the mass media has unquestioningly accepted the equation of an aging population with danger to the common good.

People over eighty-five comprise the second fastest-growing group of Americans, now outnumbering teenagers. Fear of this change rests partly on the stereotype of elders as parasites expensive to maintain. In fact, older Americans will contribute to economic growth by continuing to work after age sixty-five (a choice many are forced to make), spending their IRAs, and buying goods and services. They contribute a great deal to their families and friends both in material and non-material terms. Their contributions are often invisible in economic calculations—taking care of a spouse, for example, helping a neighbor, teaching or guiding grandchildren, volunteering, simply being available to talk. An old woman or man who is currently not able to give to others should be seen as someone who has contributed in the past. In our society, however, with its strong future orientation, services rendered in the past or help given "do not bind the recipient for long to a demand for reciprocity," whereas in cultures with a different sense of time, strong obligations from the past live on in the present (M. Clark, "Cultural Values," 270).

THE LANGUAGE OF FEAR

Fear of an aging population is sometimes communicated in ways that suggest old persons are alien creatures, not a part of our common life. A *Boston Globe* article began, "Just as societies gird for the greatest onslaught of people ever to cross the threshold of old age" (Knox, 40). "Society" here is defined as the not-old. The war metaphor is telling. Its effect is not to inform but to create fear. The implied "we," those facing the "greatest onslaught," have no connection to the Others, who are not just different from "us" but menacing. Words like "onslaught" were also used to attack immigration to the United States in the nineteenth and early twentieth centuries.

Other examples of language used to create fear of increasing longevity are instructive. A Brookings Institution report on aging uses the phrase "senior tsunami," for example (June 11, 2007), and "age wave" is a popular usage in the media (Frey, 1). A wave can't be controlled, keeps coming, and may be harmful. Another phrase is "grey hordes" (Bytheway, *Ageism*, 60), to suggest barbarian invaders climbing over city walls. Other disaster metaphors are common—for example, the use of "flood," "epidemic of old age," or "avalanche" to describe the society that lies just ahead. Nations with aging populations face "mountains of debt . . . that could destabilize the world economy" (Longman, 34). Dire predictions such as these have been repeated uncritically until they sound familiar enough to be plausible. World economic health obviously depends on multiple factors, of which population aging is only one.

Statements suggesting that population shifts in and of themselves bring disaster imagine passive politicians and economists unable to plan or react. They assume that the economic dimension of aging supersedes all others. When writers refer to "the baneful effects of longer lives" (D. Callahan, 189), their comments are taken as self-evident facts rather than as emotionally laden value judgments. Furthermore, studies of the impact of population aging overlook subgroups such as childless elders, in Asia and Europe as well as in the United States, and the outcomes of population aging cannot be assumed to be uniform across society (Kreager and Schroeder-Butterfill, 27).

Another word that deserves attention is "entitlement," which conveys an impression of selfish demands made on taxpayers and the government (Ekerdt, 526). A more accurate term would be "deferred compensation," to acknowledge that people over sixty-five are both contributors to the system and its beneficiaries. And, if Social Security were seen, correctly, as an earned benefit, a way to preserve living standards, or a program that shields families over the life course (Quadagno, "Social Security," 398), attempts to reduce confidence in it would appear destructive.

A Sunday *New York Times* full-page ad for Peter G. Peterson's book *Gray Dawn: How the Coming Age Wave Will Transform America and the World* pictures a huge and ominous iceberg with many jagged edges (February 14, 1999, 19). The caption reads "A Demographic Iceberg Threatens to Sink the Great Powers." Beneath the caption are alarmist quotes from conservative luminaries such as Peggy Noonan and Sam Nunn. Paul Volker, former chairman of the Federal Reserve Board, cautions that the aging of America is a "time bomb." The phrase "great powers" has a lovely Victorian ring to it, suggesting imperialist glories. Making a connection between an iceberg and a group of citizens requires a leap past logic into irrational fear. Countries with aging populations, we are told, will "stagger under their weight." The personification of a country uses emotion to convey a sense of intolerable burden. Despite its arctic setting, the ad displays a lush garden of metaphor.

Grim prophecies such as those in the book ad quoted here have been described as "apocalyptic demography" and "alarmist demographic discourse."[1] Another phrase, "voodoo demography," refers to the lack of evidence for questionable assumptions about population aging, for example, that by itself it will cause severe economic problems and that it will greatly harm younger generations (Gee, 5). Tsunamis, icebergs, and the other scare words may also be regarded as demographic demagoguery because they attempt to stir up fear by inventing a social problem.

Lenard Kaye, director of the University of Maine's Center on Aging, explains why he dislikes "tsunami": "it implies a destructive force and that's just not the case" (Hewitt, 4).

Irrational fear of an aging population began in the United States but has spread to Canada and other countries (Gee and Gutman, 1). Similarly, in the United States in the 1970s and 1980s, some conservatives imagined a homosexual takeover of America, a myth that has lost much of its potency except when the issue is marriage. The rhetorical intent implicit in the iceberg ad is to divide old from young by creating a huge disparity of interests, just as enemies of immigration in the late nineteenth and early twentieth century portrayed a great gulf between Anglo Americans and immigrants. Demographic demagoguery is a weapon used against women, people of color, and workers (Estes, "Feminist Perspective"). Beyond curbing old-age benefits, its real aim is to challenge the legitimacy of all government social welfare programs (Olson, "Women," 14). That is why conservative rhetoric about population aging is so emotionally charged. Today elderly people are scapegoated for problems they did not cause: deficits due to tax cuts, wars, bank bailouts, and the stimulus spending in 2008 and 2009 (Estes and Wallace, "Globalization," 514).

AGING POLITICS AND ECONOMICS

The Concord Coalition, created by former Republican senator Warren Rudman and others, argues that the cost of Medicare and Social Security is "exploding" and in forty years will "swallow" nearly half of U.S. payrolls. Although the Concord Coalition was more influential in the 1990s than at present, mass media reports consistently overlook the analyses that rebut its arguments. Future costs of Medicare and Social Security, for example, could easily be met if corporations were taxed today at the same rate as they were taxed in the 1950s (Minkler, "Scapegoating," 10). The name "Americans for Generational Equity" assumes inequity exists, but there is "no evidence for intergenerational warfare here in the United States" (Carstensen, *Long Bright Future*, 36).

According to Canadian studies, population aging will not lead to significantly increased health care costs, nor will a smaller number of workers be harmed by a larger number of retirees (Gee and Gutman, 2). The notion of great danger in population aging has persisted, however, in such books as *The Coming Generational Storm: What You Need to Know about America's Economic Future*, by Lawrence J. Kotlikoff and Scott Burns and *Shock of*

Gray by Ted C. Fishman. Age-blaming as well as the false assumption that elders are a homogeneous group underlie scare language about population aging (Gee, 7). Those who raise alarms about population aging are not simply policy analysts but ideologues, "ardent champions of private sector solutions to social problems" (Schulz and Binstock, 16).

Liberals, too, may have negative views of this demographic trend, but they usually do not resort to portraying old people as a monolithic and threatening group, and they are much more likely than conservatives to support social programs. Liberals may not realize, however, that fear of an aging population rests partly on prejudice and outdated ideas that cause us to focus only on problems and to overlook opportunities (Moody and Sasser, xxx).

A flaw in the thinking of groups such as the Concord Coalition is the assumption that older people live in isolation from others. In fact, most live in families, either in the same family unit or in contact with nearby or distant family members. That means, for example, that a cut in Social Security benefits might require an adult child to give money to an aged parent, a change that would clearly harm the economic interest of the younger person. Or, if a grandparent who parents because he or she has the time available returns to a paid job to cover increasing health care costs, the child suffers. Benefits to old citizens do not come from the pockets of the young and middle-aged.

Furthermore, wealth is passed downward to the young as well as upward to old citizens. Without Medicare, parents of baby boomers would have spent much more of their savings on health care. The often-cited fact that programs for the old take up one-third of the federal budget is usually stripped of its context: Without Social Security and Medicare, the old would be entirely dependent on savings or families, if they had either one. Thus payments to the old can be seen as payments the young and middle-aged need not make. Without the so-called entitlements, the old would have fewer assets to pass on to their children. Not much ability to think abstractly is required to understand that the old are a part of society, interconnected with others, not an invasive species like kudzu. Responding to fears of intergenerational conflict, geriatrician Jerald Winakur wrote that old people are not burdens but "an untapped resource, a deep well that when nurtured will give back to our families, schools, communities, and public consciousness much more than we will ever take" (3).

Words and phrases such as "epidemic," "onslaught," "tsunami," and "time bomb" denigrate old women and men. Instead of being seen in multiple roles or as having diverse economic needs, they are caricatured as parasites, "living too long, consuming too many societal resources, and robbing the young," a perception that justifies cuts in their benefits (Estes, "Critical Gerontology," 29). This viewpoint falsely assumes that young families and children are directly harmed by spending on the elderly. In fact, many of them, especially women over eighty-five and single women of color, are poor. Nearly 20 percent of old Americans are poor or near poor, the highest rate for any group except children (Minkler, "Scapegoating," 9). The claim that old-age benefits increase poverty among minority children is unsubstantiated. In fact, these benefits are especially important in minority communities because family units are interdependent (Wallace and Villa, 242).

False assumptions can influence large numbers of people, however, and the result of conservative arguments that the old Americans threaten future generations is that we have lost the social contract of the Lyndon Johnson era, according to which old people should be cared for. They were often mistreated in the past, as Robert Butler's 1975 book *Why Survive?* makes abundantly clear, but most citizens believed in providing an adequate safety net for them. "Social contract" suggests further the concept of intergenerational dependency, reciprocity across the life course, and intergenerational solidarity (Estes, "Social Security," 16).

The social contract began unraveling in America in the late 1970s, according to former labor secretary Robert Reich, who argues that it defined our sense of fairness but was not based on redistribution of wealth (21). In the past, American elders had a strong political presence but are now seen as "threatening to others" (Hudson and Gonyea, 273). Canadians, by contrast, believe in "equity and access to health care for all" (Chappell, McDonald, and Stones, 79). In the United States, humane values have been supplanted by a view of elders as an economic drain. Thus by 2007, the Medicare budget for home health care had been cut in half (Harrington Meyer and Herd, 111–12). The retirement of baby boomers will *increase* the need for home health care. Although Boomers are denounced as selfish and materialistic by some conservatives, the great heterogeneity in this group belies such stereotypes (Hudson and Gonyea 279).

The attack on "entitlements" used to evoke fear of an aging population seems ironic considering that older people are better off than their grandparents *because* of increased Social Security benefits and Medicare. "The aggregate well-being of today's aged is largely the result of a half century's governmental action on their behalf" (Hudson, 11). Conservatives have been attacking a success. In fact, the number of elders who support adult children exceeds the number who depend on them financially (Estes, "Social Security," 18–19). The white middle class benefits more than the working class from deferred compensation, and if benefits are cut, the greatest suffering will occur among the working class and people of color. They are less likely to own property or to have pensions, two cushions that help protect the economic interests of white middle-class people over sixty-five. And their interests are usually not promoted by the American

Association of Retired Persons (AARP), unless they coincide with the interests of the middle class.[2]

Conservative politicians' hostility to AARP extends far beyond partisanship, and exaggerating AARP influence is a favorite ploy to discredit it. A former senator, Alan Simpson, once condemned AARP as "evil." Women and men over sixty-five are resented for having a voice, even as muted a voice as AARP, which alienated many of its members by its support of the Medicare prescription drug bill. On the other hand, in 2005, it successfully opposed Republican efforts to privatize Social Security and sponsored "Diversity and Aging in the 21st Century," a conference at which NAACP and AARP pledged to work together (June 19–21, 2007, Los Angeles).

The dangers to the economic health of older Americans posed by conservative attempts to "fix" Social Security have been thoroughly analyzed by others.[3] I simply note that these proposals would lack credibility if widespread fear of an aging population were not part of the popular mythology. The chief beneficiaries of "privatizing" Social Security would be banks, insurance companies, brokerage houses, and health care corporations. Zeal for "privatizing" Social Security has dissipated because of the disappearance of the budget surplus; the recession; increasing economic anxiety among citizens facing job losses and steep declines in their property values; and rising gas prices; but its security remains somewhat threatened by fear of an "age wave" swamping younger taxpayers. The importance of keeping Social Security intact was reinforced by the Enron collapse, which wiped out the 401(k) retirement plans of many of its employees. Privatization changes beneficiaries into consumers and puts at a disadvantage those with few resources (Harrington Meyer and Herd, *Market Friendly*, 27).

Conservatives' success in frightening many citizens about population aging is illustrated by the results of a survey by the Employee Benefits Research Institute showing that only 52 percent of Americans current workers are confident that they can retire comfortably (Ghilarducci, 5).[4] A 2010 Gallup poll found that 76 percent of people aged eighteen to thirty-four do not believe they will get any Social Security benefits. That would happen only if Congress abolishes Social Security. Although that is extremely unlikely, "elders' political legitimacy will be under ongoing threat" (Hudson and Gonyea, 280). Multiple sources feed into the fear of vanishing benefits. An important one must be workers' fear of their own aging. With that dread already implanted, they may be susceptible to more abstract fears. If someone told these workers that a projected huge increase in the number of teenagers threatened the country's economic future, they would probably not be very alarmed.

The mass media have not communicated to citizens a far more plausible outcome than slashed benefits: With reforms and adjustments, both

Social Security and Medicare can be maintained at their present levels. The second scenario lacks drama. No scary graphics can be brought out to illustrate it. The conservative scenario imagines us victims of numbers. In fact, a modest improvement in the health of old Americans would result in Medicare savings, and a modest shift toward health promotion for old people in place of the current disease model would bring these improvements. No utopian schemes are needed to assure the continued security of old-age benefits. The *Columbia Journalism Review* judged media coverage of Social Security seriously inadequate, for example in its failure to report on the negative impact of Obama's payroll tax cut or to tell readers/viewers how proposed cuts would affect ordinary Americans (Lieberman).

Health care costs will increase with population aging, but a major cause of escalating Medicare costs is fraud. According to the National Center for Policy Analysis, Medicare fraud amounts to $33 billion each year.[5] Furthermore, the major cause of escalating health care costs is not population aging but the "aggressive use of expensive technology" (Robert Kane, 71) and thus targeting baby boomers for health care costs is a form of scapegoating (76).

Medicare recipients do not compel drug companies to test a thousand new drugs, to spend millions giving free samples to doctors, or to carpet bomb television with their commercials. The United States spends more of its GNP on health care than Canada and gets less in return, an imbalance that old citizens did not create. Furthermore, the very old cost less to care for at the end of life than people in their sixties and seventies. The ten-year MacArthur Foundation Study of Aging in America concluded, surprisingly, that once people reach sixty-five, their added years do not have a major impact on Medicare costs (Rowe and Kahn, 186). The reason is that people in their eighties are less likely than fifty-year-olds to have major surgery or dialysis. Requiring fewer resources, their care is less costly, one piece of evidence that questions the doomsday scenarios of right-wing analysts. Joint replacements are now common, however. We don't know whether breakthroughs in genetic research and biotechnology will increase or decrease the cost of health care for everyone.

Moreover, no one knows the future economic impact of population aging because the large number of variables makes predictions unreliable. While the percentage of people over sixty-five is growing, their actual numbers may not increase substantially. In the coming decades, longevity may level off. According to one calculation, human life expectancy will not exceed eighty-five years. Even eliminating cancer, stroke, and diabetes would not boost the figure to ninety-five or one hundred (Roush, 42). While it is true that the ratio of workers to retirees is shrinking (from 4.5 to 3.3 between 2000 and 2020), the trend in itself is not the menace that conservatives make it out to be. The percentage of people over sixty-five who stay in the workforce, for example, has increased from 10.8 percent in 1985 to 16 percent in 2007, according to the legal advocacy office of AARP (Associated Press, February 18, 2008), and the recession solidified this trend. If the U.S. economy grows only 1.3 to 2 percent over the next thirty to sixty years, the United States can absorb the costs of population aging without "unduly burdening future workers" (Kingson and Quadagno, 356).

Even when economics is the only lens through which population aging is examined, the cost of old Americans should be calculated not only by Social Security and Medicare but also by less obvious factors. Women and men over sixty-five have a crime rate that is remarkably low (Posner, 128). The car accident rate for male drivers over eighty-five is one-fourth the rate for teenaged males and one-half the rate for males aged twenty-five to twenty-nine (125). Even though the old as a group have fewer accidents than younger people, their accident rate per mile driven is comparable. The Insurance Institute for Highway Safety reports that drivers over eighty have a higher rate of crashes per mile driven than younger groups, and the highest rate of fatal collisions per mile driven. A Canadian study notes that older drivers show the greatest variability of any age group and concludes that age itself is not a reliable gauge of driving fitness (Tuokko and Hunter, 24). On the other hand, taking multiple medications, as many elders do, is a risk factor (34).

Posner strongly disagrees with other conservatives on the meaning of population aging. He believes that when both costs and benefits are calculated, there is "no solid basis for concluding that the aging of the population has been or in the foreseeable future will be a source of net diminution in the overall welfare of the American people" (363). No icebergs, tidal waves, epidemics, floods, onslaughts, gray hordes, or time bombs dramatize this assessment.

"Demography is not destiny."[6] In "The Fertility Implosion," *New York Times* columnist David Brooks ignores the connection between lower fertility and increases in women's standard of living, and his statement that Japan has "one of the worst demographic profiles" conflates science with moralistic elder bashing (March 13, 2012).

Although misleading, conservatives' fear-inducing rhetoric deserves study because it frames the public discussion of aging policy issues that will affect every citizen. As a result, drastic proposals for change can look moderate, and the interests of women, minorities, and the poor can be ignored (Kingson and Quadagno, 346). An example is the option of raising the retirement age for Social Security to seventy, a change that would particularly harm low-income early retirees and unemployed older workers and would result in a 40 percent benefit reduction for workers who retire at sixty-two (351). In addition, people of color would be disproportionately harmed because of their lower life expectancy.[7] Any proposed changes in Medicare should take into account women's longer lives, higher incidence of chronic illness, greater risk of poverty, and greater need of long-term care.

CONCLUSION

The issue of old-age benefits is not only economic and demographic but also moral (Vincent, *Inequality*, 147). Generational equity assumes a narrow view of reciprocity: You get back what you have given. A broader view, one that acknowledges interconnectedness, is that benefits bestowed by the generation ahead of us will be returned to the generation following us (149). A related moral issue is the limits (and dangers) of the adversarial mindset implicit in visions of generational conflict—a white, middle-class, male, competitive, Western mindset. The communal traditions of many blacks, Latino/as, Asian Americans, and Indians and the value systems of many whites, especially women, stress cooperation and harmony between generations rather than opposition and struggle. They are not the ones who formulate aging policy.

Women are especially harmed by attempts to stir up fear of population aging. Living longer than men and more likely to be poor in old age, they require stable public policies on aging that will not use emotion-laden rhetoric to justify benefit cuts. Because unfounded fears of population aging have spread widely, progressives must respond to demographic demagoguery, showing how its solutions to perceived crises would pit one group of citizens against another. The time bomb and the iceberg are after all large numbers of our mothers and aunts, our neighbors and co-workers, and ourselves. This is not a reason to ignore implications of increased longevity, but it is a reminder that numbers tell only part of the story and that other numbers give a different account. When the story is frightening, when metaphors carry the weight of argument, when the powerful feel victimized, it is time to turn on our flashlights in the dark room and find no rough beast lurking there after all.

3

❦

Sickness and Other Social Roles of Old People

Wherever meaningful social and religious roles exist for elders, physical health is only one dimension of aging. In a materialistic culture having no designated role for elders, on the other hand, the state of the body is all-important. "Our society views aging through the prism of illness" (Hazan, 20). In other societies, the old may be peacemakers or mediators. They may be keepers of traditions or repositories of special knowledge. In some African tribes, old women have the power of naming the newborn. In Asian cultures, the time of gradual loss of physical strength is thought to be the time for deepening spiritual power. In North America, minority communities are generally the only ones in which any comparably high status for the old is found. Old Indian women assume roles such as wisdom keeper, leader, and artist, for example (John, Blanchard, and Hennessy, 305). Everyone has a place in the talking circle of the Manitoba Cree, but it is the elder who begins the talk. Black women typically exert strong influence when they are old, often through their churches.

One mark of the social construction of aging is overemphasis on bodily decline. The entire meaning of old age then becomes physical loss. When old people are reduced to deteriorating bodies (which change in infinitely varied ways), they can easily be marginalized. No one regards childhood or adolescence solely as a physical condition. Seeing old age in this narrow way has many consequences, of which the most significant is the medicalization of aging.

THE SICK ROLE

Thirty years ago, medical anthropologist Margaret Clark pointed out that the old in the United States have only one important social function: getting sick. This viewpoint is even more persuasive today because of the increasingly large role corporate health care plays in aging, both in shaping public policy and in limiting individual choice. In America, where usefulness is defined as productivity, many who are old do not appear to themselves or others as useful because their paid work role has ended. In a market economy, however, they produce something of great monetary value: illness. The business of the old is to be sick.

In biomedicine, the aging body is seen as a site for "continual restoration and improvement." Thus the sick old body can be fixed by the ministrations of drug conglomerates, science, and technology (Joyce and Mamo, 99–100). Sickness is so profitable, in fact, that healthy elders who have no need of restoration or improvement subvert an increasingly dominant system of learned dependence.

As the number of young people decreases and the number of those over sixty-five and especially over eighty-five rapidly increases, biomedicine depends more than ever on the old for its profits. American elders use a third of all prescription drugs. Decreased use would result in big losses for the drug industry. If most of the old could manage without drugs and hospitals, who would fill the beds? In addition, population aging creates potential expansion for businesses that provide illness-related products and services.

If the financial interests of big medicine, insurance companies, and the drug industry were served by healthy old people, the center of aging would be health promotion and not illness. But as Carroll Estes has written, old Americans are "instrumental in the development and expansion of a large and profitable medical-industrial complex." Under capitalism, the needs of the old are commodifed ("Critical Gerontology," 26). Therefore, the illnesses of the old have far more than biological meaning; they are not just individual occurrences. Looking at illness as *characteristic* of the old, especially old women, misses its social function. A resurgence of health among large numbers of them would slow down expansion of the medical-industrial complex.

In industrial nations, the *healthy* elders are "expected to behave psychologically and socially" like sick people of any age (Arluke and Peterson, 275). To fill their social function of illness, the old must be conditioned to believe that aging is a disease requiring heavy consumption of medical services. The drug ads that saturate television encourage this belief, especially since old women and men appear in few ads for the products healthy people use. Magazines geared to them advertise medicines and props for illness. Newspapers cover the disease aspects of aging as if the two were interchangeable. Families assume that an elderly parent needs more drugs than before simply because he or she is old, and this assumption is shared by nurses, doctors, and social workers. Medicare's emphasis on acute illness rather than health promotion is a major factor in conditioning the old to see sickness as their chief concern. Instead of having federally funded recreation programs for the old, or a jobs program, we have Medicare. When aging is viewed as socially constructed, however, as something more than what happens to our bodies, the focus on illness seems skewed.

The accuracy of Clark's comment on the sickness function of the old can readily be tested by eavesdropping on conversations in a senior center or anywhere people over sixty-five gather. It is soon apparent that illness serves as one of the main staples of conversation. More significantly, old people with serious health problems gain status by having them. They quote their doctors at length, speculate about the progress of their disease, cite examples of others who have it, and manage to stay in the spotlight by emphasizing their illness. Other facets of their lives recede in importance. Sometimes elders will try to outdo each other in boasting of the severity of their condition. "Illness talk becomes competitive," noted Frida Furman in her study of older women and beauty shop culture (31). A sentence that begins, "My doctor says . . ." is a status marker for an old woman or man. It links him or her to culturally valued workers and institutions. It announces participation in an important world.

Once during a healthy-aging workshop I was conducting, a woman in her seventies said proudly and defiantly, "I live with pain." She offered no other information about herself. Apparently, she was staking a claim to be taken seriously. Without her pain, how would she present herself? The woman's pain is a physical condition, but the meaning she gives it is culturally determined. In a society where sickness conferred no status, she might experience pain but its meaning would be slight compared to its very large meaning in modern America. Or, in late life, pain that began earlier may actually "entail more suffering" once judged age-related (Gullette, *Aged by Culture*, 133). A Finnish study found that elders distanced themselves from the identity "old," except when it "served to *legitimate* ill health and inactivity (Jolanki, 262–63).

Those who come into contact with old women and men sometimes complain about their preoccupation with illness and disease. Perhaps they would have more compassion if they could see how the world of old people often excludes much of what used to make life meaningful and now focuses on illness. The old woman who constantly complains about her ailments expresses not only an individual personality but a cultural pattern. At the same time, she is breaking an unwritten rule that requires her to suffer silently. Reporting on one's physical condition is not the same as complaining, but old women often are not granted the psychic space to explore the differences between reporting and complaining.

The doctor may be the one person outside the family that an elderly woman regularly sees. Often those perceived as frail and dependent are not making new friends or discovering new interests. The importance of sickness may become magnified if isolation removes other sources of self-definition. Very old people typically have little power or influence, and society has few expectations of them. Illness is absorbing, ever changing, seldom dramatic but eventful. It fills up time. Illness may be the only process occurring in the life of an old person that others regard as meaningful. No wonder many of them emphasize health problems. It takes both an awareness that one can easily become enmeshed in the medical system and a strong ego consciously to avoid the sick role when old and ailing, or to resist exploiting sickness to gain attention.

The sick role for older Americans has grown along with the "expansion of the medical gaze into wider areas of health and social policy." The phrase "medical gaze" refers to the "discourses, languages, and ways of seeing" that shape our understanding of aging and thereby make biomedicine more powerful (Powell, 672). An example is the notion that old people need more drugs *because* they are old. As a result of the increasingly dominant role biomedicine currently plays in America, we have access to much information about our personal risk of disease and, as a result, risk may preoccupy us. As medical anthropologist Sharon Kaufman notes, "more information and increased surveillance of the body lead to enhanced risk acuity in a seemingly endless feedback loop, in the demand for more intervention" (23). In other words, America's elderly "swallow their prescribed remedies, often many simultaneously, to bring their laboratory numbers to heel" (Hadler, 13). One result is that ineffective or unnecessary medical procedures cost the United States approximately $700 billion each year (Peter Orzag, ctd. in Carstensen, *A Long Bright Future*, 171). A curb on this trend might be a greatly increased number of geriatricians, but a signal weakness in the health care system is that only one-half of one percent of U.S. medical school graduates choose geriatrics as a specialty (Hogan).

The understanding that old-age illness is partly socially constructed does not deny widespread health problems among the old, blame them for being sick, or assume they are victims. Whether we age from wear and tear or because we are genetically programmed to age, the fact is that late life and sickness are more closely linked than youth or middle age and sickness. But this general truth is no reliable predictor that any given individual will get sick, nor does it mean that a disease or health problem in old age is incurable. People fall ill for complex and mysterious reasons. Even in the case of the chain smoker who gets emphysema or the heavy meat eater with heart disease, we cannot know the brain chemistry disorders that may have predisposed them to addictions. Although programmed to accept illness as natural to their life stage, many old people navigate the health care system without becoming victims. For some, seeing a doctor is comforting and reassuring without entangling them in a sick role.

Furthermore, certain groups are sicker than others. Black women are more likely than white women to die of heart disease, stroke, and breast cancer and are less likely to get mammograms. High blood pressure is a problem for 19 percent of white women but 34 percent of black women (Flaherty, 3). American Indians have very high rates of diabetes. Poor whites as well as people of color are more likely to have been exposed to environmental toxins and less likely to have had their illnesses diagnosed and treated before they reach old age.

The sick role extends to the very end of life. Looking back on his treatment of terminally ill patients, a doctor recalled that sometimes a family asked him "to use my physician superpower to push the patient's tired body further down the road, with little thought as to whether the additional suffering will be worth it" (Bowron, 3).

Alzheimer's Disease

Today, Alzheimer's disease stands for aging in America.[1] It accounts for 60 to 80 percent of all dementia cases (dementia is the broader term) and age is the greatest risk factor.[2] At present, neither "approved disease-modifying drug therapy for Alzheimer's" nor scientifically proven strategies for prevention exist (Wierenga and Bondi, 42). The great attention paid to the disease by the media reinforces the link between aging and sickness. The devastating impact of Alzheimer's disease on individuals and their families warrants concern, but media coverage has also contributed to an unreasonable fear of aging. John Bayly's memoir about caring for Iris Murdoch (in which the great novelist is described playing with teletubbies) received far more press than any of her works. Fear of getting Alzheimer's is disproportionate to its incidence.[3] Approximately one in ten older Americans suffers from the disease (some estimates say one in eight) but media emphasis creates the impression that it is far more prevalent. Students are surprised to learn that it does not afflict most older people.[4]

Simply saying "Alzheimer's" evokes "fear and dread in baby boomers" who have seen the illness in their parents; they know that no anti-Alzheimer's pill can eradicate the disease, as an antidepressant helps a depressed person lead a normal life or as an antibiotic can cure pneumonia

(G. Small, 34). Dread also reflects the kind of life our care system has created for people who receive the Alzheimer's diagnosis (Power, 12). Scary movie images of zombies have "leaked into the popular and scholarly discourse about real people who have Alzheimer's, constructing them as animated corpses and their disease as a terrifying threat to the social order." This perception not only creates highly negative stereotypes and stigma but also the "emotional responses of disgust and utter terror" (Behuniak, 72). People with AD may also evoke our fear of being out of control. The derogatory term "demented" is applied to people with AD, who have the additional disadvantage of being able to contrast their present limited abilities with their previous condition (Scholl and Sabat, 111–12).

Loss of one's mental capacity is especially terrifying in societies like ours where rationality is so highly valued. Here Alzheimer's excludes one from the circle of life in ways not characteristic of other societies. A person with Alzheimer's becomes a manifestation of disorder rather than an individual who is ill. The ideology of Alzheimer's sharply contrasts normal aging with "total and remitting pathology; in so doing, it both denies the complex experience and the personhood of old persons it would represent and shifts attention away from the social origins of much of the weakness of old age" (L. Cohen, *No Aging in India*, 303). Social origins include learned helplessness, expectations of decay and decline, lack of health promotion programs for the old, media stereotypes, and inattention to the dangers of multiple prescription drug use.[5]

Elizabeth Markson has observed that memory loss may be a way of coping for women whose roles have disappeared, and consequently, what we term dementia may be a "social interaction and the appearance of more primitive, unsocialized, emotional or cognitive states" ("Gender Roles," 268). A similar interpretation suggests that memory loss may be an attempt to return to the "safe haven of a past universe of meaning" (Hazan, 86). Nonetheless, Alzheimer's disease is an incurable affliction, striking many people over eighty-five, the age group in which women outnumber men four to one. An important discovery is that the performance of people with AD is linked to the social context in which it occurs; in other words, not all incapacity results from neuropathology (Scholl and Sabat, 114). If we consider only exclusively cognitive function when dealing with people with AD, "we will see them as embarrassments in our 'hypercognitive society.'" Ethicists remind us that humans have many facets that "an obsessive focus on rationality tends to obscure" (Holstein, Parks, and Waymack, 230).

Consequently, a few gerontologists now explore more humane attitudes toward and treatment of people who have dementia. Two examples are *Dementia beyond Drugs* by G. Allen Power and *Forget Memory* by Anne Basting. In the preface to Power's book, William Thomas, founder of the

Eden Alternative, writes that the false equation of care and treatment serves "powerful forces inside the medical profession and the medical-industrial complex" (ix).⁶ Overdrugging Alzheimer's patients, for example, is not the same as caring for them (although the drugs may alleviate anxieties of family members); it reinforces the sick role, the slot into which they are placed. In *Forget Memory*, Basting argues that excessive fear of dementia is triggered by fear of death and fear of meaninglessness, but the "fear reflex is making the experience of dementia worse" (4). Memory is very complex, she notes, and some loss is normal. Basting shows how performing plays, songwriting, dancing, and writing create more humane treatment of dementia. When people suffer cognitive impairment, their bodies become "the primary means of self-expression" and thus performances can humanize dementia care (Kontos, 145). The same is true of singing and painting, therapeutic activities showing that vestiges of creativity remain. Gene Cohen used the example of Willem de Kooning to demonstrate "the important phenomenon of possessing an area of preserved skill" ("Creativity," 201).

In short, attitudes toward dementia care can shift from a custodial model to a therapeutic one (Graham and Stephenson, xvi). This new approach is used in the Netherlands town of Weesp, where patients live in a small complex rather than a nursing home. Cared for by two professionals, they have access to music, painting, baking, a small grocery store, gardening, and communal areas. Residents are encouraged to help with cooking and to help each other (Tagliabue, A12). If this model were used in the United States, families and friends of people with dementia could focus on what capacities their loved ones retain rather than on lost abilities. Anecdotal evidence suggests that people suffering from dementia keep some aspects of their previous religious feelings even in advanced stages of their illness and that in fact it is "one of the aspects of their identity and personality that can longest be protected and preserved" (Coleman, 169).

An insidious aspect of the sick role is that it may actually create illness. A telling example of socially constructed incapacity occurred when a group of English people in a long-term geriatric ward was moved into attractively decorated bungalows during renovation of their ward. As they began to exercise more and to perform household tasks, both their incontinence and their mental confusion declined, and they began to cast off their sick role (Townsend, 37). This dramatic change suggests that old people may perform sickness when their environment gives them the appropriate cues. If they assume their illnesses are natural concomitants of their age, they may feel fatalistic about their health. "Fatalism implicit in metaphors of deterioration, decline, and disease as aging" may prevent older adults from reestablishing their levels of physical, psychological, and social health (W. Davidson, 177). It may even prevent them from imagining recovery.

Learning to be old, then, means knowing that late-life illness has both cultural and biological origins. It means believing in one's capacity to recover completely from illness, accident, or disease in the face of skepticism or insensitivity from families and doctors. It means knowing that political and economic institutions are structured to offer some support for the sick old but very little for health maintenance or improvement.

Aside from normalizing illness, the sick role of the old is damaging because it places people in a dependent, relatively powerless position. The old woman or man who frequents doctors' offices performs subordination. His or her infirmities receive far more attention than strengths and innate healing powers. Rarely will a doctor view an old patient as capable of returning to full vigor. Rarely does a patient have the opportunity to tell the whole story of his or her illness in a way that emphasizes not only its severity but also his or her coping strategies and resilience. An old woman may escape the most blatant forms of gender bias in her medical care—being diagnosed as demented if she expresses anger, for example—but gender may determine how seriously her symptoms are taken and whether or not a psychotropic drug is prescribed.

A *New York Times* essay, "What's Making Us Sick Is an Epidemic of Diagnoses," describes "the medicalization of everyday life." Uncomfortable physical and emotional sensations used to be considered part of life but are increasingly regarded as symptoms of disease, partly because advanced technology lets doctors "look really hard for things to be wrong" and partly because of an emphasis on pre-disease or being "at risk." Not all treatments, the authors note, have significant benefits but almost all can be harmful. More diagnoses result in bigger profits for drug manufacturers, doctors, and hospitals (Welch et al.). In the era of overtreatment, when patients present their doctors with medical information gleaned from the Internet, it is useful to remember that there is "subjective core to every medical decision. . . . [D]espite many advances, much of medicine still exists in a gray zone where there is not one right answer" (Hartzband and Groopman, C3). Since late-life illness may be multi-faceted, this cautionary note is useful.

The dangers inherent in the sick role are particularly apparent at the end of life, when there are "enormous pressures from multiple sources . . . to prolong the lives of the very old who face serious or critical illness" (Kaufman, 231). Resisting these pressures or even examining them critically will not be easy for baby boomers and their families. But patients and gerontologists alike need to become more aware of "the tension between our desire to make the old body ever more malleable and to extend life because we can, and the desire for a death without technological interference" (240).

To remain healthy in old age is to defy expectations. Good luck, class privilege, college education, and high status of one's former work help increase chances of health as do exercise, good habits, and access to well-trained alternative healers. A non-conforming spirit seems essential, too. What Rowe and Kahn call "usual aging" has not been the fate of the very healthy old. Since the robust among them tend not to appear on the radar screens of policymakers, their numbers are probably greater than anyone realizes. Although unreported, late-life vigor is ordinary.

The conventional view inextricably linking disease with old age must give way to a newer idea that good health characterizes large numbers of elderly people. If those who are very healthy in their eighties and older could become known beyond their circle of family and friends, the assumption that being old is a medical condition could be challenged. Fear of an aging population rests on this belief. Fear of our own possible deterioration is surely intensified if the lives of the only old people we know are circumscribed by illness.

OTHER SOCIAL ROLES

Are there alternatives to the sick role for old women and men? Social gerontologists often call modern aging a "roleless role" because no special tasks, responsibilities, or leadership functions are expected of people resulting solely from old age. Recently it has seemed that the social responsibility of old people is to extend mid-life as long as possible so that neither they nor others will be discomfited by thoughts of what comes next. Those who favor rationing health care do not forthrightly say that the social role of the old is to hurry up and die, but they regard their prolonged living as a threat to the common good. The description "roleless role" better fits the white middle class than American Indians, Asian Americans, Latino/as, and blacks, whose communities often seem to have a variety of roles for elders. Gender bias lurks here, too, because very often a woman's caregiving role lasts for her whole life.

Service

What are old North Americans supposed to do or be? A common view is that their role is to serve others.[7] Since those who serve others are unquestionably useful, the service role has some appeal. But it masks doubt that elders are worthy in and of themselves. "Designated server" is a demeaning role for those who are old; it assumes they are a monolithic group and locates their value in action, not in being. Designated server is especially unsuited to old women, many of whom have served others all too faithfully for decades. Volunteering is often thought to mean only formal volunteer activities but the definition should be broadened to include caregiving, mutual aid, providing companionship, and running errands for neighbors (Martinez et al., 25; 31).The service ideal reflects middle-class bias, in that it disregards the fact that poor and working-class women and men have often been coerced into the service of others. Besides, conventional notions of volunteering do not consider barriers such as poor health or lack of transportation (Martinez et al., 33).

Tillie Olsen's novella *Tell Me a Riddle* describes a woman who fiercely rebels against the expectation that she tend to others' needs. She is tired and would rather sit quietly absorbed in her own thoughts than humor a grandchild by telling riddles. Service to others is not the special province of the old. They may be good at it, from practice, and they may have more leisure than others to be of use, but this worthy ideal for people of any age should not be assumed to fit them automatically. Justifying the existence of old women and men on the grounds that they serve others is narrowly utilitarian and devalues those too infirm to give assistance to others. What they can provide is opportunities for others to serve them.

In grandparenting, the service role takes a benign form, but it is not an experience universal to aging, and it is a more complicated role than before because of high divorce rates, blended families, and the mobility that allows working families to live far from grandparents and grandparents to retire far from their grandchildren. The role has also changed significantly now that many grandparents have assumed parenting responsibilities. The term "abuela," or grandmother, conveys "a romanticized image of older Chicanas that only serves to disempower women within their families and among the community" (Facio, 348). The individuality of an elderly Chicana may disappear into "abuela." Census reports indicate that American Indian grandparents are three times as likely to care for grandchildren as other Americans (Cross et al., 383). Intergenerational ties are deeply rooted in Chinese culture and, according to one study, grandparents now provide important family resources rather than simply receiving them, as in the past. Many grandparents who live with their grandchildren provide more care than mothers (Chen et al., 588–89). In the United States, especially in the shadow of the Great Recession, "the growth of grandfamilies leads to food insecurity" (*Aging Today*, May–June, 2012, 7; 10).

David Steinberg, who wrote a column called "Seniorities" for the *San Francisco Examiner*, reported that when he auditioned for television commercials featuring grandfathers, he wore a cardigan sweater because that's what grandfathers are expected to wear. The narrowness of role expectations is mirrored in the narrowness of this dress code.

As the population ages and more people over sixty-five are available to volunteer, the idea that their role is to serve others conveniently justifies the use of volunteer labor to replace the many paid workers whose jobs were cut. Volunteer labor, it is true, keeps many programs and agencies afloat, but it cannot compensate for what has been lost.

Robert Butler, a psychiatrist and gerontologist whose writings have encouraged a humanistic view of aging, sees the role question in this light: "Older persons should be custodians of the finest elements of civilization, and active guides, mentors, models, and critics. Old age should be a moral powerhouse. Otherwise, does humanity deserve its newly acquired longevity?" ("New World"). Commendable as this sounds at first hearing, it assumes that the presence of large numbers of the old requires justification. It doesn't. Butler's view expresses a need that the non-old may have for mentors, moral guides, and preservers of culture, but the existence of that need does not mean that old people should be the ones to meet it. Barbara Macdonald believed that the culture-bearer role objectifies old women, for example (75). The statement that "old age should be a moral powerhouse" in effect prescribes a role for women, because it is they who survive to deep old age. In fact, life knowledge probably equips many old women to advise well, but this role should be freely chosen, not imposed. Number of years accumulated does not predict moral development.

A related prescription is that old people should be protectors of the environment. Many retirees have become ecologically sophisticated advocates for environmental causes, using their leisure for the common good. Many march with groups such as the Sierra Club at the demonstrations against the World Trade Organization. The Colorado group Great Old Broads for Wilderness calls attention to damage caused on public lands by off-road vehicles and publishes the newsletter *Broadsides*. Perhaps late life encourages a strong awareness of future generations, of legacy, or of the transitoriness of human existence. It's likely, too, that women and men who are now over seventy remember clean air and clean water. Although the notion of old people as guardians of the environment is appealing, it is a variation of the idea that they exist to serve others.

The service role might look different if they were paid more for their labor. Designed for low-income people over sixty-five and dating from the War on Poverty of the 1960s, the Foster Grandparent Program, Senior Companions, and Senior Community Service involve relatively few elders. Senior Companions offer a stipend of $2.65 an hour. Senior Community Service homemakers earn between $10 and $13 an hour. SCS also provides free Medicare counseling staffed by volunteers and social work services. Program limitations suggest "a cultural ambivalence about older adults as serious and capable service-providers" (Freedman, "Senior Citizens," 215). This situation is especially discouraging because public institutions need so much work. Some problems in our underfunded schools might be solved, for example, if paid workers from the ranks of older women and men were given meaningful work to do in schools, mentoring, testing, or tutoring. The boredom and loneliness of many nursing home residents might be alleviated if paid workers their own age visited them frequently.

In late life, people will keep on doing what they have been doing, especially if they are healthy. Others will learn something new or discover talents and abilities unknown before. Some will take up a cause like literacy or community work such as hospice. Some will be the mainstays of their parishes, congregations, synagogues, or covens. For some the role of bereaved spouse will be defining. As the population ages, caregiving will be the social role of an increasing number of middle-aged and old women.

An attractive example of self-help is the Village Movement, begun in Boston. Villages meet needs of elders who choose to remain in their own homes. They are self-governing and self-supporting grassroots, membership-based organizations (Poor, Baldwin, and Willett, 112–14). They vary in response to members' needs and coordinate services of screened volunteers and providers. Villages Movements have developed without federal or state funding and outside of the traditional aging services network; they promote volunteerism, civic engagement, and intergenerational connections (113).

Wisdom

Another common view is that old people hand down their wisdom to others. This notion fit societies in which the survival of the young directly depended on acquiring the knowledge possessed by tribal elders. Among Pacific Coast tribes, for example, the art of catching salmon was passed down to the young. An understanding of how to behave, how to handle disputes, how to choose a partner, whom to avoid, and how to interpret the natural world all depended on received wisdom. Where to find medicinal plants, how to make tools, or how to fashion baskets reflected accumulations of knowledge whose possession gave status to old members of the group. On the other hand, in a technological society, in which information rapidly becomes obsolete, the wisdom role of the old all but disappears. Today a grandparent may impart knowledge, but with the dispersion of families and the proliferation of information, few grandparents have knowledge that a young person absolutely needs to survive. The life experience acquired by some elderly women and men, valuable as it is, does not provide a widely sanctioned guide role for them, partly because age segregation is common now and individualism highly valued. In addition, cultural diversity and the dissimilarity of our various North American traditions preclude a common guide role for older people, but particular forms of it exist among specific groups—American Indians, for example, or newly arrived immigrants.

The role of wise elder appears to require a scarcity of candidates for the honor. In colonial America, where few lived to be old, that attainment carried with it an aura of having been favored by God. Now, with millions surviving past seventy-five and eighty and many becoming centenarians, figuring out what is special about them is difficult. A Georgia study of centenarians and personality that focused on black people and whites in Georgia and used both self-reports and reports from family members found the centenarians low in neuroticism (they were neither anxious nor fearful) and high in conscientiousness. They tended to have high levels of competence and extraversion (P. Marshall et al.). Most centenarians are women, and although most have ailments, others are in "remarkably good shape" (Weil, 31). Those who live to 100 tend to have genetic protection against the diseases that shorten life.

The most comprehensive study of wisdom and aging, the Berlin Wisdom Model of Paul Baltes and his colleagues, examines various components of wisdom—for example, the ability to deal with problems, a deep understanding of human nature, tolerance, and the capacity to deal with uncertainty (Kunzmann, 1232–33). Wisdom seems to require integration of cognitive power with a high degree of emotional development. Sadness may come instead of happiness, however, as one sees friends fall ill and decline or experiences loss of power and ageism. Stanford studies by Laura Carstensen and her colleagues found, on the other hand, that compared to younger people, older participants less often have negative emotions, exercise better control of them, and rely on a "complex and nuanced emotional thermostat that allows them to bounce back quickly from adverse moments" (Hall, "Older," 64). Another perspective is that wisdom is a "process rather than a final state of being [and] collective wisdom seems a better goal that individual wisdom" (Whitehouse and George, 294–95).

The wise elder is a comforting notion in times of upheaval and rapid change. But the automatic linking of wisdom and age overlooks the fact that not all of the old are wise and that the characteristics of modern North America are manifestly not conducive to developing wisdom at any age. Those who attribute wisdom to the old romanticize them. This link is popular with young and middle-aged feminists, who understandably wish to counter ageism, for example by referring to the "wisdom . . . emerging from a lifetime of experience" as if this were universal.[8] A better way to honor old women than by invoking positive stereotypes is to value individual temperament and creativity. In some, wisdom will be a striking feature, but only in some. Or it will characterize certain aspects of an old woman's life but not others. The wisdom born of a deep understanding of one's own life experience differs from the wisdom that transcends an individual story.

At the same time, the wise elder archetype deserves some place in the modern scheme of aging if only because of its powerful, ancient, and cross-cultural manifestations. Surely old women and men who are highly developed emotionally, intellectually, and spiritually are worthy of being named wise elders. Whether they would choose this designation is another question. Recognizing high attainment in an elder requires both a generosity of spirit and freedom from ageist stereotypes on the part of a younger person.

Retirement

Some gerontologists believe retirement is merely a position, not a role involving special rights and duties or determining social relationships (Atchley, *Social Forces*, 251). Retirees identify themselves by their former work, especially when meeting someone for the first time, suggesting that the retirement role has limited meaning for them. Since work has more status than leisure, the retiree who names past work links himself or herself to what is valued. Paradoxically, retirees may be engaged in the most complex, demanding, and absorbing work they have ever undertaken, but it will not be defined as "work" if it brings no wage. (Retirement is analyzed in chapter 7.)

Gender Shifts

An aspect of social role and aging is the process by which some men take on traits and attitudes thought characteristic of women, such as nurturing, and women become more assertive. This late-life gender bending may become more common as gender stereotypes lose some of their formative influence, if that is a result of more women entering professions and more men growing through fatherhood. The later work of Georgia O'Keefe reveals an "adventurous, expansive, self-asserting" woman. By contrast, older men increasingly stress "their self-control, their friendly adaptability, and even their passivity."[9] Does this observation best fit white middle-class people? O'Keefe's late-life independence resulted in part from good fortune, a male partner who opened the doors of the New York art world to her.

I saw evidence of gender shifts at the Montefiore Senior Center in San Francisco, where I observed women in their eighties leading groups in which old men were rather quiet participants, even though some had retired from professions in which their dominance was assured (labor union president, for example). The men were outnumbered, but that alone should not have been responsible for their willingness to defer to women. One man memorably did not illustrate this pattern of late-life androgyny. He stood up in a discussion group and yelled, "Where are the men?" I explained that women outlive men. "Why is that?" he roared, and answered his own question: "Because women don't take good care of their husbands!"

From the vantage point of their nineties, Matilda White Riley and John W. Riley envisioned a society in which retirement would be replaced by alternating periods of leisure, work, and education; education would truly be lifelong; paid-work opportunities would be available to people of all ages; and old age would not be considered a burden (33). Some baby boomers will want to work until age 70 or older, especially women who finished their degrees in their fifties or sixties.

Colleges and universities keep older adults on the fringes, however, with weekend courses, "senior college," continuing education classes, and noncredit work. A major barrier to achieving an age-integrated society, according to John W. Rowe and Robert L. Kahn, is the unwillingness of many colleges and universities to adjust schedules and requirements "to encourage intermittent or sustained course work by adults of all ages" (196). "Encourage" is the key word here. At present, students over fifty or sixty are merely tolerated; colleges and universities are set up to serve eighteen- to twenty-five-year-olds. There is no biological reason for restricting education and work to youth and midlife, but the association of old age with decline seems to justify this custom. In the 1980s, however, the University of the Third Age was developed in Britain and Australia to offer low-cost higher education to older people. No previous education is required, and professors and administrators donate their time. A current trend in the United States is the establishment of retirement communities adjacent to universities, an excellent opportunity for affluent elders to continue learning. Senior colleges draw a broader range of students. Especially valuable are the Osher Life Long Learning Institutes known as OLLI (Moody and Sasser, 104).

What if old women and men have no particular social role simply by virtue of being their particular age? The great diversity of this population, its size, the increasing number of minority elders, the growing gap between rich and poor, and the fragmentation of society all support this view. Shaped by decades of influences and accidents of race, class, and gender, those who happen to be over seventy or eighty may find other aspects of their being more salient than their chronological age. If they have no social roles unique to their life stage, then their value cannot be grounded there, in utility and service. The idea that old women and men have special roles is condescending. They have the same roles as others. They choose them based on individual temperament, energy level, family needs, beliefs, habits, locale, income, friendship, skills, and time available rather than age.

Stories, Reminiscence, and Life Review

Another possibility, however, is that a social role for the old might be found in storytelling, reminiscence, and life review. The meaning older people see in their lives is part of the larger system of social and cultural meaning (Black and Rubinstein, 3). Life review was described by Robert Butler as a process marked by the return of memories and past conflicts that can lead to "resolution, reconciliation, atonement, integration and serenity. It can occur spontaneously, or be structured" ("Butler Reviews," 9).[10] Barbara Myerhoff hyphenated "re-membering" to distinguish it from ordinary recollection. It is a process of "focused unification" in which the "members" are our past selves and the people important to our story. In "re-membering," the creation of an aesthetic or moral framework for a story may be preferable to fullness of detail ("Rites and Signs," 320). Solitude is conducive to reminiscence and the ability to reminisce signifies cognitive health (Cappeliez and Webster, 187). Some reminiscences come up spontaneously while others are deliberately evoked (189).

Life review usually cannot be done alone; a recipient is needed to make the narrative coherent (Myerhoff and Tufte, 252). When the listener is young, the shared stories create intergenerational continuity (255). Women and men who live to be old accumulate much material to draw from, and the stories they write down or tell others constitute a legacy. Kathleen Woodward describes reminiscence as less analytical than life review and likely to create an "atmosphere of a certain companionableness" ("Telling Stories," 152). When reminiscence is the focus of writing groups, it becomes a "highly malleable process subject to others' influence," so that the story is not simply a record of an individual's thoughts and feelings but a "social product" (Ray, "Social Influences," 57). In one life-writing workshop, participants presented "multiple and conflicting representations of old age" in their narratives (Ray, "Researching," 179). The patronizing view of old people as dwelling too much on past events misses an important dimension of reminiscence: The past is not simply over but "continually lived out in new terms as its storytellers speak of life" (Gubrium and Holstein, 297). A vehicle for expressing this continuity is reminiscence theater, developed by groups such as Elders Share the Arts in Brooklyn.

Elders recounting their stories seldom follow the actual sequence of life events, a choice that probably heightens interest for their hearers. When a life review is elicited by an interviewer, he or she must be aware that if another interviewer spoke with the elder, the result would be a different story (Black and Rubinstein, 7). Looking back over one's past may hold special significance for members of stigmatized groups, particularly if survival strategies are a theme. Reminiscence and life review are healthy antidotes to the sick role: They can be useful tools for improving the quality of life of old adults, including those who are mentally impaired or recovering from trauma (Kunz and Soltys, 176). Given the tendencies to project wisdom onto the old and to ask them to serve others, however, the emphasis in storytelling and life review should be as much on the pleasure and satisfaction of the elder as on the enlightenment of the audience.[11] (For narrative gerontology see chapter 10.)

CONCLUSION

The dramatic twentieth-century extension of longevity was caused by changes in sanitation, health care, and diet, notes Alice Rossi, but these "environmental changes" (as opposed to genetic) could be reversed by other environmental changes so that future generations in developed societies may not necessarily live as long as present generations have: "It is therefore only an optimistic faith in the persistence of improved diet and health that underlies the prediction that future generations in Western societies will be healthy, long-lived creatures, and that the age composition of society will be increasingly tipped to an older population" (112).

AIDS has already lowered longevity rates in Africa. Some doctors speculate that the present obesity epidemic in the United States will shorten lives (Olshansky et al., 1139).

The rise of HMOs and the concomitant loss of patient-centered health care have been especially harmful to old people, whose chronic illnesses need closer attention and a wider range of treatments than mainstream, drug-oriented medicine can provide. If most provisions of the Affordable Care Act are put into practice, this situation may change. Until then, sickness will consume more of elders' time, money, and attention than it should, and other social roles diminish in importance. The very healthy old women and men for whom this is not true find their individual solutions to the "roleless role" of old age, but few structures support them. Our sense of late-life possibilities may change as healthier women and men, especially those who are middle-class, choose activities and roles never before thought compatible with "old." For many poor and working-class Americans and for people of color, greater longevity may mean longer periods of chronic illness. The future dominance of the sick role will depend not only on elders' level of health but also on cultural attitudes magnifying the importance of sickness in their lives. Thus the investigations of medical anthropologists and sociologists will be crucial in illuminating the sick role. With population aging, pressures to expand the sick role for profit will intensify. Awareness of these pressures and resistance to them will mark those who have learned to be old.

4

✣

Overmedicating Old Americans

People over sixty-five make up 13 percent of the U.S. population but use 34 percent of the prescription drugs (some estimates say 45 percent). According to Jane Brody's health column, more than 40 percent of people over sixty-five take five or more medications, and each year, one-third of them experience a serious bad effect such as "a bone-breaking fall, disorientation, and even heart failure" (*New York Times*, April 17, 2012, D7).[1] Attention paid to the high drug costs for elderly people, while necessary, narrows public discussion of the drug issue. Medication management and compliance are topics gerontologists usually consider. The unasked larger question is more abstract: Should the old be taking as many drugs as they now take? This chapter offers a context for discussing an issue that has many more dimensions than economic.

The focus here is not on drugs taken for short periods for specific acute illnesses but rather with long-term use, especially of multiple drugs for chronic conditions. Most health problems associated with aging are chronic—arthritis and high blood pressure, for example. A typical reaction to statistics showing extremely heavy drug use by people over sixty-five is that the old need more drugs *because* they are old. But someone who steps outside the circle of medicalized aging has to wonder whether this is really so; whether drugs on the scale they are now being used are benign, health-inducing agents or instruments of social control; whether profit is not a hidden but defining factor in high drug use. It may be true that as a group elderly patients need more medical care than others, but the equation of medical care with drugs is socially constructed.

In this culture, accepting the inevitability of multiple drug use is an essential part of learning to be old. Overmedicating old people results from three interlocking problems:

1. The multinational, multi-billion-dollar pharmaceutical industry has the money and power to control markets and heavily influence the way Americans think about aging.
2. As medicine and gerontology have increasingly become advocates of prescription-drugged aging, they have exaggerated the benefits of drugs, downplayed their risks, and left unexamined the assumption that multiple drug use promotes healthy aging.
3. The opposing, countercultural view is not taken seriously by professionals or by the mainstream media.

Together these developments create a serious threat to the health of older Americans. Understanding why requires a brief examination of body changes with age, adverse drug reactions, the drug industry, doctor training, pharmacy practices, the U.S. Food and Drug Administration (FDA), cultural attitudes, and alternatives to the present system.

CHANGES WITH AGE

Changes in height and weight as we age influence our reactions to drugs. Because metabolism slows down and organs tend to function less efficiently, drugs can have a very powerful impact on aging bodies. Loss of lean body mass affects the way we retain and eliminate drugs. In women, the percentage of body fat goes up from about 36 percent to 48 percent; fat-soluble drugs like sedatives and anti-anxiety medications are more concentrated in fatty tissue ("Drugs and Older Women," 5). Blood vessels stiffen and decreased blood flow impedes the circulation of drugs and nutrients. Cerebral blood flow decreases by 25 percent. With less water in our bodies, drugs are more concentrated than in younger bodies. The filtering function of kidneys does not work as well in older people, resulting in drug accumulation. Decreased liver function can affect the way some drugs are metabolized, leading to toxic levels (Cameron, 10). The brains of older people are more sensitive to drug side effects than younger brains (Lamy, "Actions," 9).

Because the lining of our intestinal walls loses cells, we cannot absorb what we take in as efficiently as before, and because our stomachs empty more slowly, drugs remain in them longer (Bonner and Harris, 90). Age changes in hormones mean that drugs have a stronger impact on us. The elderly are more likely to develop drug-induced hypoglycemia (Lamy,

"Geriatric Drug Therapy," 123). If poor diet causes protein deficiency, the impact of a drug may be intensified (Beizer, 14).

ADVERSE DRUG REACTIONS

Each year, 100,000 Americans or more die of adverse drug reactions, one million are severely injured, and two million are harmed while they are hospitalized, making ill effects from drugs one of the greatest dangers in modern society and one of the leading causes of death, according to Thomas J. Moore, an authority on prescription drugs (*Prescription*, 15). The incidence of adverse drug reactions is estimated to be twice to three times greater among the elderly (Gomberg, 95). For them, the physiologic response to drugs is much more scattered and the predictability of drug action is much less certain than in younger people (Lamy, "Geriatric Drug Therapy," 122). Adverse drug reactions can occur at any age but are more likely to be "catastrophic in the frail elderly" (Hadler, 161). Approximately 17 percent of hospital admissions of people over seventy are caused by adverse reactions to drugs. Not all of these reactions are caused by overmedication, but gerontologists surmise that it is the most common cause. Because adverse drug reactions are missed or falsely attributed to a disease, geriatricians say "any new symptom in an older adult is a drug reaction until proven otherwise" (Steinman).

Forty percent of the respondents to a survey by AARP reported side effects from their medications. Overprescribing psychotropic (mood-altering) drugs is a leading cause of adverse reactions (Arluke and Peterson, 282). Cough suppressants can cause drowsiness, unsteadiness, and constipation in the old. Prolonged use of antacids causes constipation and can weaken bones (Bonner and Harris, 95). Analgesics containing codeine can cause dizziness and fatigue and increase the effect of most other drugs (Bonner and Harris, 99). Other common reactions to overmedication include impaired movements, memory loss, confusion, anxiety, palpitations, restlessness, insomnia, blocked thyroid function, mood swings or other emotional imbalances, blurred vision, urinary retention, potassium depletion, gastrointestinal pain or bleeding, involuntary movements of the arms and legs, and lessening capacity to smell and taste.

In addition, overuse of drugs can cause nutritional depletion resulting in such problems as hearing loss, anemia, breathlessness, and weakness. Among nutrients lost are vitamins A and C and beta carotene, all thought likely to help immune systems ward off cancer. Drugs that should not be prescribed for people over sixty-five include some tranquilizers and sedatives, antidepressants, arthritis drugs, pain relievers, dementia treatments, blood thinners, and muscle relaxants. Depression as a side effect of drugs is not limited to tranquilizers and other mood-altering medications. Anti-inflammatory drugs, medications for high blood pressure and high cholesterol, antihistamines, and antibiotics may all cause depression. Milder forms of depression are easily dismissed as natural to aging (Moore, *Prescription*, 201). Old women are especially at risk for having treatable symptoms attributed to aging itself.

Alcohol and tobacco interact with prescription drugs, increasing risk factors for elderly people who take multiple drugs. Some arthritis medicines, for example, interact with coffee and alcohol to damage the lining of the stomach. When sleeping pills mix with alcohol, breathing can be impaired to a dangerous degree. Many people over sixty-five use both alcohol and prescription drugs. Concurrent use of these two substances even ten or more hours apart can make drugs much more toxic (Lamy, "Actions," 11–12).

Unrecognized drug interactions can lead to a false diagnosis of Alzheimer's disease. Although the extent of this problem is hard to determine, it is likely to increase as the aging population increases. Mental function can be impaired by both prescription drugs and over-the-counter medications: steroids such as prednisone, drugs used to treat heart problems and high blood pressure, drugs prescribed for stomach ailments, psychiatric drugs, Parkinson's drugs, and treatments for anxiety and insomnia.

An underlying cause of adverse drug reactions is the use of short-term studies before drugs are marketed and the unmet need for long-term studies after an approved drug has been on the market. Long-term studies have been strongly recommended by Dr. Clifford Rosen, director of the Maine Center for Osteoporosis Research. Another underlying cause is that older people are "consistently excluded from clinical trials, though they are the largest users of tested and approved drugs and devices" (D. Perry, 1).

Of all the adverse consequences of drugs, the effect on cell division is probably the danger most underestimated, according to Thomas J. Moore. It does not show up in routine tests of new drugs, and it may result in large numbers of bone marrow injuries (*Prescription*, 108). When cell birth and death are disrupted, cancer, birth defects, and blood disorders may result (*Prescription*, 92). Drug catastrophes are not dramatic like plane crashes but tend rather to be "slow, insidious, and difficult to see" (53). Studies of potentially dangerous drugs that should not have been prescribed for the elderly are summarized by Moore. In a nationwide sample of more than six thousand people, 23 percent received drugs that were inappropriate. Using Medicare data, the General Accounting Office found that 17 percent of the drugs prescribed for the old were the wrong ones (Moore, *Prescription*, 121). These figures probably only hint at the risks run by those over sixty-five who use prescription drugs. Unforeseen side effects not apparent during testing come to light only after the drug is in widespread use, and even more alarming, deaths and injuries from drugs are "vastly underreported" (Stolberg, "Boom," A18). Since old people use so many drugs, they suffer disproportionately from unforeseen side effects and the underreporting of deaths and injuries. For them, a wise precaution would be to avoid any drug on the market for less than a year.

Are women more at risk than men? They appear to metabolize some drugs differently, especially psychotropic ones. A report by the National Center on Addiction and Abuse at Columbia University (CASA) states that women over fifty-nine get addicted to alcohol and prescription drugs faster and on smaller amounts than other people, that women are much more likely than men to be given a prescription for a tranquilizer by their physician, and that the use of sedatives and sedating antidepressants doubles the risk of falls and fractures among older women ("Report," 2–3). For either sex, taking more than four prescription drugs is strongly associated with increased fall rates (Rao, 81). Common sense suggests that women's smaller body size and hormone changes mean that standard doses of medications are too high, but the susceptibility of older women to side effects has not been studied. "Either no one thinks it's important, or if they do, they don't have funding," according to Katherine Sherif. It would be useful to know, for example, if drug prescribing should take hormone replacement therapy into account. Dr. Sherif points out that the FDA now requires that women be included in clinical trials but does not require that study results be broken down by gender. Particularly frustrating is the fact that women must be included only if there is evidence of gender difference, but the evidence comes from research.[2]

Although adverse drug reactions affect the old who live independently or with families as well as those who are institutionalized, the problem is especially serious among nursing home residents. Since this population is largely female, the problem of overmedicating nursing home residents is a women's issue. Some drugs have very similar names, resulting in mix-ups. Many falls in nursing homes result from overmedication. Nursing home residents are often given psychotropic drugs—50 percent according to some estimates and 80 percent according to others. Anti-psychotic drugs designed to treat schizophrenia and bipolar disorder are now routinely given to nursing home patients to control aggressive behavior caused by dementia. These drugs raise blood pressure and may cause weight gain. Nearly all studies showing drug benefits for nursing home residents were sponsored by the drug manufacturers (Power, 24). These drugs have significant side effects including stroke, pneumonia, and cognitive decline (24). Ira Rosofsky, a psychologist who worked for many years in nursing homes, offers this summary in his memoir *Nasty, Brutish, and Long*: "The elderly—whether in nursing homes or not—represent a license to print money for the pharmaceutical industry. The average nursing home resident ingests about ten drugs a day—predominantly gastrointestinal, analgesic, cardiovascular, and psychoactive" (9).

Geriatricians are concerned that in many cases, no precise diagnosis indicates a need for these powerful drugs (Agronin, 389). Even when a diagnosis of dementia is accurate a very serious problem remains: Psychotropic drugs have not "demonstrated efficacy for most of the behavioral symptoms" shown by nursing home residents who suffer from dementia (Sherman, 36). Some doctors find however that drugs can benefit dementia patients, but psychotropics are now so common that the American nursing home in the early twenty-first century is more like a psychiatric institution than a medical one (Agronin, 389).

Women who live long enough to be placed in nursing homes may thus be transformed into psychiatric patients, not because of their individual needs or conditions but because they are a captive market for the drug industry. Those with mild dementia may need one or two drugs, but they are almost certain to be given several. Because of the "bench depth of public relations personnel at pharmaceutical companies" mainstream dementia stories focus on a cure from science rather than on strategies available now for improving dementia care (Basting, *Forget Memory*, 38).

Gerontologists who write about prescription drugs sometimes use the word "polypharmacy" to refer to multiple drug use. While this term has an authoritatively scientific and neutral sound to it, "polypharmacy" can also be defined as a situation in which a person is given too many drugs, is kept on drugs for too long, or is given "exceedingly high doses" (Michocki et al., 441). The precise extent of overmedication remains uncertain. The acknowledgment by geriatric pharmacologists that many drugs prescribed for the old are probably unnecessary or ineffective is somewhat misleading because drugs are powerful agents that alter body chemistry; thus they are not "ineffective" in the usual meaning of having no effect.[3]

Non-biological factors contributing to adverse reactions are drug-swapping by the old, poor doctor-patient communication, and non-compliance on the part of the drug user. Some elderly patients obtain prescriptions from various doctors so that no one doctor or one pharmacist sees the complete picture of their drug consumption. Patients may not tell their doctor what over-the-counter medicines they take. They may not understand, for example, that long-term use of laxatives for constipation can damage their intestines. Others may neglect to mention herbal medications they are on, anticipating the doctor's disapproval. Latinas/os may not discuss remedies they obtain from a local botanical shop. Limited English, hearing loss, extreme deference to doctors, and a sense of powerlessness on the part of the patient are also factors in incomplete drug assessment.

Doctors who know the most about adverse drug reactions in late life, geriatricians, seem to be the most cautious about prescribing drugs. The majority of old women and men are not treated by these specialists, however. One solution to the problem of overmedication is an increase in the number of geriatricians. Their wise prescribing advice is "start low, go slow" (Winker, 56).

Periodic reevaluation of drugs is crucially important for old people. Drugs should have standard labels giving clear and precise information about how to use them. They now come with inserts that are intended to describe side effects, but inserts typically omit information about the most severe ones (Stolberg, FDA, A23). Armed with the full story of their medications' risks, consumers might balk at taking them. It would also be helpful if inserts clearly specified "geriatric dosage." More research is needed to define these doses (Beizer, 16). Other needed reforms include systematic collection of information about prescribing through computers to eliminate mistakes from illegible handwriting and to allow easier doctor-pharmacist cross-checking of medications (Moore, *Prescription*, 170).

Juxtaposing the bodily changes with age and adverse drug reactions and taking into account the high cost of medication, an impartial person might conclude that old people should take *fewer* drugs than others, not more.

THE DRUG INDUSTRY

In the past decade, critiques of the drug industry by medical experts inside the system have added depth and breadth to the case against this powerful institution. Previously challenged by leftists, feminists, and a few renegade doctors, the industry now faces scrutiny from mainstream authorities, notably Marcia Angell, Arnold S. Reiman, and Hugh Brody.[4]

Elders benefited from Medicare Part D, prescription drug coverage passed in 2003, creating a new market for the drug industry. Industry influence was felt in the provision forbidding the government to negotiate for lower drug prices, a reform that would have saved an estimated $60 billion in co-payments and deductibles. A major improvement with the Affordable Care Act of 2010 is the gradual elimination of the so-called doughnut hole (a gap in coverage) by 2020. Elders using Part D must pay the total cost of their prescriptions between $2800 and $4550.

Americans pay 38 percent more for drugs than Europeans (Trager, A13) and wholesale drug price differences between the United States and countries such as Canada and Australia range from 25–68 percent higher ("Researchers," 8A). After Maine representative Tom Allen introduced legislation that would require drug companies to sell to pharmacies at the same lower prices given to the government and HMOs, the industry predictably launched a fervent defense of the escalating cost of drugs, claiming that research on new drugs would be threatened if elders paid less for their drugs. Allen replied in plain language: "Here you have the most profitable industry charging the highest prices in the world to senior citizens" (S. Campbell, 1A). Drug company propagandists do not mention either that industry research is heavily subsidized by taxpayers or that the "me too" drugs flooding the market are designed not to create new medical knowledge but to increase their profits. New drugs to fight malaria and other tropical diseases are needed, but the industry spends virtually nothing on them (Buell, A11). The exorbitant cost of prescription drugs did not become newsworthy until the middle-class old were hurt.

Aggressive promotion of drugs meant for long-term use is much more common than it was a decade ago, especially through television ads. The industry spends $10 billion a year marketing drugs (Buell, A11). Smart marketing transformed Claritin, a "moderately effective medication that had difficulty getting approved" into a blockbuster drug (Hall, "Prescription," 40). Jerry Avorn, a Harvard pharmacology expert, wrote that promotional material from drug companies is aimed at increasing product sales "even when they are not the best choices. This distorts the communication of risks and benefits, and raises medical expenditures" ("Prescription Drugs," letter to the *New York Times*, July 11, 2011). Echoing this concern, and focusing on the fact that antidepressants may be dangerous for elderly patients, Nortin Hadler wrote that doctors and patients have been "fooled to think otherwise by egregious marketing schemes that take advantage of unconscionable shenanigans with the data" (*Rethinking Aging*, 164).

When pills are sold like potato chips or Pepsi, artificial needs for medicine are created to a degree that suggests brainwashing. Page after page of drug ads litter the front sections of many magazines today. False or misleading claims in drug ads have been documented, and they are most likely to occur in the drugs most heavily promoted (Adams, A24). Doctors are deluged with free samples, and often their only knowledge of a new drug comes from salespeople, who are unlikely to discuss side effects. Kaiser Permanente of northern California banished drug companies for six months for offenses that included offering doctors $100 to attend company-sponsored dinners and filling out forms for them to sign in order to get their pharmacies to stock a drug. The "free" supplies, dinners, and vacations provided for doctors by drug companies are not free at all but paid for by their elderly patients.

Other abuses have come to light as a multi-billion-dollar industry has sprung up to take over the testing that drug companies used to do themselves. A ten-month investigation by the *New York Times* found that doctors conducting drug research often have limited experience and run tests unrelated to their medical specialties. They receive a bounty for getting patients into drug trials (unbeknownst to the patients) and those who recruit the greatest number get a special reward: They are listed as the authors of drug studies even though the real authors are ghostwriters using information provided by the companies themselves (Eichenwald and Kolata, A28).[5]

Patents on drugs are monopolies that let pharmaceutical companies raise prices higher than free-market levels (Sager and Socolar, 29). Elderly consumers are especially harmed when pharmaceuticals pay manufacturers of generic drugs to keep the drugs off the market, so that their more expensive version is the only one available. The cost of these payoffs and the unavailability of generics contribute greatly to the dramatic increase in the cost of medications.

This practice may be banned in Europe. A striking example of drug industry greed appeared several years ago when thirty-nine pharmaceuticals sued to prevent South Africa from providing generic drugs to people with AIDS, an outrage that public opinion stopped. Drug companies challenged a Maine law passed in 2008 that bans the practice of pharmacies selling information on doctors' prescribing habits to drug representatives. These are rare instances of the industry experiencing a check of any sort. Their interests are promoted by an army of federal lobbyists—625, according to a *Public Citizen* report, more than one for every member of Congress. The lobbyists are often former members of Congress and their aides.

The economic and political dimensions of overdrugging are complex but may be reduced to a single inference: safety is too costly. When patients' right to be protected from harm collides with drug companies' drive for profit, "safety loses," Thomas J. Moore concludes. In his view, the current system is organized to promote maximum drug sales, not consumer safety (*Prescription*, 162). Those who take the most drugs risk the greatest harm. When problems with a drug turn up, as in the case of Halcion, pharmaceuticals have the power to go to court, lobby Congress, petition the FDA, "bombard the news media, pressure medical journals, and influence doctors," regardless of the facts of the case. Most of the information known about drugs is controlled by the industry. This is too much power to be concentrated in a global business (162).

Problems with prescription drugs are likely to increase because the integrity of medical research and medical journals has been compromised by their ties to the drug industry. The former editor of the *New England Journal of Medicine*, Marcia Angell, acknowledged that researchers are swayed toward more favorable findings on products of companies who pay them (Associated Press, May 18, 2000), and the *Journal* apologized for violating its own conflict-of-interest policy by publishing nineteen articles on drugs whose authors had financial ties to drug companies (*New York Times*, February 24, 2000, A15). An issue of the *New England Journal of Medicine* ran ads for twenty-eight different drugs, making it look like a trade publication. The drug industry attempts "the deliberate seduction of the medical profession, country by country, worldwide [and soon] unbought medical opinion will be hard to find" (le Carré, 12). The implications of this judgment for old people who use prescription drugs are ominous.

A closely related problem that has not drawn journalists' attention is that the integrity of gerontology has also been compromised because its conferences and publications are subsidized by pharmaceuticals and therefore papers challenging drug industry hegemony will not be found. Silence about the link between the giant pharmaceuticals and gerontology prevents a critical examination of drugged aging either as a philosophy or as a practice. Journals read by gerontologists and geriatricians feature ads in which dreamy-looking old women (never men) smile out at the reader to show the benefits of tranquilizers. Gerontologists can admit that adverse drug reactions cause thousands of hip fractures each year and other problems causing billions of dollars annually, that one-third of nursing home residents take more than eight drugs a day, and that research on the effects of multiple prescription drug use is lacking (Lyder et al., 55–56); and geriatric nurses can suggest that because of the large number of deaths from adverse drug reactions, noncompliance (failure to take medicines) is sometimes the best choice (Fulmer et al., 47); but no one can name the present system a public health disaster for old women.

At gerontology conferences, alternative medical practitioners are not invited to lecture on what they have learned from the drug-free treatment of elders. The suppression of this knowledge is indefensible. It limits public discussion of healthy aging to corporate voices and their echoes in gerontology. If information about drug-free treatments is not made available, how can elderly people determine whether the organizations and publications focused on their issues can claim any degree of objectivity? How can they learn about alternatives to drugged aging if the industry's point of view is the only one allowed into print or into conferences? What is the real cost of this stultifying orthodoxy?

DOCTORS, PHARMACISTS, AND THE FDA

An underlying cause of chemically dependent aging is that mainstream doctors are not trained to be healers of the whole person. Theoretically with each patient a doctor has a choice: non-drug remedies or drug treatment. But the doctor usually sees the choice more narrowly: which drug to prescribe.[6] Only a few U.S. medical schools have full departments of geriatrics, in contrast to *every* medical school in Great Britain, and geriatrics is an unpopular specialty. HMO pressures on doctors to see as many patients as possible lessen the quality of care for all, but especially for old patients, who may have several different ailments requiring a combination of individually tailored treatments. Few doctors have time for a thorough review of a patient's drug-use history in relation to current symptoms. In an office visit that may be as short as fifteen minutes, they cannot perform a physical examination, determine whether to change medications, and adequately educate patients about them (Knight and Avorn, 111). In addition, doctors may not know the age-appropriate dose of a drug or the information may not be available, making the choice of a medication a trial-and-error process in which undetected mistakes outnumber corrected ones (Atchley, *Social Forces*, 363). Doctors sometimes do not change their prescribing habits when the FDA notifies them that a drug now in widespread use has been found to have adverse side effects that did not show up in clinical trials.[7]

Medical training may reinforce rather than challenge ageist stereotypes. Even when a doctor consciously acknowledges these stereotypes and avoids patronizing behavior, he or she may not be aware of subtle changes in elderly patients caused by medication or may attribute observed changes to the aging process itself rather than to multiple drug use. As a result of all of these factors, establishing the right dosage, guarding against drug interactions, and monitoring use carefully are "beyond the capacity of medicine as it is currently organized" (371).

If adequate safeguards against overdrugging do not exist at the doctor's office, the risk to the old is compounded by changes in pharmacies. Harried pharmacists now sometimes work twelve-hour days, increasing the likelihood of error, and they have little time to advise customers about appropriate use of medications, as they used to do (Stolberg, "Boom," A18). Managed care pressures on pharmacists result in drug switching to save money. The drugs treat the same disorder but differ chemically and have different side effects. Equally disturbing is the huge gap between the small FDA budget and the "deep pockets of the industry it is supposed to regulate" (Mann). Twenty-one safety evaluators at the FDA monitor the 3,200 drugs in current use. An additional ten pharmacists monitor medication errors, and ten epidemiologists research safety reports and drug use patterns.[8] Ideally, the number of FDA workers protecting consumers ought at least to equal the number of lobbyists who represent pharmaceuticals. Older people are "consistently excluded from clinical trials, though they are the largest users of tested and approved drugs and devices" (D. Perry, 1). Although the FDA screens new drugs, a big loophole creates safety risks: Testing periods are short, typically a few weeks or months for drugs meant to be taken for the rest of a person's life. Clinical trials for Prozac, Paxil, and Zoloft, for example, lasted only six weeks despite the fact that they are recommended for long-term use (Moore, *Prescription*, 177–78).

In the 1980s, approval of new drugs took three years, a process that offered consumers some protection. Other problems are that the FDA is not required to collect data on deaths and injuries from prescription drugs, a serious impediment to protecting the public (Moore, *Prescription*, 46; 175), and that it does not require drug companies to test for interactions before a new product is approved (Eastman, 16). Safe use would increase if drug approvals were not permanent but were reevaluated every five years to determine if safer alternatives had become available (184). Finally, the FDA cannot prevent the development of "me too" drugs that are far more costly than those already on the market.

RELATED SOCIAL AND CULTURAL ISSUES

Americans are well known for liking quick fixes, and taking a drug for a medical problem is certainly easier than changing diet, increasing exercise, or reducing stress. This cultural preference for a fast solution may predispose elderly people to expect doctors to prescribe drugs for them and to feel disregarded if they are given none. If they believe they need more drugs than before because they are old, an accumulation of drugs will not prompt questions, especially if their friends who are old also take several a day. A recent commercial for a hotel chain booms "more is better," another American cultural value that encourages overdrugging.

The more frequently old women and men see mainstream doctors, the more often they get prescriptions for drugs, and the more likely they are to get sick from side effects, if they take several drugs. Also troubling in the encapsulated world of medicalized aging is the discovery that independent researchers often cannot replicate findings in studies sponsored by drug companies (Epstein, 60).

Are the old sedated *because* they are old? "It may well be that in the minds of legislators and the public, keeping older people sedated is an acceptable idea" (Gomberg, 94). How much social control, especially of frail and dependent old people, is appropriate? Do racial and ethnic differences affect drug prescribing and monitoring? Do they affect drug impact? Stanford gerontologist Gwen Yeo cites a study suggesting that old Asian Americans may need only one-half of the drug dose prescribed for whites (76). Will baby boomers demand more careful drug prescribing as they age? Is drug coverage through Medicare an adequate solution to high prescription costs for low- and middle-income families? Will old citizens be scapegoated if their consumption of expensive drugs is blamed for driving up health care costs?

Prescription drugs have been in use only since World War II, and heavy medication of the old is a fairly recent phenomenon. Thus people now in their eighties have been exposed to drugs for only part of their lives. In twenty years, however, most people will have been in the drug culture all of their lives. Heavy drug use by the old is now so embedded in American culture that a booklet titled *Using Your Medicines Wisely: A Guide for the Elderly*, published by the Department of Health and Human Services, provides space for eleven different drugs to be recorded, in an attractive insert with the remarkably misleading title "Passport to Good Health Care." This official publication sends a subtle but powerful message: taking eleven different drugs a day is usual and acceptable. This "passport" is an excellent example of the social construction of aging.

Given the extent and seriousness of adverse drug reactions among people over sixty-five and considering their heavy drug consumption, it is logical to suppose that some of what we call "aging" is actually a cumulative reaction to prescription drugs, especially to multiple drugs taken over a long period. Those who live with elderly relatives and the elderly themselves may well believe that problems they experience result from a slowing-down usual for their age. While some decline is normal for many women and men, drug-induced decline is not, but the two may be hard to separate today. Americans have paid too much attention to drug benefits and not enough to their risk (Moore, *Prescription*, 29). Clearly the overdrugging of the old is related to the large number of children now on Ritalin. Both trends signal a "large-scale chemical control of human behavior" (Moore, *Prescription*, 22), whose implications are both profound and unstudied.

ALTERNATIVES

If all of the alternative healers in the United States—chiropractors, homeopathic doctors, acupuncturists, herbalists, massage therapists, ayurvedic doctors, and naturopaths—profiled five patients over seventy whom they had treated for ten years, we could get a glimpse of drug-free aging that is currently unavailable. Indeed, drug-free aging is unthinkable to most Americans. Drugs keep alive some elders who would not have survived earlier, but we do not know how others would fare if they were relatively drug free or if 75 percent of them were treated by complementary medicine. Having no basis of comparison to drugged aging, we cannot be confident that drugs are the universally and necessarily beneficent products that their makers would have us believe. We must take this on faith. Individuals over sixty-five who have chosen alternative medicine do have a basis of comparison, however, and their decision to end prescription drug dependency frees them from conventional, corporate-sponsored belief. Elders who have left drugged aging must tell their stories. Those killed by inadvertent overdrugging unfortunately cannot tell theirs.

The drug industry relies on arguments from authority—its own authority—to persuade elders that multiple drug use is safe for them. If drug-free aging were studied systemically through longitudinal studies of a large number of diverse people, preferably two-thirds female, aged sixty-five to one hundred, we could eventually distinguish between the late-life conditions that can be treated effectively only by drugs and the ailments and illnesses best treated by other means. If most health plans covered a wide range of alternative care, the playing field would be more level. A truly free market would allow drug treatments to compete with non-drug treatments.

In a comprehensive and illuminating article on the placebo effect, Margaret Talbot notes that because illnesses are treated aggressively in this society, "we know less about their natural history—what would happen if we did nothing" (38). This viewpoint has an intriguing application to aging: What if in some cases nothing was done to treat chronic illness? It is such an article of faith that the old need a great deal of medical care that this suggestion seems heretical. If Talbot is correct in stating that a placebo "probably works through a certain kind of expectation, generated by empathic care" (58), then expectation of improvement and empathy are powerful healing forces.

In England and Germany, where homeopathy is widely practiced, non-drug treatment of the old is more prevalent than it is in the United States. In Japan, Western drugs are available but an elderly person would usually not be on as many as four drugs, and doctors prescribe traditional Asian remedies as well as drugs.[9]

Imagine a drug-free nursing home—impossible from the viewpoint of medicalized aging but neither an oxymoron nor a utopian vision. In such a home, doctors using complementary and alternative medicine would show what their methods have to offer old adults and they would work together. If a resident's health problems were not helped, a drug would be considered and very carefully monitored. The remaining life energy of residents would not be sapped by multiple drugs. Many would be able to dress themselves. Food choices would not be regimented. If residents wished to express their sexuality, staff would not interfere except in cases of harassment. The prudish monitoring of sexual behavior in nursing homes has been called "iatrogenic loneliness" by doctors who envision more humane settings for end-of-life care (Miles, 40). Off drugs, nursing home residents would be more likely to express their intimacy needs and staff would be encouraged to understand sexuality as a basic human need for connection (38). Drug-free residents might not value or be capable of sexual expression, but they would be more like their former selves when not heavily sedated.

A unique and valuable program supervised by Marilyn Gugliucci, director of Geriatric Education and Research at the University of New England, places medical students in nursing homes *as residents* for two weeks. Among other benefits, including increased empathy for old persons, this aspect of medical education should allow students to see directly the consequences of overmedicating nursing home patients.

CONCLUSION

In 1975, Robert Butler warned Americans about the high cost of drugs, deaths from adverse drug reactions (30,000 annually then, 100,000 now), the "far too cozy relationship" between doctors and drug companies, and the conflation of natural aging with slowing down from sedatives (*Why Survive?* 200). Elders are the citizens most harmed by these trends; it is they who suffer when "health" and "care" are stripped from health care for the sake of profit. If they take multiple drugs for chronic conditions, their lives may be shortened or made more difficult by illness created and maintained to benefit the pharmaceutical industry. Overmedication is likely to increase because the second-fastest-growing segment of the elderly population, people over eighty-five, is most likely to be institutionalized and to be given multiple drugs. Medicare Part D has the potential to improve the lives of people over sixty-five but it may also cause overuse of prescription drugs (Bishop, 432).

In a sense, women and men on multiple drugs squander their health allotment because these powerful substances interfere with the body's healing powers, but old people who suffer side effects from prescription drugs should not be blamed for their plight. Many, especially old women, are denied the experience of aging—whatever it might be for them— because the chemicals in their bodies are literally changing who they are. And their doctors have unwittingly taken control of their aging.

Although complementary (alternative) medicine is reaching more elders, especially those who are white and middle-class, and the folk remedies that some people of color and some whites rely on are better understood, mainstream medicine has a near-monopoly on the health care of elders. An insidious feature of this monopoly is that the most profitable businesses in America promote the myth that aging is a disease for which their product is the appropriate remedy. Pharmaceuticals have joined the tobacco industry as a high-profile threat to the public good. Their practices—the suppression of generic drugs, for example—deserve far more scrutiny.

In a review essay on drugs and the elderly, two medical school professors acknowledge that the science underlying current prescription practice is "distressingly thin, especially considering the central roles that medications play in the care of elderly adults and the much reduced margin for error that makes prescribing for them such a challenge" (Knight and Avorn, 111). Pondering this candid assessment might prompt one to ask how drugs became so central to aging, without an adequate science base. The plausible explanation is that culture and the profit motive more than biology or health dictate heavy drug use by people over sixty-five. The primary reason many elders take six or eight drugs a day, or more, is not that their health will benefit but that the drug companies need new markets. An aging population offers more territory for their expanding empires.

The two parts of the statement quoted above, thin science and central roles, collide. What is missing is an admission that the old risk being harmed, perhaps greatly harmed, by current prescribing practice. What is missing is the recognition that drug-induced aging may now pass for normal aging. Older people on medications need to know that the combination of the "thin science" behind the drugs they take and the fat purses of Pfizer et al. leaves them open to exploitation and danger. Learning to be old requires keen skepticism about the widespread use of multiple prescription drugs. It may mean questioning one's trust in medical authority for the first time. And families of elders must balance their solicitude for the loved one's well-being with knowledge of the potential dangers of drugs and consider that their parent or grandparent may need far fewer drugs than he or she is on, or no drugs at all.

Many older women and especially women over eighty are needlessly and dangerously overmedicated. In the absence of drug tests designed specifically for old bodies and able to differentiate old women from old men, prescribing multiple drugs for them is a custom that rests more on belief than evidence. The overdrugging of the old is a tragedy of unfathomable proportions. It cries out for a scientist/writer like Rachel Carson to sound the alarm that will wake up Americans of all ages.

5

❧

Healthy Physical Aging

The biggest issue in healthy aging is the eventual fate of the Affordable Health Care Act (Obamacare). Passed in 2010, upheld by the Supreme Court in 2012, and scheduled to be fully implemented in 2014, ACA, the most significant change in American health care since Medicare and Medicaid were passed in 1965, drew ferocious opposition from Republicans. Provisions already in place have benefited older Americans, for example, the free yearly health screening and the elimination of pre-existing conditions as a reason to be denied insurance. The Roberts Supreme Court ruled, however, that the Medicaid expansion part of ACA is unconstitutional, a decision that harms low-income citizens not eligible for Medicare. Despite falling short of the preferable reform, or Medicare for All, ACA is a signal achievement that leaves room for improvements in the future.[1] It has been called "a leap ahead for women's health care" (Cathcart and D'Arcangelo, A5). Older women will benefit from several provisions:

(1) Preventative care including mammograms and bone density screenings will be expanded; (2) insurance companies will not be able to drop people for pre-existing conditions; and (3) gender rating—charging women more for coverage simply because they are women—will end.

Four decades of research on healthy aging indicates that much of what we call "aging" results from lack of exercise, smoking, other addictions, poor nutrition, falls, and stress. How much of the decline seen as normal aging is due to preventable chronic illness? Perhaps as much as half. Thus the challenge is to distinguish the late-life conditions that truly are unavoidable from those caused by disuse and lack of movement. But this distinction is often lost in mainstream health care for elders, and age denial keeps many who are under sixty from realistically assessing their chances of reaching eighty intact.

Gene Cohen and other gerontologists have marked a shift from thinking that illness necessarily accompanies the aging process to understanding that late life illness is not normal. Research on resilience in late life, for example, shows a shift from a definition of resilience as coping or adjusting to a broader conception of "recovery, plasticity, regenerative capacity, and maintenance of health function" (Fry and Keyes, 2). Increased susceptibility to disease often accompanies aging, however. Age-dependent conditions (those that rise steadily with age) include vision and hearing loss, type 2 diabetes, hip fracture, Parkinson's disease, dementia, pneumonia, incontinence, and constipation. Measurements of health and ability to function show gradual rather than precipitous changes with age, according to the Baltimore Longitudinal Study of Aging. A link may exist between inflammation due to chronic infection and aging, but more evidence is needed to confirm this (Rose, 14).

One definition of healthy aging, "minimal interruption of usual function, although minimal signs and symptoms of chronic disease may be present," lists its components as exercise, nutrition, stress management, support from family and friends, and spirituality (Schmidt, 35). This is a good definition because it does not sharply separate health from impairment or disability.

Homeostasis, a state of equilibrium in different but interconnected parts, is a useful concept for healthy aging. When people say they are "fighting" cancer, they speak as if confronting an external enemy instead of an imbalance in their bodies. If old women and men think of aging simply as decay, they overlook a fundamental life characteristic, our capacity for "self-repair" (Bortz, *We Live*, 41).

These views are fairly comprehensive if the focus is on individuals. But as soon as the focus shifts to social structures, the notion that we are responsible for our health in old age, repeated for example in Rowe and Kahn's *Successful Aging*, seems questionable. Healthy aging has great relevance for women because they live longer than men and experience more chronic illness and disability as they age. Although the problems they face are created partly by the health care system itself, women are encouraged to see their health status only in individual terms and expected to find solutions on their own.

Chapters 5 and 6 offer a highly selective look at the complex subject of healthy aging. Chapter 5 discusses the elements of healthy physical aging and chapter 6 considers its political dimensions. In few subjects are the hopeful aspects so intertwined with the grim.

EXERCISE

In the midst of many unanswered questions about aging and contradictory health research reports in the mainstream media, it is reassuring to know that scientific evidence definitively proves the benefits of exercise for older people, not only for those already fit but also for those who have led sedentary lives before beginning to exercise and for frail elders as well. Moreover, relatively modest exertions can lead to significant improvements. It is not necessary to exercise heroically, like Doris Haddock of Dublin, New Hampshire, who spent thirteen months walking across the country, ten miles a day, to call attention to campaign finance reform. Haddock was ninety at the time she completed her walk in 2000, a remarkable feat for a woman who had both emphysema and arthritis.[2]

Exercise prolongs life, even for people who have chronic illness and disability (Kaplan, 42). It improves all bodily functions, including our immune system, and improves mood, cognition, and memory (Bortz, *We Live*, 191). Exercise protects against adult onset diabetes, and strength training (resistance training) enlarges muscle fiber in older women and men, improves balance, and burns calories (Rowe and Kahn, 105–6). It can also lessen arthritic pain. The MacArthur Study of Aging found that people with higher mental function were also more likely to be physically fit and, surprisingly perhaps, the level of emotional support a person received strongly predicted his or her chances of staying fit over time (Rowe and Kahn, 123).

In "Aging and Activity," a fascinating essay that combines evolutionary biology, anthropology, and medicine, Walter Bortz notes that our bodies are designed to keep moving to find food. What is normal bone, he asks, "our own crumbly type or that of our ancestors, which could outlive a sledgehammer that assaulted it?" (199). Lack of exercise leads to heart disease, muscle weakness, weakened immunity, obesity, and depression (200). Our present inactive life, which Bortz calls "zoolike," finds many of us, especially women, "languishing on the orthopedic floors of hospitals with fractured hips, spines, and pelvises; neither as a result of age nor of calcium or estrogen lack, but because of our cultural disuse. There are no broken hips in the jungles of Borneo" (*We Live*, 130). Here the social construction of aging is succinctly stated. The Industrial Revolution made us more sedentary than our agricultural ancestors, but Bortz observes that cultivating land requires less physical movement than hunting and gathering. The recommendation that vigorous exercise be undertaken on alternate days rather than daily derives from the optimal hunting frequency for hunter gatherers (*We Live*, 195). A male model slips in here but the idea is intriguing. Ideally, women and men over sixty should get four kinds of exercise: aerobic, muscle-strengthening, flexibility, and balance training (Bortz, "Aging," 211). A big benefit of exercise is cutting the risk of falls (Rowe and Kahn, 111). More generally, regular exercise decreases chances of a prolonged dying process (Bortz, "Aging," 219).

Walking to Wellness, a fitness education program for minority women that began in 1990, has motivated ten thousand women to walk. It is sponsored by the National Black Women's Health Project, founded by Byllye Avery, whose work is motivated by a racial gap: Black women are more likely to die of heart disease and breast cancer than white women, and their diabetes rate is 50 percent higher. They are also more likely to have high blood pressure (Flaherty, 3). Avery is president of the Avery Institute for Social Change.

Yoga, Tai Chi, Qi Gong

Because it builds strength and flexibility, yoga is particularly conducive to healthy aging. Older women who have lost some mobility benefit from gentle yoga postures, and stretches help them maintain balance and prevent falls. Yoga's development of the breath is an important health asset, since lung capacity diminishes with age. Enhanced self-esteem and zest for life often result from the regular practice of yoga. Two devotees who lived past 100 were Sadie and Bessie Delany, authors of *Having Our Say*, who attributed their longevity to two other factors: never marrying and eating many vegetables each day.

Older women for whom yoga twists and stretches are uncomfortable gain much benefit from Judith Lassiter's *Relax and Renew: Restful Yoga for Stressful Times*.

Tai chi is an ancient form of exercise using slow movements in precise patterns to stimulate energy pathways, improve balance, and reduce pain (Peck and Peck, 1). Simplified versions are suitable for people who are not very strong or flexible at the beginning of their practice. It is an excellent exercise for fall prevention. A study in Hong Kong of elders who do tai chi found that hip bone density improved but not spinal bone density (Woo et al., 267).[3]

Qi gong, another ancient Chinese form of disciplined movements, is very beneficial for older people. This practice increases energy and mental clarity. The version of qi gong called Falun Gong is now a mass movement with a strong supernatural element that threatens the authority of the Chinese government.

Dance therapy, movement for physical, mental, and emotional benefits, strengthens elders who cannot do yoga, tai chi, or qi gong. Classes for those with physical or psychological problems are held in clinics, psychiatric hospitals, prisons, nursing homes, and rehab centers. People in wheelchairs can move rhythmically and enjoyably through dance therapy.

Breathing and breathwork, important signs of the mind-body connection, hold promise for healthy aging. Breathing is our only function that can be either voluntary or involuntary, and it offers the possibility of using the conscious mind to modify the unconscious mind (Weil, 208).[4]

Diaphramatic breathing, inhaling from the diaphragm, is one technique for reducing stress in people with Alzheimer's disease and may lessen "negative self-stereotyping" (Scholl and Sabat).

> Whoever can swallow the breath
> Like the tortoise
> Or pull the breath in and circulate it
> Like the tiger
> Or guide and refine the breath
> Like the dragon
> Shall live a long and healthy life

> —Master Ge Heng, second-century China

NUTRITION

In a nutshell, as people age, "the obstacles to good nutrition multiply even while eating properly becomes increasingly important to optimal health" (Jane Brody, "Changing," B7). Declining sense of taste and smell, difficulty shopping, reluctance to cook for one, dental problems, and attachment to lifelong eating habits all interfere with healthy eating. Malnutrition may afflict as many as 40 percent of the old who see doctors (Bennett, 10). Less dire but nonetheless serious signs of nutritional problems common in the elderly are diminished immunity, slower wound healing, and more fragile tissue (Bortz, *We Live*, 206). The familiar notion that the old need fewer calories has been questioned as an ageist myth, but bodies that shrink need less fuel. On the other hand, the caloric needs of vigorous old women and men "remain largely unchanged" (Bortz, *We Live*, 206).

Bodily changes impact nutritional needs. The capacity of the kidneys to conserve water declines with age, for example, and our sensation of thirst diminishes. At greater risk for dehydration, older women and men should drink one and a half to two quarts of fluid a day (Rowe and Kahn, 112).

As most women over fifty have discovered, weight gain seems to accompany menopause. For those who are mostly sedentary, declining energy needs are not matched by reduced food intake, which leads to abdominal fat, which in turn leads to a greater risk of diabetes (Evans and Cyr-Campbell, 632). Because women live longer than men and have less money, nutritional deficits are likely to have a more adverse effect on them. When

Boston activist Anna Morgan was ninety-four, she volunteered for a study of elders and diet and was told the cut-off age was seventy-nine. Presumably, her nutritional needs differ from those of a sixty-year-old.[5] The lack of disseminated nutritional knowledge that would benefit older people is well illustrated by the fact that, according to the Center for Eating and Weight Disorders at Yale, federal spending on nutrition education equals one-fifth of the advertising budget for Altoids Mints (cited in Haber, *Health*, 456).

A diet including fruits, vegetables, whole grains, legumes, seeds, and nuts is healthy at any age but especially for women and men over sixty-five, whose digestive systems may be overtaxed by the usual American diet high in refined carbohydrates and saturated fats. A problem for Latinas/os is that their traditional diet of fresh food is being replaced by fast foods, junk foods, and soft drinks (Haber, *Health*, 427). Many Chinese Buddhists believe that age sixty is the time to give up red meat (Sankar, 267), a practice that helps the body maintain homeostasis. Meat eaters excrete more calcium in urine than vegetarians (Gannon, 158), and thus older women at risk for osteoporosis should consider a vegetarian diet. Over a lifetime, women lose nearly twice as much calcium as men, and 80 percent of those who suffer from osteoporosis are women (Haber, *Health*, 421).

When oxygen is metabolized, cells form by-products called free radicals. "Great white sharks in the biochemical sea, these short-lived but voracious agents oxidize and damage tissue, especially cell membranes" (Walford, 87). Free radical damage has been linked to heart disease, cancer, Parkinson's disease, inflammation, and cataracts. Antioxidants—vitamin C, vitamin E, selenium, and beta-carotene—protect cells by scavenging free radicals, binding to them, and carrying them out of the body. Air pollution, ultraviolet light, and smoking are also sources of free radicals, and the older we are, the more exposure we have had to them. Theoretically then, the best diet for an older person is one that minimizes their impact. Light eating, for example, creates fewer opportunities for oxygen to be metabolized.[6]

A perennially interesting question in gerontology is whether caloric restriction extends life. It may reduce free radical damage and preserve the capacity of cells to proliferate ("In Search," 28). Experiments in the 1930s by Clive McKay showed that mice live longer when underfed. Similar experiments were conducted in the 1960s by Roy Walford, and current research studies caloric restriction in primates. Few would give up 30–40 percent of their caloric intake to live longer, but the implications of caloric restriction are important, if only to suggest that light eating promotes healthy aging. It may be possible to mimic the effects of caloric restriction through some natural substances while avoiding the hardship of a severe cut in calories.

The role of vitamins and other supplements in warding off disease is increasingly acknowledged by mainstream medicine. Older adults deficient in vitamin B6 or B12 show symptoms that may be mistaken for dementia. Vitamin D helps the body process calcium and D deficiency is thought to be a key factor in hip fractures ("Vitamin D Deficiency," 10). Aside from its benefits for bones, calcium enhances nerve function, blood clotting, and muscle contraction, and it may protect against colon cancer and stroke. The protective effect of vitamin E against cancer has been debated, however.[7]

Herbal medicines are used by one-third of American adults; sales have increased dramatically, reaching $20 billion by 2008. The advantage of herbs over drugs is that they cause many fewer side effects. Ginkgo biloba dilates blood vessels and can improve blood flow to the brain (Haber, *Health*, 283). Saint-John's-wort is used to treat mild depression. On the other hand, exaggerated claims are made for herbs; they are poorly regulated in the United States; and some do not contain the ingredients listed on the label (Jane Brody, "Americans," D7). Faddish consumption of herbs probably wastes money of older Americans, if health concerns increase their susceptibility to unproven advertising claims. In Germany, the growing, harvesting, and processing of herbs is monitored by the government (Grady, "Scientists," D1). Thus German elders who use herbs are better protected than their American counterparts.[8]

Addiction to coffee, especially over a lifetime, is a liability Americans carry into old age. Because of physical changes with age, caffeine has more impact on old bodies than on young ones, a fact that should lead gerontologists and writers on healthy aging to regard it as "an addictive psychotropic drug" (Zuess, 93). Coffee addiction does its harm slowly and silently. Research on the possible link between life-time coffee drinking and late-life illness will not be conducted because the question is not interesting to gerontologists, many of whom, like most other Americans, drink coffee daily. It's a given to them, part of the natural landscape, not something to question.

A few doctors have begun to explore the health implications of widespread coffee consumption in the United States. In *Eat for Health*, William Manahan, M.D., lists some of the effects of caffeine that may not be recognized: It stimulates the nervous system, stimulates excessive gastric acid secretion, relaxes the bladder, stimulates heart muscle, increases urine production, raises the level of fatty acids in the blood, and raises sugar levels (9). Of particular importance for old women is the finding that calcium loss from urine doubles after consumption of caffeine (Manahan, 19). Studies show a correlation between drinking two cups of coffee a day or more and suffering bone density loss (Gannon, 64). Thus anyone with osteoporosis or at risk for developing it should consider eliminating coffee. The CD-Rom

"Bone Health and Osteoporosis: A Report of the Surgeon General" is available from the U.S. Department of Health and Human Services.

Sugar is another source of addiction. Added sugar consumption has risen significantly in the past twenty years, and, according to the U.S. Department of Agriculture (USDA), Americans now use an average of 156 lbs. of added sugar a year, 29 lbs. from traditional sugar and the rest in food. The USDA recommends using no more than ten teaspoons a day, but many people average twice that amount. The large increase in soft drink consumption since the 1980s (especially dangerous for teenagers, who now drink far more soft drinks than milk at a time when they are building bone mass), the increase in sugar consumption by people who eat fat-free foods, and the increased use of artificial sweeteners may eventually lead to an epidemic of osteoporosis (Jane Brody, "Drunk on Liquid Candy," D7).

The link between excessive sugar consumption and bone loss is particularly relevant to women, as is the strong connection between sugar and depression. Sugar addiction is comparable to alcoholism (Manahan, 77). Reducing consumption increases energy and strengthens immune function (Zuess, 145). High levels of sugar in the blood produce compounds that damage the body and over time may be the basis of age-related degenerative diseases (Weil, 71–72). Claims have been made for the healthful benefits of dark chocolate because of its anti-oxidants, but the chocolate used in studies is higher in quality than that available in stores, and most of the research is funded by the chocolate industry (Haber, *Health*, 215–16).

With a few exceptions such as Kathleen DesMaisons, researchers are not interested in the damage sugar causes.[9] We have no studies of the cumulative effect of caffeine and sugar addiction or studies of people over sixty who use little of either substance.

THE BRAIN

Brains of healthy old women and men remain intact, although the part that controls memory shrinks slightly. The ability to do more than one thing at a time declines. Older people tend to take in new information more slowly than the young, but they retain it as well. Both physical and mental exercise help stimulate brain function. Research by Marian Diamond on old rats placed in an enriched environment showed brain growth (Bortz, *We Live*, 173–74), the first evidence that the structure and chemistry of the brain could be influenced by environment (Ebersole and Hess, 794). Work by Diamond has shown increases in neuron size and in the number of neuron branches that transmit information to other cells;

nerve cells shrink in an unstimulating environment (Ebersole and Hess, 794). Current thinking is that the brain develops and maintains itself by adding new cells, a reversal of the long-held belief that the old had to expect gradual mental deterioration as cells died off (Blakeslee, D1). Neurogenesis (the capacity to generate new cells) is a sign of brain plasticity, that is, "a brain that is dynamic, constantly reorganizing, and malleable" (Nussbaum, 7). Thus researchers are beginning to explore "development, as opposed to deterioration" in middle-aged and older people (Gannon, 39). Older adults use both sides of the brain simultaneously, giving them a "deepening capacity for left brain/right brain integration" (Cohen, "Creativity," 192). Cohen relates this capacity to the motivation felt by some elders to work intensely on their life stories.

The brain continues to develop in late life, and lifestyle affects brain health (Nussbaum, 11). Paul Baltes and his colleagues theorize that the old have untested "reserve capacity" that enables them to perform at higher levels than their test scores indicate (Whitbourne, 268). Brain reserve may delay the onset of brain diseases (Nussbaum, 11). Another plausible hypothesis is that old people may use different parts of the brain than young people use to accomplish the same task.

Studies of brain differences in women and men in late life present contradictory findings, but one hypothesis is that women use both sides of the brain, whereas men appear to be restricted to one hemisphere (Kryspin-Exner et al., 541), a contradiction of Cohen's finding cited above.

A safe conclusion, however, is that studies of cognitive ability developed on young men are probably not applicable to middle-aged and old women (Gannon, 39). Moreover, perceived decline in cognitive functioning may reflect "performance measurement rather than defects in competence" (Bortz, *We Live*, 175).

This is an important caution, given the cultural bias of intelligence tests. Intelligence measures that favor a quick response put old test takers at a disadvantage and often contain material not relevant to their lives. On a test of practical information, older adults outscored the young (Gaylord, 79). Stanford psychologists found that although the aging brain processes information more slowly and less accurately than younger brains, "the subjective experience of normal aging is largely positive," and memory of emotional information remains strong (Carstensen, "Growing Older," 45–46).

In a longitudinal study in Seattle, K. Warner Schaie and his colleagues studied five thousand people aged twenty to ninety to see what happens to intellectual ability. Decline was found to vary greatly. Those who sustained a high level of mental functioning had several things in common: a high standard of living marked by above-average education and income; lack of chronic disease; active engagement in reading, travel, cultural events, or professional associations; willingness to change; an intelligent partner; the ability to grasp new ideas quickly; and satisfaction with accomplishments (April Thompson, 8). Of these seven characteristics, three directly reflect class privilege (income, health, and travel), while another (life satisfaction) is probably related as well. Intellectual competence may improve in old age (Schaie, 281). If cognitive function is thought of as functions, plural, "even moderate decline in some areas of mental functioning does not necessarily interfere" with preserving independence (Rowe and Kahn, 136). Data from 2,380 people in Amsterdam aged fifty-five to eighty-five showed those with high scores on cognitive tests tended to live longer than people with lower scores. Information processing speed was the strongest predictor of mortality (Sison, 1).

An advantage of aging brains is what Gene Cohen calls "developmental intelligence," by which he means "the maturing synergy of cognition, emotional intelligence, judgment, social skills, life experience, and consciousness" (*The Mature Mind*, xix). A study in which memory tasks were compared in young and old subjects suggests that the older adults compensated for neural decline by "reorganizing their neutral networks," although the exact way this process works is unclear (*The Mature Mind*, 21).

EMOTIONS

Emotions and illness are clearly linked, as folk wisdom has long held and mainstream medicine is belatedly acknowledging. Emotions change with age, according to speculative work in neurobiology, and one day chemical manipulations may be able to turn off negative emotions such as anger and loneliness and turn on "playfulness, nurturance, and intimacy," a prospect that raises ethical questions for the psychology of aging (Manheimer, "Review," 263). Very little psychological theory is based on the actual experience of older people, as Betty Friedan notes in *The Fountain of Age*, although she quotes Jungian analysts who believe a root cause of psychological problems in the elderly is an insistence on seeing themselves as young (461–62). This suggests that psychological strength in late life depends partly on acceptance of one's life stage and on self-esteem, and those characteristics in turn depend on freedom from internalized ageism. Friedan believes that decreased resistance to disease in elders may be caused partly by low self-esteem, a sense of powerlessness, and few opportunities for meaningful participation in society. Individual psychology is linked to social contexts.

The irascible woman or man who is not afraid to say no or to insist on his or her own way probably has a strong sense of self. One may be outspoken and contrary when a situation demands it but serene in one's usual disposition and able to let anger pass when it arises. Older women have been socialized to repress their anger, of course, and it will be interesting to see if this traditional female socialization fades with future generations. Some older women express anger indirectly through querulousness. Repression of negative emotion tamps down the life force and narrows emotional range. Being unconventional may be advantageous for old women if it leads them to express freely what they feel.

Older people are slower to anger, less likely to hold a grudge, and more likely to forgive, according to psychologist Laura L. Carstensen. They have insights "into the preciousness of life that are largely inaccessible to those who see seemingly infinite futures" (*A Long Bright Future*, 94).

Despite charges of "false memory syndrome," many health care workers understand that large numbers of children, especially girls, experience incest. David Finklehor, director of the Crimes Against Children Research Center at the University of New Hampshire, estimates that in the general population 20–25 percent of women were abused as children and 33 percent of women on welfare (DeParle, 1). Sexual violence against children is a "silent epidemic in a society fascinated by violent crime" (M.-L. Gould, 6). Our bodies store memories of what happens to us early in life, and if those events are traumatic, aches and pains, chronic tension spots, or blocked areas may be relieved or cured by recovering memories. When oral sex is forced on children too young to protest or escape, for example, interruptions in their normal breathing patterns may have long-lasting consequences such as shallow breathing rather than diaphragm breathing. One root of adult psychological problems such as addictions or relationship failures is sexual assault occurring during childhood.

What does this have to do with aging? An estimated three and a half million women over sixty-five survived childhood rape and incest, yet little is known about their experience (Farris and Gibson, 31). I believe that one of the best preparations for healthy aging is confronting memories of childhood sexual assault if they arise. This is a risky process that may trigger old feelings of shame, worthlessness, and terror. Survivors of incest and early rape often feel powerlessness throughout their adult lives even if to outward appearances they are high achievers. Their self-esteem is often low. If they escape the damage of obvious addictions to drugs and alcohol, they may be compulsive overeaters or exhibit patterns such as workaholism, perfectionism, or an extreme need to be in control. As they age, the accumulation of stresses on them can produce illness. Since the illness is rooted in a profound psychological disturbance that remains hidden, it is not likely to be considered by a doctor making a diagnosis. Healing can occur in the present only when we allow ourselves to feel, express, and release emotions from the past that we have suppressed or tried to forget (Northrup, 55).

An example of ageist bias is the belief that therapy is wasted on older people, who are thought to be incapable of growth. Clearly this is fallacious. A woman in her sixties or older who comes to understand hidden parts of her past may find that mysterious pieces of her life are now explained. If she can re-experience early traumas and integrate them into the self she is now, she will almost certainly become healthier emotionally and physically. Tense places in her body will relax. Breath work is often a key to this transformative process, which is more often circular than linear. A woman who knows what was done to her may feel a new sense of power. Her anger may channel itself into creative paths. Her pride in having survived something horrible may embolden her to take risks.

Long-term effects of violence will affect a woman's health as she ages (P. Davidson et al., 1031). Unaddressed psychological and social problems in early life "fester and compound," leading in some cases to destructive behavior such as drug abuse (1038). With incest, the past lives on, cruelly in some instances, as it does with survivors of torture. To be free of inner feelings of worthlessness and uncontrollable rage is an invaluable asset as we age. To be sure, not all therapy can accomplish such healing changes, but in most cases, women who grapple with past abuse and identify behavior patterns directly related to it are much better off than if they continue living oblivious to a truth about their childhood or living in the shadow of recurrent depression.

Depression afflicts nineteen million Americans a year, and according to one estimate, major depression strikes 1–2 percent of adults over sixty-five, and minor depression 3–13 percent (Fiske and Jones, 246). Thus some gerontologists believe that it is the most serious disorder of late life, but few studies differentiate between depression occurring for the first time after sixty-five and this affliction experienced throughout life. Clinical depression appears to be less common among elders than among younger people, but when measured by indicators such as sluggishness, feeling sad, feeling lonely, and difficulty concentrating, depression occurs frequently (Quadagno, "*Aging*," 156). According to research surveyed by Betty Friedan for *The Fountain of Age*, all physical symptoms found in older people including symptoms of Alzheimer's, in the absence of a defined disease, may mask depression "or somatic equivalents of depression, even without depressed mood" (429). Depression among older women may be caused by prescription drug interaction.

Current research shows that depression involves not only problems with brain chemistry but with brain structure itself. Stress and depression can shrink parts of the brain, and any successful treatment such as drugs or therapy creates new neurons in key areas. Investigations of neurogenesis should lead to more effective antidepressants (Goldberg, "New Life," D1).[10]

At all ages women report depression more frequently than men, and the gap is greatest for women over eighty (Quadagno, *Aging*, 156–57). Depression may go undiagnosed in the elderly because models for detecting it were developed for the young. The deficit model of aging in the mental health system—elders are not portrayed as coping, adapting, and demonstrating psychological strength—especially harms old women. Predictably, nursing home residents have high rates of depression (I. Katz, 270).

Compared to others, old women and men more frequently have depressing experiences such as loss of a partner, illness, or relocation to a relative's house or nursing home. It may be hard to distinguish between situational depression and depression originating in chemical imbalances in the brain. Depression leads to decreased physical activity and to increased social isolation. Social isolation may lead to inactivity and greater likelihood of depression (G. Kaplan and Strawbridge, 71)—a sign of the complex interplay of social and biological factors.

In 2020, the middle of the baby boom cohort, 55 million strong, reaches sixty-five. Since present mental health systems are inadequate, baby boomers will overwhelm them, and those who suffer most will be elders with chronic mental illness (Koenig et al., 674–75). A Department of Human Services report in Maine, for example, shows that 86 percent of older adults with a mental health diagnosis receive psychotropic drugs without counseling or other support services.

Physical and psychological health are connected for everyone, but their "mutually interacting association seems to accelerate with age" (Gannon, 47). Thus an old woman who has lost some ability to move about freely may be at risk for depression. The stigma of mental illness may prevent some in their seventies or older from saying they are depressed; instead they may say dismissively that they are just a little "blue" or "down" and not see getting help as an option. Doctors may be afraid of inquiring into the emotional states of older patients for fear of opening Pandora's box (Koenig et al., 235), a tendency certainly exacerbated by shortened office visits. In a materialist culture, doctors cannot ask their patients about the state of their souls, although they may know intuitively that much illness begins in the psyche. How can the psychological health of older people be improved? This is a key question for healthy aging.

The notion that healing emotions bolster the immune system, long understood in alternative medicine, is increasingly accepted by the mainstream medical community as well. Since decreased immune function is common in late life, whatever we do to strengthen it is good. Positive emotions boost two kinds of immune system cells: T cells, white blood cells that coordinate immune defenses; and natural killer cells, large white blood cells that attack cancer cells and infected cells (G. Cohen, *The Mature Mind*, 27). Immune function varies greatly, but people over seventy-five or eighty usually need longer to recover from a cold or from wounds, and their infections tend to be more serious than those of younger people. Since we cannot see our immune system or locate it in our imagination as we can our heart, it is difficult to think of strengthening it, in a way comparable to strengthening our heart by walking three miles a day. Nonetheless, the mysterious processes of getting sick and recovering can be modified somewhat by our own actions.

What are healing emotions and what does it mean to encourage them? It may simply mean awareness: If I know a certain emotion is beneficial, that recognition may help me, if only because I have shifted from acting without thought to acting consciously and deliberately. Three good examples of healing emotions are serenity, gratitude, and reverence. A common way serenity is cultivated by the old is gardening. Nurturing new growth is calming, and gardeners seem to thrive in old age. The ability to feel and express gratitude is an important part of healthy aging. In the lives of most people there are at least a few things to be grateful for. Sometimes this is just a matter of mindfulness. "I'm grateful that it is a clear night and I can see the stars." Gratitude does not depend on external circumstances, and it helps to counter the message from industrial societies that we need more of everything (Macy, 49). Speaking of herself when old, Colette expressed gratitude for each flower she passed as she walked slowly by. Gratitude for old friends must be one of the deepest pleasures of old age. Buddhist teacher Sylvia Boorstein writes, "Gratitude with no complaints is the attitude I would like to have, not only at the end of my life, but from now on" (xi).

Reverence seems more abstract than gratitude or serenity. The old who only grumble and air grievances have lost, or perhaps never had, a sense of reverence. It may grow out of the healing following a serious illness or life-threatening operation. The hard breathing that accompanies strenuous exertion or exercise can induce feelings of reverence. This emotion acknowledges the life force greater than our individual spark of life. It may make us feel puny or exalted. A group experience may evoke it, or it may be solitary. People who see the Northern Lights report feelings of reverence. This emotion may come from a flash of understanding that all beings are interconnected. In "Tintern Abbey," Wordsworth expresses reverence for nature and also for himself. To be old without a sense of reverence is an unenviable lot. If we lack the power to transcend our personal concerns, the stiffening and slowing down of our bodies signals the end of meaning. To survive into old age capable of feeling reverence requires some freedom from the prevailing materialism of our culture. Looking over one's past life as well as looking at a mountain may inspire reverence for the sheer doggedness of humans who live to be old.

COMPLEMENTARY AND ALTERNATIVE MEDICINE (CAM)

Conventional medicine has little to offer people dealing with chronic health problems or with the complex and interconnected conditions that sometimes accompany aging. Alternative or complementary medicine is safer and more effective. Its benefits deserve to be far better known, but little attention is paid to alternative medicine by gerontologists, their texts, or the media. At aging conventions, no exhibits extolling homeopathy or herbal remedies will be found alongside the booths of the drug companies that fund the events. Typically, alternative practitioners spend far longer with patients than mainstream doctors are able to, getting emotional information as well as hearing about specific symptoms. Thus they are more likely than mainstream doctors to develop a healing relationship with the people they treat. In this way, they resemble healers in other cultures. Their holistic approach to health equips them to work especially well with older people.

Healthy Aging by CAM authority Andrew Weil contains a wealth of information about physical aging and strategies for maximizing health. Weil believes that chronic inflammation is a common root of age-related diseases and that diet influences inflammation (55; 145). Two attitudes Dr. Weil associates with healthy aging are flexibility and humor (217).

The rise of alternative medicine represents a growing awareness that while allopathic medicine is good for diagnosing and treating major illness, it is not very good for keeping us well. An estimated 50 percent of Americans see an alternative practitioner. A poll by Angus Reid showed that 66 percent of Canadians believe their government should advocate the use of CAM to reduce costs to the health care system. In England, sales of herbal medicines have greatly increased (*Health and Well Being*, July 27, 2007). Of Americans using CAM, 54 percent chose chiropractors, 25 percent massage therapy, and 14 percent acupuncturists (Stolberg, "Alternative," A1). Other forms of alternative medicine include diaphragmatic breathing, progressive muscle relaxation, visualization, and meditation. Women use CAM more frequently than men (Ness et al., 522).

The implications of the growth in alternative medicine for healthy aging are both profound and unexplored. For the middle class, this development may well lead to improved health in old age.

Attacks on alternative medicine have become increasingly heated as it grows more competitive with mainstream medicine, but no level playing field is possible as long as health insurance and Medicare cover only the latter. Some plans now cover chiropractic care, however. If homeopathy, acupuncture, massage, herbal medicine, naturopathy, and ayurvedic medicine were also covered, their use would increase, and their effectiveness would be more widely known.[11]

Chiropractic

Chiropractors treat back pain and many other conditions by manipulating the spine. Poor alignment causes a number of short- and long-term problems. The traditional method of forceful correction has been supplemented by the activator, a device that allows doctors to move bones without force. The space between our vertebrae narrows as we age, reducing movement. Since spinal mobility is a key to healthy aging, chiropractic is especially important for the health of middle-aged and older people.

Homeopathy

This healing system was synthesized early in the nineteenth century by Samuel Hahnemann. It uses extremely diluted solutions of active substances to cure disease, following the principle of "like cures like"—that is, the same substance that causes symptoms of a disease in a healthy person will cure the disease in an ill person. Homeopathy is enjoying a resurgence in the United States, where it has not been as widely accepted as in Europe. Like other alternative medical systems, homeopathy pays close attention to emotional states, stimulates the body's own healing capacity, and looks for underlying causes of disease.

Osteopathy

Osteopathy is a non-invasive form of medicine that uses gentle, hands-on techniques to work on joints, muscles, and the spine. A core belief is that if any part of the body is restricted, the rest of the body compensates, resulting in pain or stiffness. Osteopathic treatment aids the nervous, circulatory, and lymphatic systems.

Acupuncture

Acupuncture is a Chinese medical system that is five thousand years old. Extremely thin needles are inserted into the body along pathways called meridians to ease pain, stimulate organs, and release blocked energy. Since acupuncture corrects imbalances in the body and restores vital energy, it is especially suited to easing the process of aging. It can help people accept the slowing down they experience in their bodies.[12]

Ayurveda

Ayurveda is an ancient Indian healing system that uses dietary change, herbs, meditation, and massage to relieve the body of toxins and restore balance. It makes use of whole plants, believing that plants contain material that counteracts side effects from the curative element. "Ayu" means life in Sanskrit, and "veda" means knowledge. In contrast to Western medicine, which considers the body and illness as objects, Ayurveda considers illness as a disruption in bodily, climatic, and social systems of balance (Langford, 11).

Rolfing

Rolfing, developed by biochemist and physiologist Ida Rolf, increases balance within the body by working on muscles and connective tissue. Stretching fascia (tissue surrounding a muscle) allows bones to become properly aligned so that bodies move in gravity with less strain. Rolfing improves posture and range of motion and alleviates chronic pain.[13] It is an excellent method for correcting tension and stresses that accumulate with age or result from injury or surgery.

Reiki

Reiki (ray-kee) is a Japanese word that means universal life-force energy. Practitioners place their hands on or near the person being treated. Reiki is used for relaxation and stress reduction, rejuvenation, alleviating pain, balancing the body's natural energies, and bolstering immunity.

Massage

Massage involves both touch and movement. Because older women are so accustomed to giving to others, receiving massage encourages balance in their lives. Massage is one of the best aids to comfortable aging because it is gentle, non-invasive, and benefits the whole body. It helps relieve inflammation and stiffness of the joints. It releases muscle tension, lessens anxiety, and induces feelings of relaxation and well-being. Massage stimulates the flow of blood throughout the body and may alleviate chronic pain. It bolsters immunity by improving lymph flow and increases tissue elasticity (Tappan and Benjamin, 338). In *The Life Cycle Completed*, Joan Erikson writes, "I am persuaded that if retired elders have regular massages, it would be amazingly beneficial" (121). Massage is especially beneficial for old women and men, who are often touch deprived. The "Insist on Hugs" chapter of Meika Loe's *Aging Our Way* stresses the importance of touch for very old people (213–23). Massage also helps counteract the dehumanizing impact of institutional care, according to a study by Canadian nursing professors. Being touched is particularly important for elders who have diminished sight and hearing (Fraser and Kerr, 238–42).

Massage is so beneficial for older people, in fact, that Medicare should cover it. Imagine a biweekly or monthly massage for anyone over seventy who wanted one.

A reasonable expense? The results would be shorter recovery periods after surgery and illness; stress reduction; delayed onset of serious illness and disability; decreased falls, leading to prolonged periods of independent living; and tonic effects hard to quantify. Although many people over seventy have not experienced massage, it is growing increasingly popular as a therapeutic practice and is now used in some hospitals and offered to some hospice patients. How to extend its benefits to more working-class elders and people of color remains a challenge for healthy aging.

Feldenkrais Method

A movement philosophy and practice especially well suited to older people, including those with limited range of movement, is Feldenkrais. Moshe Feldenkrais (1904–1984) was an Israeli physicist and judo master who developed his system of movement education by healing a knee injury. Watching babies crawl, he synthesized what he knew from science, body mechanics, and the martial arts, refining his ideas over several decades. The method has two formats: (1) Awareness through Movement group classes; and (2) Functional Integration, one-on-one sessions in which a practitioner gently touches and moves parts of the body. Feldenkrais believed that very early in life we develop habitual ways of functioning that we repeat "compulsively to the exclusion of other patterns" that might be easier and more efficient, and that we use only about 5 percent of the movements we are capable of making (Claire, 101–2). His method reprograms the brain by substituting conscious and deliberate movements for ones that cause strain. This "sensory motor re-education" can occur either consciously or unconsciously (Claire, 105).

In Feldenkrais classes, students decide for themselves what is beneficial rather than try to fit a standardized model; this is one reason why it is so effective with older adults. Another is that Feldenkrais does not envision an ideal body type, which in our culture is often the athletic twenty-year-old. The movements are done without strain on muscles and joints and thus are an excellent practice for older adults who may have accepted weakness or stiffness as natural to their aging process. The Feldenkrais method is not goal oriented.[14] The attentiveness required to make the very small movements characteristic of the practice allows students to re-evaluate the high-speed, high-stress lives many North Americans now live. Moving slowly can be a revelation, especially to people who have been on fast-forward for decades, not thinking of their bodies unless they felt pain. Feldenkrais consists of "tiny little noticings," and even imagined movements can cause microscopic muscular responses.[15]

I have observed Feldenkrais classes in which all participants were over eighty and several hampered by strokes or disabilities. It is unusual for people this age to find pleasure in their bodily movements. Slow, gradual, repeated movements give people with impairments a chance to feel physically competent and unself-conscious. The particular relevance of Feldenkrais to healthy aging is that our "nervous and muscular systems are so flexible that we can reverse previously learned patterns" (Claire, 102).

Body Mechanics

Whatever the condition of our health, the ability to be comfortable in our bodies may be a reward for living to be old, but by the time we reach sixty, our characteristic ways of moving are so habitual that they are unconscious. Often these movements unnecessarily strain backs, hips, shoulders, and necks. Thus an important aspect of healthy aging is becoming aware of body movements that may cause tension. Alternative practitioners are more likely than mainstream doctors to notice when a person's way of walking or holding the shoulders puts stress on other parts of the body. A worker who carries a lunch bucket or a briefcase in the same hand for forty years or who drives clenching the steering wheel with both hands may experience pain seemingly unrelated to the habitual movement. By changing customary patterns, we wake up dormant neural pathways. The bodily pleasure of easy movement can be experienced by many older women and men who have not been physically active earlier in life, by people recovering from strokes and injuries, and by those labeled frail. When long-held muscle tensions, including those caused by past trauma, are released by bodywork, therapy, or breathing exercises, older people may be able to experience their bodies more directly than was possible before. Discovering new movements may bring emotional and psychological benefits inseparable from the physical change. All gentle bodywork systems hold great promise for healthy aging. Experiencing many of them would be ideal.[16]

HEALTHY AGING PROGRAMS

Over the past several decades, numerous healthy aging programs have been developed for senior centers, YWCAs and YMCAs, schools, and other community sites. Health Promotion in Older Adults, a collaboration between Group Health of Puget Sound and the University of Washington, focuses on exercise, nutrition, alcohol and drug use, stress management, and home safety. Healthy aging programs have demonstrated the benefits of conscious aging by showing that loss of function is sometimes reversible, even in the very old. Some health promotion programs are called "It's Never Too Late," which sounds glib but is literally true. If more elders could be persuaded of this perhaps more would slowly change their habits. The best exemplar of the never-too-late philosophy is Jeanne Calmont, a French woman who stopped smoking at age 117 when she could no longer see well enough to light a cigarette. She died at age 122.

An excellent resource is David Haber's *Health Promotion and Aging*. Especially important are programs that focus on fall prevention because each year, 300,000 Americans over sixty-four break a hip, and three-fourths of these are women (Dembner, "Hip Fractures," 1). A Matter of Balance in Maine and other states trains community members rather than professionals to teach others how to improve balance.

Healthy aging programs have not reached many Americans, however, particularly low-income elders and people of color, and often programs last only a few weeks or months, until a grant runs out. Until they are permanent and available to all who wish to take part, the health potential of American elders will not be known.

RELATED ISSUES

The interconnecting issues of healthy aging lead to a question of particular relevance to old women. Is it possible to be severely impaired or immobile and at the same time to be healthy? Traditional gerontology, opposing health to frailty, would answer no, thereby consigning many women over eighty-five to an undesirable category. But as more women live to be very old, the paradoxical coexistence in some of major impairments and vitality may encourage broader definitions of health relative to old women. A bedridden woman would not be judged healthy by conventional norms, but if her life is enhanced by some creative activity and by close ties to a wide circle of friends, surely she is healthy.

Decline and loss of some function can coexist with good health. Adequate late-life health is a reasonable expectation for most white, middle-class Americans. Furthermore, improved health—in some cases, dramatically improved health—is a realistic hope for some women and men over sixty-five. Learning to be old means being aware that we have been so conditioned to expect decline that our late-life health expectations may be too low, and we may unthinkingly attribute to aging ailments or problems that can be successfully treated.

The conventional images of healthy aging in the media focus only on bodies, not on the power of the breath to create mind/body harmony. This may suit the tennis-playing seventy-five-year-old, but eventually she too will need other ways of conceiving of health, perhaps as a vital force not dependent upon physical vigor, or as a quality that transcends good habits and the various components of well-being considered here. Neither a woman who will never exercise again nor a woman who exercises one month but is too weak to do much the next should be made to feel guilty by the preachments of healthy aging.

Gerontologists debate whether longer lives will mean more or less late-life disability. A reasonable hunch is that these trends will occur simultaneously: an increasing number of older people remaining healthy until the end of their lives and an increasing number having prolonged, severe illness or disability (Lamphere-Thorpe and Blendon, 78). The fear of a long, slow descent toward death is so strong that most people would probably accept a short illness at the end of a healthy life. But how can Americans be persuaded that the choices they make in their fifties and sixties will affect their condition at eighty?

CONCLUSION

From one positive perspective, "our rate of decline in key respects levels out rather than accelerating, creating a plateau effect" (H. Small, 271), at least for people who reach late life in fairly good health. But it is also true that "the bright lines between health and illness or disability [are] highly problematic" (Holstein, Parks, and Waymack, 14). Some signs bode ill for healthy aging, the rising rates of obesity and diabetes, for example, and the increase in drug-resistant bacteria. The number of Americans with brain cancer has doubled since the mid-1980s. This is due partly to better detection but also to environmental causes: More people have been exposed to more chemicals for longer periods. Older adults may be more susceptible to effects of exposure to pesticides because of age-related changes in the way bodies process chemicals, according to the Environmental Protection Agency (publication Number EPA-100-F-04-901). Pesticides are used both outdoors (in weed killers, for example) and indoors (in kitchen and bathroom disinfectants). Many doctors still believe, despite evidence, that high blood pressure is a normal part of aging (Currey, 17). The current epidemic of asthma among children, especially those who are poor or black, is a troubling public health development (Stolberg, "Gasping for Breath"). World Health Organization statistics project a slight increase in breast cancer for American women over sixty between 1990 and 2020 (Caselli, 260). HMOs are leaving rural areas. Dental school enrollment has dropped 50 percent in the past decade, creating a shortage of dentists in rural areas at the same time that population aging is increasing the need for dental work.

Another danger sign is that despite the increase in the elderly population in the United States, the number of geriatricians fell by a third between 1998 and 2004 (Gawande, 53). As of 2011, only 9 of the nation's 145 medical schools had full departments of geriatrics, and half of the geriatric fellowships in American medical schools go unfilled (Gross, *Bittersweet Season*, 148).The work of these medical specialists, to "bolster our resilience in old age, our capacity to weather what comes, is both difficult and unappealingly limited. It requires attention to the body and its alterations. And it requires vigilance over nutrition, medications, and living situations. . . . When the prevailing fantasy is that we can be ageless, the geriatrician's uncomfortable demand is that we accept we are not" (Gawande, 57).

Future cohorts of old Americans will be better educated than those now in their eighties, however—a change that may lead to healthier habits and lower disability rates. Data suggest a reduction in arthritis, hypertension, stroke, emphysema, and dementia but more Parkinson's disease, heart disease, bronchitis, pneumonia, and hip fracture (Crimmins, 10). Substance abuse is more prevalent among baby boomers than in previous cohorts (Kaye, "Maine Voices"). The health benefits of better education may be partially offset by heavy use of prescription drugs, the high stress of longer work hours and harried family life, and poor nutrition, if it is true that one-fourth of all American breakfasts are eaten at McDonald's. On the other hand, the percentage of people unable to care for themselves is declining. Medical advances such as hip and knee replacements and lens replacements for cataracts significantly ease aging. A cure for macular degeneration would improve late life for many Americans.

Stem cell research holds promise for organ regeneration. Developments in the field of psychoneuroimmunology (the study of interactions of the mind, stress, and the immune system) may lead to new knowledge about aging. Hardiness, for example, formerly thought of as a manifestation of physical health, now appears to have an important psychological dimension as well (Friedan, 442–43). And yet a study of patient interactions with mainstream physicians found that only 17 percent said that psychosocial issues were discussed with their doctors (Innes et al., 43). Other studies have shown that doctors spend less time with old patients than with others.

Finally, there are the telomeres: Bits of simple repetitive DNA sequences at the end of chromosomes, called telomeres, formerly thought to be biological "junk," have been shown to prolong the longevity of cells. Experiments with a naturally occurring enzyme, telomerase, that synthesizes new caps on chromosomes, may lead to a better understanding of life extension. A study of 2,400 women and men aged eighteen to eighty-one by King's College London and the New Jersey University of Medicine found that those who exercised most had longer telomeres than sedentary people have (*AARP Bulletin*, March 2008, 28), an intriguing discovery.

Elizabeth Blackburn, Carol Greider, and Jack Szostak won the Nobel Prize in 2009 for discovering how chromosomes are protected by telomeres and telomerase. They showed that stress is related to the shortening of telomeres, an important finding because stress harms the immune system. Cancer biologist Ronald A. DePinho proposes that malfunctioning telomeres are the "core pathway" to health decline in late life, but tests that measure telomere length may provide only one clue to assessing health (Thea Singer, *Washington Post*, May 25, 2011).[17] Accelerated shortening of telomeres may be either a cause or consequence of cardiovascular aging and disease (Fyhrquist and Saijonmaa).

Signs of unusual physical capacity among a few hearty people over seventy, the snowboarders jocularly called "Grays on Trays," for example, should not be used to denigrate elders who experience the more common slow decline and gradual loss of function associated with advanced age. Selective representations of exceptionally fit old people "create a compelling mythic structure that obscures chronic illness or functional decline" and also obscures the need for health care reform (Scannell, 1416). These selective examples foster "a new dualism of super aging in which story-lines of physically fit, creative, active, adventurous ageing become oppressive and unachievable" (Warren and Clarke). We may be approaching a time in which large numbers of white, middle-class older adults exhibit a level of health that would have seemed remarkable to their grandparents or even to their parents.[18] But that promise will not extend to all of their fellow citizens. The great and growing income gap in the United States today has already created a new dualism of aging.

6

The Politics of Healthy Aging

Despite positive developments in science, medicine, and public health, the only way to make healthy aging a realistic possibility for *most* Americans is to eradicate poverty. That would not eliminate all self-destructive behavior, obviously, but even a decrease in poverty would lead to healthier aging. Although a focus on smoking and obesity may reduce health disparities, a more fundamental solution is increasing the income and the educational level of the currently disadvantaged (Herd et al., 122). The United States has the highest poverty rate in the industrialized world, and economic deprivation causes health disparities (130). Single-payer national health care could mitigate some of the damage to health caused by poverty and near poverty. "The new longevity" is now a popular slogan in gerontology. The question is, for whom?

An egalitarian spirit might prompt one to say that age levels differences. In certain instances this may be true, as for example when a retired CEO and a retired laborer are both ignored at the hardware store on Saturday morning or when a receptionist calls a famous author by her first name as she does any old woman patient. But inequalities in money, status, and power matter greatly where healthy aging is concerned, except perhaps in an Alzheimer's ward. Until we have more accurate measures of late-life health, especially for people of color and for women, the extent and meaning of difference may not be knowable. Decades of experiencing prejudice and discrimination based on class, ethnicity, or gender, or all three, exacts a serious toll on health. That is a political judgment. A spiritual or psychological perspective would emphasize wholeness and recovery from oppression.

One thing we do know is that the life expectancy gap has widened in the United States. In the early 1980s, affluent Americans lived an average of 2.8 years longer than the poorest people; by 2000, the difference had grown to 4.5 years, and it continues to expand. Growing income inequality is reflected in the growing life expectancy gap, which Peter R. Orszag, former director of the Congressional Budget Office, calls "really quite dramatic" (Pear, "Gap," 14). Thus conventional aging models cannot fit everyone. This is especially true because by 2030, non-Hispanic whites will be a numerical minority in the United States (James Jackson, Govia, and Sellers, 92).

The class bias and individualist bias inherent in "successful aging" were noted earlier. Gerontologists also urge "responsible aging," a phrase that suggests not costing taxpayers too much. "Responsible aging" puts the burden on me of making wise choices without inquiring as to my capacity to make them. When a stigmatized group is told to behave responsibly (like the "deserving" poor), unjust distribution of resources is conveniently ignored. Thus the theme of this chapter is inequality.

The complete elimination of differences in health care, a goal of Healthy People 2010, was unrealistic, given the difficulty of achieving the more modest goal of *narrowing* the race and class gap. The National Institute on Aging and the National Institute of Nursing Research funds six resource centers for minority aging whose goal is to reduce health care disparities.[1] A racial difference in pain treatment has been documented, for example, for both blacks and Latinas/os (Glaeser, D8). Even if such injustices can be remedied, a larger structural problem remains: The rapid growth in the numbers of minority elders means that current policies "designed for a homogenous population are increasingly obsolete" (Wray, 357).

CLASS

Low-income elders are far more likely than others to have restricted physical functioning or disability (George Kaplan, 45). Low socioeconomic status, as measured by occupation, income, and education, and the conditions associated with it, is a more fundamental cause of both unhealthy lifestyles and poor health than individual behavior (Robert and House, 268). This hard truth is seldom acknowledged in gerontology, even though epidemiological research clearly indicates that countries with less income disparity have "longer life expectancies and lower rates of mortality from specific diseases" (Wallack, A22). Class difference means not only that the wealthy live longer in better health but also that poor health threatens the economic resources accumulated over a lifetime (J. Smith, 282). The severity of the recession reduced economic resources for many

Americans. Noted economist Joseph Stieglitz argues that although some inequality is inevitable, the current excessive inequality in the United States is "bad for economic growth [because] it leads to underinvestment in the 'public good' including infrastructure, education and technology" ("TRB: Inside the List," July 15, 2012). Aside from determining who has adequate health care and health insurance, class determines who will feel entitled to good care. In noting the link between class and late-life health, two public health authorities observe that poverty by itself is disabling (Kennedy and Minkler, 95). According to an AARP report, one in four older workers lost their savings because of the recession (May 24, 2011).

A problem inherent in healthy aging, often overlooked, is that healthy choices and habits are to some degree middle-class luxuries. To state the problem differently, the ideas about health promulgated by gerontologists reveal middle-class assumptions about personal responsibility. To make choices that the middle class regards as healthy requires a sense of control over one's circumstances and belief that planning for the future is worthwhile or even possible. To be poor or working class often means that others control the conditions under which we live and that long-term planning and deferred gratification are meaningless. Maine, for example, has many poor residents and the highest adult rates of smoking and of asthma in the country. Self-destructive behavior among people of color may often be "a response to recalcitrant racism" that dehumanizes them and deprives them of hope (Bayne-Smith, 14). Making these connections does not absolve people of responsibility for their actions but it highlights the impact of race and class. Careful eating, exercise, and moderate drinking are choices of people whose relative freedom from addiction and self-esteem result in part from their social and economic niche.

Healthy aging advice emphasizes individual choice about smoking, drinking, and exercise "without further reflection on what is reinforcing or dictating those choices" (Hendricks and Hatch, 443). People who are just getting by, who lack education, who face prejudice at work or in housing, cannot be expected to place the same value as middle-class people on healthy habits. Many do, in spite of the obstacles, but organic food, alternative medicine, long vacations, and workshops on self-care all lie beyond their means.

ETHNICITY

The approach of intersectionality (see chapter 10) asks how identities besides ethnicity such as class and age impact health status (Koehn and Kobayashi, 137).[2] Ethnic identity comes from the interplay between an individual's belief about his or her ethnicity and what others believe it to be (Loue, 37). Generalizations about "minorities" are unreliable, given the diversity of people under that umbrella term, both between groups and within groups. Elderly black women, for example, include those who did not reach eighth grade and women with graduate and professional degrees (Jacquelyne Jackson, "Aging Black Women," 35). It is clear, nonetheless, that inadequate health care in childhood and middle age has a big impact on the late-life health of many blacks, Latinas/os, Asian Pacific Islanders, and American Indians.[3] A report by the Institute of Medicine concluded that minority Americans use fewer health services than whites but need them more (Fleming, 28). When they do enter the system they tend to get poorer care. The *Women of Color Health Data Handbook* issued by the National Institutes of Health documented significant disparities in every category studied, including access to insurance (Reed, 46). A related problem is that the number of minority nurses and doctors has declined (Fleming, 24). In emergency rooms, where many people of color get the only care available to them, most of the doctors are white.

Racism at school, at work, and in housing has life course consequences not only in poorer health but also in lower life expectancy for blacks, Latinas/os, and American Indians (Quadagno, *Aging*, 270). Cumulative disadvantage is the pattern by which those who begin life with few advantages fall farther behind as they age. Although the inequities that suppress vitality in many people of color are not a central concern of gerontology, a life course emphasis in social gerontology encourages attention to cumulative disadvantage.

Ethnogerontology gathers data not only about social inequality but also about age changes affected by ethnicity, nationality, and culture (P. Jackson and Williams, 291). Minority status *per se* reveals less about a person than interactions among such factors as health, income, and family support (Markides, "Minorities," 785). Ethnogerontology and ethnogeriatrics, the integration of aging, health, and ethnicity, are particularly important because by 2030, 25 percent of all elders will be minority elders (Wadsworth and FallCreek, 254). The number of old Latinas/os will triple by 2050, and the number of blacks will double (Binstock, 5). More than 40 percent of older black women and Latinas who live alone are poor (Hounsell and Riojas, 7). Minority women elders are most likely to be burdened by chronic illnesses (T. Miles, "Living," 55). By 2050, old Asian Pacific Islanders could number seven million, or 16 percent of their total population. By the same year, 500,000 American Indian elders will constitute 12 percent of all Indians. Besides sheer numbers, another reason that minority concerns should take up a much larger space in healthy aging studies is that cultural patterns affect the way people define illness, how an ill person is perceived by his or her group, and what health-seeking strategies are appropriate (Tripp-Reimer, 236).

Minority elders are underrepresented in clinical trials; they may react to medication differently from whites on whom the drugs were tested; they often lack health insurance; they may be unaware of programs they qualify for; and limited access to long-term care burdens their economically vulnerable families (M. Harper, 12). Lack of money keeps elderly people of color out of nursing homes, but discrimination is probably another factor accounting for low nursing home use across all minority groups (Kiyak and Hooyman, 305). Minority elders lack a voice in formulating health care policy, "bilingual and bicultural barriers abound," and most doctors will not understand their traditional customs and beliefs or the folk medicine they may be using (M. Harper, 12). In addition, their pensions are decreasing in value (Villa, 213), and many seek supplementary income from work. There is a great need for more minority health care professionals trained in geriatrics (Jacquelyne Jackson, "Aging Black Women," 42). These problems are exacerbated by the growing income gap in the United States.

A problem for researchers is that past and present studies take whites as the standard measure, so that dimensions of aging or of a disease particular to a minority group are overlooked (T. Miles, "Aging," 119). While comparative studies may be useful, conditions common to whites should not be the "explicit or implicit standard for black health conditions" (Jacquelyne Jackson and Perry, 172). A good alternative is to focus on a specific problem, disease, or issue in one population (T. Miles, "Aging," 119). Heterogeneity within ethnic groups must be studied from the perspective that factors accounting for variability between groups do not necessarily affect variability within groups (Whitfield and Baker-Thomas, 75). Another, broader challenge is to integrate population aging, cultural diversity, minority aging, and public policy.

Emphasis on the fundamental unfairness built into our social structure should not obscure the fact that minority elders act in their own behalf, bringing strengths and resources to the aging process that may be invisible to white, middle-class professionals. The advantages of membership in minority communities, racial or ethnic solidarity, for example, or interdependence, are significant, as are the unique personal histories that shape health and illness. Black elders tend to see friends as family members whom they can look to for help and encouragement, thus extending their support network. The suicide rate among elderly blacks is very low, and black women have greater bone density and greater bone mass than whites (Gannon, 155). Strong religious belief often characterizes elderly Latinas/os and blacks, and the reverent worldview of American Indians smoothes their passage into old age. Indian elders have been called "unifiers" of their families (Red Horse, 491). Perhaps the greatest advantage for older Asian Pacific Islanders, Latinas/os, and blacks is the respect given them in their communities.

Blacks

Racism has damaged the self-esteem of older black Americans and very little discussion or research tries to understand its impact (Stanford, "Mental Health," 164; 169). Over a lifetime, blacks absorb physical, mental, and emotional abuse, and to survive they stifle anger at unjust treatment (176). Misdiagnosis, overdrugging, and cultural insensitivity have marked the mental health system's dealings with black patients (170–71). Older black women and men have learned to "present themselves and their outward actions in ways that will be most acceptable" to the dominant group, but these adaptations may not be compatible with their own beliefs, needs, or circumstances (175). The health of older black women is affected not only by discriminatory experiences in their current lives but also by the cumulative impact of experiences of racism. Black women aged forty-nine to fifty-five are estimated to be 7.5 years older biologically than white women that age; stress and poverty account for 27 percent of this difference. By middle age, black women have shorter telomeres than white women (Geronimus et al., 21; 29). Whites are far more likely than blacks to get help from a family member for a down payment on a house and also more likely to get inheritances (Harrington Meyer and Herd, 93). Predatory lending rates leading to foreclosures have threatened or eliminated home ownership for many black families. Older blacks have high rates of stroke, diabetes, obesity, and chronic illness (M. Harper, 17), and a higher incidence of cervical, colon, and lung cancer than whites (K. Gould, 208).

At every income level, black women over fifty-four are only half as likely as white women to have a mammogram ordered for them by a doctor, even if they see a primary care doctor just as often (Lisa Cool, 17). Thus their breast cancer is detected later and only one-half of elderly black women diagnosed with breast cancer are alive five years later, compared to three-fourths of white women. Black women have a higher mortality rate from breast cancer partly because they are more likely to have a type of breast cancer called estrogen receptor negative disease, which is more difficult to treat (Haber, *Health*, 426). In addition, the death rate from heart disease in black women aged sixty-five to seventy-four is double that of white women of the same age (Fahs, 115–16). Hypertension is a bigger problem for black women than for black men (Taylor, 112). On the other hand, black women have lower rates of Alzheimer's disease than white women.

Compared to whites, blacks are more likely to live in cities where they are exposed to air pollution and crime. Both blacks and Latinas/os are more likely to live in overcrowded housing in dangerous neighborhoods and to have higher rates of lead poisoning, injury from fire, asthma, and gas poisoning (Harrington Meyer and Herd, 102). Blacks are more likely to have hazardous jobs and greater exposure to workplace toxins. Black women are sicker than whites when they see a doctor, perhaps because of low income, trouble getting child care, fear of hospitals, or fear of becoming a guinea pig (Edmonds, 208–9). Feeling a need to work regardless of health, they may overestimate their health as a way of coping, or they may believe illness is their cross to bear (213–15). Older blacks are two to three times as likely as whites to give health problems as their reason for not working (Wallace, 260). Raising the age for Social Security benefits would therefore be harmful to them. Another study found that among Medicare recipients, blacks were 50 percent less likely than whites to have bypass surgery, angioplasty, or hip replacement (Harrington Meyer and Herd, 104). Compared to whites, blacks' hypertension is more prevalent, more severe, and more likely to lead to disease and death (Svetkey, 64).

Shortcomings of existing research are the inadequate size of black samples and the lack of longitudinal studies that would shed light on the process of aging among blacks (Jacquelyne Jackson and Perry, 121; 143). It has been thought that blacks who reach sixty-five are more likely than whites to survive to seventy-five, either because of a lower incidence of heart disease or because they must be hardy to reach their mid-sixties, but this apparent advantage may be based on faulty data (Jacquelyne Jackson and Perry, 142).

Latinas/os

Latinas/os are a very diverse group including not only recent immigrants but those who live on land formerly owned by Mexico. Stressors that may affect their health include limited education, low income, and difficult transitions from rural to urban life (Torres, 213). This transition is especially hard for elders driven out of Central America by war who speak only Spanish. Their American-born grandchildren may speak only English. Those who are illegal aliens may fear getting help when they are sick. An executive order by the Obama administration in 2012 ended deportation of young people brought to the United States as children by undocumented parents. Hostility to immigrants from Mexico and Central America must be stressful for those who are its targets. The Arizona immigration law that encourages racial profiling (SB1070), partly upheld by the Supreme Court in June 2012, caused some Latinos to leave the state, a difficult uprooting especially for long-time residents.

More than 20 percent of Latina/o elders have incomes below the poverty level, compared to less than 10 percent of Anglos. Most older Latinas/os have no pension and do not receive Social Security. The systems developed by the dominant culture to manage health may be alienating to Latinas/os, who respond better to surrogate family approaches to services. Latino health varies by country of origin, with Cubans enjoying better health than Mexicans (Herd et al., 123).[4]

Chronic health problems are found in 85 percent of older Latinas/os. Nearly three-fourths have some health impairment that restricts their activities (Kiyak and Hooyman, 304). Latinas have the highest rate of cervical and uterine cancer among all women, and Mexican-American and Puerto Rican women are twice as likely as whites to have diabetes (Minority Women's Health website, Department of Health and Human Services). Latinas/os are more likely than whites to die from infections, flu, pneumonia, and accidents (Markides, Coreil, and Rogers, 197). They tend to have high cholesterol (M. Harper, 17). Problems among Mexican Americans include lack of awareness of hypertension and the stress of poverty leading to depression. On the other hand, they have less osteoporosis and arthritis than non-Hispanic whites. The Sacramento Area Longitudinal Study in Aging is following 2,000 Latinas/os to determine whether heart disease risk is related to dementia.

Asian Pacific Islanders

Asian Pacific Islanders are the most diverse minority group in language, in the culture of their country of origin, and in the circumstances of their arrival in the United States (Louie, 147). Little is known about their health status because national surveys inadequately sample them (D. Yee, 43). Health care needs of recent arrivals from Laos, Cambodia, Korea, and the Philippines differ from those of Chinese American and Japanese American elders born here (46–47). Nearly three-fourths of Asian Pacific Islanders live in California, Hawaii, and New York. Although they are healthier in late life than members of other minority groups, they have higher rates of tuberculosis, hepatitis, anemia, and hypertension than whites (B. Yee and Weaver, 41). They have high rates of cancer—stomach cancer for Japanese Americans; lung and breast cancer for Hawaiians; and pancreatic cancer for Chinese American women (M. Harper, 17). Among older Filipino Americans, diabetes is common (Yeo and Hikoyeda, 94). The late-life health problems of Asian Pacific Islanders result from low income, lack of adequate health care throughout life, likelihood of working at physically demanding jobs, language barriers, and distrust of services from the dominant culture that has historically discriminated against them.

Sixty-five percent of Korean American women have never had a Pap smear (Lisa Cool, 17). Asian Pacific Islanders are more at risk for osteoporosis than are other people of color, but they are less likely to die of heart disease than blacks, Latinas/os, American Indians, or whites.

Adapting to the high-sodium American diet appears to have increased their susceptibility to high blood pressure. They may take herbs that interfere with drugs and cause serious side effects (B. Yee and Weaver, 41). Chinese Americans typically believe that health is maintained by balancing opposite forces in the body, yin and yang. Vietnamese immigrants explain many illnesses by bad wind in the body, released by rubbing the back (Yeo, 75), beliefs that will not be understood by white doctors. Among Asian-American immigrants, tuberculosis and hepatitis B are major problems.

A mental health issue is that standardized psychological tests are unreliable for diagnosing problems of Asian Pacific Islanders. Because of the stigma attached to mental illness in their communities, they may express psychological problems through physical symptoms such as stomach upset or fatigue (Louie, 151). Older Chinese American women have three times the suicide rate of white women (Yeo and Hikoyeda, 94). High levels of stress and anxiety among Korean Americans living in big cities have been linked to racial discrimination (Louie, 152). Refugees from Southeast Asia experience relocation depression and post-traumatic stress disorder (Yeo and Hikoyeda, 82). A strength in the Asian Pacific Islander communities is the traditional high status of the elder, but "declining expectations of filial piety" are also characteristic (Yeo and Hikoyeda, 80). Asian Pacific Islanders in California have high rates of hypertension (Stavig et al., 677). This problem is worse for Filipino Americans than for the more prosperous Japanese Americans, an instance of class as well as ethnicity affecting health.

Unlike other minorities, Asian Pacific Islanders have longer life expectancies than whites; it is not clear if this greater longevity results from some genetic protection or from factors such as exercise or diet. They have lower death rates from heart disease (Markides, "Minorities," 784). Asian-American women in Bergen County, New Jersey, lead the nation in longevity, typically living to ninety-one. Asian-American women in general outlive low-income black women in the rural South by thirteen years.

American Indians

A major difference between Indians and other minorities is that a far greater proportion of them, 53 percent, live in non-metropolitan areas (AARP, *A Portrait*, 7). The number of Indian elders doubled between 1980 and 1990 (8). Indians have the poorest health of all minorities and the shortest life expectancy. They experience "accelerated aging" and often spend years in disability (John, 409). Those fifty-five and older who live on reservations have impairments comparable to those of non-Indians over sixty-five.

Compared to whites, American Indians have higher death rates from car accidents, alcoholism, and pneumonia, and they are ten times more likely than whites to have diabetes (M. Harper, 17). These problems are exacerbated by poverty, overcrowding, malnutrition, and distance from hospitals. Men are sicker than women, having three times as much emphysema, twice as much cancer, and 1.5 times the heart disease (John, Hennessy, and Denny, 54; 57). Indian women have higher rates of gall bladder disease and diabetes than Indian men but their life expectancy is 20–25 percent longer (John, "Native Americans," 408). They are less likely than white women to get breast exams, mammograms, and Pap tests. American Indian caregivers report low levels of caregiver burden, highlighting the strength of reciprocity in their communities (Jervis, 300).

Knowledge of Indian aging is "rudimentary and incomplete" compared to knowledge about other minority groups' aging and to that of whites (John, "Aging," 84). Because little is known about chronic health problems among Indians, an especially important goal of the Native Elder Research Center at the University of Colorado is to train Indians to do aging research.

The Indian Health Service, difficult to get to for Indians living in cities, focuses on young people and families rather than elders (Kiyak and Hooyman, 305). In addition, the IHS is better equipped to treat life-threatening problems than chronic ones, to the detriment of the 20 percent of Indians over fifty-five for whom arthritis is the leading cause of impairment (John, Hennessy, and Denny, 68). A study of Navajo showed that hypertension increased with age and weight. Greater exposure to the dominant culture since the 1930s may be a factor in the high incidence of hypertension among Indians.

The diabetes epidemic in their communities seriously threatens the health of American Indians. The Pima of Arizona, for example, have the world's highest diabetes rates. Their traditional low-fat diet protected them but their current diet is 40 percent fat. Native Seeds, a group promoting preservation of ancient crops, collaborated with nutritionists and conservationists from the Seri, Tohono O'odham, and Pima tribes and from the Sonora Desert Museum to determine that native foods dramatically reduce blood sugar levels and improve insulin production (Montgomery, "Return").

The study of Indian aging did not begin until the 1970s. Before then, work on elders was based on an anthropological model, which in turn was based on assumptions about "primitive" cultures. Unlike whites, they consider aging "a natural process to be embraced," and they readily define themselves as elders.[5] Research has not adequately considered diversity within the Indian population or the specifics of Indian women's aging (John, Blanchard, and Hennessy, 309–10). Moreover, health research on old Indian women is limited by small sample size, narrow focus, and the selection of only a few tribes, precluding valid generalization (300). Today, a great need of Indian elders is a comprehensive, culturally competent, long-term care system made up primarily of community-based services rather than institutional care (John, "Native Americans," 411).

Although diversity exists within American Indian tribes, the cultural value of great respect for elders remains consistently strong. Elders are viewed as cultural transmitters, oral historians, and wisdom keepers. A Michigan study found that a strong motivation for care of grandchildren is the grandparents' memories of trauma and abuse suffered in government boarding schools. They are therefore reluctant to seek support from mainstream services (Cross et al., 383; 378).

Ethnogerontologists use "culturally competent" to indicate health workers' responsibility to learn and adapt rather than simply have good feelings and intentions, as the earlier phrase "culturally sensitive" suggested. Western biomedical notions conflict with indigenous peoples' conceptions of illness (Jervis, 299). North American Indians, for example, may value family members who have dementia if they are seen to be communicating with the spirit world. Dementia is a Western diagnostic category; native North Americans may refer instead to childlike behavior or sickness (Hulko et al., 319).

Some Indians use vapor baths to treat disease, for example in the sweat lodge. One consequence of drug companies' support of U.S. medical schools is a turning away from water therapy, which remains widely used in Europe (Nikola, 5).

Immigrants

Immigrant elders in the United States include both newcomers and those who have lived here thirty years or more. Vietnamese elders may suffer from war trauma. Immigrant elders tend to be caregivers rather than care-receivers, performing household tasks, supervising homework when both parents work, and serving as the person designated to pray (Trease). Often they are not authority figures, as they would be in their native countries, because they lack resources and familiarity with American culture. They may offer advice but have no power. Furthermore, family life is no guarantee of security: They tend to suffer from depression, isolation, loneliness, and boredom and may be too busy caregiving to get on with their own lives. Besides the economic value that immigration provides to California, large immigrant families help to balance population aging (Trease).

Immigration now and for the next twenty years will have a greater impact on American society than at any time since the 1920s and 1930s, but gerontologists have not yet become involved in the issue (Torres-Gil). Researchers who study immigrants, people of color, and working-class Americans must examine closely both their own values and the cultural relevance of their theories "instead of assuming that they are universally appropriate scientific truths" (Dilworth-Anderson and Cohen, 497).

GENDER

For a woman, learning to be old means learning to cope with medical professionals who may be unresponsive to her needs and uncomfortable with assertive old women. Most older women can expect to be treated by doctors who have no specialized knowledge of aging and little time to take the medical histories that would distinguish disease from normal aging. In the United States, women are twice as likely as men to seek preventative help, but this leaves them open to being dismissed as "whiners, complainers, and hypochondriacs" (Gannon, 51). A large-scale study in Canada and the United States of gender differences in patient-doctor relationships found that women doctors allow more time for patients to talk (Lorber, 46).

Heart disease is the leading cause of death or disability among older women. Their heart attack symptoms may be back pain rather than the more familiar signs of chest and arm pain, and thus they may not be diagnosed as readily as men. After a heart disease diagnosis, women are less likely than men to get an implanted defibrillator to control irregular heartbeats (Garner, 282).

Women are less likely than men to be given clot-dissolving drugs during a heart attack and are referred less often for carotid surgery to prevent strokes ("Our Mothers," 196). Much more research is needed because "too many women die too soon from cardiovascular disease" (Garner, 281).

Other instances of age and gender bias in health care have been well documented. Women are underrepresented in clinical research and trials and also in health care leadership roles, leading three Australian researchers to conclude that the needs of older women "will not be adequately addressed until women play a more significant and authoritative role in the administration and governance of health" (Davidson, DiGiacomo and McGrath, 1040). Data from four thousand breast cancer patients showed that older women were significantly less likely than younger ones to receive a two-step surgical procedure, first biopsy and then tumor removal (Hynes, 336). When these two steps are combined, little time is spent evaluating the results of biopsy (336). Elderly women with breast cancer are less likely than young women to undergo lymph node dissection, regarded as essential to treatment ("Our Mothers," 195). Although half of

U.S. women diagnosed with breast cancer are over sixty-five, in clinical trials evaluating new drugs for treating breast cancer, fewer than 10 percent of the participants are sixty-five or older (Currey, 17).

Compared to men, women are 50 percent more likely to have arthritis (Harrington Meyer and Herd, 97). Old women suffer more chronic illness, including hypertension, gall bladder conditions, and intestinal diverticula. Thyroid disease or other endocrine problems may be an underlying cause of immune system breakdown. Autoimmune diseases such as Hashimoto's thyroiditis, lupus, and rheumatoid arthritis are far more common in women than in men (Kalache, Barreto, and Keller, 38). Women also have higher rates of restricted activity and spend more days in bed (Verbrugge and Wingard, 115–17). Women have more vision problems but better hearing. They use more medication, both prescribed and over the counter, and take more psychotropic drugs. A detailed study of Medicare recipients found a large gender gap: Women spent 22 percent more of their income on medications than men spent, and more than half of the people whose drug spending exceeds the coverage allowed by Medicare Part D are expected to be women (Wei et al., 447–48).

Why are old women sicker than men their age? This question, which seems logically to be one of the most important in gerontology, has not attracted much attention. Women's "greater survival at every impairment level" (Ory and Warner, xxix) is a plausible biological explanation. Since women are more likely to perceive health problems than men, more apt to discuss symptoms with others, and more likely to see doctors, their poorer late-life health may reflect more reporting of illness than more actual illness (Verbrugge and Wingard, 135). On the other hand, it is conceivable that women are sicker in old age than men because their lives have been more stressful. Before becoming old, they juggled multiple roles and often worked in unchallenging jobs (123). Another explanation that gets at the cultural roots of the problem is that the health care system is geared to women of child-bearing age, not to older women. If all social causes of their late-life illness were reduced, so that women felt more productive, experienced less stress, and got aerobic exercise, they would be likely to have fewer chronic health conditions (Verbrugge, "The Twain," 184). But the social causes of older women's health problems may increase rather than decrease, as more women take on the stressful job of caring for aged parents.

Social conditions such as poverty, widowhood, and caregiving place a woman at risk psychologically, and if she enters the mental health system, "her vulnerability continues" (Rodeheaver and Datan, 649). A false diagnosis of psychosomatic illness is more likely to be given women than men, especially poor women, immigrants, and those with an earlier psychiatric diagnosis. Age may be a factor as well because older women's health is not well understood and thus a doctor may disregard or underrate physical symptoms by considering them psychosomatic. In addition, older women's low social status may lead to "low believability and authority, which, in Western medical settings, puts a person at risk for receiving a psychosomatic diagnosis" (Wendell, 143).

Chronic pain among older women is a neglected area of research (Roberto, 5). Non-drug treatments such as heat and cold applications, relaxation exercises, ergonomics, and transcutaneous electrical nerve stimulation (TENS) are effective, but information about their specific application to older adults is limited (5). When research priorities that ignore the needs of millions of older women are juxtaposed to the heavy marketing of painkilling drugs, the politics of healthy aging comes into focus.

The problem of death or injury from falls is most serious for people over seventy-five. Each year, 300,000 people break a hip, and 500,000 suffer vertebral fractures, leading to annual medical costs of $14 billion (McDonald, A16). Another estimate is $60 billion, not counting the indirect costs to family and friends of the injured person (Fahs, 124). Many nursing home admissions result from falls, and hip fractures are increasing faster than can be explained by population aging (Pousada, 456). Although weak bones are blamed for falls, a more likely cause is weak muscles from disuse (Bortz, "Aging," 201). Poor balance or unsteady gait also cause falls. Gait-measuring devices that analyze walking patterns in elderly women and men may play a role in reducing falls. A study outside of the office of a healthy aging researcher showed that women over eighty could walk only halfway across the street before the light changed (Kaplan and Strawbridge, 69), a fall risk created by the environment. Traffic lights should be timed to accommodate old women, not harry them.

Women who suffer hip fractures deserve longer and better rehabilitation than is now available to them; restoration of full function should be the goal. When current practice emphasizes accommodating problems, it indirectly encourages dependency (Estes, "Aging Enterprise Revisited," 140). Lack of health promotion programs and unsafe home environments make falls a structural as well as an individual problem. The voices of women who have experienced falls must be incorporated into research and recovery programs. Old women who have not fallen realistically fear that they will. How does this fear limit them physically and psychologically? Much more work needs to be done on the connection between prescription drugs and falls. Drug-induced lethargy, confusion, and dizziness erode the power of old women.

Many fewer women are taking estrogen since the Women's Health Initiative's study of hormone replacement therapy was stopped three years early because of evidence of increased risk for breast cancer, heart attack, and stroke in women taking estrogen-progestin. Breast cancer rates in women have declined, apparently because of the sharp drop in the numbers of women taking estrogen replacements. Moreover, a study published in the *Journal of the American Medical Association* (*JAMA*) found that estrogen had not improved cognitive function in women with Alzheimer's disease (Mulnard et al., 1013). According to a later *JAMA* report (March 2008), increased cancer risk does not end when a woman stops taking estrogen. Women should be more aware that drugs are not tested long enough "to be sure (presumed) benefits truly exist" (Moore, "Why Estrogen," E1). The observational studies suggesting a benefit for heart health from estrogen may have overlooked a possible link between affluence, leading to better health and more exercise, and estrogen use. The refusal of many health plans to cover the bone density test that would let a woman gauge her risk of osteoporosis complicates the estrogen question. Bone density tests should be considered a routine part of older women's health care, and may be if the Affordable Care Act is fully implemented.

The idea that women should protect themselves against heart disease and osteoporosis by taking a costly drug fits in well with medicalized aging. These diseases have been "re-conceptualized as being *caused* by menopause without adequate scientific research to support this conclusion" (Gannon, 137).[6] We need a large body of data from long-term studies in which women of color are well represented to re-evaluate the hypothesis that a sound diet and regular exercise offer sufficient protection against heart disease and osteoporosis. The myth that aging requires drugs for routine management has led to the neglect of diet and lifestyle as the primary means to achieve healthy aging (Willett et al., 553).

Complete regeneration may not be possible for most ill older women, but Americans are so conditioned to expect deterioration with age that restoration of function is not aggressively pursued. The powerful, often insidious side effects of drugs, especially multiple drugs, noted in chapter 4, keep women from discovering what natural aging might be for them. Some new drugs may benefit them, but generally speaking, the healthiest aging is drug free or nearly drug free.

Drugs can suppress sexual desire and cause sexual dysfunction, for example. The sexuality of old women, a subject of mirth in classical literature and in popular culture today, deserves far more attention. The sex drive of healthy old women remains fairly constant, although lack of partners is a problem for heterosexual women, two-thirds of whom over sixty-five are single, compared to one-fourth of their male peers (Porcino, 117). The obvious importance of masturbation for women in this age group is a taboo topic in gerontology. For some women, thinning of the vaginal walls and decreased lubrication cause discomfort during sex. Orgasms are shorter than those experienced by younger women (Neuhaus and Neuhaus, 76). For some postmenopausal women, testosterone cream increases libido. Whatever her age, an older woman is entitled to "the freedom to explore and expand her sensual, sexual self" as long as she lives (Weg, 220). For many old women, touch deprivation is potentially threatening to health, an issue that neither feminists nor gerontologists have begun to address. Commenting on the sexuality chapter of her book *Growing Older, Getting Better*, Jane Porcino laments the few options for intimacy for older heterosexual women. "We should do more touching of each other. I think it's as important as any other facet of life for us after fifty" (quoted in Downes, 33). A key to healthy sexuality in late life is rejection of cultural images that portray old women as ugly and asexual. When Viagra was in the news, a television station looking for a gerontologist to comment called me. I said that the topic of masturbation among old women interested me more. "You can't say that on television," the reporter hissed. Older men's sexual needs are front-page news, while older women's are draped in silence.

Combined loss of companionship and the income drop that accompanies widowhood create health risks for heterosexual women over sixty-five, some of whom will be widows for thirty years or more. Half of the women over sixty-five are widows, and four-fifths are widows at age eighty-five. Black women are widowed earlier than white women. If men's deaths could be postponed even an average of one year, the economic gains (and indirectly the health gains) for heterosexual women would be significant. Although lesbians have an advantage in partner life expectancy, their bereavement is more likely to be hidden. Both urban lesbians and those living in rural areas fear eventual isolation from other lesbians in a nursing home (Butler and Hope, 2).

Medicare is increasingly inadequate. "It doesn't pay for what most patients need or want" (Gross, "Medicare"). Today people over sixty-five spend an average of 20 percent of their annual income on health care gaps in Medicare coverage. The health care costs of single, older women consume more than a third of their annual income (Estes and Close, 324). Thus Medicare has lost its original purpose of providing comprehensive health care coverage. A large drop in federal payments for home health care has forced many Medicare patients to stay longer in hospitals and nursing homes (Pear, "Medicare," A1). Agencies have turned away the most disabled, fearing their care would cost more than agencies could be reimbursed (A18). This slashing of benefits shows how relatively powerless the elderly in America really are: A potent "gray lobby" would have beaten back this assault on its constituents. The National Association for Home Care reports that the total number of home care visits has been cut 55 percent since 1997. These cuts have had especially bad consequences for minority elders and their families (Binstock, 17). Most of their oldest old live outside of nursing homes and thus have a special need for home care (Wallace and Villa, 413). Lack of home health care endangers blacks, Indians, and Latinas/os, who are twice as likely as middle-income whites to have chronic diseases that limit their activities (Kiyak and Hooyman, 303–4). Medicare Part D, the prescription drug benefit, potentially could lessen the health disparities between white, middle-class people and people of color and low-income elders, however (Bishop, 429).

Medicare is a prime example of the male model of aging in the United States. According to the Older Women's League (OWL), it covers more health expenses for elderly unmarried males than for unmarried females, for example (Steckenrider, 247). Medicare is based on the traditional illness model, "an acute-phase model, grafted onto a time of life when chronic problems predominate" (Bortz, *We Live*, 267). Since men tend to get the acute diseases and women the disabling chronic conditions, Medicare is more aligned with men's needs, and thus it does not sufficiently protect women from preventable health problems (Steckenrider, 246–47). Many more women than men require home care, but Medicare covers intermittent nursing care rather than the expenses of food preparation, bathing, dressing, or transferring out of bed (Steckenrider, 251). The failure of Medicare to cover health maintenance results in "specific discrimination against minority and poor women" (Healey, "Confronting Ageism," 7). Because Medicare reimburses elders for very few preventative measures, it pays much more later on for serious illnesses, an example of wastefulness and of unfairness to women because it is they who would benefit most from early disease detection or prevention (Steckenrider, 254), in not only longer but healthier lives. If the Affordable Health Care Act is fully implemented in 2014, the problems with Medicare may be alleviated. Medicare was originally intended to be a first step in health care reform, with extended benefits coming later. It was not conceived of as a handout but rather "a benefit paid for in advance by its ultimate users," but now its benefits do not match what is most needed, chronic care (Gross, *Bittersweet*, 203). The apparent impossibility of achieving Medicare for all in the United States shows the great disadvantage of placing profit at the center of the health care system.

As old women and middle-aged women increasingly understand how little we can expect from mainstream medicine or from government, and as we recognize that we are now chiefly valued as a big market for prescription drugs, we may see the disadvantages of confronting old age health challenges on our own. The creation of healthy aging circles like the consciousness raising groups of the 1970s might be a good strategy. When a grassroots response directly connects an ill woman to a support group, the providers of help benefit as well as the woman being helped (Stoller, 17). Self-help is not a very satisfactory response to the profit-driven American health care system, but it is better than accepting the passive victimization encouraged by the status quo. The self-help groups envisioned here might also advocate for reforms that would benefit older women—federally funded fall prevention programs, for example; nutrition programs geared to low-income women; more respectful treatment of old women by doctors; and disability studies.[7]

Since women outlive men and have poorer health in late life, drug industry abuses will have a disproportionate impact on them. New Zealand is the only country besides the United States that allows drug ads on television. Direct-to-consumer mass media ads totaled $166 million in 1993 and $4.2 *billion* in 2005 (Donohue, 659). Marcia Angell believes these ads "mislead consumers far more than they inform them" (125). She and other medical researchers note that the industry devotes more resources to advertising than to research and development. Basic drug research is done by academics and the National Institutes of Health (Hugh Brody, 78); one-third of cancer drugs, for example, were developed by federally funded research but profits from sales went to the drug industry (93)—not exactly a model of free-market enterprise. Furthermore, research papers are often written by drug companies, not by the doctors whose names appear on the articles.

Preventative care and health promotion may improve if the Affordable Care Act is fully implemented. Pushing back even a year or two the onset of illness and disease would result in significant savings. The health care dollar is divided as follows: 97 cents for disease, less than 3 cents for prevention, and half a penny for health promotion (Haber, *Health*, 21). Increasingly, older women may see this resource allocation as irrational and dangerous to their interests. Are citizens entitled to good health in old age? If we were, half of the health care dollar would go to health rather than disease, and drug-free care would be available to all. Women would be the chief beneficiaries of such a reform. Health promotion in this country is a women's issue yet to be discovered by feminists and an aging issue that concerns too few gerontologists.

Doctors may cover up their ignorance of aging or lack of interest in the complicated problems an old woman often presents by saying "it's old age." When hearing this, a woman in her eighties, socialized to treat doctors with extreme deference, may find it hard to challenge this interpretation or get a second opinion. Urinary incontinence, for example, is twice as prevalent among women as among men. Despite the opinion of doctors who think aging inevitably brings incontinence, it can be alleviated or cured (Sharpe, 15). When women now in their fifties reach old age, they will probably be less inclined than their mothers to defer to doctors, but what may not change is their doctors' limited understanding of the aging process, of ageism, or of gender and racial differences in health care. On the other hand, women now fifty have a good chance of being treated by a woman doctor when they are seventy-five. And it is possible that geriatric knowledge will become more integrated into medical practice than is now the case.

A persistent problem is the near invisibility of older women's health concerns in widely used texts. In one text, for example, three articles out of fifty examine old women's issues and two are devoted to mid-life. Another text has a unit called "Special Issues for Older Women" in which the focus is disease. Changes in journalism as well as textbooks are needed. A large-scale content analysis of mass media by the National Council on Aging (NCOA) found that one in four news stories about older women's health omitted crucial information such as sample size, other research on the same topic, or control of variables. Breast cancer was overemphasized, relative to its incidence, and heart disease underemphasized. Clearly, women need more reliable sources of health information, for example from newsletters published by the Brandeis Center for Women's Aging and the Center for Women's Healthcare at Cornell and from articles and books created by older women themselves, such as the 500-page resource book *Ourselves, Growing Older* by the Boston Women's Health Collective, and *The New Ourselves, Growing Older* (Doress-Worters and Lasker Siegal).

In research and in practice, health promotion has been slow to recognize how significantly class, ethnicity, and gender influence the health of older women. Furthermore, it tends to accept "current social structures and power relationships as functional for society and for women" (Ward-Griffin and Ploeg, 284). Ideally, health promotion research would make its assumptions explicit and involve older women in research design. Such changes would begin to address the problem of research subjects' relative powerlessness to account for their experience in their own way. As Sally Gadow notes, an ethical issue as important as access to health care is "access to meanings that establish the woman at the center of her own health" ("Whose Body?" 295). It would be illuminating, for example, if old women investigators interviewed 100,000 women over seventy with health problems. As corporate control over health care tightens, it is all the more urgent that older women interpret their own experiences. When a false dementia diagnosis is given an old woman who takes six different medications a day, or when depression is overlooked because the doctor thinks an old woman has much to be sad about, ignoring women's stories becomes oppressive.

Older women are more diverse than any other group in their health status, and many are psychologically strong, despite all the obstacles to good health that they face (Rodeheaver and Datan, 652). Compared to men, they exhibit "greater intrinsic (genetic or hormonal) robustness" (Verbrugge, "Gender," 35). The life expectancy gap between women and men has narrowed slightly, however, because more women are dying of lung cancer (Verbrugge and Wingard, 108–9). The health of older women in the future will depend on many factors including disease patterns, environmental risks, new technologies, "society's conception of the value of life" (Lamphere-Thorpe and Blendon, 79), and the status of health care reform.

A hopeful sign is that feminists are looking closely at the ways women's health is conceptualized by researchers. It is now obvious that just as blacks' aging or the aging of American Indians deserves to be studied in and of itself, not only in comparison to whites, the health of older women and especially of women over seventy-five must be studied apart from men's health.

CONCLUSION

In general, older men, whites, and people with a high level of education and income are healthier than older women, blacks, Hispanics, and those with lower levels of education and income (Harrington Meyer and Herd, 96). Many agree with two Harvard professors of medicine who argue that only a single-payer system "can save what we estimate is the $350 billion wasted annually on medical bureaucracy and redirect those funds to expanded coverage" (Himmelstein and Woolhandler). Universal health care is a "social right, not a consumer product" (Quadagno, *One Nation*, 6).

Demographers at the Department of Health and Human Services reported in April 2008 that for the first time since 1918, life expectancy is decreasing among some low-income American women in the deep South, Appalachia, and Washington County, Maine. Among likely causes are poverty, high rates of smoking and diabetes, limited access to health care, and consumption of unhealthy food. Another factor is that low-income citizens, unlike middle and upper-income people, have little access to health information on the Internet (Brown, 1). The DHHS report demonstrates the significant impact of social class on aging.

To a large extent, aging was something that just happened to our mothers and grandmothers. Often its attendant problems were denied and its possibilities unnoticed. Women now young and middle-aged have an opportunity to age more deliberately and mindfully, with a sense of options and strategies for self-preservation. This will be easier for white, middle-class women than for women of color.

The possibility of greatly improved health in old age, through alternative medicine, health promotion programs, and bodywork is exciting. But the blitzkrieg of prescription drugs nearly obliterates creative thought about this prospect. Nowhere are the limits of Western thinking and Western medicine more starkly revealed than in attitudes toward the health of elderly people. Alternative medicine and bodywork, influenced by Eastern philosophy, have much more to offer. Full use of them and comprehensive healthy aging programs in every community would not only eliminate the need for multiple prescription drugs; it would radically alter our conception of aging.

A current challenge for policymakers is to pay serious attention to the "nonfatal conditions and difficulties in doing desired activities that compromise life's value in later life, especially for women" (Verbrugge, "Gender," 70). If health and research priorities focused on delaying the onset of chronic conditions such as arthritis or lessening their severity, American elders could "gain precious years of comfortable aging" (Jacob Brody, 30). The economic consequences of not postponing illness or dysfunction are "staggering" (Butler, "Revolution," 3). More important, the damage done to women, the cost that is not quantifiable, remains hidden. If health care continues to emphasize disease, health problems will be redistributed so that conditions that "bother and disable but do not kill" increasingly mark individual lives (Verbrugge, "Disability," 93). This prediction is ominous for women.

A society that spends relatively little for preventative care in effect creates illness for its older citizens, and the frailty and dependency that often accompany late-life illness appear to be natural rather than partly the result of health care policy. The current incidence of illness among old women and men, far from being inevitable, is more determined by culture than biology. Without this understanding, our expectations of late-life health will be too low.

But the situation is more complicated than misdirected priorities. The ideology of individualism that determines the priorities is hidden in directives to eat carefully, exercise, and so on. When the individual is the "basic unit of social analysis" then the focus is individual behavior rather than structural patterns such as the distribution of wealth and power, and health education is assumed to be the best way to prevent disease (Tesh, 161). The assumption that health is controlled by the individual runs counter to the "interdependence and collective responsibility valued by many ethnic minority elders" (B. Yee and Weaver, 43). Individualist philosophy shields corporations and government from responsibility for their major roles in creating illness (environmental pollution) and sustaining it (inadequate regulation of polluters and drug companies). The older we are, the greater the cumulative impact on us of corporate and governmental action or inaction.

Whatever our personal characteristics or individual choices, therefore, our late-life health may be determined or greatly influenced by forces beyond our control, even if class privilege benefits us. As geriatrician Christine Cassel has said, the social and economic challenges of aging are greater than "unlocking the biological mysteries" ("Ethics," 63). Now that we have the knowledge to maintain and in some cases improve the health of older women and men, we lack both the regard for elders that would lead to wise health care policy and a collective commitment to our own future well-being.

7

✣

Class, Ethnicity, Sexual Orientation, and Gender

Gender, class, and ethnicity strongly determine how well Americans age. Class may be the most important of these intersecting factors. While not the whole story of aging, economic determinism is often ignored because it does not fit the middle-class worldview of many gerontologists, advocacy groups such as AARP, or the mainstream media. The strong impact of class and ethnicity on American aging is powerfully illustrated by a World Health Organization (WHO) report on "healthy life expectancy," which measures life expectancy by factoring in diseases and disabilities. In the WHO ranking Japan comes first and the United States twenty-fourth.

Rich Americans are judged the world's healthiest people, but our overall ranking is lowered by the relatively poor health of people of color and poor Americans, and by cancer, heart disease, and violence. Life expectancy in the United States is lowered by lack of health insurance, racial disparities, high obesity rates, and relatively high rates of infant death before age one.

Nevertheless, many Americans mistakenly believe that their health care system is the best in the world.

This chapter considers class, ethnicity, sexual orientation, and gender in relation to aging and then examines caregiving and retirement as institutions that show their convergence especially well.[1]

CLASS

Ethnicity and class give gender specific meanings and at the same time, class and ethnicity acquire specific meanings through gender (Calasanti and Zajicek, 121–22).[2] While it is true, for example, that older women are far more likely to be poor than older men (a gender difference ignored when gerontologists say that Social Security and Medicare have reduced poverty among "the elderly"), older women of color are more likely to be poor than white women. The meanings of designated family caregiver for a female will depend on her class and ethnicity. Gender in itself is significant, however, for as Amanda Barusch notes in *Older Women in Poverty*, longevity increases women's risk of old-age poverty, a gender difference that cuts across all groups of women (xxxiii).[3]

At the same time, ethnicity and class are also strong predictors of late-life poverty (Barusch, xxxiii). In Europe, the poverty rate of old women living alone is negligible, but it is high in the United States: Germany, 2.4 percent; Sweden, 1.7 percent; France, 0.8 percent; the Netherlands, 0 percent; and the United States 17.6 percent (Barusch, xx). While approximately one-third of all older women in the United States are poor or near poor, this designation applies to 58 percent of black women and 47 percent of Latinas (Malveaux, "Race," 172). Of women living alone, nearly 20 percent are poor (Hartmann and English, 121).Those most likely to be poor are women of color over eighty-five who live alone (Davis, Grant, and Rowland, 81). Seventy-five percent of old people who live alone are women, and those who live alone are more than four times as likely to be poor than couples (Harrington Meyer and Herd, 4).

Widowhood increases an older woman's poverty risk (Barusch, xxxiii); half of the widows who are poor today were not poor before the death of their husbands (Davis, Grant, and Rowland, 82). Another estimate is three-fourths (Steckenrider, 239).

Poverty statistics do not reveal the extent of hardship. If they were calculated on the basis of income left over after medical expenses are deducted, the proportion of elderly poor would greatly increase (Davis, Grant, and Rowland, 85). Another factor not taken into account is the difference in the cost of living across the country. Workers retired from unskilled occupations experience a greater level of disability in old age than middle-class people, and they are more likely to smoke and to be obese. The most common cause of bankruptcy in the United States is medical bills, a sign that economic status and class status are intertwined. According to a University of Wisconsin report, although Americans are living longer, the gains disproportionately benefit better educated citizens (*New York Times*, April 12, 2012, A12).

The long-term consequences of class difference can be illustrated by simple examples. A middle-class professional woman in her twenties can afford to buy an IRA each year, but the woman her age who cleans her office cannot. Forty-five years later, the former may have accumulated several hundred thousand dollars, the latter nothing. To acquire this wealth, all the first woman has to do is to keep breathing (assuming her IRA is not gutted by a recession). Very likely, her husband has a secure job that, like hers, will provide a pension. Their child care expenses take a smaller percentage of their salary than of the office cleaner's wage. Moreover, the working-class woman's parents will probably need her caregiving help sooner than the parents of the middle-class woman. If the working-class woman and her husband manage to save enough for a down payment on a house, they may be denied a mortgage because of redlining, a form of discrimination that will never impede the upward mobility of the middle-class couple. In late life, home ownership is often the key to financial security, but when working-class people of color own a home, it may have declining value in an inner-city neighborhood (Malveaux, "Race," 188). Between 2007 and 2012, 1.5 million older Americans lost their homes through foreclosure, and millions more remain at risk (Trawinski).

Little attention has been paid to class in relation to aging even though structural systems of inequality are "reproduced and eventually reinforced" in old age (Lopes, 94–95). Class, ethnicity, and gender play a large role in determining not only access to education and jobs but "to the opportunities those jobs allow or the limitations they impose" (Atchley, *Social Forces*, 451). A major limitation lies in earnings: A black woman earns 65 cents for a dollar earned by a man and Latinas 57 cents (Hooyman and Gonyea, "Feminist Model," 155). The more familiar figure, 79 cents, masks racial/ethnic disadvantage and does not apply to women over fifty-five. They earn 66 cents for a dollar earned by a man, and the gap widens as they age (Older Women's League, 300).

White women frequently fare better than blacks or Latinas/os, male or female, and white families are better off than minority families, in part because they are more likely to have pension income (Dressel, 116–17). Elderly minority women should be differentiated from the men in their communities, however, as well as from older white women (Ketayun Gould, 212).

The economic status of older women is a "map or mirror of their past lives" (Malveaux, "Race," 168). Unemployment levels for black women, for example, tend to be twice those of whites or Latinas (Malveaux, "Gender," 230). While numerous women work in sex-segregated jobs, many black women work in jobs segregated by race as well; they are chambermaids, cleaners, nurses' aides, and welfare service aides (231). Many black women who work in private homes do not have Social Security benefits. Besides the labor market disadvantage of sex and race, a black woman shares in the disadvantage of her spouse or family members, giving her a triple burden (233). Moreover, when black men are unfairly treated by the criminal justice system, their retirement is jeopardized and the future financial well-being of the women in their families is undermined as well (235).

Gerontologists allude to the "cumulative disadvantage" of older Americans whose lives have been characterized by physically demanding jobs or unemployment, poor housing, inadequate health care, and low levels of education. Because of cumulative disadvantage across the life course, certain groups are particularly disadvantaged—blacks, Hispanics, and the unmarried (Harrington Meyer and Herd, 22). Gerontologists rarely examine the other side of the coin, middle-class cumulative *advantage*. The gains in longevity in the past two decades for example almost all went to people whose incomes were above average (Ghilarducci, 5). A good education, white-collar jobs that do not cause bodily harm, health insurance, sufficient money for a healthy diet, and control over many life circumstances do not guarantee good health in old age, but they make it likely rather than exceptional, unless a person's genes or bad luck interfere. Middle-class privilege operates in less obvious ways, too. When I speak to a doctor or a banker from this class position, I am taken seriously. In an emergency, I probably have a friend or a relative with enough disposable income to help me out. I carry an invisible sense of entitlement that may be reflected in my gait and demeanor as well as in confident speech. Being middle class gives me the privilege of being oblivious to class. I can believe that my favorable circumstances result from my own individual effort.[4]

ETHNICITY

Within the elderly population, the percentage who belong to minority groups will grow at an even faster rate than the white majority (Dilworth-Anderson and Cohen, 487). Current trends that work against all of the elderly are especially onerous for minority elders—the increase in out-of-pocket medical expenses, for example, and Medicare cuts in home health care. "The Economic Crisis Facing Seniors of Color" reports that while all Americans have suffered from the recession, its effects have been "truly devastating" for African Americans, Latinos, and Asian Americans hoping to retire. The foreclosure crisis has disproportionately affected black and Latino families, draining over $213 billion in wealth from their communities. The report also notes that the federal poverty line fails to consider factors such as the high cost of health care, housing, and transportation for elders on fixed incomes (Kleyman).

The development of ethnogerontology, the study of ethnicity and aging, may encourage advocacy through organizations such as the National Asian Pacific Center on Aging, the National Caucus and Center on Black Aged, the National Hispanic Council on Aging, and the National Indian Council on Aging, but no single national organization advocates for all minority elders. An improved model of healthy aging would begin with a definition that goes beyond absence of disease and infirmity to include factors that affect health, such as educational opportunity, good housing, and safe neighborhoods. The health of poor people and people of color is undermined by the *new morbidity*—that is, threats to health from domestic violence, drug abuse, crime, and the "pervasive sense of inferiority that is the result of discrimination" (Angel and Angel, 1156).

Ethnicity and class come into sharp relief in studies of life expectancy: Many people of color do not live long enough to collect their Social Security benefits. Christopher Murray of the University of Washington School of Public Health has found that black men in Washington, DC, live an average of fifty-eight years and Indian males in South Dakota, sixty-one years. Raising the retirement age to seventy would mean that even fewer black men and Indian men than today would live long enough to gain Social Security benefits.

Much work on minority aging focuses on families. Gerontologists have suggested, for example, that closely knit communities may not survive for future generations of Pacific Asian elders because of the increasing social and geographic mobility of younger community members (Kiyak and Hooyman, 309). Elderly Pacific Asians feel conflict between traditional communal family values and the American emphasis on self-reliance, "making them loath to ask others for support" (309). Is the role of honored elder declining in some communities? Vietnamese elders are now being placed in nursing homes in America, a practice not condoned in the past (Haber, *Health*, 429). Elderly blacks are known to adopt "fictive kin" by turning friends into family. The aging experiences of urban Indians differ from their counterparts on reservations. Although great diversity exists within families considered "minority," they have more in common with each other than with middle-class families, particularly their shared experience of racism (B. Yee, 75).[5]

Recently ethnogerontologists have begun to look beyond families. A life course perspective emphasizing aging as a process should encourage future researchers to view Chicano or Latino elderly in relation to their earlier lives (Wallace and Facio, 345), not simply in relation to whites. Big economic gaps exist within groups; Japanese Americans are better off than Korean Americans or Vietnamese, for example. Moreover, "gender and class dominance transcends the family and continues into old age" (348). Qualitative research may be better suited to discovering subtleties of ethnicity than survey research (C. Johnson, 308), for ethnicity is both subjective and flexible (Linda Cool, "Effects of Social Class," 265). When Chicano aging is studied through the family, women appear only as wives, mothers, and grandmothers (Facio, 339). Many older Chicanas would like to be seen not only as grandmothers but also as cultural teachers (342).

Another theme in ethnogerontology is that too heavy an emphasis on social inequality overlooks people's strengths. Gerontologists need to know not only how Chicanos are disadvantaged, for example, but also how they fashion meaningful lives (Wallace and Facio, 347). If quality of life is examined through many lenses, strengths inhering in social networks and spirituality will be seen (Kiyak and Hooyman, 311). In the face of "social and political imprisonment," blacks have shown a powerful will to survive, and their elders deserve to be understood through their own history without being compared to others whose circumstances are far more favorable (Stanford, "Diverse," 117). Ethnicity provides "continuing self-identification and communal belonging at a time when the older person begins to experience the diminution of his or her conventional identities formed on age, sex, or occupation" (Linda Cool, "Ethnicity," 267). Further ethnographical research should show that diversity education improves the behavior and skills of trainees in gerontology and geriatric care (Yeo and McBride, 106).

Problems with studies comparing people of color with whites were noted in chapter 6. Whites become the norm, gender disappears, and an implicit judgment is that people of color need to "catch up" to whites. The few studies that have looked at differences within groups are seen as interesting only to minority researchers (Stanford and Yee, 17). Comparative work assumes that gender, ethnicity, and age are "fixed, immutable, biologically based individual properties with predictable (if as yet undetermined) behavioral and social consequences" (Dressel, Minkler, and Yen, 276–77). Studies of adjustment to old age based on whites have not considered the meanings of this concept for blacks, Latinos, Asian Pacific Americans, or Indians. For them, aging may more likely signify a process of survival, and the struggle to survive "in fact may mean that an individual has developed strategies to keep from adjusting" (Burton, Dilworth-Anderson, and Bengtson, 132).

Will the growth of ethnogerontology encourage white, middle-class gerontologists to rethink the meanings of "minority"? This question became less theoretical with the release of census figures showing that "minorities" are now the majority in 48 of the nation's 100 largest cities.

By the year 2030, 25 percent of those over sixty-five will be people of color (Angel, 503). Could Asian Pacific women, Indians, Latinas, and black women be imagined as central actors in aging America, not as "special"? To themselves, after all, they are not special, only to the dominant group.

The usual rationale for studying Latino, black, Asian Pacific, and Indian elders is to serve them better, but this could happen without changing their marginal status. Mainstream gerontology could absorb ethnogerontology without being transformed itself. Or new thinking about diversity could become "an energizing force for understanding aged people and aging in this country" (Stanford and Yee, 20), not only the aging of particular groups. For a conservative field like gerontology, however, adopting multicultural perspectives may be a slow process.

The discipline would be enlivened by the application of theoretical writing by women of color to aging. Aida Hurtado explores the meanings of multiple identities, for example, through "shifting consciousness," the ability of many women of color to move from "one perception of social reality to another, and, at times, to be able simultaneously to perceive multiple social realities without losing their sense of self-coherence" (384). Shifting consciousness would be valuable for old women who can see with ironic detachment the ways others project "old" onto them, without internalizing ageist attitudes. Surviving the dominant culture's influence requires, in the words of Paula Gunn Allen, "an uncompromising commitment to multiplicity" (*Off the Reservation*, 78). The theory arising from an understanding of multiplicity may not conform to Western notions of logic and abstraction for, as Barbara Christian writes, "our theorizing (and I intentionally use the verb rather than the noun) is often in narrative forms, in the stories we create, in riddles and proverbs, in the play with language, since dynamic rather than fixed ideas seem more to our liking. How else have we managed to survive with such spiritedness the assault on our bodies, social institutions, countries, our very humanity?" (336). Rarely in professional settings are gerontologists encouraged to think of women of color in these terms or to reflect upon the meanings of whiteness for individuals or for the organization and perpetuation of gerontology itself.

The late Gloria Anzaldúa formulated "marginal" theories, partly outside and partly inside Western frameworks, seeking out the "in-between, Borderland worlds" (xxvi). This stance responds to colonization and social invisibility but is far more than defensive, for it makes space for subjectivity and declares intellectual freedom from an either/or, dominant/subordinate paradigm. What are the "in-between worlds" within aging? Maria Lugones observes that the Anglo world may construct her, a Latina, in ways she does not understand or would not accept, "and yet

I may be *animating* such a construction, even though I may not intend my moves, gestures, acts in that way" (631). Something similar must occur when people who have many identities are perceived only as old.

SEXUAL ORIENTATION

Like women of color, lesbians are "special" and unlikely to be seen as norms for aging. Nearly all published work on women's aging assumes heterosexuality; a few studies mention lesbians. Media images of lesbians exclude those who are old. Paradoxically, old women in general are seen stereotypically as asexual, while old lesbians, when they are noticed at all, are perceived only through their sexuality (Fullmer, Shenk, and Eastland, 137). They differ in ethnicity, class, education, income, and degree of identification with the gay and lesbian community. Because of slowly growing acceptance of lesbian and gay identity, future cohorts of old lesbians will include many more who have been out of the closet for most of their lives. Lesbians who were once married often have supportive children and grandchildren, although others have been rejected by their families. Some have speculated that the resilience needed to cope with a stigmatized identity helps older lesbians adapt to aging, but it may also be true that the special stresses of their lives, especially if they have been fired from jobs, lost custody of children, or been otherwise harmed, have long-lasting consequences. Work on lesbian aging arises from a political motivation—to increase visibility and to debunk myths, and also from "the natural curiosity of gerontologists in studying an undocumented minority" (Gabbay and Wahler, 14).

Lesbians have the same concerns as heterosexual women as well as particular concerns—a desire to live in a retirement setting where they can be open about their lives, for example, fear that a partner's role might not be acknowledged by medical workers, and fear of confinement in a nursing home where being gay is not acceptable. Bereavement leave is a benefit heterosexual women can take for granted and most lesbians cannot. Pension plan benefits and Social Security benefits are unjustly denied survivors of lesbian partnerships. Some advantages enjoyed by many old lesbians are a life history of self-reliance and high status within lesbian communities. Having been free to de-emphasize or entirely disregard conventional notions of female attractiveness, many seem to accept their aging bodies with equanimity. Those who were tomboys when young tend to retain their physical competence.[6]

Lesbians now in their seventies and older differ significantly from a younger cohort because being known as gay or lesbian was far riskier than it is today and sometimes led to loss of jobs and housing, loss of child custody, banishment from churches, and verbal and physical attacks. While these injustices and prejudices still exist, lesbians now in their sixties and younger are likely to have developed self-esteem and a sense of group solidarity through the women's movement and gay liberation, and those who choose to be open experience affirmation. Whatever their level of political awareness or identification with political movements, older lesbians form a variety of friendship groups and mutual aid networks, and informal care for disabled or old lesbians is common both in rural areas and in cities (J. Barker, 65–66).

Studies of aging sexual minorities have recently become more numerous and detailed. Although they are illuminating, little research is based on large samples and thus far there are no longitudinal studies of older gay men, bisexuals, and transgendered persons. Full-scale ethnographic studies of the lives of older lesbians do not yet exist (J. Barker, 38). An estimated 40 percent of lesbians have been married, and 25–33 percent of them have children (45). We need to know more about the coming out process after age sixty-five, for example, about the particular issues facing LGBT people of color, and about the hardships caused by gay elders who do not receive Social Security survivor benefits. How will external and internalized homophobia impact our aging process?[7]

A survey of 1,300 LGBT elders in San Francisco conducted by Open House found that gay elders have no more money than their heterosexual counterparts; have more disability and higher rates of chronic illness; and are more likely to be single, childless, and live alone. Sixty-five percent have a B.A. degree.

According to the Administration on Aging, HIV infection rates are increasing among young black gay men. Men who stayed negative for a long time are now getting infected at age fifty or older. Women make up 13 percent of people with HIV/AIDS in the sixty to sixty-nine age group. Caregivers of partners with AIDS fear negative reaction to their sexuality, loss of contact with lesbian and gay friends, and loss of control of their personal circumstances (Elizabeth Price, 517). Caregivers use various strategies to maintain their relationships after onset of illness or disability. One lesbian, for example, changed her name so that she and her partner could pass as sisters (519).

Aging organizations overlook HIV/AIDS, and AIDS groups are geared toward younger people. Since AIDS may mimic diseases associated with late life such as arthritis, memory loss, wasting, and pneumonia, older people may get diagnosed later. Those most at risk often get the least help. With the first generation of AIDS survivors, the effects on aging of long-term heavy use of prescription drugs is unknown. Survivor fatigue, depression, and ageism within the gay community are other issues (Hollibaugh, Campbell, and Olivera).

In 2010, the Administration on Aging, of the Health and Human Services department, awarded SAGE (Services and Advocacy for Gay, Lesbian, Bisexual and Transgender Elders), a three-year, $900,000 grant to create a national resource center on LGBT Aging. SAGE opened a full-service senior center in New York City in 2012. Other groups working on gay aging issues include Open House in San Francisco and the National Association of HIV over Fifty. Open House and a non-profit developer plan housing units for all income levels in San Francisco. Old Lesbians Organizing for Change (OLOC) has raised consciousness about ageism within the lesbian feminist community. The first nursing home for gay people opened in Berlin in 2008.

Elders who transition to the other sex late in life face particular challenges. Age-related health concerns may make surgery riskier than for younger people, for example, and their social roles are more entrenched. Speech patterns and mannerisms may thus be harder to change. Transitioning elders face dating difficulties and critical legal issues, protecting benefits from Social Security and the Veterans Administration, for example. Work issues are also more complicated for those who transition before full retirement. They often lose their jobs and if they have hidden their trans histories cannot reveal their past employment history without revealing their previous name and identity (Cook-Daniel, 4–5). The 2005 Maine gay rights law is one of the few state laws that covers gender-based discrimination, a protection for transsexuals.

Research on older lesbians, gay men, bisexuals, and transgendered people raises some of the same issues as research on people of color: Will the concerns of the group be distorted as they are filtered through the lens of the dominant group? Are the interests of the group served by this research? How will it be used? Research on gay aging will benefit heterosexuals as well, shedding light for example on friends as caregivers, a common pattern in the gay community, where friends often become family.

In the past three decades, the multidisciplinary field lesbian/gay/bisexual/transgender aging has "moved from the hidden recesses of secret support groups into the full range of activities and services," and now gay gerontologists must ensure that LGBT elders representing "the full spectrum of diversity" are included in research and receive all services they are entitled to (Kimmel et al., 10). A plausible prediction for the future is that an increasing number of people will enter late life with same-sex partners and an increasing number of people will choose same-sex relationships after divorce or widowhood (Arber, 57).

GENDER

The best examples of gender gaps in aging are caregiving and retirement. Class and ethnicity interweave with gender in the examples that follow.

Caregiving

Currently, 80 to 85 percent of eldercare in the United States is provided free, by family members and friends (Eaton, 38). Caregiving covers everything from occasional help for a relative who lives on his or her own to twenty-four-hour total care for a person in the same home. Although some men provide care, 70–80 percent of home care for elders is provided by women (some estimates say 90–95 percent). Daughters-in-law are more likely to be caregivers than sons and sisters more likely than brothers. Thus the commonly used term "family care" is a euphemism for women's work.

The productivity of older women is largely invisible, yet the value of their elder care is an estimated $400 billion annually (Holstein, "Ethics and Aging," 257). Moreover, since the recession began, 47 percent of workers who are also caregivers used up all or most of their savings for care.[8] Caring for older family members is low status, "emotionally binding work" (Hooyman, "Women," 229). Ninety-five percent of paid caregivers are women (McLeod and Roszak, 12). They number more than 500,000, mostly poor, predominantly black women or recent immigrants who receive the minimum wage and no benefits (Holstein, "What," 3). These women have been compared to garment workers and sweatshop workers (McGeehan, C13).

Several trends have significantly altered the caregiving landscape, including longer lives, smaller families, delayed childbirth, higher divorce rates, and growing numbers of blended families. Today many families have two or more generations over sixty-five, and thus a woman in her sixties or seventies may be caring for an aged parent. In the past four decades, the proportion of fifty-year-old women with living mothers has risen dramatically, from 37 percent to 70 percent (Margolies, 138). The biggest difference between caring today and in earlier times, however, is the large increase in the number of women in the labor force. But business and government still operate as if "an unpaid army of caregivers" were available at home (Toner, 29).

The added duties of caregiving are obscured by their seemingly commonplace nature (Holstein, "Home," 236). The assumption that women are naturally suited to caregiving rests on a belief in separate spheres for women and men that blocks women's access to economic benefits and "thereby perpetuates their powerlessness" (Hooyman, "Women," 221–22). This issue is complicated for feminists because many have attributed a special caring capacity to women and have seen women's customary caregiving role in a positive light. The emotional and psychological benefits possible in the role can be acknowledged at the same time that substantial and sometimes hidden costs to care providers are identified.

Not only is the hard work of caregiving unpaid labor; performing it actually penalizes women because it often takes them from the workforce entirely or forces them to cut back on their hours or turn down promotions. Not all caregiving is performed by women who also work outside the home, but those who do often find that home duties negatively affect job performance and evaluation. In a study by the Coalition of Labor Union Women and the National Policy and Resource Center on Women and Aging, among women who lost time at work, 31 percent used sick leave to cover caregiving duties, and 69 percent took unpaid leave (Alcon and Bernstein, 47). Another study found that Latina and Asian American caregivers were more likely than whites to have taken a leave of absence from work to provide home care (*Family Caregiving*, 33).

A less immediate but potentially catastrophic problem is that caregivers who work outside the home suffer long-term economic losses by having lower incomes, smaller pensions, and lower Social Security benefits than they would otherwise have had. The loss is even greater if money not contributed to accounts that use pre-tax wages to accumulate retirement funds is considered. According to a June 2011 MetLife study, lost wages, pensions, and Social Security of elder care providers is nearly $3 trillion a year. The loss for an individual female caregiver is $324,044.

Thus women caregivers who are coerced into self-reliance not only sacrifice their time and energy (often willingly) but their future financial security as well. This huge sacrifice is taken for granted. Its magnitude is analyzed neither by feminists nor by gerontologists. This particular exploitation of women is not as dramatic as unequal pay or domestic violence, but it contributes to their subjugation. An interesting gender difference was found in a Swedish study of people over 85: When talking of their past experiences, men recalled being strong and active, while women remembered the burden of domestic work and family caregiving. The researchers described these traditional female roles as "hidden subordination" (Alex and Lundman, 311).

From another angle, care of aging relatives cost U.S. businesses for absenteeism, workday interruptions, and supervisory time. A 2010 MetLife report estimated that U.S. companies lose $33.6 billion a year in lost productivity from workers who care for an elderly relative. They tend to have more illness than other workers, and they are costly to replace when they leave they jobs to work at home.

Men have the advantage of doing one job, while many women do two, one paid and the other unpaid. As long as women's position in the labor market is subordinate to men's, "strong economic pressures reinforce the traditional assignment of unpaid caregiving work to women" (J. Allen, 223).

Women of color and working-class women suffer disproportionately because they are clustered in low-paying jobs that are not waiting for them after a caregiving period, jobs that offer fewer benefits than middle-class women receive. Poor women do not have husbands with professional jobs whose income can ease the financial strain of caregiving. Assuming that an elderly Chicana will automatically take on a caregiving role reinforces her subordinate status and assumes that family is the only significant part of her life (Facio, 338). According to the National Alliance for Caregiving, Asian American and Latina caregivers were significantly younger than whites and were more likely to have out-of-pocket expenses for caregiving (*Family Caregiving*, 8; 24). Sixty percent of them, for example, report spending between $100 and $1,000 each month on their parents' basic expenses (Hounsell and Riojas, 9). Women's financial sacrifice to provide care is a major cause of their late-life vulnerability to poverty (J. Allen, 224).

A theme of *Age through Ethnic Lenses: Caring for the Elderly in a Multicultural Society*, edited by Laura Katz Olson, is that the traditional value of great respect for elders, leading to caregiving within families, is in flux. It is affected by differences between native-born and immigrant elderly, social mobility of younger family members, language differences, out-migration from rural areas, intermarriage, and generational differences heightened by assimilation. The cultural emphasis on filial duty does not eliminate the need for public programs and services. Many elderly immigrants share the experience of Polish immigrants: Old women and men have a place of honor in the family, but they may not have family members here in the United States who can help them. Moreover, they are shut out of the formal care system because they do not know about it, they wish to conceal their undocumented status, or because the services "represent a shameful failure of the family system of care" (Berdes and Erdmans, 184).

Compared to white, middle-class women, poor women and women of color have more chronic illness and disability. Even though they are the old who most need care, they are the least likely to have access to services (Hooyman and Gonyea, "Feminist Model," 153). A review of studies since the mid-1980s on race and ethnicity as influencing care for a person with dementia showed that blacks and Latinas/os as compared to whites reported less depression and stress; had less sense of care being burdensome; and were more likely to cope through faith or prayer (Connell and

Gibson, 355). Future studies of differences within the black community and among Latinas/os will give a more nuanced view of caregiving experiences and attitudes. An issue for some Asian Americans is that dementia tends to take away a second language, and often the only available adult day care is for English speakers (Goodman, 111).

Caregiving studies have documented a wide range of physical and psychological illnesses experienced by care providers. Like other women they tend to have less autonomy and control at work compared to men, and when this stress is added to the stress they experience from their heavier responsibility for domestic work and caregiving, illness may result (Harrington Meyer and Herd, 101). Despite these problems women are motivated by emotional bonds, a need to help others, reluctance to turn to community resources or institutions, and the unavailability of other family members. Women provide care because their family role leads them to see few alternatives (Rizza, 68). In interviews, caregivers express satisfaction in closer relationships with parents as well as a rewarding sense of discovering new strengths and abilities (70). The experience of working at a paid job while caregiving is "not as uniformly negative as it is sometimes portrayed"; work provides a welcome break from "all-encompassing" home responsibilities, for example (Scharlach, "Caregiving,"383). A study of caregiving among Plains Indian families found low levels of burden and high levels of reward. Reasons include a sense of reward from helping an elder, physical closeness of families, shared caregiving tasks, and, a crucial factor, reciprocity: Elders are seen as continuing to give to others, not merely taking (Jervis, Boland, and Fickenscher).

When noting that family care of the elderly is unpaid, it is important to remember that caregivers do emotional work as well as chores and tasks. If forced to leave a paid job to provide home care, women feel cut off from opportunities and even from their aspirations (Healy). When external resources such as respite care and affordable home health care are limited, and the elderly parent suffers as a result, the caregiver may blame herself and not the current caregiving system. Her sense of inadequacy and the parent's experience of insufficient care may cause family conflicts that seem private but also reflect large social problems (Healy).

Caregiving opens up other emotional issues as well: It tends to be lonely work; a caregiver may lose a sense of control over her life (Abel, "Family Care," 75); and caring for a dependent parent may trigger unresolved resentments (76). A major difficulty for caregivers is the "chasm between their overriding sense of responsibility and their ultimate powerlessness" (Abel, *Who Cares*, 76). They also find it hard to exert authority over a parent (105). Focus on the care recipient may entail less time and attention for other family members. One study reported that mother-daughter conflict was heightened by the increased dependence of the mother. Both mothers and daughters felt a tension between the daughter's social needs and her filial responsibilities (Brandler, 50; 53). A study of urban white women caring for a chronically ill older parent found that feelings of resentment, anger, and frustration were "so threatening that they were not dealt with directly, except in the most secure families. Seemingly small issues became the targets permitting expressions of feeling" (Archbold, 43).

Psychological explanations of caregiving are limited because women are not "uniformly nurturing and expressive." In addition, psychological explanations take the nuclear family as the ideal and overlook a structural problem: The current system overvalues masculine traits in the public arena and undervalues feminine values expressed in the home, and thus caregiving is seen as a personal issue (Hooyman and Gonyea, *Feminist Perspectives*, 22–24). In this framework, caregiver stress is emphasized rather than the social reorganization that would make caregiving more equitable and humane (Abel, *Who Cares*, 66). A study of paid caregivers in New Zealand notes that caregiving is regarded as inherently female work and that male workers were more reluctant to address intimate issues. The workers felt that they were less likely than family members to become ill from stress (Kirkman).

Chapter 2 linked the socially constructed fear of an aging population to conservatives' goal of shrinking federal government. Increased emotional burdens on women have resulted from the "increasing devolution of responsibility from the federal to local levels along with cutbacks in federal funding and the privatization of care," and as public agencies that have traditionally served poor women have cut services, the reduction in public support has intensified gender and racial inequalities (Hooyman and Gonyea, "Feminist Model," 164). Caregivers' right to public support has not been recognized (Hooyman and Gonyea, "Feminist Model," 162; Quinn-Musgrove, 106).

Another issue is the neglect of old women and men without family members to provide care. In the future, many more elders will have no children to care for them (Abel, *Who Cares*, 177), a problem in Europe and Asia as well as in North America (Kreager and Schroeder-Butterfill). A feminist analysis of caregiving potentially benefits men as well as women because it "bridges home and work and ensures choice for both sexes" (Hooyman et al., 11). A situation that has yet to be analyzed in gerontology occurs when one person in a couple needs assisted living but the other one does not. What are the risks for the wife or husband (or unmarried spouse) when the pace of life in assisted living is not suitable for them?

A problem at the heart of caregiving is the dichotomy between dependency and autonomy, noted in earlier chapters, an example of either-or thinking that undermines the self-respect of old Americans. How can dependency be disassociated from failure? How can overrated (and partly illusory) autonomy be seen as a relative rather than absolute value? Instead of apologizing for no longer being totally self-sufficient, could an old woman say to her daughter or son, "I need help and you have an opportunity to provide it." This sounds ludicrous but only because we are conditioned to believe autonomy means self-reliant separation from others. In the case of driving, an older woman who must give it up might say to herself, "I am *worthy of being driven* at this stage of my life."[9] The American Occupational Therapy Association maintains an Older Driver Web site at www.aota.org/olderdriver.

Wanting to be self-reliant and not wanting to be a burden, older women will "often ask for less help than they need, even at their own peril" (Holstein, "What," 3). The overused phrase "the burden of care" deflects attention from the ways in which caregiving can be mutually beneficial or positive, as well as a source of difficulties. The general term "burden" does not identify particular problems or distinguish between economic and psychological hardships. If I feel I *am* a burden, that differs from feeling that my situation creates challenges for my caregiver. The unreflective use of "the caregiving burden" objectifies older people and fuels alarmism over the growing size of the elder population (Arber and Ginn, *Gender*, 130). Furthermore, emphasis on *burden* "devalues the act of caring—caring about as well as caring for" (Wenger, 374). When caregiving is defined as a burden, its "structural and cultural roots" become invisible (Holstein, "Home Care," 235). Caregiving is understood not so much as a duty or a burden among many Chinese, Filipinos, and Vietnamese who have settled in the United States. A common saying among them is "When I was young and helpless, my parents cared for me. Now that my parents are old, it is my turn to help them."

The term "eldercare" reinforces the stereotype that old women and men are inherently dependent, like children. It also fails to acknowledge the presence of reciprocity in intergenerational relationships (Matthews and Campbell, 131). Similarly, the sharp split between caregiver/care recipient overlooks the effort the receiver may expend in taking care of herself (Ray, "Postmodern," 677). In a study in British Columbia, 94 percent of caregivers interviewed said they found rewards in their work, growing closer to the care receiver, for example (Chappell, McDonald, and Stones, 320).

Proposed reforms to the present system include reimbursement for family caregivers, Social Security credit for years spent caregiving, greater involvement of men, and a more family-sensitive workplace. Pay equity should be seen as a caregiving issue because wage inequality reinforces the tendency for women to be the ones to leave paid work in order to provide care at home (Foster and Brizius, 70). Other proposals are the creation of caregiving accounts for every adult through Social Security, used to pay for services (68–69), and a Caregiving Corps modeled on the Peace Corps (McLeod and Roszak, 10). Imaginative planners envision "carebots" that roam around the house making sure that a person with dementia has not wandered away or that an elder has not fallen (Emerman, 12).

While significant, these changes would not get at the underlying problem that the United States, alone among industrialized nations, relies on an ethic of individualism to abdicate its responsibility for the care of elderly citizens. As long as caregiving is seen as a private duty rather than a "public value," the economic disadvantage suffered by women who do the work will limit their participation in society (Hooyman, "Women," 234–37). Caregiving is both a "profound personal experience and an oppressive social institution" (Hooyman and Gonyea, *Feminist Perspectives*, 24). Whether women give care or receive it, whether they are unpaid in the home or underpaid outside the home, gender prescribes their role.[10]

RETIREMENT

In the institution of retirement, male privilege, class privilege, and white privilege grandly converge, filling the stage of late life with operatic fullness. In comparison to other countries, the United States shows the greatest inequality among elderly persons (O'Rand and Henretta, 2). Conditioned to seeing retirement only in personal terms, many Americans miss the big picture of socioeconomic advantage and disadvantage. Media images of affluent elders at play deflect attention from the many whose lives do not fit this picture. In addition, elders pay a greater proportion of their income on property taxes, and more than others on medical expenses, despite Medicare (A. L. Campbell, 43).

Women's worker benefits are about three-fourths those of men (Harrington Meyer and Herd, 73). Their retirement income is lower than men's because of their lower pay, interrupted work histories, and workplace gender segregation. Greater responsibility for care work also lowers their retirement income (6). Other factors that increase women's poverty risk relative to men's are their greater likelihood of being retired a long time, of losing a spouse, and of having a chronic illness (C. Price, 9). Pensions are inadequate or reduced by discrimination (Barusch, 186). Fifty-five percent of men over sixty-five have pensions but only 32 percent of women, and women's pensions average one-half as much as men's (Tyson, 8). Working-class women and women of color fare worse than white women because their wages and the wages of their spouses and families are lower and because the good educations that lead to good jobs are frequently denied them.

Men spend an average of 1.3 years out of the labor force compared to 11.5 years for women (Davis, Grant, and Rowland, 82) or 14.7 years by the calculation of the Older Women's League (300). This gender difference is extremely significant: If a woman has fewer than thirty-five years of earnings, a zero is averaged into her Social Security calculation for each of those years, in effect reducing her benefits (Williamson and Rix, 47). Defining an older woman's caregiving years as "zero years" is blatant gender discrimination. Women are penalized for doing the work society expects of them. Social Security benefit losses for caregiving are greatest for workers with low and moderate earnings (O'Rand and Henretta, 93).

Low wage workers earning less than $15,000 a year are nearly all women, and since women spend more years in retirement than men, inflation takes a higher toll on their income than it does on men (Hartmann and English, 117; 126).

The system still operates with the outmoded assumption that retirees are male wage earners and stay-at-home spouses, and provides more benefits for them than for two-earner couples. Even worse, when the husband in a one-earner couple dies, his widow receives 67 percent of their total Social Security benefit, compared to 50 percent for the survivor of a two-earner couple. Thus Social Security clearly favors traditional marriages (O'Rand and Henretta, 95). Often a woman who has worked for many years is entitled to higher Social Security benefits as the wife of a retired worker than as a retired worker herself; her benefits are no greater than if she had never worked. Moreover, the payroll taxes she contributed to the system decreased her disposable income (Dailey, 94). Social Security bias toward married women is particularly harmful today, when marriage rates are decreasing and rates of single parenthood increasing (Harrington Meyer and Herd, 15).

Social Security accomplishes some income redistribution that benefits lower-income workers but in its present form, it "overdelivers retirement income to economically advantaged workers and underdelivers retirement income to low-income workers" (Atchley, *Social Forces*, 464). Two mechanisms that disadvantage the latter are the exemption of wage income over $110,000 from Social Security taxes and the exemption of income from interest and dividends (Bergman and Bush, 42). Eliminating these generous and unmentioned gifts to the affluent would be fairer and fiscally sounder than "privatization," the stealth attack on Social Security in the guise of reform.

President Clinton proposed voluntary private plans in *addition* to Social Security, but the later proposal to "privatize" some payroll tax deductions would create risk in a secure system. Who would shoulder the greatest risk? Those whose retirement income depends most heavily on Social Security, women, people of color, and the working class. In addition, any of the changes needed to pay for "privatization" would disproportionately harm them: increased payroll taxes, decreased benefits, an increase in the eligibility age, or an increase from thirty-five to thirty-eight as the number of years used to calculate benefits. Privatization's welfare for Wall Street would be very costly for many Americans. The ghost of FDR still haunts conservatives. Privatization, the biggest proposed change in Social Security since its inception, would be their exorcism ritual.

Only recently has women's retirement been examined through the prism of their own life experiences.[11] "The particular mix of paid and unpaid work shifts constantly throughout our lifetime, and continues to do so whether we are officially retired or not" (Onyx and Benton, 100). Little is known about the impact of retirement on women's identities (C. Price, 10). A sense of identity for some seems to be maintained by expanding their roles after retirement (154). Thus researchers should not assume that home life is the focus of retired women's lives (156). According to Barbara Cabral, the nearly exclusive pre-retirement focus on financial planning "overshadows the need to prepare for the complex psychological, spiritual, social and sometimes physical aspects of retirement after decades of constant employment."[12]

Retirement is not a meaningful concept for the many Americans who have to keep on working, mainly people of color and low-income workers. Blacks do not fit the norms by which retirement has traditionally been marked: age sixty-five, sharp distinction between work and non-work, income from sources besides Social Security, and self-identification as retired (R. Gibson, 120). For black women and men alike, work is lifelong and discontinuous; they are the "unretired retired" (125; 122). Because white men earn more than black men, black women who receive spousal benefits receive less than white women (Harrington Meyer and Herd, 77).

The conventional view of retirement does not fit middle-class white women very well either. Retirement is a dubious proposition for those who began careers in mid-life and do not wish to end them at sixty-five. Moreover, women do not retire from housework. Increasingly, women over sixty-five are working for pay, but it is not clear that they want to. "Women have multiple needs and priorities—not just for wages but for time spent on family, friends, community, and on themselves" (Johns, 42–43). An Australian study of professional women makes a similar point: Retirement means not just a switch from active involvement in a job to leisure, but readjustments, "a finer balance of time and energy to allow a more creative and satisfying engagement with the many sides of life and self" (Onyx and Benton, 107). In the future, then, retirement will not be as sharply differentiated from work as it is now, and it will require multiple measures (Hatch, 136). It will be an unfolding process, seen as a phased transition involving "fluctuations in and out of work" (Hooyman et al., 16).

"Bridge jobs"—part-time, temporary paid work that spans work and retirement and offers the advantage of flexibility and income—disguise the compulsory nature of retirement under our economic system. Since full employment is impossible, some people must be kept out of the work force. Retirement is not simply leisure, the early bird special, and senior discounts on Tuesday; it is a mechanism for income reduction. The mechanism is ageist but more importantly, to the extent that women, people of color, and the working class reach retirement with already lowered incomes, it reinforces discrimination.

Formerly understood only as role loss, widowhood now prompts researchers to consider complexities and variations, cultural diversity as well as "the intersection of wealth, health, and class" (Martin-Matthews, 339). More than 17 percent of non-married elderly women are poor (Anzick and Weaver, 1). Nearly four times as many widows live in poverty as do wives of the same age, according to the Older Women's League (301). Many women have limited savings and only 18 percent have pensions (299). Social Security, pensions, and savings or investments are considered the "three stools" of retirement, but because of the high poverty risk for unmarried women over sixty, husbands have been called the fourth stool for [heterosexual] women (Johns, 15). "Explicitly or implicitly, many women have staked their economic futures on their marriages" rather than on their own work history (Hartmann and English, 121). Pensions and Social Security are based on "a misperception that marriage is permanent" (Harrington Meyer, "Family Status," 472). The divorce rate of older women and men has been increasing four times as fast as the overall growth of the elder population (Moody and Sasser, 301). For women, this trend brings an increased poverty risk (Hatch, 135). In particular, the marriage rate for older black women declined significantly from 1990 to 2000, so that linking Social Security benefits to marital status particularly disadvantages them (Harrington Meyer, "Declining"). Another danger sign is that the eligibility age for Social Security will increase to sixty-seven, and women who take retirement at sixty-two will get 75 percent of their total benefit compared to 80 percent today. Many black households will continue to be headed by women, some of whom will work "off the books" where they will not accumulate benefits (Malveaux, "Race," 177).

Women who do have pensions may have the defined contribution kind, in which the value depends on fluctuating markets, rather than the traditional defined-benefits pension, which guarantees a fixed payment. The essence of this pension shift is that risks inherent in retirement savings are transferred from employers to workers, and from groups to individuals (Harrington Meyer and Herd, 85). This trend contributes to growing inequality among older women (90).

In short, the present system is inadequate for many, for women caregivers, for workers in low-paying jobs with few benefits, "and for increasing numbers of workers, male as well as female, in a 'new economy' characterized by more frequent job changes and less paternalism on the part of employers" (Johns, 36). Uncertainties and risk will mark the retirement of baby boom women, fewer than 20 percent of whom should feel secure about it (Dailey, 8; 124).

Proposals to reduce inequities in the present system include using twenty-five years rather than thirty-five to determine Social Security benefits, to take caregiving years into account (Malveaux, "Race," 177); making widow's benefits a larger percentage of a couple's benefits (Anzick and Weaver, 12); encouraging men to share caregiving responsibilities equally; lifting the cap on wages taxed for Social Security; and ending the disadvantage for two-earner families. Their survivors would get the same benefits as survivors of one-earner families (Burkhauser and Smeeding, 13). Social Security is the only source of income for one-fifth of older people, and for two-thirds it comprises 90 percent (Calasanti and Slevin, *Age Matters*, 7). Teresa Ghilarducci has proposed guaranteed retirement accounts in addition to Social Security that would be professionally managed and pay out annuities (5). The IRA/401(k) model has failed, she believes, because do-it-yourself pension planning cannot match expert planning.

In 1981, a presidential panel recommended national pensions to supplement Social Security, an idea that seems unthinkably progressive today, when a woman's marital status still plays such a large role in deciding her retirement income. Whatever her personal choices and individual circumstances, her late-life income is largely determined by family and workplace structures and by public policy (O'Rand and Henretta, 70), policy that favors the white middle class. A 2012 report titled "Breaking the Social Security Glass Ceiling: A Proposal to Modernize Women's Benefits" by Carroll Estes, Terry O'Neill, and Heidi Hartmann, calls for caregiving credits for children or elderly parents and for permanently lifting the $110,000 earnings cap on Social Security contributions ("New Report," 10).

CONCLUSION

The dynamic interplay of class, ethnicity, and gender with aging is not yet well understood. It is obvious, however, that women's old-age poverty is directly linked to a sexual division of labor whereby much of women's work earns neither wages nor credit for retirement (Harrington Meyer, "Family Status," 466–67). For many, the seeds of late-life financial struggle are being sown today. Thus the connection between women's caregiving and their retirement needs more attention (C. Price, 150). As the aging population grows, inequality is likely to increase (O'Rand and Henretta, 207). The widening gap between classes in the United States today "causes pain far beyond economic suffering," concludes bell hooks, "denying us the wellbeing that comes from recognizing our need for community and interdependency" (158). These non-material values, embodied by caregivers and particularly relevant to aging, are our real source of wealth.

Whatever individual differences mark our experience of aging, this process is profoundly shaped by gender, class, and ethnicity. Theoretically, this needn't be so. If advantages and disadvantages were more justly distributed, our aging differences might chiefly reflect our biological inheritance or the care we took of ourselves earlier in life. Most Americans become uneasy at the thought that individual effort counts for little. As long as the U.S. rank on the WHO healthy longevity scale is a shameful twenty-four, however, extolling individual effort will only disguise the many forces that determine how we age.

8

✿

Ageism

Ageism is mentioned in litanies of social problems such as racism, sexism, and homophobia but it is more often invoked than analyzed. Although the term "ageism" was first coined by Robert Butler in 1969, awareness of it as a social, political, economic, and moral problem is still so low that the fields of health care, gerontology, and women's studies provide numerous examples. No credible public figure would condone sex or race discrimination, but the harmful impact of age discrimination has been denied or trivialized by Supreme Court justices.

The tenacity of ageism is not surprising, given its deep roots in Western culture and the absence of a mass movement of old people, comparable to civil rights, women's rights, or gay and lesbian liberation, to challenge it. People over forty are targets for an astonishing range of insults, including birthday card jibes, and the mass marketing of fear and ignorance of aging through these cards elicits few protests. The message that being old is funny or embarrassing is so ingrained that many old women and men take this view of themselves, at least in social groups. Biased attitudes reinforce discriminatory practices, such as firing older workers and maintaining an educational system focused on the young.[1]

Fear of death is a major source of age bias. The limited use of hospice is one sign of powerful death denial in the United States. To call our society "youth-worshipping" is an understatement. Television programs are written by and for the young. When large numbers of women and men over sixty-five move to a community, their migration brands them a "gray peril," as feared and unwanted as the late-nineteenth-century arrivals in California who were branded the "yellow peril" (Longino, 449).

Discussions of individuals' ageist attitudes and behaviors stress the psychology of stigma and prejudice, but understanding ageism requires looking beyond individuals to its structural roots, taking power relations into account (N. Thompson, 379). Two ground-breaking books of the 1980s, *Look Me in the Eye* by Barbara Macdonald and Cynthia Rich, and Baba Copper's *Over the Hill*, examine one structural root of ageism, women's subordination in the patriarchal family.[2] Their analysis shows that while women are victims of ageism, they may also be its perpetrators.

An ageism motif runs through the preceding chapters, in the irrational fear of an aging population, the dominance of the sick role, the lack of programs designed to preserve the health of older citizens, and the exhortation to keep busy in order to prove one's worth. Ageism may coexist with other oppressive attitudes and actions. A Latina in her seventies who receives inferior health care, for example, may experience three layers of prejudice simultaneously, based on her sex, her ethnicity, and her age; but in her own family, she may be highly regarded. While ageism intensifies negative treatment based on ethnicity, gender, or sexual preference, it deserves separate scrutiny. In this chapter, I consider sources of ageism—stereotypes, the focus on appearance, internalized ageism, and overemphasis on "old" as a category.

STEREOTYPES

The British gerontologist Alex Comfort, better known for *The Joy of Sex* than for *A Good Age*, defined ageism as the belief that "people cease to be people, cease to be the same people, or become people of distinct and inferior kind, by virtue of having lived a specified number of years" (*A Good Age*, 35). Ageism has also been described as "beliefs and practices that prevent us from functioning in an optimal way" (Gullette, *Agewise*, 34). According to Bill Bytheway, ageism is an "ideology upon which dominant groups justify and sustain the inequalities between age groups" (*Ageism*, 116). Because it can be either conscious or unconscious, individuals may perpetrate it or be victimized by it, whether or not they are aware of the process (Levy, "Unconscious Ageism," 335). Robert Butler compared ageist stereotyping to racism and sexism ("Ageism," 243). The link to racism and sexism is a rhetorical device that highlights the damage caused by ageism, but the analogy falters by comparing lifelong identities to one we have for only part of our lives. Secondly, ageism is unique because anyone can live long enough to become a target of ageist stereotypes. A final distinction is that women and people of color accept those designations for themselves, whereas many people over seventy or eighty, perhaps most, spurn "old" as an identity. Discrimination based on age is just as irrational, arbitrary, and unjust as race and sex discrimination, and in all three cases, one's appearance determines the classification. We lack a good word to designate a specific kind of ageism, bias toward people with dementia (Basting, *Forget Memory*, 26).

Men as well as women experience ageist bias, but men do not face the "primal loathing" old women evoke merely by existing (Copper, 19). Women over sixty or seventy naturally do not want to think of themselves as objects of scorn, but "primal loathing" shapes the ways aging plays out for them. Although the taunt of "dirty old man" is cruel and nasty, it lacks the fierce contempt of "old hag." The terms "shrew" and "crone" are more intensely negative than terms for old men such as "geezer" and "old fart." Lately, "geezer" has appeared in newspapers and magazines to cover both women and men, and this contemptuous term appears even in the title of a *Scientific American* article, "From Baby Boom to Geezer Glut."[3]

Ageist stereotypes require dualistic thinking. Sharply differentiated pairs such as old/young, black/white, feminine/masculine impart reassuring familiarity, with one valued over the other. In the past two decades, gender differences have become less rigid and black/white no longer frames our increasingly multicultural society, but old/young remains as fixed as ever, blurring the complexities of aging and defining the old as less worthy than others. "A cleaver-sharp binary between beauty and the so-called ravages of time, between health and disability, figured as old age, is encoded daily in the stories and advertisements in the mass media" (Woodward, *Figuring*, xvi).

Older people are often thought to be incompetent, selfish, and a threat to the economic security of others. They are viewed as poor, disabled, and isolated from their families (Quadagno, *Aging*, 9), as the "culturally residual, the decrepit, the distorted, and finally, the alien in the new world to come" (Russo, 27). Old women are reviled as grumpy, frumpy, sexless, and uninteresting. Their prototypes are the wicked witch, the bad mother who is needy and neurotic, and the comical, powerless little old lady (Copper, 14). A study of ageist and sexist stereotypes in Disney movies found old women depicted as ugly, evil, and power hungry, as well as devil-like, greedy, and crazy (M. Perry, 206; 208). Ageism also underlies assumptions that it is "natural" for old people to have lower expectations than others, to have less control over their lives, or to have less need to be mobile.[4]

An old woman who fails to be cheerful will be thought "bitter, mean, complaining" (Healey, "Growing," 61). When one of these labels is affixed, it may expand into an identity rather than mark a passing mood. Just as young women may be typecast as virgins or whores, old women face similar restrictive and distorting stereotypes of grandmother, hag, or spinster.

Folklore is a rich source of negative attitudes toward old people, especially old women. In fairy tales, for example, an old woman who is kindly at first may turn out to be a witch. Meeting an old woman on the road brings bad luck, a folk belief epitomized by the saying, "If the devil can't come himself, he sends an old woman." In German fairy tales, the old draw vitality from the young, and those thought to have lived too long can be killed. A saga describing a tenth-century famine in Iceland tells of the old being thrown over cliffs.[5]

On his travels, Gulliver encounters the Struldbrugs, who are frozen in old age and can never die. They are "peevish, covetous, morose, vain, talkative," envious, impotent, incapable of friendship, "dead to all natural Affection . . . and cut off from all Possibility of Pleasure." Gulliver pronounces the Struldbrugs "the most horrifying sight I ever beheld; and the Women are more horrible than the Men" (Swift, 181–83). The title of Anthony Trollope's 1882 novel *The Fixed Period* refers to a law passed by citizens of an island independent of England to kill people before they reach sixty-eight. This modest proposal is defended as a rational, progressive, and modern way to bypass the miseries of old age. But the first candidate for euthanasia balks, and England sends a battleship to depose the island's president and block the law.[6]

An examination of English cartoons revealed three predominant themes: failing eyesight, failing memory, and reduced sexual activity (Bytheway, *Ageism*, 63). An analysis of drug ads in physicians' journals found that the old were depicted as "disruptive, apathetic, temperamental, and out of control" (Levin and Levin, 91). Behind many of these caricatures is the unconscious fear of a strong old woman.

Accusations of witchcraft often targeted old women but the large body of scholarship on the witch-craze does not focus on the *age* of victims (Feinson, 437). Why were old women vulnerable? Scholars have noted that they were blamed for stillborns, crop failure, and male impotence. In her book *The Crone*, Barbara Walker states that old women in particular were called witches because of the survival of an ancient archetype, the destructive Crone Mother (13). The old woman who could kill with her gaze could also cause death by curses (58). In addition, an accusation of witchcraft was a good way to get rid of poor women too weak to work and seen as economic drains (132). Any woman living outside of male control—a single woman, a widow—could be singled out. If a woman accumulated medical knowledge or gained a special understanding of the natural world or animals, or if she were suspected of reading philosophy or dispensing spiritual advice, she could be labeled a witch (141). It seems plausible that old women, who had the most time to acquire knowledge, would have been the most threatening. The witch-crone was a woman "who reserved her powers for herself" (Arber and Ginn, *Gender*, 38).

The author of a sixteenth-century book on witchcraft describes witches as "old, lame, bleare-eid, pale, fowle, and full of wrinkles, poore, sullen, superstitious and papists" (qtd. in Chase, 122). Old Protestant women who were lame, bleare-eid, pale, and fowle were apparently exempt from blame.

Even though the witch hunts occurred centuries ago, they lasted so long and their fury was so intense that their influence has not been entirely erased. "The real threat posed by older women in a patriarchal society," Barbara Walker concludes, "may be the 'evil eye' of sharp judgment honed by disillusioning experience, which pierces male myths and scrutinizes male motives in the hard, unflattering light of critical appraisal. It may be that the witch's evil eye was only an eye from which the scales had fallen" (122). Sharp judgment and critical appraisal may not be necessary to make some old women threatening. Merely withdrawing attention from men may be enough.

It is unnerving to acknowledge that hatred of old women is an important strand in Euro-American culture. In many other cultures, by contrast, postmenopausal women gain power and status. The witch craze is like a toxic waste site covered up for a long time but still emitting poisons. The hatred of old women that is its legacy is fairly well concealed in our society by sentimentalized images of grandmothers, patronizing deference to "granny," and the invisibility of most women over sixty-five in politics, the media, and business. Barbed insults and jokes directed at old women give a glimpse of the residual hatred, as does an assumption that illness, silent suffering, and even deprivation are natural concomitants of their old age.

Certain words, phrases, and ways of speaking communicate negative stereotypes. Someone who says grandparenting "keeps me young" offers a pious falsehood. Attributing youthfulness to old women, intended as praise, reinforces the idea that being old is bad. When a woman over sixty is addressed as "young lady," she can be certain that her age has been seen as a deficit. "Young at heart" suggests fun-loving and active, while the unstated contrast "old at heart" by implication means boring, passive, and a "wet blanket" (Palmore, 91). Gerontologists perpetuate ageist language by using "young-old" to distinguish people under seventy-five from the "old old." These tags imply a sharp separation between groups, with the really old set down a notch from the slightly old.

In the introduction to Imogen Cunningham's collection *After 90*, portraits she took when she herself was over ninety, the photographer is praised several times for her "youthful qualities," as if energy, whimsy, and intense professional commitment are to be found only among the young. The introduction rises to a crescendo of condescension when the photographer is described as "this ageless, frisky, elfin creature, a crone in a black wool cloak, our heroine of the camera, bright-eyed, quick-witted, and working—even after ninety" (M. Mitchell, 23). Cunningham's great force of personality is lost in "frisky" and "elfin" and the word "creature" distances her from us. Even the word "our" is revealing, the equivalent of a pat on the head. Cunningham's statements quoted in the introduction make clear that she did not see herself as a heroine; this false identity is grafted onto her. The surprise in the last phrase, "even after ninety," patronizes the photographer.

Language is ageist when it expresses surprise that an old person retains his or her competence or assertiveness, as for example in phrases that begin "still creative at . . ." and "still attractive at . . ."(Williams and Giles, 151). "Tired" is sometimes a code word for old, and "older" a euphemism for "old." The comparative term takes youth or mid-life as the norm. The popularity of "feisty," used especially for old women, reveals surprise that vigor, assertiveness, or strong opinions are expressed by a person over sixty. A pamphlet from Old Lesbians Organizing for Change asks, "Would you call Superman 'feisty'?" Another belittling word is "spunky," used on old women but better reserved for spirited pets.

No magazines or products are labeled "anti-black" or "anti-woman" but "anti-aging" is a very common label for commercial products, including books. Being against aging is like being against pregnancy or season change. The currently popular phrase "senior moment," used to call attention to forgetfulness, is oppressive. A twenty-year-old who forgets his or her car keys or leaves a burner on does not say he or she is having a "twenties moment." Implicit in "senior moment" is acknowledgment of status loss. "The frail elderly" sounds like an innocuous phrase but suggests an identity that is meaningful only to service providers. In a group of twenty elders given this designation, individual differences are probably far more important than similarities.

Psychologists and communications researchers study "elderspeak," observed in interactions between people of different ages. Elderspeak is characterized by a slow rate of speaking, simple sentence structure and vocabulary, and repetitions. It is "not necessarily cued by older adults' comprehension problems" (Kemper and Harden, 656). Studies of elderspeak provide good empirical evidence of ageism. Other researchers use "patronizing speech" to describe speech directed at old women and men that is marked by careful articulation, a demeaning tone (either overbearing or overly familiar), superficial talk, and in its most extreme form, baby talk (Hummert, 162). In a study of patronizing speech, subjects denied they were treated differently because of their age but agreed that others were (Williams and Giles, 151). Among the stereotypes that evoke patronizing speech are old people as severely impaired, curmudgeonly, and depressed (Hummert, 164).

Patronizing speech damages the self-esteem of elders. Moreover, the unsatisfactory social exchange between the two speakers affects the younger as well, for it reinforces negative stereotypes (Hummert, 165–71). Doctor-patient interaction studies have shown that compared to young patients, old patients are addressed with less respect and less patience, given less precise information, and asked fewer open-ended questions (Williams and Giles, 138). Patronizing speech in medical settings occurs in the tone, simplicity, or brevity of the communication.

Ageist language is particularly dismaying when used by writers on aging. The book titled *Coping with Your Difficult Older Parent* creates a category out of certain behaviors that may be interpreted quite differently by the parent. Behavior the parent herself might acknowledge as stubborn or angry is just behavior, not an identity. Even worse is another title, *Working with Toxic Older Adults*, from a leading publisher in gerontology.[7] This insulting label reveals the sinister side to the helping profession's dominance of aging. Once a person in a relatively powerless position has been stigmatized as "toxic," he or she can easily be disregarded. Labeling an old person "toxic" effectively erases the possibility that his or her needs and desires may not coincide with the services provided by the "helper." In both of these book titles, the old person is seen as marginal, while the point of view expressed is that of an authority. A pronounced Us versus Them mentality is apparent here. No book titles target "difficult adult children" of old women and men.

Ageist stereotypes play out in the media, the law, the workplace, and the family.

Media

Television has been called a major source of ageism (Palmore, 98). On television, "women can now be forty or fifty but they must look thirty" (Mellencamp, 316). Lucille Ball was in her forties when "I Love Lucy" began its run in 1951, but she played a twenty-nine-year-old (316). The age difference between male and female television anchors is dramatic. The popular Angela Lansbury was whisked off stage, suggesting that one visible old woman on television, Barbara Walters, is considered enough. Representations of blacks and women have evolved since the 1950s, but where aging is concerned we are still in the era when Jack Benny's jokes about his 39th birthday were a staple of mainstream humor. Lifetime television viewing leads to negative views of aging and the aging process and ageist attitudes may negatively impact health (Harwood, 9). An analysis of television commercials showed that 12 percent portrayed people over fifty, nearly three-fourths of whom were male. They tended to pitch health and hygiene products or food (Quadagno, *Aging*, 7). Television commercials would probably not depict old women with any sensitivity, and thus their increased appearance might reinforce rather than weaken negative stereotypes. At the same time, the absence of old women from this mirror of American life suggests a social consensus that they do not matter.

A study of magazine ads and television shows in England found several assumptions: The ageing body is a problem for women and thus requires remedial work; women are morally responsible for bodily upkeep; they should try to look ten years younger; they can 'triumph over time' if they buy solutions to visible ageing (Coupland).[8] A study of the impact of sexualized media images on Australian women over sixty found examples of self-objectification, as women expressed shame and embarrassment about their appearance. They were well aware, however, of their personal qualities and strengths that were independent of physical appearance and were also aware that media marginalized them "both as subjects and consumers" (Hine, 643). A study of newspaper images of old people in Ireland found patronizing tags like "grannies" and assumptions of frailty and infirmity, so that old people were placed outside of mainstream Irish society (Fealy et al.). Older women are "exceptionally under-represented" in magazine ads in the United States, Great Britain, Germany, India, and China (Scholl and Sabat, 106). In films, men are portrayed as enjoying an active, vigorous old age, whereas women project images of decline, a pattern that has not changed in sixty-five years (Markson and Taylor, 137; 155–56).

Today the media avoid overtly racist or sexist messages in advertising or programs (with the obvious exception of talk radio). Covert prejudice and misrepresentations still occur. What is unique about ageism is the crude directness with which prejudice is communicated on radio and television, in newspapers, in news magazines, on talk shows, and even in publications geared to an older audience. Stephen Colbert wrote in a *New York Times* column that "the elderly look like lizards" (October 7, 2007), an astonishing sneer that would not survived an editor's red pen if the target had been any other group.

A face cream commercial gushes that in an experiment, women "were given a chance to look years younger," as if that were a great benefit any woman would be thrilled to receive. Other ads urge people to cover up or de-emphasize their age—ads for creams that cover up liver spots, for example, or ads for hair dyes. The message is that being old is undesirable, something to disguise in order to be acceptable. A telling example of the force of this prejudice appeared when a dermatologist concerned about the increase in skin cancer told San Francisco reporters that young people were still sunbathing and could not be discouraged from the practice by warnings about skin cancer. He found another, scarier warning: Tanning will make you look old early.

In the media, old women and men are portrayed as sick, as needing help, and as costing too much. An obstacle to combating ageism is the dearth of realistic, complex images of elders. How different media images would be if aging were seen as a process rather than an affliction. The vigorous old are not featured in the media unless they perform some remarkable feat. Ordinary, healthy old people are invisible except to their friends and families. The covers of *Modern Maturity*, the AARP magazine, used to feature affluent-looking heterosexual couples in their early fifties wearing warm-up suits. Now young celebrities appear on the cover, with an occasional middle-aged star such as Susan Sarandon. If you look old enough to join AARP, you can't be on the cover. The failure of the media to present varied images of old women "reinforces an unattainable cultural standard"—that aging must be fought at all cost (Bazzini, 542).

Workplace

The Age Discrimination in Employment Act (ADEA), making it illegal to use age as a criterion in hiring, firing, and layoffs, was passed in 1967 and amended in 1986 to end mandatory retirement from most jobs. ADEA cases differ from those relating to discrimination by race, national origin, and sex, or those filed under the Americans with Disabilities Act (1990), however, because they allow neither compensatory nor punitive damages (International Longevity Center, 93).

Stereotypes about older workers persist, despite evidence that they are as efficient as other workers, have a lower rate of absenteeism and a higher rate of job satisfaction, are less likely to be injured on the job, and continue to learn. Nevertheless, some managers see older workers as resistant to change, unimaginative, cautious and slow, less physically competent than younger workers, uninterested in technology, and untrainable (Atchley, *Social Forces*, 234–36). Resentment against older workers has been voiced during the recession, with the accusation that they are holding onto jobs that could go to younger workers. Studies have shown a positive correlation, however, between labor-force participation among the elderly and youth employment. At times, older workers "crowd out" younger workers, but there are "myriad ways in which older workers also increase employment among the young" (Glaeser). Age discrimination in hiring is thought to be both the most prevalent form of discrimination against older workers and the most difficult to prove (International Longevity Center, 78). In a study of work, women, and ageism in England, subjects felt strongly that they had much to offer employers but were not given a chance to demonstrate their abilities (Grant, 54). Those who worked part-time because of family care-giving responsibilities found they were ineligible for promotion. They noted some progress toward equality but felt that it was "too slow, too little, and too late for them" and questioned whether legislation could tackle age discrimination (62).

A worker already perceived as less competent because of racial or sex bias is further disadvantaged if age prejudice figures in decisions to cut his or her job rather than another's. Layoffs in many American companies in the past two decades, especially in the recession, disproportionately affected older workers, some of whom did not realize they were "older workers" until they lost their jobs. Once out of work, they remain unemployed much longer than younger workers and experience a greater earnings loss in their next job, if they find one (Palmore, 120–21). Between 2008 and 2012, the number of unemployed older job seekers doubled. The economic cost of the lost productivity of unemployed workers over fifty has been estimated at $60 billion annually (107).

At work, sexism and ageism may be interconnected. A study of a large geriatric center in England found that female nurses treated male residents better than women. Nurses knew far more about the lives of the men and were more likely to describe women residents as difficult. The researcher speculates that caring for old women threatened the nurses because each day they had to face images of their own future lives, and thus they distanced themselves emotionally from the women (Evers, cited in Bernard, 636). Nurses can be unconsciously ageist if they have a fatalistic attitude about the usefulness of their help. Thus nursing education must demonstrate the "heterogeneous experience of old age," so that nurses see older people in various diverse contexts, beyond a biomedical lens (Phelan, 898–99).

The Law

A 2009 Supreme Court decision, *Gross v. FBI Financial Group*, made it harder for older workers than for other protected groups to win discrimination cases. Previously, a worker needed to show only that age was a substantial motivating factor in an employer's discriminatory action, not the sole factor. In this ruling, the Supreme Court "disregarded long standing legal precedent" and set "an unfairly hard standard to meet" (*New York Times* editorial, March 30, 2012, A24).[9] In 2000, the Supreme Court ruled 5–4 that state employees cannot go to federal court to sue over age bias (*New York Times*, January 12, 2000, A1). Sandra Day O'Connor wrote that age discrimination is unlike sex or race discrimination, reasoning that old age "does not define a discrete and insular minority because all persons, if they live out their normal life spans, will experience it." The logic of the former justice was seriously flawed because at any given moment, the old *are* a minority group: 13 percent of the population. If old workers are discriminated against, it is no comfort to tell them they escaped this treatment when they were young. Furthermore, forcing individuals out of the workplace because of their age has social and economic costs that conservatives on the Supreme Court do not recognize.

A Southern worker in his early fifties was fired after a new supervisor repeatedly mocked him for being as old as Methuselah. The state court ruled that he was not a victim of age discrimination. Historically, members of minority groups have gone to federal court because their rights were not fully protected by state courts. State workers prevented from taking age discrimination cases to federal court have fewer legal protections than other citizens.

Families

Two works cited above, Barbara Macdonald's *Look Me in the Eye* and *Over the Hill* by Baba Copper, examine the family's role in fostering ageism. Young women are conditioned to align themselves with powerful fathers rather than mothers and to see older women as servants of both their fathers and themselves (Macdonald, 40). Old women's "labor energy," that is, favors or services provided without reciprocity, is available to all family members (Copper, 22). An older woman may unknowingly trigger in a younger woman anger she feels toward her mother. The older woman then finds herself "bearing a burden of projected hostility" that mystifies her (Copper, 24).

The grandmother's place is in the home; her role defines her so strictly that "her right to exist depends on her loving and serving." She is not supposed to believe that her last years are as important as her grandchildren's early years (Macdonald, 105–6). An old woman may feel a sense of helplessness when her capacity to serve others diminishes (Sceriha, 310). Grandmothers represent the past—memories of them evoke nostalgia—and thus their present concerns go unnoticed (Copper, 10–11). The traditional family is not set up to nurture late-life development.

Not all women are grandmothers, of course, but the role extends to all, for it envisions the model old woman as passive, cheery, devoted to others, and easily controlled. A study of film images of old women over many decades found that when they were portrayed as powerful, it was usually within a family setting (Markson and Taylor, 153).

Just as no single Asian Pacific woman or black woman can speak for all, no single old woman can represent everyone over sixty-five. The burden of representation may fall on her, however, if she is the only old woman in a social group, at a public forum, in a college class, or in a family.

In some families and social settings, old women assume the guise of a clown. This is a strategy for age denial: "I'm not old, I'm just eccentric!" (Macdonald, 92). I have often observed old women mocking themselves, as if to include themselves in a circle of fun rather than risk being targeted by others' derisive humor. Is this dynamic more likely to occur among white women than women of color? Among women once considered beautiful? Is it more characteristic of women in their eighties or nineties than of younger women? Old women do not have to act like clowns to be treated like mascots.

A subtle form of ageism in families is the unstated assumption that old women need less space than others, not only physical space but psychic space as well. The mother-in-law apartment is typically small. Some old women may move and speak as freely as men but all have been conditioned to see male dominance of space as natural. Baba Copper noticed that "the ground ceded to me by those who pass me on the street had shrunk" (29). In late life, a woman may restrict her space needs from an unconscious belief that others' needs are more important than her own, especially if she lives with children and grandchildren. A nursing home room, often shared, is the final stage of shrinking physical and psychological space.

APPEARANCE

Bodies change. Faces become lined and wrinkled, and loosening flesh takes away their firm definition. The face in the mirror may be grandmother's face. Breasts sag. Knees and ankles thicken. Upper arm flesh hangs down and abdominal fat accumulates. Pubic hair and underarm hair thins. Joints stiffen. Fingers lose some dexterity. Within these common changes are myriad individual differences.

One of the biggest obstacles to women's complete self-acceptance in late life is the judgment that loss of attractiveness (by conventional norms) is a tragic fact of life rather than a belief that can be examined and repudiated, like the belief that blacks are less intelligent than whites or that women are inferior to men. The judgment that old women's bodies are unattractive is so pervasive as to be almost inescapable.[10] Few women can regard even their mid-life bodily changes with complete equanimity. Disdain for old women's bodies is "very similar to the distaste anti-Semites feel towards Jews, homophobes feel towards lesbians and gays, racists toward Blacks—the drawing back of the oppressor from the physical being of the oppressed" (Rich in Macdonald, 143).

Is this problem as onerous for women of color as for white women? One way to find out would be through extensive interviews with women of different ages that would take into account class differences and differences between women of color born here and those who have come from other countries. Literary images shed light on this question. Poets such

as Judith Ortiz Cofer, Lucille Clifton, and Mary TallMountain have described old women's bodies with loving detail, for example in "Paciencia"
(Cofer), "Miss Rosie" (Clifton), and "Matmiya" (TallMountain). The poets
express unique sensibilities and should not be read simply as cultural representatives. Puerto Rican, black, and Athabaskan cultures differ greatly
from each other. Nonetheless, the stark difference between the poets'
positive views of old women's bodies and the contempt expressed by
M. F. K. Fisher (see below) is striking. For Cofer, Clifton, and TallMountain, power resides *in* old bodies; they make no distinction between
weak/bad/defeated flesh and indomitable spirit.

Women, especially white women, face a double standard, according
to Susan Sontag: Men are judged as "face and body, a physical whole,"
while women are identified with their faces. The range of acceptability is
much wider for men's faces than for women's, and their well-worn faces
are thought to convey maturity, character, and experience. A woman's
face, on the other hand, is valued for staying the same. Ideally, it is a
mask.[11] Old men often want much younger women for wives and companions. Men's fear of an "all-engulfing mother" is intensified when
women are old (Woodward, "Tribute," 87). In 1873, the radical feminist
theorist Matilda Joslyn Gage wrote that a woman who no longer interests
men sexually was thought to have "forfeited the right to live" (quoted
in Mollenkott, 4). Although much has changed for women since Gage
wrote, the perception that old women's bodies are ugly has not changed.
"Old women vanish from ads when they lose their sex appeal for men,
appearing only to sell food they can cook and medications they can take,
or being foolish in a modern female version of Uncle Tom" (Reinharz, 78).
Another sign of the double standard is that no equivalent of the irrational
fear of old women exists for men (Sceriha, 313), no equivalent to "primal
loathing."

The relentless emphasis on appearance pressures some women to fit
into a youth-centered culture by choosing face-lifts and other alterations
to their bodies. Those who when young tried to be as thin as possible are
victimized again. Some women who get face-lifts say they want to erase
the difference between the way they look and the way they feel inside, but
this rationale divides us into "our corpus, which drags us inevitably into
our dreaded old age, and our spirit, which remains forever young." This
age denial through "artificial dissection" results in a split self (Andrews,
301). Though portrayed as glamorous, face-lifts are actually mutilations,
a fact powerfully revealed in a series of self-portraits Anne Noggle took
immediately after her surgery. Her swollen and bruised face looks like the
face of a woman who has been beaten.[12]

In *Facing Age*, Laura Hurd Clarke reports on three sets of interviews of
women aged fifty to ninety conducted over ten years. Their comments

reveal that appearance is a "battleground on which cultural capital is won and lost, and beauty work is a deeply political and often unconscious . . . act that is circumscribed and required by ageist and sexist ideologies" (135). Self-surveillance and strict discipline over bodies are themes in *Facing Age*. Many women in the study cannot comfortably look in mirrors or examine photographs of themselves. Several interviewees resist internalized ageism, however. Hurd Clarke interviewed physicians who perform cosmetic surgery to get their perspective. They want to help older women "achieve congruence" between the way they feel inside and the way they look (80–81).The website of the American Society for Aesthetic Plastic Surgery states that nine billion surgical and non-surgical procedures were performed in 2011. Hurd Clarke believes that cosmetic surgery will become increasingly popular with baby boomers.[13] Another study of women's attitudes toward cosmetic surgery found that some women who wanted surgery used liberal feminist language of freedom and individual choice, while others valued new aspects of themselves outside of physical appearance and thus did not choose surgery (Brooks, 300–301).

Do baby-boom women of color feel pressure to change their faces and bodies? A large, unexplored topic. Lesbians probably less so than heterosexual women. Class difference must enter in here. However free many women of color or many lesbians may be of pressures to hide marks of aging, they are no less subject to ageist bias than white, heterosexual women. In her memoir *I Love a Broad Margin to My Life*, Maxine Hong Kingston, sixty-five, asks for example if she is still pretty and concludes that "It all depends on the light" (5).

If large numbers of baby-boomers—men as well as women—alter their faces to pass as young, we will all be deprived of seeing the whole range and variety of aging faces. Audre Lorde wrote in *The Cancer Journals* that pressure on women like herself to disguise the fact that they had lost a breast deprived her of knowing who shared her experience. So, too, with the banishment of faces that look fifty, sixty, or seventy. In a way, the age denial that cosmetic surgery represents is a superstition as powerful and irrational as any observable in so-called primitive societies. Praying to rain gods and cutting out one's wrinkles and sagging face flesh express two kinds of magical thinking. People who have their faces altered try to escape the wrathful gods of inexorable change. Their cosmetic surgeon is Zeus. If they pretend they are not old, they won't really *be* old. No mockery is directed at their delusion; it is too widely shared to be named make-believe.

Hurd Clarke believes that feminists are not immune from negative body image and thus from internalized ageism. The growing prevalence of cosmetic surgery demonstrates the limited influence of feminism on aging attitudes. More girls play sports in schools today, thanks to Title IX pioneers of the 1970s; more women work in professions previously closed to them; sexual harassment has been identified as a barrier to working women since the 1980s; and in the 1990s, many women of color entered professional schools. Where aging and appearance are concerned, on the other hand, no comparable progress can be claimed.

The "anti-aging" movement among dermatologists, cosmetic surgeons, and sellers of products tries to claim scientific legitimacy for itself but relies on metaphor. Through battlefield metaphors, for example, the enemy becomes the process of aging itself (Vincent, "Science," 950; Hurd Clarke, 127). Implicit here are the ideas that old people are the defeated and old age cannot be a positive or fulfilling time of life (Vincent, 957). The claims of the anti-aging movement have been skeptically reviewed by biogerontologist Leonard Hayflick (see chapter 1, note 10).

The shame of aging is perpetuated when old bodies are hidden from view. Young naked female bodies are everywhere, including the magazine section of the Sunday *New York Times*, but where can naked bodies of old women be seen? This is terra incognita. The absence of naked old female bodies deprives women of all ages from knowing what old bodies look like. This deprivation is both aesthetic and psychological. The ways beauty can be expressed through old female forms are yet to be known, although a few artists are breaking the taboo. The cover of Kathleen Woodward's *Figuring Age: Women, Bodies, Generations* is a photograph by Jacqueline Hayden of a nude, one-breasted woman over sixty, sitting on a stool with her arm resting against her raised knee.

Book cover photos of Betty Friedan and Madeleine Albright picture women thirty years younger than they were when their books were published: two notable woman over sixty-five with easily recognizable old faces are pushed back into a closet of youth, the better to enhance their market value. The cover of a Jane Fonda biography makes Fonda look eighteen. The stamp honoring Barbara Jordan, issued in 2011, portrays a very young woman. A *New York Times* ad for Roger Ebert states that he has been a critic for forty-four years but the photo in the ad makes him look twenty-five (August 31, 2011). A youthful image is so prized that many older people want to freeze early images of themselves and pretend that image is the real one. Newspapers that run obituary photos taken forty or fifty years earlier reinforce age shame when they could instead depict old women and men as they really look or run both a current and an old photo.

Looking old can lead to being ignored. Perceiving a woman over sixty as asexual because of her appearance is a way to ignore her. Lucille Clifton writes:

> Sometimes other people don't bring the same level of attention that I bring to them, and sometimes that makes me sad, or angry, as the case may be.

For instance, I've been widowed for ten years, and have noticed that other people, especially men, do not always notice my human characteristics but are quick to pin a label on me: poet, for example, or professor. Sexually and romantically, they are interested in women of my daughter's age. It hurts my feelings. It puts me in a slot, and I go uneasily into slots of any kind. (53)

How does an older woman find the courage to accept bodily change? What values or emotional history let her acknowledge what she sees happening in her body without trying to alter it? She may never have been much influenced by conventional beliefs about female beauty. She may grasp the connection between profit and culturally induced body loathing. Whatever her ethnicity, she may have aunts and grandmothers whose power or life satisfaction does not come from looking a certain way or denying their age.

INTERNALIZED AGEISM

Just as colonized people may internalize messages about their own inferiority, many old women feel ashamed of their age. This is the most insidious form ageism takes. Consciously working through the negative associations with age that are nearly universal in this society requires effort. If she does not continually examine her ageist notions, writes Shevy Healey, "false expectations and assumptions cloud and diminish my ability to actually experience my life" ("Confronting Ageism," 47). Internalized ageism keeps people from accurately assessing their own abilities and even worse, sets them up to "rationalize unfair assessments from others" (Bodily, 251).

People who are old themselves appear as likely as or more likely than others to perpetuate ageist stereotypes by their jokes and comments, but at the same time they know far better than others that these stereotypes distort and demean them. Studies of attitudes toward the old among people of various ages found less complex views of aging among the young and more complex and more positive attitudes among the old themselves (Hummert, 165), a sign of resistance to internalized ageism. A study of attitudes toward aging in Japan concluded that although Japanese elders held many negative opinions about their own age group, they also had strong self-concepts protecting them from what would otherwise have been "the damaging effects of social environment" (Levy, "Inner Self," 142). The mental gyrations needed to exempt oneself from membership in a group others assume one belongs to, however, would seem to complicate self-understanding and to require vigilance. A similar process of distancing occurs among old women and men in the United States. The assumption that being old is shameful is illustrated by the oppressive practice at some senior centers of fining members who use the word "old" (Palmore, 110).

Age passing, pretending to be younger than you are, is a form of internalized ageism. Copper speculates that it may be easier for small, "cute" older women than for their "more bulky peers" (31). Another self-defeating strategy is to say "nothing has changed but our bodies," a split that erases "the unique insights of our time of life" (11).

Why is internalized ageism common among elderly people apparently more common than either internalized racism or internalized homophobia? One explanation is that by the time a young person has grown old, she or he has spent fifty years expressing and internalizing negative stereotypes of aging (Levy and Banaji, 66). Some people, especially those with a close tie to a grandparent, may escape this common experience.

Apologies for slow movements reflect internalized ageism. I recall many times when an old woman boarding a San Francisco bus apologized for what she perceived as her slowness. The cultural bias favoring speed is so powerful that slow movements mark inferiority. As some colonized people identify with the dominant group rather than their own to deflect stigma, some old women call other old women "little old ladies," thereby evading an undesirable category.[14]

The hunch that internalized ageism may negatively affect not just self-esteem, motivation, risk taking, and other hard-to-measure traits but physical capacity as well is supported by a study of gait speed and swing time (time spent with one foot in the air while walking). To test their hypothesis that activating positive stereotypes could partly reverse age-related changes in walking, researchers had subjects aged sixty-three to eighty-two play a video game that exposed them to either positive or negative stereotypes about the old. Those given positive stereotypes showed significant increases in walking speed and swing time. Researchers concluded that stereotypes of aging "apparently have a powerful impact on the gait of older persons" (Hausdorff, Levy, and Wei, 1346). The mind-body link evident here was replicated in other studies: In one, internalized negative stereotypes of aging were shown to influence cardiovascular function (Levy, "Eradication," 579) and in another, older people exposed to negative stereotypes of aging demonstrated shakier handwriting than those exposed to positive stereotypes (Levy and Banaji, 60). This work should inspire other researchers to think about measurable effects of ageism. [15]

A study of Canadian women at a senior center who view themselves as "not old" discusses this labeling as a way of "negotiating" aging and concludes that it helps the women contradict negative stereotypes. Most of their statements suggest, however, that the strategy does not work, comments for example on the ugliness of their bodies (Hurd, 431–32). The women feel a sharp separation between themselves and those they designate as old. All are widows, though, a status that definitely coincides with being old. Additionally, the women are well aware that illness could take the "not old" mantle away from them (430). One of the chief ways they lock in "not old" is by being busy (427). Choosing "not old" requires a degree of self-deception because women must deny that aging is a process, one that includes them. Living in a society in which they are ruthlessly judged by physical appearance, they trust that the trivializing self-characterization of "young at heart" gives them protective cover. The reprieve is only temporary. The various rationalizations of the "not old" are often regarded as cute by others, a sure sign of their transparent failure.

Instead of rebuking women who exhibit internalized ageism, however, it is fairer to adopt a double consciousness that recognizes both the harm this stance of shame causes and the heavy weight of cultural baggage that makes full self-acceptance and honest disclosure of age difficult. An especially poignant example of internalized ageism comes, surprisingly, from a writer who has described other people's aging with unusual insight and sensitivity, M. F. K. Fisher. The afterword to her book *Sister Age* is luminous, but in an interview she reports:

> My husband told me that every self-respecting woman must have a full-length mirror in her house, to see herself from top to bottom cruelly. Mine is facing me at a distance of about ten feet from my bed when I get up in the morning. About a year ago I realized—I sleep without pajamas or a nightie— I suddenly realized I could not face walking toward myself again because here was this strange, uncouth, ugly . . . toad-like woman, long, long thin legs, long long thin arms, and a sort of shapeless little toad-like torso and this head at the top with great staring eyes. I thought, "Jesus! Why do I have to do this?" So I bought some nightgowns. I felt like an idiot. But I couldn't face it in the mornings. If I'm going to hide myself I want to *hide*. And I have long-sleeved, high-necked, long-to-the-ground granny gowns. They're pretty. I hate them. I'd much rather not have to wear them. But I will not face that strange, that humanoid toad walking toward *me* in the morning.[16]

In this paroxysm of body-loathing, Fisher reduces herself to "it," sharply separating "it" from "me," the true self residing outside of her body. The contortion demanded by the rules of a dead husband is shocking.

OLD AS A CATEGORY

Learning to be old means being conditioned to "lean on the concept of age" (Bodily, 254). It becomes a ready explanation. Children's books typically portray old characters as if age were their defining characteristic (Sorgman and Sorensen, 120). Once designated "old," writes Barbara Myerhoff, we are "sharply separated" from the members of society deemed useful, full participants, usually "without reference to individual desire or capability. Here nature and culture stand at great remove from each other" ("Rites and Signs," 320). A keen awareness of our individual desire and capability allows us to resist the total category of "old," while at the same time accepting the facts of bodily change and the inevitability of further change.

When "the old" are constructed as a group, they are seen as uniform, with their numerous differences blurred so that they become an "aging melting-pot," and other identities are "pushed aside by the potent age stereotypes" (Spector-Mercel, 75). This may be truer for white people than for people of color. When Barack Obama is eighty, for example, his identity as a black man will be just as salient as his age.

The well-intentioned Age Page in some newspapers assumes a uniformity among elders that does not exist. Just as the now-defunct Women's Page inadvertently revealed inferiority through segregation, the Age Page signals specialness where it has no bearing. The arbitrary chronological marker of sixty-five creates a class of people who get important benefits, are denied resources and opportunities available to others, and suffer "denigration ranging from well-meaning patronage to unambiguous vilification" (Bytheway, *Ageism*, 14). The other meanings of "old," including decline, shift like colored pieces in a kaleidoscope. The category looks fixed because it is familiar and provides a convenient way to rank people. The self-confident ease and assertiveness of the well-off white old may insulate them from contemptuous treatment, but if institutionalized, they devolve into the merely "old," and if cared for at home, they enter into the unequal power relationship of caregiver and care recipient. At a time when most people acknowledge that a woman worker's lower pay does not result from her personal shortcomings, we are much less aware that decline among the old is created by social policy as well as by individual bodily processes.

Just as a heightened sense of racial difference interferes with communication, a heightened sense of age can impede straightforward and unself-conscious interaction. If I speak to an eighty-five-year-old woman with a strong awareness of her age and thus her difference from me, a category unnecessarily shapes our communication. If socialized to see this difference as extremely important, I will have trouble letting it fade back into relative insignificance, even after I suspect that seeing "old" limits my perceptions. The woman can probably do most of what she has done in the past; focusing on her losses rather than her continuities gives too much weight to the conventional meaning of "old." If, trying to be helpful, I grab the arm of an old woman as she crosses the street because I think she needs help, I lean on the concept of old. If I assume a friend will enjoy discussing Medicare with me because she is old, I see her in monochrome. Conditioned by ageist stereotypes, I see helplessness where it does not exist or focus on the medical and economic dimensions of aging as if they were its totality.

I learned what I missed by seeing only "old" while teaching a class called "All About Aging" at the Montefiore Senior Center in San Francisco. The students were amused that a woman under fifty presumed to speak on this topic to an audience made up of people over eighty. One woman who sat near the front of the room paid close attention and made perceptive and lively comments. Not long after the class ended, I was amazed to see her in the hallway of the center, groping her way along slowly and uncertainly. She could barely see. If that had been my only impression of her, age and infirmity would have been the most striking aspects of her identity. But in class I had seen her as a competent and fully functioning individual. Another woman at the center wore a long coat and a babushka. "Old" was my only impression of her until one day when she joined a group chatting in the hallway and mentioned that she had lived in China and spoke Mandarin. She then became an individual and the category "old" no longer covered her like a blanket.

In *Look Me in the Eye*, Barbara Macdonald claims old as an identity, and in *Over the Hill*, Baba Copper writes, "I take to myself the word everyone seems to fear" (75). The parallel to ethnicity, sex, and sexual orientation is implicit, but a woman who takes on the identity "old" has no mass social movement to back her up. Writing in the 1980s, Macdonald and Copper tended to see old women as a monolithic group, as acted upon by an ageist culture but not as having influence upon it. At the time it seemed obvious that old women should counter ageist stereotypes by proudly calling themselves old and that their well-known reluctance to do so signified internalized ageism. They needed consciousness raising to adopt Gray Pride. Now their reluctance seems more complex. It may well be that resisters to the designation "old" neither deny their bodily changes nor believe that their interests are the same as those of younger women. Perhaps they sense that "old" erases their individual differences and creates a separation from others that they do not feel, or even an artificial separation from their former selves. Being old may be a less salient identity marker than black, female, or gay, because it fits only part of our life span. All stereotyped notions about people of color, women, and gay people are demonstrably false, while a key stereotype about late life, the equation with illness, is harder to dismiss because old age and illness are undeniably associated. The stereotype is *equating* the two.

A study of a group of old people in northern England found that they monitored each other to see who was crossing a threshold—from normal aging, which included slowing down, over to "real old age," marked by loss of mental acuity and inappropriate behavior. Those they saw as old were no longer regarded as their equals. "Old" is not simply projected by younger people but is also a social category older people themselves create (Degnen, 76–78).

A problem with embracing "old" as an identity is that it facilitates social control. Even the innocuous phrase "the tasks of aging," popular among psychologists who study late life, implies that "old" is a tightly fitting identity with requirements imposed by others. "Task" is a good word for strivers and doers; it seems unsuitably standardized for a group as diverse as people over sixty-five or seventy, some of whom may live for another thirty years. The expectation that the old will be docile illustrates the coercion implicit in the category "old." When Celia Gill vigorously protested the introduction of plastic tablecloths in the nursing home where she lives, she was threatened with expulsion (Associated Press, January 10, 2002). Her age, ninety-four, was a key factor in her new notoriety.

Learning to be old means avoiding what British scholar Molly Andrews has called "the seductiveness of agelessness" (301–18). Being old has specific meanings. It can mean vulnerability to stereotyping, for example. But more positively, Andrews believes that "development is the project of a lifetime" and thus living to be old is an accomplishment (310).

This view of late life as unique is shared by Barbara Macdonald, Cynthia Rich, and Baba Copper.

Bill Bytheway sheds light on the problem of age as a category when, reporting on a group of English elders, he concludes that "even though they acknowledged a popular belief that age statuses are defined by chronological age, they actively resisted the application of these statuses to themselves" ("Age Identities," 474). When old people choose not to identify with their age group, their strategy may effectively exclude them from a negative social identity but "the dissociation may be psychologically harmful to the extent that they reject an important part of themselves" (Weiss and Lang, 162–63).

Whatever their personal feelings about "old," elderly people live in a society in which others will so designate them and the identity engulfs them. If the numerous, strong differences among people over sixty-five come into focus—differences of social class, education, income, political affiliation, health status, interests, degree of community involvement—"old" seems a fairly unimportant identity marker. This insight does not help me respond effectively when medical workers and others address me as "young lady." Elderly people delude themselves when they claim to be only as old as they feel; assuredly they are as old as their internal organs. In her account of participating in the film *Strangers in Good Company*, Mary Meigs writes that the old women in the film thought of themselves as "semi old," until the director's request for a nude swimming scene proved that they were really *old* (cited in Chivers, 92).

The author of *Old Maine Woman*, Glenna Johnson Smith, writes that she likes the "strong, earthy, honest sound of 'old woman'" (99) adding, "I suspect many of us can say hello to the mirror and admit that we live more comfortably with this less-than-perfect old face and body than we did with our teenaged or twenty-year-old selves" (100–101). "Old woman" is indeed strong, earthy and honest, and saying hello to the mirror with equanimity a goal for any woman.

Despite ambiguities associated with old as an identity, group consciousness among old women and men is highly desirable, because social change will not occur unless these members of a denigrated group identify with each other (Williams and Giles, 151). Thus the Older Women's League, Old Lesbians Organizing for Change, and the Gray Panthers make combating ageism their special agenda.[17] "Old" can be thought of as an affinity group rather than an identity. Such groups form, grow, dissolve, and spring to life again depending on circumstances. Within affinity groups, "old" can seem fluid and indeterminate, relevant to this situation or issue, irrelevant to that. It may not be necessary to take on "old" as an identity to feel completely at ease with one's physical appearance or the number of years one has lived. Much space exists between denying age and claiming it as an identity.

CONCLUSION

To be truly comfortable in old age one must have a keen perception of ageism—its prevalence, its destructive impact on self-esteem, and the particular harm it does to women. An ageist birthday card may seem funny to family and friends; a comic's joke on television or an older person's self-deprecating humor may seem amusing. On these apparently trivial words and commercial products, the scaffolding of ageist stereotypes holds firm. The prejudice implicit in these stereotypes obscures a fundamental truth: At sixty-five, a woman is "still in process" (Macdonald, 41). So also at eighty-five or ninety.

Ageism is a form of oppression that harms not only its targets but also those who express it (Laws, 11). An eloquent passage in *Over the Hill* elaborates this point:

Ageism screens communication between young and old women like a one-way mirror—the old can see the young, aided as they are by memories of their own youth, but the young cannot—or will not—see their future in old women. Sensing that vital information may be hidden on the other side of the mirrored surface, the young press their faces against the barrier, only to scan their own reflections nervously for the imperfections of age. The old, on the other side, watch with sadness, recognizing their own denial of aging in the young women's faces. (Copper, 57)

A similar theme is expressed by Evelyn Rosenthal when she writes that younger women "look past us and through us as if by denying our existence they will magically avoid growing old" (6). "Anti-aging" is not just a marketing slogan but a stance toward life.

A possible defense against the distortions of ageism and the shame it engenders is simultaneously seeing what age means to others and what it means to ourselves. If we experience continuity with our past selves and feel as worthy as before, dismissive judgments based on age may be less wounding. Conscious aging entails mindful resistance to stereotypes, those implicit in the increasingly popular "geezer," for example, a demeaning tag that insults men and erases women in one fell swoop. The study of age bias in numerous fields—sociology, psychology, economics, linguistics, consumer behavior, communications, and medicine (Wilkinson and Ferraro, 354)—may encourage change.

In the 1970s, Alex Comfort wrote that ageism is "not only idiotic but anachronistic, and the old to come will not acquiesce in it" ("Age Prejudice," 8). Will baby boomers live up to Comfort's expectation or will they find themselves engulfed in oppressive stereotypes? Ageism is probably too deeply rooted in American culture to be eradicated by mere population aging. Ageist stereotypes can be challenged by facts, but strategies to combat them may not change beliefs and behavior because powerful interests are served by ageist attitudes (Angus and Reeve, 141). If legislators and corporate leaders, for example, resist spending money on retraining workers over fifty, ageism benefits them.

The struggle against this injustice is worth pursuing, however, even if it presently concerns only a few. Like advocates for civil rights in the 1940s and defenders of women's equality in the 1950s, critics of ageism today find their voices drowned out. But better health, an analysis of ageism, a stronger drive for self-determination than their grandmothers could express, and the support of like-minded friends may inspire many old people, especially women, to accept their aging without shame or apology.

9

⚜

Countercultural
Gerontology

Previous chapters have shown that aging is far more than illness and loss, although these accompany aging for many people. In conventional thought, aging is not only a scary descent into decrepitude but aging people are unattractive. Mainstream gerontology has uncritically accepted the dominant biomedical view of aging according to which human aging requires medical intervention and the individual is the unit of analysis (Estes, Binney, and Culbertson, 51). This model is acceptable not because of its intrinsic merit but because of biomedicine's great power. The important problems of aging, rooted in issues of class, ethnicity, gender, politics, economics, and demographics, do not lend themselves to biomedical solutions (60). Furthermore, the biomedical model conveys the false impression that modern medicine alone is responsible for the longer and healthier lives of older people, ignoring the key role played by social improvements—in sanitation, housing, and education (Estes, Biggs, and Phillipson, 85).

But "there is a world elsewhere," as Coriolanus defiantly says when he is banished from Rome, the world of countercultural gerontology. Various strands of thought converge to create it. The term "countercultural gerontology" identifies both an attitude—skeptical, questioning, asking what is missing—and a body of work. Its components are humanistic gerontology, critical gerontology, and feminist gerontology (chapter 10 describes feminist gerontology). Countercultural gerontology resists fixed categories, certainties, and dictates about "successful" aging. Learning to be old does not require sustained study of aging, but some familiarity with countercultural gerontology may usefully equip one to age consciously and comfortably. This chapter describes humanistic gerontology and critical gerontology. It examines an important element of aging often overlooked by mainstream gerontology, prescribed busyness, and two of its antidotes, creativity and spirituality.

THE HUMANITIES

The humanities study meaning and interconnection and address complex questions that have no definitive answers (Kivnick and Pruchno). They include literature, philosophy, history, anthropology, cultural studies, religion, and art (both visual and performance). Although the phrase "the humanities" now includes interdisciplinary studies on gender and ethnicity as well as global issues, narrative social science, and legal theory, "the arts and humanities are still concerned with mysteries—those things that have no definitive explanation" (Cole, Ray, and Kastenbaum, 7). In fact, the mysterious aspects of aging are easily overlooked, for example in research purporting to explain Alzheimer's or in catalogues of healthy aging choices and more obviously, in "anti-aging" rhetoric.

Humanistic gerontology has been both corrective and illuminating—corrective in balancing ideas about aging set forth in the natural sciences and social sciences, illuminating in its new perspectives on aging. Humanities scholars argue that the "facts" about aging do not provide a neutral, objective understanding of late life, but rather a value-laden interpretation. A deep tension between the humanities and mainstream gerontology arises from the difference between "prediction and control versus interpretation and self-actualization" (Moody, "Humanities," 413).

The humanities seek to restore a spiritual and moral dimension to aging and to resist management of old age, concerned that many aging policies foster dependency and fail to nurture basic strengths (Moody, *Abundance*, 11). This insight is reinforced by anthropological studies, for without romanticizing pre-literate, pre-industrial societies, anthropologists show that Western societies have "dealt with aging far less directly and less satisfactorily than many simpler societies" and that in America, old people are a "dislocated group—societal refugees—structurally alienated and unabsorbed" (Myerhoff, "Aging," 107; 126). This summary helps to explain why old Americans are feared, why sickness is such an important role for many of them, and why busyness is culturally prescribed.

The humanities implicitly challenge prescriptions for aging based on materialism, for the "accumulated capital of a lifetime of human experience has no direct equivalent in the economic marketplace" (Hazan, 19). The "productive aging" model comes from this marketplace, but paradoxically it is not material enough, for it retreats from the material conditions of advanced old age. Someone with Alzheimer's, for example, can hardly be productive in a marketplace sense. Meaning for that person must therefore be found in more capacious views of aging.

Humanities scholars do not simply counter negative views of aging with positive ones—the pains, deprivations, and shriveling of the self that may accompany aging are starkly revealed in modern literature—but seek to move beyond the either/or thinking shown by the division of aging into positive and negative elements (Achenbaum, 426). This split occurs when writers, including feminist writers, contrast an old woman's diminished body with her spirit, always called "indomitable," as if the latter resides somewhere outside of her body. Another example is the supposed incompatibility of erotic power and old age, sometimes juxtaposed to highlight dissonance.[1]

Metaphors transcend limiting dualisms. Aging is a journey (Cole), an "abundance of life," (Moody), or a time of ripening. Aging is a kaleidoscope, its shifting images neither good nor bad. It is a mask that both hides and reveals identity (Hepworth, 28). In popular culture, toughened and wrinkled old skin is abhorrent. Metaphorically, such changes express "the greater intricacies, the finer articulations, that are possible in the person for whom reality has become multi-layered, folded upon itself, woven and richly textured, a reality no longer ordered in the familiar linear fashion, but now a world filled with leaps, windings, countless crossings, immeasurably more intricate and perhaps also more true than the world of one-dimensional thought" (Berg and Gadow, 226).

The contrast between a one-dimensional view of aging and a many-layered one is evident in the differences between two portraits of eccentric and "difficult" old women, Hattie in Saul Bellow's story "Leaving the Yellow House" and Flo in "Spelling" by Alice Munro. Both Hattie and Flo are surly and acrimonious, but Hattie is also repulsive and drunken.[2] In her, old age itself appears loathsome. Munro on the other hand elicits affection for Flo through a complex blend of humor and irony. Dementia is disruptive but does not make Flo grotesque.

In an interview recorded when she was in her late seventies, Munro offered this philosophical comment on aging:

> Now I am more conscious of the possibility that everything could be lost, that you could lose what filled your life before. Maybe keeping on, going through the motions, is what you have to do to keep this from happening. . . . This may be the beast that's lurking in the closet of old age—the loss of the feeling that things are worth doing. (*Paris Review* interview, 429)

Does late life illness or incapacity increase the risk that things no longer seem worth doing?

Regarding the loss of what filled your life before, Sherry Turkle writes that not long ago, people walked on beaches looking up "at the water, the sky, the sand, and at one another." Now they walk with heads down, texting.

Prescribed Busyness

The inequalities outlined in chapters 6 and 7 tell a story of aging, especially women's aging, often obscured in discussions of late life. What else is missing? An awareness that busyness has the force of a prescription for elders in this society. Just as they receive social approval for being sick and accepting sickness as their natural condition, they are expected (when not sick) to stay as busy as possible. Resistance to the path of illness and prescription drug dependency is easily justified because health is valued. With busyness, however, the defense is less obvious because lack of busyness can be equated with laziness, withdrawal from others, or lack of imagination. Women typically are busy for most of their lives. Late-life busyness may be a trap for them, however, encouraging age denial, numbing feelings, and keeping them in familiar grooves.

Learning to be old means following the direction "Be busy," for busyness is equated with worth, mental competence, and "successful" aging. When workers approach retirement, colleagues ask what they will do with their time, and later, the new retirees commonly report that they are as busy as ever. This accomplishment meets with social approval. Sitting around, doing nothing, having no plans, looking out the window for hours at a time are all frowned upon. To admit to not being busy invites suggestions for remedying this unfortunate condition. "We are busy people" is the boast of residents of Sun City, Arizona. There people "race with time" and "fill time so that they will not be swallowed by emptiness. And they avert their eyes when the ragged tooth marks of time begin to appear around the edges of a neighbor's mind or body" (Kastenbaum, 178).

Old women and men who keep busy resemble the young and the middle aged, at least in one respect. Busyness has nothing to do with frailty, disability, slowing down, dependence. It encourages emotional distance from those no longer able to boast of a crowded schedule. Perhaps the emphasis on busyness is a way of keeping the terror of aging at bay, as Kastenbaum's gloss on Sun City suggests. Busyness blocks recognition of one's future self as (possibly or probably) unable to be busy. It is a shield, even an amulet.

When Connie Goldman titled her series of radio interviews with artists over seventy "I'm Too Busy to Talk Now," she offered a positive image of late-life vigor and creativity, but behind the title lurks a shadow of a prescription: For a good old age, stay busy.[3]

A belief that the old are intrinsically worthy or that life beyond wage earning is intrinsically good runs counter to a belief that busyness is redemptive for them. Busyness is a utilitarian value. It is an unimaginative expectation to hold for people in late life. Accepting busyness allows one to overlook the possibility that old age has meanings not shared with midlife. In addition, by uncritically applauding busyness, gerontologists have reinforced a pragmatic view of aging and, until recently, have de-emphasized the possibilities of late-life spiritual development.

In Tennyson's famous dramatic monologue "Ulysses," the speaker values his former life of adventure at sea and chafes against his present idleness. Telling his companions that old age is a time for honor but also for toil, Ulysses urges them to set out with him once more. The lure is fresh experience and action itself:

> How dull it is to pause, to make an end,
> To rust unburnished, not to shine in use!

From the poetry of Victorian England to the pages of *Modern Maturity,* pausing is linked to rusting.

Activity and engagement differ from busyness in being more mindful and allowing space for inactivity and reflection. These broad descriptions are hard to apply to an individual's choices and schedule, of course; one person's level of activity would be far too busy for another. But a distinction can be made between busyness and the more purposeful and thoughtful engagement with life suggested by *Vital Involvements in Old Age,* the title of a book by Erik Erikson, Joan Erikson, and Helen Q. Kivnick (1986).

Prescribed busyness functions as social control. It is a hidden rule. Old women and men who hurry from one task or appointment to the next have no time to notice that their age group is disfavored or to ask what they have in common with other old people. What if no social approval accompanied a crowded schedule? Would older women and men stay busy then? Some would have to decrease their activity in response to health problems, loss of energy, or declining incomes. For others, leisure is not an option. Many more black women than white women remain in the labor force when they are aged sixty to sixty-five, for example.

A common justification for busyness is that it is healthy. For some, it may be true that staying in harness is healthy, but the health benefits of retirement are well documented. Robert Atchley found for example that walking for exercise was far more common among retirees than among people the same age who still worked, and he concluded that the false link between retirement and physical and mental harm serves to emphasize the value of work (*Social Forces,* 260).

Why is the idea that busyness is desirable so firmly rooted in our ideology of old age? It protects a person from suspicions that she or he may no longer be capable of busyness, and it "tames the potentially unfettered pleasures of retirement to prevailing values of engagement that apply to adulthood" (Ekerdt, 138–39). What are these unfettered pleasures and why must they be tamed?

We could have an "ethic of repose, with retirees resolutely unembarrassed about slowing down to enjoy leisure in very individual ways," says Ekerdt, or we could espouse an ethic of "hedonism, nonconformity, and carefree self-indulgence" as appropriate for late life (138–39). To choose either repose or happy hedonism in old age, Americans would have to throw off the Puritanism that underlies prescribed busyness and find value in being as well as in doing. Since this is unlikely to happen, options less extreme than either repose or hedonism would have to be encouraged.

As a supposedly desirable mark of aging well, busyness is related to gerontologists' prescriptions for "productive aging" discussed in the Introduction. At first glance, this worthy goal seems unassailable. Who would defend its opposite? Many years before the buzzword "productive aging" gained currency in gerontology, the anthropologist Margaret Clark noted, however, that "the value placed on work and productivity in our culture, and the implementation of this value through social sanctions, constantly impinge upon the aged individual's self-perception and a struggle for adaptation follows" (*Culture and Aging*, 17). Gerontologist and ethicist Martha Holstein has offered several other reasons for questioning this norm. Productive aging may come to be defined as paid work; it may reinforce traditional patterns of work inequality that have harmed women; and by setting a narrow standard for a meaningful life, productivity obscures the complexities of old age. In Holstein's view, emphasizing productivity can devalue the relationships women create as primary caregivers of the old and as recipients of care and "hide the creativity and moral integrity that are developed and realized in these relationships" ("Productive Aging," 26). Another danger is that the productivity model may discount those who are not vigorous and independent, thus intensifying the negative attitudes toward frail or impaired elderly citizens (27).

Moreover, older women are "least likely to be the 'gatekeepers'" who define productive aging and thus they risk living by others' norms (Holstein, "Women's Lives," 236–37). At the same time, it is they who can benefit most from a "reimagining of old age" (236). A woman who resists busyness, who moves to her own inner rhythms, need not find her self-worth through accomplishment. She may find pleasure in relaxing the ego drive that busyness often requires. But as Ram Dass observes, we Americans are uneasy in "retirement from achieving" (83).

Productivity interprets aging through values of growth, energy, activity, and accumulation when a broader vision is needed, one that stresses "altruism, citizenship, stewardship [and] creativity" (Moody, "Age," 36; 38). The latter do not require physical stamina to be enacted. As Theodore Roszak observes, productivity as an old-age ideal makes the loss of physical stamina especially frightening (108). Keeping busy creates an illusion of invulnerability and control that cannot be sustained. A human culture is only possible, writes Thomas Rentsch, if humans understand their lives not only in production, consumption, and domination of the natural world but also in "their materiality, corporeality, fragility, and vulnerability" (271). Busyness draws attention away from our vulnerability. In particular, it may deflect attention from subtle bodily changes that may or may not be significant.

Slowing down can only be seen as a problem in traditional, biomedically based gerontology, but suppose that slowing down is not primarily a symptom but an opportunity to be more attentive, so that we no longer "finish quickly with one experience in order to hasten on to the next" (Berg and Gadow, 225). The idea is not compensation for loss (although that may be a part of healthy aging) but opening to something not available before, stretching beyond one's past experience. Busyness has aptly been called "a hedge against emptiness," not an inevitable condition but something chosen (Tim Kreider, *New York Times* blog, June 30, 2012). Since even elders feel pressure to be productive and in tune with a fast-paced society, "downshifting and taking time for self [are] all the more important as a counter-balance" (Loe, *Aging Our Way*, 88).

It is useful nevertheless to relate productivity narrowly to aging because older workers are often pushed out of the labor market, and widespread layoffs and unemployment caused by jobs moving overseas have limited outlets for many workers over fifty to be productive. Paradoxically, older people are urged to stay busy while opportunities to be busy at paid work are decreasing, especially with the recession. To maintain a good self-concept in late life is difficult because social worth in our society depends on productivity, and elders find themselves "stripped of the power to freely produce" (Stannard, 13). The absence of a wide range of well-paid flexible jobs for people over sixty is a structural problem that is disguised as a personal problem when workers are told to retrain, adapt, accept lower wages, or take early retirement. Lack of opportunity to be productive in paid work is made worse by the inadequacy of lifelong learning programs, either academic or technical.

Volunteer work may preserve a self-image of usefulness. It is urged on older Americans as a way to keep busy, but as Baba Copper points out, projects needing the work of elders, especially of old women, are typically designed by others (86). In *Prime Time*, Marc Freedman predicts that volunteers of the future will expect to be in charge of activities rather than simply providing extra hands.

Models of "productive aging" or "good aging" are inherently coercive. Nearly always they are proposed by the non-old. Rather than illuminating aging they reveal the anxieties and needs of the non-old. In much gerontological writing, notes Margaret Urban Walker, late life meaning comes "either through 'productive aging' in which we keep 'busy' . . . or through a final project of life review" in which we "prove to ourselves and to others that at least we *were* socially acceptable persons before our adulthood expired" ("Getting Out of Line," 104)—that is, that we *used* to be busy.

An excellent study of retired women and volunteering shows the limits of social engagement as a norm for all elders. Volunteers who were interviewed found much satisfaction in their work. "Nonvolunteers" included women tired of taking care of others who wanted time for themselves. A third group, whose work in retirement was taking care of family members, deserved recognition as volunteers, in the view of the authors, but did not count their family work as volunteering. Retired women discover multiple ways to find meaning in later life (Nesteruk and Price). Another study agrees that the social engagement recommended in mainstream gerontology is too narrow; it overlooks the constraints on choices developed in previous decades (Rozanova, Keating, and Eales, 33). Thus the advice to age well by being engaged fits privileged older adults, not all elders. If a better message is not developed, marginalized groups may be blamed for their poor health (32–33).

If being old in America were seen as a natural process, models for doing it properly would be unnecessary. Some have proposed that the definition of productivity be expanded to include not just paid work but a wide range of socially beneficial activities (Alan Walker, 374). Caregiving would be an example. But as long as caregiving is uncompensated labor that women are expected to make large sacrifices in order to perform, calling it productive will not gain for it the respect given to paid work.

In her book *Be an Outrageous Older Woman*, Ruth Jacobs tells of a woman who expresses frustration at having scheduled events every night for two weeks. "Yet this same woman becomes anxious if her calendar is not filled" (98). Learning to be old means noticing whether a busy life is truly satisfying or simply conforms to social expectation. The old, knowing they are expected to be busy, will say they are (Ekerdt, 140–41). Nonstop activity can thus become a "professional and cultural ideal" that both conditions and pressures elders (S. Katz, *Cultural Aging*, 133).

Not surprisingly, some dissent from this orthodoxy. It may be hard to redirect one's focus in late life if hard work has been central to one's identity, but outgrowing busyness can be liberating and exhilarating. This discovery shapes "Just Desserts," a personal essay by Hila Colman in the *New York Times Magazine*. At eighty, she felt pressured by thinking of all the things she felt she had to do, or that others believed she should do: find a hobby, take classes, work out at a gym, devote money and time to looking younger than her age. Then she decides that her old age will be different from her youth because old age is a new experience. Not having commitments or demands on her time is a luxury. She resists inducements to become busy. "I am tired of being useful," she concludes. "This is my time to enjoy the quietness of just being, of stopping to look and feel and think, of indulging myself. Time for myself at last" (84).

This is hardly hedonism, simply healthy non-conformity. The expression of one woman's values, "Just Desserts" reflects the experience of many women who have worked hard all their lives taking care of families, responding to others' expectations, overtaxing themselves meeting multiple responsibilities. At some point, they want to stop. Another writer in her eighties who enjoyed "the quietness of just being" was Florida Scott-Maxwell. Written in the 1960s, her small book *The Measure of My Days* has become a classic. "Goals and efforts of a lifetime can be abandoned," she writes. "What a comfort. One's conscience? Toss the fussy thing aside. Rest, rest" (119).

Slowing down is seen negatively when it means only bodily change, but this dimension of aging is more complicated. "The great benefit of slowing down," writes Carl Honore, is "reclaiming the time and tranquility to make meaningful connections—with people, with culture, with work, with nature, with our own bodies and minds" (177). A mind-body connection is also recognized in the observation that late life is the time when "our being slows on all levels in order to experience situations and persons with more attentiveness and care than is possible when a youthful, fast-paced metabolism and an energetic, vigorous body inspire us to cover great distances at high speed, to finish quickly with one experience in order to hasten on to the next" (Berg and Gadow, 225). Maybe a purpose of late life, then, is to recover physically and psychologically from the busyness binge of the previous decades.

CREATIVITY

Another good antidote to prescribed busyness is creativity. The scholar most identified with the study of creativity and aging, the late geropsychiatrist Gene Cohen, defined creativity as "bringing something new into existence that is valued." Once researchers had distinguished late life illness from aging itself, the next step, according to Cohen, was considering "potential beyond problems," the best example of which is creativity. His

"Creativity and Aging Study" showed that sustained creative activities improved both mental and physical health (Creativity, 183–86). He believed that creativity is a "universal life force, a drive we are born with, built-in by evolution [that promotes] ongoing psychological growth throughout the life cycle" (185). Health promotion for elders works best, Cohen thought, when combined with creative activity (197). In his book *The Mature Mind: The Positive Power of the Aging Brain*, Cohen wrote that creativity may be triggered by the experience of loss, as new skills and talents become apparent (175).

It would be worthwhile to study the late-life creativity not of artists such as Kathe Kollwitz, Louise Nevelson, and Georgia O'Keefe, compelling as their stories are, but rather of women whose creativity could not flourish until they were in their seventies or eighties. It may take a lifetime for conventionally socialized women to throw off self-doubt and focus intently on whatever engages them. The ninety-year-old narrator of Doris Grumbach's powerful novel *Chamber Music* embodies the unexpected, emotionally deepening changes that may accompany old age. Creating in some form is a way past despair, bodily decline, or the absence of friends who have died. Drawing and painting, singing, gardening, laughing, breathing deeply, and being surprised all hold promise for our still-developing selves.[4]

Middle-class children have become overscheduled and subject to busyness pressures previously felt only by adults. They no longer roam about unsupervised or go long distances on their bicycles. Whatever these trends suggest about childhood, one meaning for the life course is clear: Late life is now the only period characterized by ample free time. The growth-inducing possibilities of contented idleness, disappearing from childhood and unattainable by most workers, will increasingly be found only among the old. Creative pursuits will be a long-deferred gratification. Creativity itself, among those whose primary work is not artistic or intellectual, may in time be associated with old people.

In *Composing a Further Life: The Age of Active Wisdom*, Mary Catherine Bateson writes that "aging today has become an improvisational art form calling for imagination and willingness to learn." Increased longevity will allow the discovery of unexpected possibilities (19). Bateson notes that women have always lived "discontinuous and contingent lives" (quoted in Friedan, 246). This is probably more true of heterosexual women than of lesbians, although many lesbians experience the discontinuities of motherhood, and older lesbians are likely to have gone through the discontinuity of closeted lives followed later by more open lives. How do life improvisations of women in their nineties differ from those of women in their seventies?

A good example of improvisation in a working-class setting is Mary Wilkins Freeman's story "A Mistaken Charity" (1887), in which sisters run away from an old-age home to which they have been sent. Middle-class norms of propriety and dress and unfamiliar food displease them.

Notions of creativity are rooted in a particular time and place, although playfulness appears to be a cross-cultural sign of creativity. In small-scale societies, the old may be expected to pass on what is known without any embellishment reflecting their individuality, as individuality is understood in large, technological societies. However we conceive of it, creativity is an important aspect of late life, and a useful antidote to prescribed busyness. Pondering the manifestations of creativity may help correct the cultural myth of aging as inevitable and total decline. A summary of research on creativity and aging by Beth Baker suggests that activities such as painting, singing, and writing convey health benefits, for example by stimulating the growth of new brain cells in the cerebral cortex (*Washington Post*, March 11, 2008). Singing benefits upper body muscles. It not only reduces stress and increases alertness but also speeds recovery from infections, heart attacks, and stroke, according to researchers at Canterbury Christ Church University (Fishman, 293).

Making new connections with one's past illustrates creativity. In an NPR interview, for example, Lisa Simeoni asked Alfred Brendel why he recorded works he had already recorded years ago (April 28, 2000). Going back to a Mozart sonata after a long time, he explained, can "start a new chain of experiences." Creativity is usually thought of as an individual trait, but it depends on opportunities for expression and on a receptive audience (Hendricks, "Creativity," 96). Alice Walker has said in interviews that as a child she thought of becoming a musician but her family had no money for a piano and then she thought of becoming an artist but there was no money for paints. Writing was within her means. Walker's landmark essay "In Search of Our Mothers' Gardens" pays tribute to old black women artists whose quilting and gardening nurtured their creative talent.

A dimension of creativity is playfulness, a trait associated with childhood but one that elders may value, as concern with what others think slips away. "With age can come a new feeling of inner freedom, self-confidence, and liberation from social constraints that allows for novel or bold behavior" (G. Cohen, "Creativity," 195). A good example is the Raging Grannies, a social activist group begun in Victoria, BC, that now has chapters in more than fifty Canadian cities and towns and one in New York City. They deliberately play off stereotypes of old women. The Grannies create street theater, parodies of songs, and antiwar chants and they wear outrageous costumes and hats (Caissie).[5] In late life, the earnestness of one's earlier pursuits may seem overwrought, given a sharpened awareness that all paths lead to the grave. When playful, we are fully in the present moment and unselfconscious, and often this side of ourselves appears only with intimates (or, as with the Raging Grannies, in group solidarity). The t-shirt illustration of a stick figure hiking with the caption: "Aging: the Ultimate Extreme Sport" shows a playful attitude toward late life. The Dalai Lama's playful spirit is one of his most engaging characteristics.

SPIRITUALITY

Another good antidote to the busy ethic is an awareness of spiritual values. By "spirituality" I mean attitudes, beliefs, and practices expressed privately or in small groups, independent of formal religious institutions, or an inner awareness of meaning that transcends the ordinary. Baby boomers speak of "spirituality" while older generations prefer the word "religion" (Coleman, 168) but the words differ somewhat. Atheists, for example, or pagans, may embrace spirituality. In his book *Spirituality and Aging*, Robert C. Atchley explores these questions: how does spirituality manifest itself in everyday life? What does it mean to grow old spiritually? How does spirituality affect identity and self? In *Still Here*, a book full of insights about aging and spirituality, Ram Dass asks, "What has all this been about?" and "Where am I in the flow of all this?" The old in America think they are supposed to keep busy, he notes, but "slowing down, drawing in, can open us to some of the most fruitful experiences of life" (52).

In "Touch of Grey," Olivia Ames Hoblitzelle writes that considering the possibility that the aging process has a sacred dimension is both "countercultural and radical." We find time precious, for example (28). For Buddhists, aging consciously "involves staying open to the sometimes harsh realities of what's happening to the body-mind. It is also about knowing what our inner resources are, and what will sustain and keep us inspired as we meet the challenges of later life" (29).

Gerontologists have linked church participation to psychologically healthy aging, but evidence linking the two is "far from overwhelming." On the other hand, some studies provide evidence that religious people live longer than the non-religious (Coleman, 52). Does religion take on a distinctive character or meaning in old age? Research to date gives mixed results (Dillon). In discussing the notion that religion benefits older people, Moody and Sasser note that correlation is not causation (32). More certain is that Christian ministers can be "surprisingly ageist" about older people's need for "spiritual sustenance and challenge," and in their focus on attracting the young (Coleman, Mills, and Speck, 134). A problem in studying religiosity and spirituality is the assumption that these are fixed, stable characteristics. Some people feel loyal to a religion but question it (Coleman, 28).

From a spiritual perspective, the pressure we can feel to be "instantaneous and concise . . . interferes with our ability to listen to ourselves and discover what we care about" (Haney, 47–48). Consciously listening to ourselves, as for example in meditation, has demonstrable benefits. In fact, this practice improves brain function both psychologically and neurologically. Meditation training allows people to "respond reflectively rather than habitually or automatically" (Newberg, 86), a shift that deepens breathing.

The social networks provided by churches are perhaps as beneficial as religious belief itself.[6] Unitarians, Quakers, and black churchgoers seem especially supportive of the old. Ruth Jacobs reports in *Be an Outrageous Older Woman* that after her divorce she found that all of the activities at her church were organized for couples. In her new Quaker group, by contrast, she feels like a "full-status person, not a second-class person" (98). Even though churchgoing is far from universal in America, gerontologists tend not to study old agnostics, atheists, pagans, witches, or people who have left congregations and synagogues to find their own spiritual paths.

The confluence of aging and spirituality has several sources. Since the 1970s, humanities scholars have published work speculating on the meanings of age.[7] Second, within mainstream religions awareness of the aging of congregations has led to programs and publications linking spirituality to aging. Examples are the Institute of Spirituality and Aging, founded in 1992 and affiliated since 1994 with the Graduate Theological Union in Berkeley, and the Center for Aging, Religion, and Spirituality at Luther Seminary in St. Paul founded by Rev. Mel Kimble. A third influence has been the proliferation of groups growing out of the Spiritual Eldering Institute founded in Philadelphia in 1986 by Rabbi Zalman Schachter-Shalomi, now known as the Sage-ing Guild, and "Conscious Aging" programs sponsored by the Omega Institute for Holistic Studies.[8] The popularity of "conscious aging" has been related to the aging of participants in alternative movements of the 1960s (Atchley, *Social Forces*, 294). The Forum on Religion, Spirituality, and Aging of the American Society on Aging (ASA), a national, multidisciplinary group, holds an annual conference and links participants through ASA's website. In addition to these groups are others hard to document, for they consist of spontaneously forming friendship groups among old women and men interested in the spiritual dimension of aging.

Also contributing to interest in aging and spirituality are New Age beliefs, feminist spirituality, American Buddhism, and the various mind-body techniques associated with Esalen, such as humanistic psychology, massage, and altered states of consciousness. Although the term "New Age" has become so elastic as to be nearly meaningless except as a marketing tag, the phenomenon has profoundly altered many Americans, especially in the middle class, and will undoubtedly shape the ways they age. Whatever techniques or practices they espouse, those influenced by New Age beliefs look for meaning that busyness cannot provide.

Those who have adopted spiritual practices identified as Native American have been rebuked for cultural appropriation, however. Indian writers such as Beth Brant, a Mohawk, who link nineteenth-century theft of their land with theft of their religion today, make a powerful moral claim. Whites drawn to the cosmology and ceremonies of Native Americans understandably seek something meaningful, but they can never recreate the context in which the beliefs, rituals, and practices are rooted. Certainly, respect for elders is one feature of Native American culture that others wish were part of their own. In an unusual instance of bridging cultures, some elderly Navajo in Arizona spend summers with their families on reservations and winters in nursing homes.

A spiritual approach to aging recognizes the elements of mystery and ambiguity in the process, sees the futility of struggling against it, and challenges us to find value in growing old (Holstein and Waymack, 198). This may be hard for women who have garnered praise for beautiful bodies and youthful appearance. A study of older Swedish women found that although they commented negatively on bodily changes, they felt pride in their bodies when dressed in their best clothes (Krekula, 165).

In feminist spirituality, the central place of old women is recognized, for it was they who lost influence in the rise of patriarchal religion. Writers such as Charlene Spretnak and Starhawk explore pre-Christian spiritual traditions in which women are honored. Feminist spirituality has strong links to the environmental movement, and feminists revere Hildegard of Bingen, the medieval German mystic, healer, abbess, composer, writer, and visionary ecologist. Feminists value Hildegard's concept of "greening power," a translation of "viriditas" by Matthew Fox.[9]

A counter to prescribed busyness is the idea that aging is a time for personal growth. An "often invisible gift of age," writes Martha Holstein, is the freedom "to discover ways to flourish that are personally satisfying" ("Women's Lives," 240). Growth may be construed as a spiritual or moral task; so it is for May Sarton's Caro Spencer in *As We Are Now*, who says, after being put in a nursing home, "I intend to make myself whole here in this hell" (4). She wants to avoid the "corroding impurity" of the rage she associates with suicide (13). Personal growth may seem suitable to late life when a person has fewer responsibilities, has less ego need to be competitive, is less constrained by the opinion of others, and is motivated by the knowledge that time is short (Kalish, 126). Some old women are still caregivers, however, and when those they care for have dementia, the responsibility is heavy.

Personal growth is an aspect of aging comfortably. For some it may mean that racist, sexist, homophobic, or fat-phobic messages lose some of their power to wound. The death of a critical or authoritarian parent or spouse may allow an older person to grow into greater self-acceptance. Or a caregiver may feel compassion for the first time for a parent whom she now experiences as vulnerable. Whatever form growth takes, many artists and writers see aging as "becoming oneself" (Rentsch, 263). Extremely busy lives leave scant room for that quest. At the end of an engrossing story of escape from calcified systems of belief and practice, from a "universal viewpoint," Don Hanlon Johnson writes, "Now I could relax into particularity" (219). That phrase sums up what aging might be.

Both *The Miracle of Mindfulness* by Thich Nhat Hahn and *Mindfulness* by Ellen Langer describe the value of paying attention and living in the present moment. This practice allows one to face the slow physical decline usual to aging. Not necessarily to *accept* it, although for some, acceptance of this change is part of a spiritual practice. In her essay "Aging as a Russian Doll," Leonore Friedman writes, "If we don't spin stories of failure and humiliation, what's happening is not a private, personal tragedy, but just what's happening in the great scheme of things" (77). One can practice mindfulness at any age, of course, but busyness is an obstacle for paid workers, parents, caregivers, and others. Retirement or a change to part-time work may be the occasion for adopting a spiritual practice such as meditation, unless non-work life becomes as busy as working life used to be. Meditation helps improve brain function both psychologically and neurologically. This training enables people to "respond reflectively rather than habitually or automatically" (Newberg, 86), a healthy response at any age. The sense of having enough time is a luxury in our society. Practices that change our relationship to time help us become aware that busyness is often self-inflicted. Undeveloped parts of the self may send out faint signals when we make time for quieting down and reflecting.

Silence is part of spirituality. People now over seventy must remember well a time when noise was less polluting, no boom boxes or Blue Angels roaring overhead, no blaring television commercials, no beepers going off in concerts or movies, no jet skis, ATVs, or leafblowers, no Muzak accompanying "please hold." Retreating from the assault of noise is challenging at a time when farmland falls to developers and hillsides are flattened by construction. Few Americans can easily get to totally quiet places. For an old woman or man who has lost a partner, silence must be desolating. And between spouses who have been unhappily together for decades, silence is neither calming nor comforting. But for the old who choose to turn inward to reflect on the meanings of their experience, silence is welcome. Silence restores the psychic energy that busyness depletes. It brings surprising (and sometimes unwelcome) insights. Healing touch offered in silence is a rare gift. In old age, if we have no family or friends nearby to turn to, silence can be a protector.

Late-life spirituality has been viewed as a compensation for loss of physical strength and mobility, but that is a limited notion, separating mind from body. Spirituality is rooted in the body, especially in breathing. Any breath work is useful to the old because our respiratory systems tend to weaken as we age. Focusing on the breath allows us to become more aware of our natural body rhythms and the relationship of parts of the body to each other. Asian practices now popular in America such as tai chi and qi gong encourage mind-body unity, as do yoga, meditation, and the various bodywork methods described in chapter 5.

Spirituality grounded in the body requires frankness about decline and loss of capacity. To speak of this honestly, writes Barbara Hillyer, an old woman "must defy the cultural prescription of false cheerfulness." Details such as fear of falling and fear of sight or hearing loss will counter our expectation "that an old feminist continues to be superwoman or is always optimistic about her aging" (55). After Doris Grumbach published her memoir *Coming into the End Zone*, some readers complained that she had been too negative when she reported signs of physical decline (*Extra Innings*, 126–27). They wanted a favorite author to filter out the bad news.

A tendency among some old women and men to pare down to essentials may reflect spirituality, whether it is manifested in an ordinary way such as giving away possessions or moving to a smaller home or apartment or more interiorly by shedding old prejudices, grievances, antipathies, or competitive feelings with siblings. If one likes slowing down and being quiet, worldly goods matter little. The mall may appear a surreal circus. Lightening our load of accumulated possessions goes along with turning inward, not to tune out the external world but rather to lessen its intrusiveness. When this happens, one develops a heightened sense of integrity, in the old meaning of completeness. This impression is conveyed by writers over eighty such as Doris Grumbach, Florida Scott-Maxwell, and M. F. K. Fisher.

Learning to be old means noticing that where materialism sets the tone, determines priorities, and assesses meaning, the old lose value. Moving quickly is so valued in our culture, for example, that old women and men typically apologize when they are aware of moving more slowly than others. How could old women using canes or walkers believe their pace is not inferior, only different? What subtle harm does the speeded-up quality of much of American life cause the old? Appropriate to late life is "a consciousness of the value of slowness, of pausing, of calmly looking backward" (Rentsch, 271). Whether or not such values are associated with spirituality, their psychological benefit seems obvious.

Without an awareness of spiritual values, it is hard to connect the youth-worshipping materialism of American culture with the corresponding denigration of the old. Nineteenth-century American writers worried about the production/consumption model overtaking the ideals of the founders. The Transcendentalists, for example, linked conformity to materialism. Walt Whitman proposed that emotional bonds between men might create spiritual values as a counterweight to dehumanizing industrialism. Margaret Fuller believed that democracy could flourish only through women's cooperative energy, "self-dependence," regard for old women, and respect for citizens of diverse backgrounds (Avallone, 140).

In recent decades, big business has pushed itself into spheres that were formerly somewhat independent of it: education, the arts, national parks. If you admire the view at Mirror Lake in Yosemite today, for example, you stand near a sign announcing that a major oil company gave money to the park. "Corporations are remaking our public institutions and space" (Schor, 9). What all of this means for old women and men is that the values of commerce are now even more pervasive in American society than they were in the time of Whitman, Emerson, Thoreau, and Fuller, and that the materialism that tends to devalue the old is even more rampant than it was in the nineteenth century or even a decade ago.

A counterweight to this devaluation is offered by gerontologist Lars Tornstam: "gerotranscendence." Among its elements are increased feelings of connection to past and coming generations; increased awareness of a cosmic life force; decreased interest in superficial social contacts; decreased interest in material goods; and decreased self-centeredness (41). These attributes may well be found among elderly people compared to those who are middle-aged, but the assertion that gerotranscendence is universal and culture free (45) seems highly questionable, especially since the research on which the concept rests was limited to Swedish and Danish subjects. Advantages of the theory of "gerotranscendence," on the other hand, are that it seeks characteristics of old age that distinguish it from midlife and that it is free of the judgments implicit in "successful aging."[10]

The sheer number of older people now living emphasizes a spiritual dimension to life or at least a non-material dimension. A significant part of the population is no longer caught up in the production of goods and services, in the cycle of "getting and spending" as Wordsworth succinctly described life in the industrial age. Therefore the meaning of their lives must be more than material. Otherwise, they are simply drags on everyone who does produce. Many believe this, of course, for example proponents of rationing health care for old adults. They do not see either the economic value of the informal, unpaid work performed by many older persons, especially old women, or the more abstract value of their friendships, knowledge, and life experience. Individuals who are old naturally see value in their own lives and regard their continued existence as desirable, but they are aging in a society that undervalues anyone deemed unproductive. By conspicuously not working, elders implicitly challenge the very great value placed on work in our society.

CRITICAL GERONTOLOGY

Gerontology covers a wide territory, from cells to organs to individual aging to large populations across continents. Gerontologists work in many disciplines, but they lack a unifying core of knowledge and models of interdisciplinary research (Estes, Binney, and Culbertson, 50). In popular usage, gerontology and geriatrics (the study of late-life diseases) are sometimes synonymous terms, so that the distinction between old-age illness and old age itself is blurred.

Mainstream gerontology, explicitly or implicitly, focuses on management of the aging process, whereas critical gerontology offers interpretations marked by tentativeness, contradictions, and contingencies, insights leading to a sense of possibilities rather than management. To that extent it exemplifies postmodern thought.

Critical gerontology brings perspectives from economics, the social sciences, feminism, and the humanities to bear on aging. Beginning in the late 1970s and becoming especially prominent in the past decade, critical gerontology is essential because mainstream gerontology's hidden assumptions and value-laden interpretations mask issues of power, class, ethnicity, and gender. Critical gerontology not only questions conventional ways of thinking about age but also the discipline of gerontology itself (Zeilig, 8). At its heart is the understanding that "we need to change our minds about what 'age' can be" (30). Critical gerontology challenges the primacy of quantitative studies in aging, incorporates historical and philosophical perspectives on late life, and analyzes the influence of cultural images of aging (Ray, "Coming of Age"). In these ways, it broadens the scope of gerontology.

Critical gerontology has been described as a "thought-space, a magnetic field where thought collects, converges, and transverses disciplines and traditions," a description that intentionally suggests fluidity, for "theoretical instability and indeterminacy" are its strengths (Stephen Katz, *Cultural*, 86; 91). If mainstream gerontology is a lumbering elephant, critical gerontology and feminist gerontology are the nimble gazelles in the same territory. Although the two are closely related, seeing them as distinct is useful because only feminist gerontology makes women's issues central. Studies of health issues specific to old women and studies of old women's attitudes toward their bodies are more likely to come from feminist scholars. Only they will tackle the problem of the shame, even revulsion, that some, perhaps many, old women feel at the sight of their bodies. Critical gerontologists have taken the lead on globalization as it relates to aging but feminist scholars now investigate it as well (see chapter 10 for feminist gerontology and globalization).

Political economy, a springboard for critical gerontology, examines the role of capitalism and the state in building systems of "domination and marginalization of old people" (Estes, "Theoretical," 231). Estes coined the phrase "the aging enterprise" to denote all of the service providers, agency workers, policymakers and other professionals who foster dependency in old people and exert control over them ("New Political Economy," 25). Critical gerontologists examine institutions that reproduce power arrangements and inequalities in society and serve their own interests (Estes, Biggs, and Phillipson, 21). Influenced by Foucault's writings and aware that issues of power and domination are seldom addressed in mainstream gerontology, critical gerontologists ask how old people are managed and what forms their resistance to management takes. Older Americans are often "processed and treated as a commodity" by age policies that segregate, stigmatize, and isolate them (Estes, *Aging Enterprise*, 2). Are the helping professions now less involved in direct social care and more involved in surveillance? (Powell, 671). Critical gerontology questions the intrusion of the market in areas such as care, where "it doesn't fit and so does harm" by becoming instrumental and task-driven rather than person-centered care (Holstein, "Ethics and Old Age, 638). Market-driven intrusions retain the language of person-centered care, however.

Political economy usefully balances the "previous overconcentration on individual adjustment" and calls attention to the unequal impact of state policies on different groups of older citizens (Alan Walker, 69; 72). It also refutes the notion that population aging will inevitably lead to fiscal crisis (S. Katz, "Critical," 9). Critical gerontology offers a "vision of what is possible" (Estes, Biggs, and Phillipson, 152).

One possibility, according to moral economy, is reciprocity. The mutually beneficial relationships of elderly people with others were noted in chapter 2. Moral economy challenges the view that the individual is an "autonomous moral agent" (Robertson, 85), considers obligations as well as rights, and takes questions of need out of the marketplace where they are commodified (86). An accurate picture of the transfer of wealth between generations might show aging parents keeping an unemployed daughter or son "afloat in the swirling waters of the global economy"

(Roszak, 38). Without a framework of reciprocity, elderly persons are typecast as economic burdens.

A problem in mainstream gerontology is that diversity is seen as relating to a particular group rather than involving a power relationship between oppressed and privileged groups (Calasanti, "Incorporating Diversity," 155). Research on difference makes the dominant group the unacknowledged norm, while research that asks why groups are divergent "relates the dominant group to racial/ethnic groups and all groups to each other" (148). (Cultural diversity is discussed in chapters 6 and 7.)

A study of women's retirement in conventional gerontology might stress individual responsibility, while critical gerontology asks what structures make it difficult for many women to accumulate savings over decades of work. A life satisfaction study might conclude that travel contributes to well-being in late life, whereas a critical gerontologist would note the class bias underlying such a finding. Measurements in life satisfaction studies convey a sense of linear time and assume that subject and questioner share the same understanding of life satisfaction. Measurements cannot reveal the "multiplicity of life"; they overlook social ties, and they view subjects' lives as completed (Gubrium and Lynott, 31–37). Aging can be thought of as "non-linear, simultaneous loss-gain" (Manheimer, "Wisdom," 435). Such a perception of time would make conventional testing and measurement difficult, and these have been important to gerontology because the discipline has presented itself as "hard" like science, not "soft" like the social sciences and the humanities. [11]

Social stratification processes set old people apart; thus a critical analysis is needed to uncover "how such processes happen and how they might be changed" (Vincent, "Globalization," 268. *How they might be changed*— here the social justice concern of critical gerontology is apparent.

Critical gerontologists challenge the dominant biomedical model of aging that conceives of human conditions as requiring medical intervention and makes the individual the unit of analysis (Estes, Binney, and Culbertson, 51). Mainstream gerontology has uncritically accepted this model not because of its intrinsic merit but because of biomedicine's great power. The important problems of aging, rooted in issues of class, ethnicity, gender, politics, economics, and demographics, do not lend themselves to biomedical solutions (60).

Critical gerontologists question the so far unchallenged central place of prescription drugs in aging. A good place to start would be demanding that the FDA reinstate its ban on television drug advertising. The United States and New Zealand are the only countries that allow this dubious practice. Much more work needs to be done on the connection between prescription drugs and falls. Drug-induced lethargy, confusion, or dizziness erodes the power of old people.

Critical gerontology questions how much of our understanding of dementia is biological and how much results from "social interpretation and framing" (Holstein, Parks, and Waymack, 221).

Within a biomedical framework, aging problems result from bodily decline or the failure of individual adjustment, not from state policy or social inequality (Townsend, 19). Significantly, concepts of adaptation or adjustment are applied not only to elders but also to children, the sick or disabled, immigrants, prisoners, and rehabilitated criminals (Hazan, 21). Studies of individuals can be illuminating, however, if they tell how people "resist rather than succumb to the pressures associated with growing old" (Phillipson, *Reconstructing Old Age*, 139).

Both gerontologists and aging policymakers have heralded "productive" aging and "successful" aging as strategies for social acceptance of elderly persons, but critical gerontology and feminist gerontology ask what assumptions underlie such positive-sounding terms. Individual responsibility and work, undergirders of successful aging and productive aging, omit much that makes late life valuable, and leave behind individuals whose bad luck, class disadvantage, hard physical labor over decades, or lack of time for knowledge of self-care make "successful" or "productive" aging meaningless except as attempts to lift stigma from old age. Hidden in these phrases is the assumption that we control our own aging and thus have a duty to maintain ourselves in ways that require a minimum of state support. They reveal either/or and hierarchical mindsets (Holstein and Minkler, 791). The now-popular "anti-aging medicine" has similar limitations (Holstein, "Feminist Perspective"). Striving for these ideals requires self-discipline and self-monitoring on the part of the old person, whereas loosening up requirements imposed from the outside may free old women and men to age consciously and creatively on their own terms.

Traditionally, gerontology has been grounded in positivism, the philosophy of knowledge based on observable phenomena that can be measured. Under its influence, gerontology has focused on aging as disease or deficiency (Manheimer, "Wisdom and Method," 427). In contrast, critical gerontology claims that the nature of scientific data cannot be separated from subjective elements such as the researcher's point of view (Lynott and Lynott, 301). In other words, knowledge is variable, relative, subject to different interpretations, and facts pass through our "perceptual filters" (Hendricks, "Generations," 32), which include our ideas, research methods, and politics (Hendricks and Achenbaum, 33). In place of the certainties of positivism are a recognition of pluralism, fragmentation, cultural diversity, and subjectivity (Polivka and Longino, 198).[12]

As chapter 7 argues, our perceptual filters often obscure the meanings of class, ethnicity, and especially gender in aging. In surveys assessing elders' attitudes, making future plans is equated with good morale and mental health, for example, but the capacity for planning implies sufficient resources and control over one's life, characteristic of middle-class people, not those who are just getting by. Similarly, the researcher may design a questionnaire that assumes age is a primary status when that is not the case for many blacks, Chicanos, Asian Pacific Islanders, and American Indians, for whom survival is the main concern (Dressel, Minkler, and Yen, 280).

Critical gerontology and feminist gerontology share the goal of freeing old persons from political, economic, and social domination. Both aim to shed light on the subtly coercive messages that tell old adults how to be old and consign them to a fixed category. Both contest the paradigm of loss that influences much mainstream gerontology, a skewed and partial perspective. "To contest loss is not to dismiss it, or deny it as an experience," according to medical anthropologists Janice E. Graham and Peter H. Stephenson. "Rather, it means confronting, questioning, adapting, negotiating, incorporating, and at times surmounting it in ways that confer meaning onto life" (xv). Critical perspectives on aging such as this one are especially beneficial for women because longer lives may be disproportionately influenced by social structures, flawed assumptions underlying research, overemphasis on loss, and attempts to privatize either Social Security or Medicare.

Taken together, the work cited here in the humanities and critical gerontology and the social science scholarship influenced by the humanities is the most vital theoretical force in gerontology today. With feminist gerontology it has the potential to transform the way North Americans think about aging. But two large obstacles stand in the way: The humanities have so far had little influence on gerontology as a whole, and their practitioners have yet to find a large, public audience. The ten-year MacArthur Foundation study of aging excluded humanities specialists (Achenbaum, 425–26). Moreover, when journalists or television interviewers need comment on some aging issue, they turn to doctors, scientists, government officials, or demographers, not to philosophers, critics, or artists (430). Thus one-dimensional views of aging are perpetuated. Learning to be old requires at least as much familiarity with the humanities as with the social sciences.

CONCLUSION

An increasing number of Americans will live twenty-five or thirty years in retirement, an opportunity for meaningful leisure and enjoyment that their parents and grandparents could not have imagined. Instead of responding to this demographic change with a set of values appropriate to late life, however, we have only midlife's emphasis on work and productivity. Unwisely, by "celebrating efficiency, productivity or power, we subordinate any moral claim for the last stage of life in favor of values that ultimately depreciate the meaning of old age" (Moody, "Age," 34). This is not only shortsighted but manifestly sexist if "productive aging" becomes a rationale for weakening public support of the oldest old, the poorest of whom are usually women (Holstein, "Women's Lives," 240). Through the humanities we gain "clarity out of the chaos . . . and immeasurable complexity we face as human beings" (Whitehouse and George, 300). Nowhere is this complexity and the need for clarity more evident than in old age.

What would constitute a moral claim for the last stage of life? One component could be a belief that the survival of many to old age is intrinsically good, like the infinite variety and abundance of the natural world (at least before species began to disappear at an accelerated rate). The long-lived whose talents have fully flowered show the rest of us something about human potential. At any age we benefit from contact with those in whom the life force is very strong. As recently as twenty years ago, the full spectrum of life was not as apparent as it is today. Long-term emancipation from work offers possibilities for growth, pleasure, enjoyment, and awareness now barely imaginable. Without that hope, old age is still inherently good, even allowing for all of the misery and degradation that often accompany it. To accept the proposition that old age is intrinsically good it is not necessary to hold religious views. A moral claim for the last stage of life must clearly separate aging from disease. The despair of some old women and men who are chronically ill or cut off from others seems a natural response to their hopeless situation, but that has been misread as a reason to devalue old age itself.

The insights of the humanities and critical gerontology deepen the meanings of old age available through science and social science. Robert Butler described lengthening lives as "the triumph of survivorship" (Butler and Lewis, xv). His word suggests a good, like friend*ship* or fellow*ship* and it connotes luck. "Survivorship" also suggests some action on our part. Each human who reaches eighty is a model of regeneration and adaptation. In *Healthy Aging*, Andrew Weil calls wrinkles and white hair "banners of survivorship" (115).

Centenarians tend to be resilient, mellow, and positive, often surprised by lasting as long as they have and amused by their singularity. So much threatens human life at every turn that mere survival surely deserves to be celebrated. Whatever survivorship means in the future as more people attain it, busyness is too limited a value to have a central place in its definition. It fits only the hearty survivors and ultimately even they will fail to live up to it. Behind the busy ethic is the secret wish that midlife will extend indefinitely.

With its scope, expansiveness, and blurred boundaries, countercultural gerontology offers not only challenge and resistance but new ways of thinking about aging, for example the convictions that "aging is a time of life that is as integral to our personal evolution as any other," and that elders, including those who are frail, enrich our society (Hadler, 172). A present-day manifestation of the sometimes utopian American visions of a better life, countercultural gerontology harks back to the protest movements beginning in the 1960s and earlier to the Transcendentalists. It fosters conscious aging, marked by resilience, adaptations to physical change, interdependence, and a playful, creative spirit. Fear of the unknown and uncontrollable is natural, and attempts to ward it off through busyness are understandable. But the inexorable process of change sweeps away our protective cover of busyness and deposits us, ready or not, at the border of old age.

10

✣

A Feminist's View
of Gerontology and
Women's Aging

Teaching courses on women's aging at the University of Maine and the University of Southern Maine made me keenly aware of different placements along the life course. For my students, even those who are middle-aged, old age is far off, like a trip to Mars. For me it is as imminent as the next baseball season. Classes like mine are unusual; I hope they will become more common. After all, age gets much attention in our society. How bizarre it would seem if one of my students did not know her age. On the other hand, age denial and other forms of ageism described in chapter 8 will persist, despite baby boomers' confidence that their cohort is entering a new era of aging. For now, a certain curious, contrarian temperament may be required to look squarely at late life, especially through the lens of gender.

In class we note that the labels "young" and "old" determine who has more and less power. Apparently we do not take on the identity "old"; it befalls us and requires others to give it meaning. Like gender, aging can be performed. I perform this identity when I repeatedly take the elevator to class, while students use the stairs. Older than some of their grandmothers, I wear clothes not so different from theirs but feel an age gulf when talk turns to popular culture.

As I expound the social construction of aging, I wonder if I should not instead be speaking of leaky bladders, impaired night vision, and morning stiffness. I shrink from such personal revelations, but in an effort to demystify women's aging, I come to the first class session wearing shorts and a tank top so that I can comment in some detail about what happens to aging bodies. Students pay rapt attention as I display a beginning dowager's hump, flesh falling away from upper arms, and age spots. Some students look embarrassed when I mention thinning pubic hair. "How did they like your cellulite?" a colleague asks afterward. While I take seriously students' fears of aging, I want gently to help them detach from fear by showing them a body neither trim nor athletic that is fine. "You'll save a lot of money when you no longer need tampons," I tell them.

Honesty requires my acknowledgment that I would like to have their metabolism, vision and hearing, taut skin, and thick foot padding, but for me the pleasures of being my age far outweigh the physical disadvantages.

In class we consider how old women become the Other when we feel emotional distance from them and imagine big differences between us. An old woman becomes old not by any words or gestures, necessarily, but simply by having projected onto her younger women's culturally shaped notions of what old is. Her statements may be evaluated by younger women as being progressive "for her age," for example, or she may be seen as walking vigorously "for her age." Younger women may express surprise that she "still" bikes or hikes.

After considering women's studies' neglect of aging, this chapter gives overviews of feminist gerontology and narrative gerontology and then examines issues relevant to women's aging not covered in previous chapters.

WOMEN'S STUDIES

Why are old women missing persons in women's studies at a time when nearly all of its founders are over sixty-five? Reproductive issues, workplace inequality, multicultural issues, and violence against women have claimed our attention during the past thirty years. Another reason why women's studies has not taken on aging issues is that academic gerontology is a small field compared to sociology, literature, history, psychology, and anthropology, where feminists have long been influential. Most of those who work in the field of aging are women, but that majority in itself has not ensured a feminist viewpoint, and thus far the benefits of collaboration between women gerontologists and women's studies faculty have not been realized. Another possible reason for age avoidance is that to confront aging would require us to acknowledge likeness to our mothers, rather than the radical difference we exulted in. We suffer from "mother flu," writes Natalie Angier, adding, "We daughters, like pit vipers, have nonretractable fangs" (254).

Moreover, aging indisputably changes bodies, and we in women's studies have not wanted to locate too much meaning in bodies. If anatomy is not destiny, neither should biology be destiny. From Mary Woll-stonecraft forward, feminists have argued that women's inferior status comes not from our bodily differences from men but rather from custom and tradition. Given the need to find explanations outside of bodies, we in women's studies have averted our gaze from women over sixty, even if we are over sixty ourselves. Although aging, like gender, is socially constructed and culture determines the meanings we ascribe to physical changes, bodies matter.

Women's studies students and professors, like others, are influenced by academic fashions, and aging is emphatically not a trendy subject. We may unconsciously avoid the topic, knowing that old people, especially women, are stigmatized. Internalized ageism may afflict us, in other words. Like others, feminists resist physical changes and the diminishment of our social power, and thus aging has not seemed to be a promising subject for study (Arber and Ginn, *Gender*, 30). Irrational terror of female aging casts a long shadow, writes Baba Copper. It divides generations and "robs women of the continuity of identity necessary for successful feminist resistance" (55). Irrational fear is harder to examine in the classroom than wage discrimination or abortion.

Articles on old women rarely appear in periodicals aimed at a women's studies audience or in our texts, and old women are still marginalized at women's studies conferences. A notable, valuable exception is the Aging and Ageism issue of the *NWSA Journal* (National Women's Studies Association), edited by Leni Marshall (Spring 2006).

Betty Friedan laid out many of the issues in *The Fountain of Age* (1993) but her book had little impact. *Look Me in the Eye: Old Women, Aging, and Ageism* by Barbara Macdonald and Cynthia Rich is occasionally mentioned, but Baba Copper's *Over the Hill: Reflections on Ageism between Women* (1988) is rarely cited and out of print. These books were original and provocative enough to inspire a body of work on ageism or the development of many courses on women's aging. That did not happen. Perhaps one day large numbers of feminists will focus on aging with the same awareness of injustice that we brought to studies of reproduction, work, racism, and violence against women. Then "old" in women's studies will no longer mean fifty and menopause, and the great diversity among women over sixty-five and seventy-five will be acknowledged.

We in women's studies must recognize three major demographic trends: (1) the shift to an aging population; (2) the increasing longevity of women; and (3) the particularly rapid increase in the number of minority elders. These changes will profoundly shape the lives of North American women in the twenty-first century. Failure to incorporate knowledge about these three trends in our teaching and writing will undermine the credibility of women's studies as a discipline.

FEMINIST GERONTOLOGY

I point out to students that *geron* is Greek for "old man," and thus gerontology is literally the study of old men. The term was coined in 1903 by the Russian biologist Ilya Ilyich Mechnikov, who won the Nobel Prize in medicine. I propose "gerastology" instead, the study of old women from a feminist perspective, knowing that my coinage will not catch on. The phrase "feminist gerontology" is somewhat deficient, suggesting a body of knowledge given a particular slant sometime after its creation. Gerastology begins in feminism. A small but growing number of scholars, from Canada, Europe, and Australia as well as the United States, have created an impressive body of work in the past twenty-five years, combining gerontology with disciplines such as sociology, literature, nursing, cultural studies, and anthropology. In pre-twenty-first-century writings on old women, the focus tended to be on ageism, health, and retirement.[1] We now have more nuanced studies of health, retirement, and ageism, and other aspects of aging as well. "The aging woman" has been replaced by "aging women," and the extreme diversity of those so designated is clearly recognized.

Feminist gerontology stresses power relations and ways power influences not only female and male identities but also their disparate life chances (Netting, 241). Both in theory and in life, writes Margaret Walker, unequal power distributions "will tend to reproduce themselves and each will tend to reinforce and legitimate the other" (*Moral Contexts*, 207–8). Feminist scholars are usually keenly aware of power differences between researcher and subjects, an issue not likely to be raised in mainstream gerontology.

Feminist gerontology has come of age. Since much about old women is either unknown or understudied, our work is exhilarating, and the possibility that it could actually benefit women connects us to the aspirations of the heady days of feminist thought in the 1970s. We believed then that knowledge would free us, which it did to some extent, but knowledge as an edifice has been dismantled, and much as we like to think of our work as emancipatory, that hope may be unrealistic. On the other hand, if the ways we are "aged by culture" (to borrow Margaret Gullette's phrase) become better understood, some old women may defy ageist stereotypes and thereby become more free. Or they may simply like themselves just as they are.

Because little work has focused on very old people, Meika Loe's *Aging Our Way*, on people over 85, is exemplary. Loe brings her subjects to life through extensive quotations and descriptions and skillfully interweaves interpretive commentary. A common thread among those who age in their own way is the value placed on moderation and restraint—in eating, spending, seeking medical care, and pacing their daily lives. A "life-long spirit of conservation and prudence" also characterizes Loe's elders (70ff.).

Strength and Change

These have been noted in previous chapters illustrating the dangers and opportunities of women's aging. Feminists stress "agency," the concept that women's actions are not completely determined by their circumstances. Even though women are "variously molded" by social location and by cohort, they resist "denigration and domination by whatever means available" (Markson, "Communities," 501). Literary examples bear this out. In Alice Walker's short story "The Welcome Table," for example, an old black woman expelled from a segregated church finds her own path to Jesus. In "Trifles," a play by Susan Glaspell (1916), farm women conceal evidence that would convict their neighbor, a woman who has killed her abusive husband, of murder. Forms of resistance to domination differ in a group as heterogeneous as old women. Those sustained by an ethic of sturdy individualism will make different choices from those of women who live collectively or are nurtured by support groups. Class privilege will insulate some older women, but at the same time it may also pressure them to alter their bodies to disguise signs of physical aging.

Crosscultural research demonstrates that in many societies, women's power and status increase with age. Old women are not only energetic and capable; they are leaders (Linda Cool and McCabe, 108). Thus obstacles to old women functioning as powerful figures in mainstream North American society are cultural, not biological. Certainly many old women were and are powerful among American Indians—Onondaga women of the Iroquois nation, for example. In *Women: An Intimate Geography*, Natalie Angier summarizes anthropological evidence suggesting that "selection favors robustness after menopause" because the food-gathering skill of a grandmother helps increase the survival chances of her grandchild (248). A proponent of the "grandmother hypothesis," Kristen Hawkes, writes that "increased longevity in our genus is a legacy of the reproductive role of our ancestral grandmothers."[2] Thus robustness after menopause could be seen as usual, not anomalous.

Some old women give each other informal help, an important aspect of women's aging that may be invisible to social science researchers. A drawback to documenting this help might be appearing to show that old women's needs can all be met privately, for example that the gaps created by cutbacks in home health care and in Medicaid can be filled by individual effort. "Peer care" is an alternative to institutional care or care provided by families. Peer care envisions networks of old women developing ways of care that they "both construct and manage" (Fiore, 247).³ As women's longevity increases, such networks will be invaluable.

Old women's potential for change, a theme touched on in earlier chapters, is expressed metaphorically by Gloria Wade-Gayles:

> I was always interruptible, always accessible and available. . . . I was like a plant from which one takes cuttings. A piece for this one, a piece for that one. . . . Although there were times I could feel the blade, I did not regret the cuttings. They strengthened my roots. . . .
>
> But there is a time when a plant should be left still, when the number of cuttings should be reduced, when it should be left undisturbed in the light of its own nourishing suns. Now is that time for me. (20)

A survey of work on women's aging concluded that processes are more important than events; women go through changes and transformations such as the one Wade-Gayles describes. We need primary sources to illuminate these changes: hundreds of diaries, letters, reminiscences, oral histories, novels, poems, plays, interviews, speeches, essays, and dialogues between women who differ in class and ethnicity. The Canadian Film Board's outstanding documentary *Strangers in Good Company* offers glimpses of the past and present lives of diverse old women, one of whom, Mary Meigs, in her book *In the Company of Strangers*, described the process of making the film and some changes women experienced through their participation.

The importance of primary sources is emphasized by Wade-Gayles when she writes that she cannot find books in which black women describe their aging. She wants accounts that show how "racism exacerbates ageism, which is further exacerbated by class" (14). Unfortunately, many prominent black writers have died before becoming old, including Audre Lorde, Pat Parker, Barbara Christian, Toni Cade Bambera, Rhonda Williams, June Jordan, and Octavia Butler. In "Indian Summer," Paula Gunn Allen reports seeing "virtually nothing written by elder women for elder women that is connected to my own experience of this part of my life journey" (186).

For many in North America, the biggest change in old age is the end of driving. The loss of this ability signals social, religious, recreational, and aesthetic losses for old women and marks official obsolescence (Carp, 256). How does a woman withstand this private shame? For some, no longer driving may be a relief, but this change may also be life-diminishing. We have no rituals for this important late-life passage. Our cultural values of self-reliance and autonomy encourage some old women and men to drive long past the time they can do so safely. Perhaps they associate no longer driving with loss of self.

Methods

Some feminists have turned away from quantitative analysis, while others believe it can be useful either by itself or in combination with qualitative methods. Quantitative work on elders must be balanced by research with them so that the work is shaped by their perceptions and concerns. Old Lesbians Organizing for Change (OLOC) has a slogan about research: "Nothing About Us Without Us." It is sobering to know, as *JAMA* reported, that one in five elders has taken prescription drugs such as tranquilizers and antidepressants that leave them susceptible to falls (December 12, 2001), but what is the subjective experience of this statistic for individual old women?

Feminist scholars value reflexivity, by which we mean an awareness of the ways our identities—shaped by particular circumstances of time, place, gender, ethnicity, region, and class—influence our work, and conversely, of the ways work shapes identities (Crawford and Kimmel, 3). Gerontologists, on the other hand, have been "singularly unreflective about their craft" (Estes, Binney, and Culbertson, 63). Feminist methodology considers the particular life experiences of (disadvantaged) older adults that "culminate in a difficult old age" (Hooyman et al., 10). Collaboration is also valued as well as interdisciplinary work.

The inadequacy of individualism as an aging model is illustrated by a dilemma for women in small, rural communities. Lack of public transportation may be a large impediment to healthy aging, but they must cope with this systemic failure as if it were their individual problem. Have they aged "unsuccessfully"? In this case, a social and economic problem unrelated to bodily change may decrease old women's mobility and thus lessen their strength and energy.

Feminists have questioned the emphasis on competition that often accompanies individualism and the belief that each person's interest is sharply separated from that of others (Grimshaw, 175), a belief underlying exaggerated fear of an aging population, for example. Since the lives of many women involve service to others, feminists grapple with the difficult problem of staking out a claim for their own interests while attending to those of others (184).

Theories

Standpoint theory presupposes that people will develop different knowledge frameworks depending on their experiences and their circumstances (Hirschmann, 167) and that knowledge is particular rather than universal (Hekman, 25). But do women have access to a special knowledge, leading them to a "truer (or less false) image of social reality than that available to white men?" (Harding, 185). A black woman's standpoint has a "legacy of struggle" at its core (Collins, "Defining," 581).

Some have claimed for old women a special knowledge of aging. Shevy Healey believed for example that gerontology credentials do not create aging experts; old people themselves are "the only experts available" ("Diversity," 109). But aging is not only an individual process; it is a social construction whose workings are often hidden from view. Healey gives too much weight to personal experience. Being old by itself does not produce an understanding of biological aging, the ways that other cultures conceive of old age, or the intricacies of the federal aging bureaucracy. Gerontological knowledge is admittedly limited, partial, and contested, but some familiarity with it can inoculate against social control. The idea that old women have a special knowledge of aging is attractive—but which old women? Feminist theory posits that "women" is not a universal category. If the same is true of "old women," who are the privileged knowers of aging? Those who have paid the closest attention might be one answer.

The term "intersectionality" was introduced by legal scholar Kimberle Crenshaw. It refers to the *simultaneous* interactions among multiple dimensions of social identity (for example, sex, gender, age, visible minority, and immigration status) that are "contextualized within broader systems of power, domination, and oppression" (Koehn and Kobayashi, 136). These intersections are at play in relation to our identities, our dealings with others, and at the point of policy formation (136). Moreover, intersectionality recognizes that "even oppressed groups include dominant and subordinate members" (Roseberry, 28). To show the advantage of an intersectional approach, Toni Calasanti notes that viewed through a gender lens, the poverty rate of women is higher than men's but incorporating race reveals that old black women have a much higher poverty rate than white women ("Theorizing Feminist," 473). An intersectional lens suggests that an older black woman's "sense of empowerment may be especially nuanced to manage racist and sexist prohibitions on her assertiveness" (Mitchell and Bruns, 122).

Terminology

Feminist gerontologists question the term "the elderly" to designate people over sixty-five or seventy because it objectifies them and is commonly used in connection with the "burden" old persons supposedly inflict upon society. The term "treats its objects as if their identity is subsumed by their being elderly . . . and represses the fact that they are persons with full and complete human lives" (Overall, *Aging*, 223). Another term, "the aged," has disappeared from gerontological literature, perhaps because it connotes a pitiful state. Stock phrases such as "the dependent elderly," "the frail elderly," or "the burden of care," should also draw our scrutiny. The facile use of the word "empowerment" by some feminist gerontologists (in the way "diversity" and "multicultural-ism" are invoked as feel-good words) suggests a benevolent regard for those seen as less able than themselves. Who has asked old women what power means to them?

Models

Young and middle-aged feminists sometimes project their wish for a certain kind of old woman on old women generally, and the resulting roles can be limited. Barbara Macdonald resented being seen as a repository of history or hearing that she resembled some younger woman's grandmother (124). In "Future Plans," Maine poet laureate Kate Barnes imagines herself in old age

> answerable to no one. Then I shall wear
> a shapeless felt hat clapped on over my white hair,
> sneakers with holes for the toes, and a ragged dress.
> My overgrown gardens a jungle.

These images appeal to younger women because they evoke unconventionality or eccentricity, but will more old women than young be temperamentally drawn to unconventional styles or behavior? When feminists project onto old women a wish that they be rebellious or unruly, we romanticize them.

The recognition that old women are often excluded from research and from the "cultural spaces of visibility and power" (Freixas et al., 55) sometimes leads to a compensatory exaggerated praise that seems patronizing. The statement that old women have "complex and subtle lives" (56) for example, suggests qualities inherent in the condition of being old and female. Unquestionably, the generalization fits the lives of *some* old women in *some* specific aspect of their lives.

Doris Lessing saw the risks in becoming a model for others, citing Bertrand Russell, who was "canonized as this dear sweet old man" before being unfairly attacked by disillusioned fans and disciples. The acclaimed novelist reported that "I myself have had to fight off attempts to turn me into a wise old woman" (302).

The crone image attracts young and middle-aged feminists because it conveys power and pride. In many societies, the crone was the "crown citizen" (Labowitz, 228) who was free to speak out (Onyx, Leonard, and Reed, 176). Although these notions are appealing, crones exemplify the social construction of aging by replacing negative stereotypes (ugly, withered old women) with positive ones; they still assume that chronology confers fixed meanings. Declaring women over fifty wise and powerful simply by virtue of their age obscures their individuality; it is a way of not seeing them. Those who think that an old woman *continues* to develop will not put her on a pedestal. Invoking positive stereotypes shows an understandable wish to take the sting out of aging, but instead makes signs and emblems of old women.[4]

Furthermore, when women are positively stereotyped as crones, white women mistake their experience for universal experience. The crone is a European figure taken over by whites to compensate for the denigration of old women in their culture. Blacks, Latinas, American Indians, and Asian American women are not burdened by this tradition. Figures analogous to the crone may be familiar to them—*curanderas* in Latina culture, for example—and many grew up with grandmothers and other female relatives who were powerful and revered.[5] Feminists have been more willing to reify a few extraordinary old women than to notice the many whose lives may resemble their own. The quality of May Sarton's work won her an audience, for example, but scarcity made her an icon.

Work by age theorists offers new perspectives on late life, for example, Margaret Gullette's books *Aged by Culture* and *Agewise*. Kathleen Woodward's essay "Against Wisdom" challenges a positive stereotype about aging and considers the uses of old women's anger. Woodward edited *Figuring Age: Women, Bodies, Generations*, which includes analyses of painting, photography, and depictions of old women in television and movies, accompanied by striking reproductions. In a *Figuring Age* essay on Carol Channing's revival of "Hello, Dolly!" Anne Basting concludes that Channing has changed and that "staying the same is really quite frightening" (260). An issue of the *Journal of Aging Studies* devoted to feminist gerontology, edited by Toni Calasanti, and the writings of Ruth Ray, Martha Holstein, Carroll Estes, and Anne Wyatt-Brown, among others, demonstrate that this focus potentially benefits all old people, not only women.[6]

Feminist Critiques of Aging Research

As objects of study, old women have been seen as a discrete group with knowable characteristics that remain fairly constant. Researchers usually have higher status than their subjects. They study the most easily accessible subjects, typically those most like themselves. Conclusions or questions from studies frame future studies, and within this closed circle, the artifice is well concealed. Narratives of aging that stress activity, contribution, and independence need to be examined for "patriarchal assumptions about what is worthwhile activity" (Mitchell and Bruns, 120). An emphasis on volunteering, for example, "socializes citizens to pick up the slack when the social safety net has gaping holes" (Netting, 246).

Traditional gerontological research has three basic flaws, according to Linda Gannon: androcentrism, biological determinism, and dualism (9–10). Men's lives are the point of reference or the standard for measurement, and men have the power to define what is normal. In retirement research, for example, the practice has been to study men and then later add women as the different other rather than beginning with women's experience (Krekula, 160). The Baltimore Longitudinal Study of Aging began in 1958 and carried on for twenty years without women. Gerontology students are often assigned readings in the life stage theories of Erik Erikson and Daniel Levinson, male models in which values such as separation, achievement, and autonomy are valued, "to the neglect of attachment, connection, and relationship." Thus when these models are used to explain women's adult development, women may appear "inferior, incomplete, or deviant" (LeVande, 168). Moreover, the Erikson and Levinson models miss differences among women as they age (168). Feminists have studied attachment, connection, and relationship among children and adolescents but not among old women (171). Late in his life, Erikson modified his belief in the particular province of old age by acknowledging that wisdom does not characterize this life stage if it has not been present long before (Hoare, 192).

Biological determinism makes reproduction women's primary purpose and thus views menopause as a "deficiency disease," not as a life transition (Gannon, 9). Differences between women and men or between whites and minority groups are attributed to biological differences. Women are often treated as a homogenous group; researchers have focused on the high rates of osteoporosis among white women, for example, overlooking the fact that osteoporosis is less common among middle-aged and old black women. Dualism creates sharply opposed pairs such as female-male, public-private, body-mind, subject-object (Gannon, 2–6). The problem is not only oversimplification and distortion but valuing one group (e.g., youth) at the expense of its opposite (age).

When gender appears as a variable in quantitative research, it "flattens women into a single dimension, ignoring their heterogeneity" (Lopata, 116). Gender's impact is complex and pervasive, for the lives of old women tend to be marked by lower incomes, more chronic illness, stronger support networks, more social activity, loss of spouse, and longer lives (D. Gibson, 443). Early work used population samples that were flawed because they excluded people in institutions (mostly women) and excluded the oldest of the old (Herzog, 138; 140). In studies based on surveys and interviews, snippets of information about old women are often presented to illustrate some theme or situation, but the whole woman disappears in the data.

Research on older women has been limited by the assumption that they develop only through family roles and thus future studies should emphasize their individuality (Sinnott, 150–51). Alternatives to family focus and family dependency need to be explored and future work should expand the meaning of "families" to include those created by gay, lesbian, bisexual, and transgendered elders. Studies should no longer use the blanket category "unmarried" to cover divorced women, those separated from male partners, widows, never-married lesbians, and never-married heterosexual women. The remark that women "might actually prefer a slightly shorter life expectancy if the consequences were to increase the utility of their lives when old by making it more likely that they would have male companionship" (Posner, 280) takes for granted women's subordination to men, and assumes not only that all women are heterosexual but that all heterosexual women want male companionship late in life. "Utility" is the wrong measure for old women's lives.

Utility matters in another context, however: More women than men suffer hip fractures. The fact that 25 percent of hip fracture patients return to their previous level, 25 percent die, and the rest are permanently incapacitated to some degree sounds predictable or inevitable until one learns that in Scandinavian countries, 76 percent of hip fracture patients go home and are found to be doing well a year later (Margolies, 33–34). Three-fourths of *Americans* who suffer broken hips should be mobile a year later. Fall prevention deserves as much attention from researchers and from the media as breast cancer.

Feminists may ask why reminiscence, a popular theme in gerontology, is now referred to in some publications as an "intervention," a word that shifts its focus from a creative process to a managerial skill. A person's life story may be all that remains under his or her control. Social workers, health care providers, senior center directors, and others attribute good intentions to themselves when they speak of "empowering" old persons, but the exercise of professional power over them remains largely unexplored. In an essay on nursing ethics, Sally Gadow notes that in clinical settings, "the discrepancy between the hidden body of the professional and the exposed body of the patient is not just an expression of power: it is one of its sources" ("Covenant," 9). Reminiscence is another kind of exposure, in the presence of one who need make no personal revelation herself, one whose power derives in part from not being known. (Other aspects of reminiscence are discussed in chapter 3.)

Mainstream gerontology has tended to marginalize women of color or to neglect them altogether. In research involving several ethnic groups, the usual approach is to take the white population as the standard measure and then compare other racial and ethnic groups, but a limitation of this method is that aspects of aging or of disease unique to groups besides whites will be missed (Miles, "Aging," 119). Simply adding information about black aging to the gerontology curriculum will not be sufficient to change stereotyped attitudes; black studies courses are needed as well (Conway-Turner, 586). Compared to gerontology, women's studies has been far more receptive to anti-racism work and has been more likely to require students to read works by public intellectuals such as bell hooks, Patricia Williams, and Gloria Anzaldúa. Although these writers do not treat aging directly, their analyses of racism, popular culture, the law, difference, and interlocking systems of oppression could influence social gerontology.

Although published studies of older white women greatly outnumber studies of American Indian women, Asian Pacific Islanders, black women, and Latinas, the Women's Studies International database lists numerous master's theses and doctoral dissertations on older minority women. Topics include health, stress, poverty, grandparenting, exile from one's native country, social support, cultural beliefs, widowhood, and leisure. Women of color have an advantage over white women in that they are more likely to have extended family networks, but this may also mean that more demands are placed upon them. Many grandmothers are serving as parents, for example.

Narrative Gerontology

Narratives are the heart of feminist gerontology and should count as gerontological knowledge. Whether fictional or autobiographical or in the form of oral histories, they provide the nuance, complexity, contradiction, and incongruities of old women's lives. A problem for feminist gerontology is that we have far too few personal narratives, especially ones that depict the lives of women of color (as noted above by Gloria Wade-Gayles and Paula Gunn Allen). If our goal is "to listen to and interpret voices from the margins" that are too often ignored (McDowell, 24), oral histories are needed. In them, an old woman herself can be the interpreter. *Their Memories, Our Treasures*, the second volume of oral histories produced by Spelman's Independent Scholars and edited by Wade-Gayles, presents the life stories of twenty-three southern African American women aged 60 to 104. Comparable projects involving other women of color or, for example, rural white women, would be invaluable. Because of "double consciousness," the keen awareness black people have of both the dominant culture and black culture, black women's life stories reflect both social accommodation and resistance to white cultural norms; the authors maintain their self-definition within their community (Etter-Lewis cited in Ray, "Feminist Readings," 125).

Introducing their *Guide to Humanistic Studies of Aging*, the editors state that the "rediscovery of narrative as an essential form of seeking and representing knowledge" has greatly influenced gerontology. Narratives counteract the overemphasis on scientific knowledge of aging; subjective knowledge is equally important (Cole, Ray, and Kastenbaum, 10). According to the concept of "reading our lives," stories we tell are "vast, open-ended texts, flesh and blood novels" whose meaning unfolds over time (Randall, 22). Narratives offer insight into physical aging in that they explore our relationship with our bodies and the meaning we attach to our bodies (Kenyon et al., xiii).[7] Usually identified with the humanities, narratives of aging also inform recent research in gerontological social work (Barusch, "Narrative Gerontology," 3) and sociology (see above, Loe). Narrative gerontology can offer critiques of social policy (Zeilig, 11).

What motivates old people to tell their stories? Gene Cohen speculated that the right brain comes into play, the side associated with "imagination and curiosity" ("Creativity," 194). Some limits of narrative gerontology are that our lives lack the forward thrust of narratives. They are uncertain and fragmented and do not point to a moment of revelation (Zeilig, 19). They may do just that however, as in this observation by Frances Partridge, one of the last survivors of the Bloomsbury group, written in her diary when she was 101: "I want to die, to get out of the world, but I am not sure how to do it. I also can't stop wanting to get well. One has a life instinct, which struggles" (qtd in Bytheway, *Unmasking Age*, 143).

Ronald Blythe interviewed elderly residents of an English village and presented their stories interspersed with his own observations in *The View in Winter*. Allan Chinen's *In the Ever After* is a collection of elder tales (fairy tales having an elderly protagonist) from many cultures. Barbara Myerhoff found her elder tales among retired Jewish residents of Venice, California; *Number Our Days* is the title of her book about them and a documentary. Kristin Langellier studies the role of memere (grandmother) stories among Franco-Americans, stories that often highlight large families, hard work, poverty, discrimination, and religion as a force for cultural preservation. In a memoir about her participation in the German resistance written late in her life in Berlin, Marion Yorck von Wartenburg wrote that being old was easier for her than being young and concluded that "You live more through your being than through your actions" (80).

In *Beyond Nostalgia*, Ruth Ray describes narrative themes of people she works with and the impact of groups on the writing process.

Fictional portraits of old women by nineteenth-century writers Sarah Orne Jewett and Mary Wilkins Freeman depict strong-willed characters, and memoirs by contemporary writers such as Florida Scott-Maxwell and Doris Grumbach reveal a variety of attitudes toward aging and candid comment on bodily decline. One of the most engaging nineteenth-century portraits of an old woman is Sarah Orne Jewett's protagonist in "The Flight of Betsey Lane." In this story, old age is regarded as normal. The ailments and complaints of Betsey and her friends, who live at a poor farm, are carefully detailed, but illness and aging are not equated. A spirited, independent woman, Betsey leaves the farm to make her first long trip from the Maine village where she has spent her whole life. Jewett imagines a woman having the most meaningful experience of her life in old age. Few contemporary writers have glimpsed that possibility.

Memoirs of old people guided by professional writers or shorter works that come from groups such as Ruth Ray describes in *Beyond Nostalgia* show that "old" divorced from context means little. Stories that trace the twists and leaps in the speech of women who have Alzheimer's give a human dimension to pathology, in Elinor Fuch's "Making an Exit," for example, a poignant and humorous account of her mother. Jane Rule's novel *Memory Board* depicts dementia with insight and grace.

In *The Measure of My Days*, Florida Scott-Maxwell describes her surprise at experiencing turbulent emotions in her eighties when she expected to be serene. Narratives supply the emotions of aging, but women's narratives may not risk strongly negative emotions. "Rarely found in women's life writing (particularly that of white, middle-class American women) is the language of willfulness, agency, mobility, fearlessness, independence, criticism, anger, combativeness, or outspokenness" (Ray, "Feminist Readings," 119).

A power struggle between a social worker and an elderly Russian client who refuses to leave his dirty, cramped room in San Francisco is the theme of Isabelle Maynard's "The House on Fell Street." The narrator gradually realizes that the needs of her client—from his room he can hear Russian nuns chanting overhead—are more important than the needs of the system she serves.

In an essay on Native American storytelling and cultural transmission, Leni Marshall observes that elders may not always be wise but those who are connected to their culture do have the "greatest accumulation of collective history and knowledge . . . and they are respected for just having the knowledge, and for transmitting it . . . usually in the form of stories" ("Kiss," 38).

In Val Napoleon's story "My Grandmother's Skin," Headache is a trickster who dreams about the beauty of old women, "about the beauty of lines and wrinkles and bodies of all shapes and sizes. . . . She suddenly sees all kinds of aging women all around the world—not simply old but as changing and transforming into other kinds of beauty" (85).

RELATED ISSUES

Bodies/Embodiment

A focus on old bodies has seemed oppressive in that it objectified old women, but feminist gerontology "recovers the territory of the body . . . [by asserting] subjectivity and reflexivity" (Twigg, "Body," 71). Bodies are simultaneously material and socially constructed (Calasanti, "Ageism," 9; Laz, 505). A particular dilemma for older women is that appearance is the "principal dimension of embodiment" (Laz, 514), and wrinkles, pouches, sagging skin, and age spots may lower self-esteem. Old bodies change but changes are not just deterioration (Chivers, xxv). "Our bodies are more fluid and flexible than we often realize, characterized by plasticity and malleability" (McDowell, 39). This generalization is unhelpful for the bodies of very old women (unless they have practiced yoga, tai chi, or qi gong) and perhaps also for women in their seventies and eighties who cannot be as physically active or flexible as they once were. Bodily distinctions are crucially important in the "production of inferiority" (McDowell, 48), and old women's bodies are viewed not only as inferior to those of both younger women and older men but even as loathsome. In her ethnographic study of a beauty salon in the Midwest, Frida Furman learned that old patrons both felt ashamed of their aging bodies and resisted cultural norms of beauty and thinness (12–17). They also found advantages in growing older. "Resistance" is a stance young and middle-aged feminists *want* to find among old women—but as Julia Twigg points out, "resistance is a profoundly ambiguous term." And the tension between age denial and age resistance cannot be easily resolved ("Clothing," 299).

Another study that examined older women's attitudes found that baby boomers were less willing to age "without intervention" than older women, who tended to accept their physical changes (Hurd Clarke and Griffin, 198). Feminist therapy encourages older women who have a "habitual self-critical body-monitoring attitude to become aware of the chronic anxiety this causes and the disconnection from inner awareness (Mitchell and Bruns, 124).

The strategy of trying to look younger masks fear of the label "old." Identities such as black or gay carry within themselves no inherently negative connotations, while "old" refers partly to decline. Terms such as "successful aging" or "productive aging" gloss over this fact. Some degree of deterioration seems to be an inescapable fact of late life, although preventative medicine or universal health care would no doubt reduce the severity and delay the onset of conditions that cause deterioration. When young and middle-aged feminists offer indiscriminate praise to old women, they avert their gaze from their own eventual fate. Lillian Rubin neatly captures her ambivalence when being praised for looking younger than her eighty-two years: She loves to hear this but also feels shame because it is important to her not to look like *them* (old persons) "even while I know that I'm one of them" (47). When a social worker in her fifties stopped dyeing her hair, a colleague responded to the change by saying, "I admire you but I'm not ready to look ugly."

Old women who dress in a way others consider inappropriate may be scorned as "mutton dressed as lamb," a phrase applied only to women (Twigg, "Clothing," 295–96). Knowing themselves to be devalued as old, women may cope by saying their bodies are not really important, or not really who they are, strategies bound to cause frustration and distancing from their bodies. Can we learn to look in mirrors with detachment, noting what we see as simply what we see, placing no value judgment upon appearance and saying, "This is the face I have now"? A twinge of regret for the way we used to look can be experienced and then released.

A survey of twenty-six studies examining feminist beliefs and body image found that these beliefs correlated with lower drives for thinness and less dissatisfaction with bodies, although women felt they were still susceptible to objectifying messages about thinness (Murnen and Smolak, 187). In these studies, black women expressed more satisfaction with their bodies than women in other groups (188; 194). Possible reasons for the apparent protective benefits of feminism are (1) critical thinking encouraged by feminism could help prevent "internalizing oppressive cultural messages"; (2) feminist emphasis on collective action may promote self-reliance; and (3) feminists may be empowered to choose their own self-interest rather than follow the cultural imperative of focusing a great deal of attention on their bodies (194).

Clearly, a challenge for feminist gerontologists is to address mind-body splits apparent when women say, for example, that they have not aged inside themselves, as if self and body were at odds. A similar split appears in a *Boston Globe* article about the artist Alice Neel. The nude self-portrait Neel created at age eighty is not reproduced, merely described: "Sagging breasts and belly are offset by a chin lifted so high her head grazes the top of the canvas. Inevitable defeat of the flesh is here but not of the spirit" (Temin, C1). This equation sets off the bad flesh from the good spirit, although the chin, as flesh, complicates the effort to praise the artist and

simultaneously present her as a victim. In this article, as almost everywhere else in American culture, an old woman does not speak for herself
but is spoken for. Old flesh can only be judged "defeated" through resolute youth worship. As long as the disdain for the aging female body expressed here is the dominant viewpoint, the individuality of old women
will be obliterated. They will be typecast as carriers of pathos.

In her essay "The Embodiment of Old Women: Silences," Barbara
Hillyer asks why so little has been written about the physical changes
women experience. Silence about them makes the aging female body "an
unspeakable subject or at least beneath notice" (53). Discussing physical changes should be a normal part of self-care for women as they age.
Instead, menopause is considered the most important physical event for
older women, accounts of "successful" aging focus on activity or accomplishments as if old bodies don't matter, and gerontologists do not in-
quire about physical changes unless they point to diseases or social problems. If an old woman talks of stiff joints or an unsteady gait, she may be
dismissed as a whiner. An old woman who honestly describes her bodily
experience rebels against the expectation that she be cheerful (48–55).

How can we teach ourselves and each other to heed our aging bodies? What constitutes close and loving attention to them? The study of
old bodies could encourage us to perform ordinary actions like sitting,
walking, standing, and driving more comfortably. How can we breathe
more easily and more deeply? Imagine a massage club for old women. No
body shame here, no apologies for wrinkles, sagging skin, or thickened
middles. No self-denigrating humor. That may be the last remnant of internalized ageism to root out, self-mockery for being old.

Disability

Although equated in popular culture, aging and disability are not the
same. Emphasizing this point should not overlook connections, however.
For some, disability and illness are normal aspects of aging (Wendell,
136) and others may live in disabling home environments (Oldman, 797).
The disability rights movement provides a model for collective action by
old people for themselves because people with disabilities have "wrested
control from professionals, at least in limited ways" and have become involved in both research and service development (Oldman, 796). Feminist
philosopher Christine Overall concludes that for both disability and aging
"the supposedly fixed biological foundation for each—namely impairments and old age—is socially created, sustained, and elaborated" ("Old
Age," 131).

Disability, like old age, is hard to comprehend from the outside. The
myth of bodily control oppresses both disabled people and old people

(Morell, 230–31). To understand aging bodies, we need more work like Mary Felsteiner's "Casing My Joints: A Private and Public Story of Arthritis," in which she explores the meanings of rheumatoid arthritis as a women's disease.

Housing

To refute the stereotype that old people are lonely or isolated, gerontologists cite statistics about frequency of contact with families, but quality of contact eludes measurement. Suppose that living alone, the pattern for more than half of women over seventy-five, is not conducive to optimal physical and psychological health. It is true that many old women report a preference for living alone. They like the freedom from obligation. Would daily contact with a circle of friends better satisfy companionship needs? Old women alone in their houses, apartments, or rooms may pay a high price for the extreme individualism of our culture. Living alone, considered a personal choice, is, perhaps more significantly, a conditioned response to social circumstance.

Communal or group living for older women is imagined only as confinement in board and care houses or nursing homes. But if a group of women pool their resources, they could have individual dwellings and common areas—dining room, laundry room, recreation room, reading room—an arrangement that might better suit them than living with families or living alone, the only choices now commonly available. Cohousing allows older adults to live interdependently as housemates or neighbors. Many women could not envision such an arrangement because their lives center on family rather than friends. But families are not organized to meet the needs of old women, while alternative living could be so arranged. Why does housing designated for older people assume that they will be a married couple or a single woman? Why not have units for two or more women living together? (Burwell, 202). Another arrangement is LAT—Living Apart Together, common in Scandinavia and Germany and likely to become increasingly common in North America. Age-segregated housing, a choice that may not enhance the well-being of older people because it narrows social contacts, could be balanced by intergenerational housing, an arrangement Gray Panther founder Maggie Kuhn chose and advocated.

In the absence of coordinated national efforts to make U.S. cities more age-friendly, the formation of community initiatives to support aging-in-place is a promising development, especially since benefits are available to people who are not affluent. The initiatives support traditional American values such as self-help, independence, and consumerism (Scharlach, "Creating").

Abuse

In mainstream gerontology, elder abuse is usually thought to result from caregiver stress, or from dysfunctional family patterns. These explanations overlook gender, just as the term "teen violence" disguises the fact that most perpetrators are male. Since current approaches to elder abuse obscure the role of men as perpetrators (Whittaker, 147), a feminist alternative is to locate elder abuse in the patriarchal family (156). While noting that women may also be abusers, this perspective asks how power operates in different contexts (152). Dualistic thinking leads us to think of a woman as a battered woman *or* an abused elder but not both, and many older women do not perceive themselves as battered women and thus do not seek battered women's services (Vinton, 87).

A study of domestic violence among rural aging women found that geographic isolation, low income, lack of social services, and the strong values of self-reliance and distrust of outsiders all complicate the problem of abuse (Teaster, Roberto, and Dugar, 636–37). Other factors were the presence of firearms and religious belief in male rule at home. Advocates for abused elderly women report that abusers will place a walker or wheelchair beyond the reach of the victim or hide her glasses so that she cannot clearly see a check she is asked to sign. One study found that abusers were more likely to be adult children than spouses (Moody, *Aging Concepts*, 6th ed., 232).

An extensive national survey of elder abuse in Ireland found that the most common forms were financial abuse and psychological abuse and that abuse existed across all classes. Authors speculate that much abuse is not reported because the victim is either frightened or prevented from reporting by cognitive loss (Naughton et al.).[8]

The Office of Financial Protection for Older Americans, part of the Consumer Financial Protection Bureau created by Elizabeth Warren, is headed by former Minnesota attorney general Hubert H. Humphrey III.

Globalization

Both traditional gerontology and humanistic gerontology have considered age and aging "almost exclusively from inside the nation-state" (Kunow, 300).[9] Feminists have pointed out, however, that although policymakers for governmental bodies focus on aging in general, the needs of women specifically are relegated to non-governmental organizations (P. Davidson et al., 1032).

Where the issue is health care, gender-neutral policies may create harm or bias. Thus the needs of women will not be adequately addressed until women play a more significant and authoritative role in the administration and governance of health" (1040). In all countries, the long-term impact of gender-based violence will affect a woman's health as she ages (1035).

Another global issue is the gap in life expectancy between the developed and developing worlds, termed "astounding." In Japan, life expectancy is seventy-nine for men and eighty-six for women but in Sierra Leone, the numbers are thirty-nine for men and forty-two for women (Carstensen, *A Long, Bright Future*, 48–49).

The term "globalization" calls to mind money, markets, and labor, but a result of globalization is "a new kind of aging" in which family and social life will stretch across continents and different kinds of societies (Phillipson, "Ageing," 117). The meaning of home will become unstable, for example (Phillipson, "Dynamic Nature," 148). Thus gerontologists will need deeper, less culture-bound understandings of concepts such as identity and late-life transition.

The growing power of transnational finance and global corporations raises questions about the nature of citizenship and the related rights of citizens to health and social care (Estes, Biggs, and Phillipson, 143). Globalization may increase inequities that shape individual and collective aging, especially for older women, as the role of the state in providing economic and health benefits is reduced (Estes, "Critical," 93). Although contemporary Western culture highly values individual autonomy, powerful forces stand against it, including outdated nationalisms, various fundamentalisms, and the desire of transnational companies to create a global culture through "relentless marketing, deregulation, and privatization" (Polivka and Longino, 188). What will this mean for the concepts of autonomy and empowered aging?

Linking the concept of global to age makes a "resolute effort to take age—and the populations designated by that term—outside national denominations and to deliver them instead into the invisible hands of global markets (Kunow, 296). This results in a shift from claims to commodities. Clearly, "the mysteries and paradoxes of late life do not translate easily into the instrumental reason of the market" (317).

Along with this sobering assessment, feminist gerontologists must grapple with the fact that women in many countries reject the values associated with capitalism such as pluralism and individualism (King and Calasanti, 154). What happens across continents will be far more complex than "linear progressions toward democracy" (153). The U.S. economy will increasingly depend on imported labor, for example, nurses from the Philippines, many of whom will provide both paid care for elderly persons and unpaid care for family members, while at the same time sending money home. Migrant Asian women are paid less than migrant men but they consistently send home more of their pay. Perhaps as many as half of Filipinos depend on money provided by overseas workers (Calasanti, "Context," 141). An increasing number of women, especially Latinas, will grow old influenced by two cultures because they left their native country to find work. How will that situation influence their aging process?

Another issue is the export of U.S. aging models to countries for which they are inappropriate. Programs such as senior day care and Meals on Wheels in India, for example, benefit only relatively well-off Indian elders, not the vast numbers of the elderly poor (L. Cohen, *No Aging*). Questions about the colonialist implications of overseas sales of prescription drugs aimed at old people are far more likely to be raised by critical gerontologists and feminists than by mainstream gerontologists. As Big Pharma expands its global reach, increased scrutiny of the industry is essential.

Future Work

Many topics remain to be more fully investigated, for example, old women victims of domestic violence; the impact of disappearing pensions on women now middle-aged; Social Security care credits that acknowledge the economic and social value of elder care; the negative impact of multiple prescription drugs on old women's bodies; media images that denigrate old women; differences within groups such as Asian American women and Latinas that have implications for their aging; and the social isolation that may accompany hearing loss. More community-based, participatory research is needed (Holstein and Minkler, 790)—for example, studies of women's involuntary retirement, since one of its chief causes is an elderly parent's need for care. How badly has the recession harmed people over sixty-five?

We know that ethnicity, gender, class, and aging are intertwined, but to grasp this generalization more fully we will need longitudinal studies of diverse women that include personal narratives, not merely answers to questionnaires. Such work may also shed light on frailty as multifaceted and changing so that the phrase "the frail elderly" no longer serves as a core identity. We know too that older women are not simply victims of circumstance, but however marginalized, act in their own behalf, but exactly how this plays out for individuals and groups can be made clearer through examples.

CONCLUSION

Postmodernism complicates the relationship between advocacy and academic specialization by questioning previously taken-for-granted categories such as "woman" and "old" and by challenging the validity of authoritative statements. But feminists cannot easily reject authoritative theoretical or political statements because women are oppressed and feminism aims to improve women's lives (Gagnier, 24). While it is probably inevitable that academic feminists reject a belief in "one single unseamed reality 'out there' composed of facts which researchers can establish as the 'truth' about social life" (Stanley, 263), there is a danger in seeing all as relative and contingent—for from this perspective, suffering and the political action that aims to alleviate it seem remote or futile. In addition, the current emphasis on fluidity of identities, ambiguity, contingency, and pluralism can reinforce popular culture's excessive individualism and thereby foster "a myopic politics of personal self help" (Wylie, 171).

Twenty-five years from now when most of the baby boomers have reached sixty-five, the economy may not be strong and elders' daily lives may resemble the lives of old Americans before Social Security and Medicare (Binstock, " Responsibility," 304). Neither the government nor scientists can predict the impact on longevity of global warming, biochemical terrorism, air and water pollution, genetically modified foods, or the increasing use of antibiotics and hormones on farm animals. In thinking about present-day women's greater longevity, gerontologists, especially feminist gerontologists, must ask not only what benefits it confers but also how it is suppressed by social policies that deprive many old women of adequate incomes and health care.

Aging has been called the "ultimate challenge in a woman's life, testing the limits of her resources and capabilities" (Gaylord, 64–65). Because her resources and to a lesser extent her capabilities will largely be determined by the politics of aging, feminist gerontologists must be skeptical of "successful aging," "productive aging," or other prescriptions that disguise inequality and power difference. "One size fits all" aging models will not do for women. Pressures to keep busy, for example, can coerce old women into prolonging the service role that gerontologists, including some feminist gerontologists, have deemed appropriate for them. As a group, feminists understand well the social construction of gender but not the social construction of aging.

The most pressing question is how can we—we old women; we service providers inside and outside the home; we researchers, students, and teachers; we providers of products and services—improve the health, well-being, and social standing of women in late life? The question assumes a double focus: the lives of old women and the professional work made possible by those lives. Thirty years ago, Nancy Datan wrote that old women are doubly disadvantaged by the "narrowing horizons of old age" compounded by ageist bias and discrimination, but at the same time, their late-life potential is greater than that of men (124).

Today the horizons of old age are less narrow for both women and men, but Datan's paradox still defines women's aging—both danger and opportunity.

Whatever students take away from Women and Aging, I hope that their fears will be eased. Specific concerns are realistic—poverty, loss of mobility, age discrimination—but the generalized fear of getting old is an insidious and debilitating fear that feminists must bring into the light. If my students' aging will mirror others' attitudes about how it should unfold and if these attitudes are socially constructed, how much freedom will students have to age in their own ways, and how can they determine what their own ways are? Years from now, hyperawareness of their age by others may construct images that they will have to notice in order to resist. They will then share with people of color, poor women, and disabled women the need to expend psychic energy deflecting distorted images of themselves.

We feminists cannot return to an essentialized, sentimentalized, and ultimately patronizing view of old women as either uniformly wise or universally oppressed. By virtue of their experience and their placement in the social hierarchy, some old women may indeed have a special knowledge of aging, and previous neglect of this knowledge gives it great importance. But the category of wise old woman can be relinquished. At this unique, historical moment of a burgeoning population of old women, meaning lies in particulars. Having few models, we improvise. Later, perhaps, we organize.

Conclusion
The Paradoxes of Aging

Aging is full of contradictions, ironies, and paradoxes. Our chronological age is both meaningful and meaningless. Nothing special, the aging process is made special by fear, denial, and the belief that it is a problem or a disease, all attitudes that are culturally determined. Our aging bodies carry these meanings because we age here, now. Old women and men are resented for their costly illnesses, but the health promotion programs that would keep them well are denied them. In this society, we have low expectations of elders, many of whom have untapped potential for social good. The loss of what they could offer is hard to calculate, but the incidence of late-life depression, alcoholism, and sickness would probably decline if meaningful social roles were available for them. The role of wise elder cannot be translated to industrial societies, but neither can the discarding of the old characteristic of American society continue. As their already large numbers grow, the gap between capacity and opportunity must be addressed.

In late life, our bodies demand more attention, but giving them too much is a trap because it leads to the sick role and overdrugging. Decline is thought to be the main theme of aging, and yet for many old age is a time of ripening, of becoming most ourselves. For women it may be both freeing and limiting—freeing if latent power and creativity can be expressed; limiting if chronic illness or lack of money narrows life possibilities. Aging is increasingly a female phenomenon; yet health care, public policy, and gerontology have not adapted to the rise in the numbers of women over eighty, and women's studies continue to focus on the young and middle-aged. Our aging population is multicultural, but the institutions that deal with aging tend to be monocultural.

Paradoxically, aging is both within our control and beyond our control. How much of each depends on class, ethnicity, and gender. Grasping this paradox is liberating for it says our responsibility is only partial. Norms such as "successful aging" and "productive aging" put the whole burden of aging well upon us. Instead, we might grade Social Security or Medicare as unsuccessful or unproductive. Comfortable aging or conscious aging, possibilities rather than models, recognize the social forces of aging. The preceding chapters have attempted to shed light on these forces and to suggest the limits of individualism as an aging philosophy. At the same time, individualism in the sense of non-conformity may be stressed too little in aging. Old people who ignore ageist messages march to their own drummer. Women who outgrow subordination to men, who know their own minds and speak for themselves, are non-conformists.

Another paradox is that "each of us is still and, at the same time, no longer the person we used to be. . . . Ageing is constant, complex, and slow. It does make a difference to our lives and our relations with others, despite the continuity implicit in our personal identities" (Bytheway, *Unmasking Age*, 21). For some, change will be the most important mark of aging, either physical change or developmental change, while for others, continuity will be more apparent.

A third paradox is that the many agencies and organizations for old people, run by caring professionals, have a rather uncaring dimension. They not only assume need (and sometimes create dependency) based on the arbitrary classification of "senior citizen," but also assume a match between elders' needs and existing programs. Many of these organizations could be run by elders themselves, or elders could decide that other services would better suit them. Or they could decide that whatever their needs, they do not fit neatly into an age-segregation model. Pieties about the wisdom of old people notwithstanding, they are often treated like people who require management. Aggregation of "the old" is convenient for service providers, but may not be in the best interest of elders themselves. Even the term "elder," which apparently conveys more dignity than "senior citizen," may be an unwelcome, superimposed designation.

Learning to Be Old is about resistance to the all-encompassing category of "old" that places such strong emphasis on *difference* from others. The notion that aging is mainly biological must be resisted because it obscures cultural aging. Even as a biological process, aging can be misunderstood if our capacity for repair, regeneration, and healing is underestimated. I have urged resistance to white, middle-class male bias in gerontology, to ageist stereotypes, to prescribed busyness, and to scapegoating old people for population aging. I have tried to depict women over sixty-five as very diverse. I have outlined countercultural gerontology.

Examples from other cultures demonstrate that the way we age now in America is only one way. Some castes in Nepal, for example, have the custom of carrying a person through the village in a palanquin once she or he has attained the age of sixty, a celebratory event quite different in spirit from our own age markings.[1]

Resistance to medicalized aging is now extremely difficult, but we can at least be aware of its dangers and limitations, especially for women. Above all, *Learning to Be Old* urges resistance to overdrugging, to the unacknowledged power the drug industry now exerts over our aging and would like to exert over the aging of people in other countries. Beyond resistance, we need to imagine new ways of understanding and experiencing late life, ways that emphasize development in the face of some decline. The body-mind split will have to be overcome. The stigma attached to frailty and dependence will have to be lifted. A change in consciousness similar to that brought about by the civil rights movement and the women's movement will be necessary to achieve these transformations.

From stories, poems, plays, memoirs, oral histories, and interviews with elders have come complex and illuminating interpretations of aging, and as more old women write and tell about their experiences, the many dimensions of their aging will be better understood. If the humanities play a larger role in shaping our common awareness of late life, if they can balance biomedicine and social science, new ways of knowing aging may be possible. Power, resilience, and rediscovery of skills and knowledge are themes, for example, of *Two Old Women*, an Athabaskan legend retold by Velma Wallis. Abandoned in a time of famine, the women survive against great odds and eventually save the lives of their tribe. In the Nevelson gallery of the Farnsworth Museum in Maine is an abstract etching of a woman titled "The Ancient One" (1953–1955). Neither fear nor revulsion is projected onto the figure, and she is not romanticized. In this striking work, Louise Nevelson transcends the social construction of aging. Will others be able to do the same?

Notes

Note: Citations are abbreviated when works are cited in full in the references.

PREFACE

1. The free screening for people over sixty-five in the Affordable Care Act is an example of policy favoring healthy aging.

INTRODUCTION

1. In her excellent critique of successful aging Julia Rozanova notes that elders who cannot afford the products and social engagement recommended by promoters of successful aging may be blamed or stigmatized (221).

2. Brent Green, "Internal Colonialism vs. the Elderly," *Berkeley Journal of Sociology* (1979): 129–49. Green adopts a concept first applied to black Americans by Robert Blauner.

1 CULTURAL MYTHS AND AGING

1. For an overview of anthropological work, see Christine L. Fry, "Social Anthropology and Aging," in *The SAGE Handbook of Social Gerontology*, ed. Dale Dannefer and Chris Phillipson (Los Angeles: SAGE, 2010). See also Barbara Myerhoff, "Rites and Signs of Ripening: The Intertwining of Ritual, Time, and Growing Older," in *Age and Anthropological Theory*, ed. David Kertzer and Jennie Keith (Ithaca, NY: Cornell University Press, 1984); Sharon Kaufman, "The Age of Reflexive Longevity: How the Clinic and Changing Expectations of the Life Course

Are Re-shaping Old Age," in *A Guide to Humanistic Studies in Aging*, ed. Thomas R. Cole, Ruth A. Ray, and Robert Kastenbaum; and *Contesting Aging and Loss*, ed. Janice E. Graham and Peter H. Stephenson.

2. Jacqueline Hayden's work was featured in Zoe Ingalls's "In the Unrelenting Eye of the Camera: Images of Our Own Mortality," *Chronicle of Higher Education*, January 7, 2000, B2. Illustrating the article is a striking nude photo of a woman crouching that evokes power and intensity rather than mortality.

3. I tell Frieda Walter's story in more detail in "Old in Spirit: A Gerontology Internship" in my edited collection of literature about aging, *Fierce with Reality* (Topsham, ME: Just Write Books, 2007).

4. A profile of geriatrician Linda P. Fried, dean of the Mailman School of Public Health, describes her extensive research on frailty: Karen Pennar, "A Firm Diagnosis of Frailty," (*New York Times*, June 26, 2012, D1).

5. Jason L. Powell's essay on aging theory discusses Foucault's ideas about resistance.

6. "Paul's Case," from *The Troll Garden* (1905), has an intriguing homoerotic subtext.

7. This theme is comprehensively treated in Lois Banner's *In Full Flower: Aging Women, Power, and Sexuality: A History* (New York: Knopf, 1992).

8. See Kathleen Woodward, "Against Wisdom: the Social Politics of Anger and Aging."

9. Margaret Morganroth Gullette's book *Declining to Decline* (Charlottesville: University Press of Virginia, 1997) discusses aging as a fall from grace.

10. Leonard Hayflick disagrees with the leaders of the Human Genome Project, who believe that when the genome is fully understood the aging process can be manipulated. He thinks they miss the distinction between "aging, a process that is not under genetic control, and longevity determination, which indirectly is" ("From Here to Immortality," *Public Policy and Aging Report* 14, no. 2 [2004]: 5). See also "Anti-Aging Medicine: The Hype and the Reality—Part II," *Journal of Gerontology: Biological Sciences* 59A, no. 7 (2004): 649–51, and "Anti-Aging Medicine: Fallacies, Realities, Imperatives," *Journal of Gerontology: Biological Sciences* 60A (2005). The claims of anti-aging medicine are persuasively refuted by Arlene Weintraub in *Selling the Fountain of Youth* and by Alan Peterson and Kate Seer, "In Search of Immortality: The Political Economy of Anti-Aging Medicine" (*Medicine Studies* 1, no. 3 [2009]: 267–79).

2 FEAR OF AN AGING POPULATION

1. "Beyond Apocalyptic Demography" is the title of Anne Robertson's essay in *Critical Gerontology: Perspectives from Political and Moral Economy*, ed. Meredith Minkler and Carroll L. Estes (Amityville, NY: Baywood, 1999). Stephen Katz uses the phrase "apocalyptic demography" in *Disciplining Gerontology* (Charlottesville: University Press of Virginia, 1996). See also James H. Schulz and Robert H. Binstock, "The Phony Threat of Population Aging," chapter 2 in *Aging Nation: The Economics and Politics of Growing Older in America* (Westport, CT: Praeger, 2006).

2. In *Aging for the Twenty-First Century*, ed. Jill Quadagno and Debra Street (New York: St. Martin's, 1996). Quadagno points out that benefits for the old do

not cause child poverty and that Social Security is a high-profile target for conservative attacks because the United States, unlike Europe, does not have a wide range of family support programs (413–14). As *New York Times* columnist Bob Herbert wrote, "Mugging the nation's grandparents by depriving them of some of their modest, hard-earned Social Security retirement benefits is hardly an answer to the nation's ills" (January 25, 2011, A23).

3. See for example "Social Security—It's a Women's Issue" by the National Council of Women's Organizations' Task Force on Women and Social Security (Washington, DC: NCWO, n.d.). See also Madonna Harrington Meyer and Pamela Herd, *Market Friendly or Family Friendly: The State and Gender Inequity in Old Age* (New York: Russell Sage Foundation, 2007).

4. The survey date was March 2012. Twenty years ago, the figure was nearly 75 percent, according to Ghilarducci. A 2007 survey by the Employee Benefits Research Institute showed that two-thirds of workers did not believe Social Security and Medicare would give them benefits comparable to those received that year.

5. Fraud in the system is thoroughly documented by Laura Katz Olson in *The Not-So-Golden Years* (Lanham, MD: Rowman & Littlefield, 2003). The website of the U.S. Department of Health and Human Services states that Medicare fraud has become more elaborate. Under Obama, the number of Medicare fraud investigators has been increased.

6. "Demographics Is Not Destiny," published by the National Academy on an Aging Society, also concludes that no crisis looms because many factors will determine the solvency of Medicare and Social Security. See Ellen M. Gee and Gloria Gutman, eds., *The Overselling of Population Aging* (Oxford: Oxford University Press, 2000) and Robert H. Binstock, "The Doomsters Are Wrong," *AARP Bulletin*, March 2007, 33.

7. A fact sheet from the Office of Minority Health reports that U.S. blacks live five years less than whites. American Indians live six years less than the rest of the U.S. population, according to the Indian Health Service. The Institute for Health Metrics and Evaluation at the University of Washington (June 15, 2011) reported that life expectancy for black women ranged from 69.6 years to 82.6 and for black men, 59.4 to 77.2. Christopher Murray of the University of Washington School of Public Health found that Asian American women in Bergen County, New Jersey, have the nation's highest life expectancy—ninety-one years. White women in Stearns County, Minnesota, live to be eighty-three. The rates for low-income residents of the Northern Plains are seventy-six years for men and eighty-two for women. States with the highest life expectancies are New Hampshire, Vermont, Rhode Island, Connecticut, Utah, Washington, North Dakota, and Minnesota. People in certain professions tend to live long lives: nuns, professors, symphony conductors and other musicians, scientists, actors, artists, journalists, clergy, and doctors (Carstensen, *A Long Bright Future*, 92–93).

3 SICKNESS AND OTHER SOCIAL ROLES OF OLD PEOPLE

1. For current thinking on AD see Simon D'Alton and Daniel R. George, "Changing Perspectives on Alzheimer's Disease: Thinking outside the Amyloid

Box," *Journal of Alzheimer's Disease* 25, no. 4 (2011): 571–81; Claudia Chaufan et al., "Medical Ideology as a Double-Edged Sword: The Politics of Cure and Care in the Making of Alzheimer's Disease," *Social Science and Medicine* 74, no. 5 (2012): 788–95.

2. Funding for research on AD, $500 million per year, is much less than the National Institutes of Health spend on cancer research, 6 billion, and on heart disease, 4 billion (*Aging Today*, May–June 2012, 3). Since heart disease kills more elders than cancer, NIH priorities are skewed. According to the Alzheimer's Foundation, the National Institute on Aging receives 3.6 cents for every dollar Congress allocates to the National Institutes of Health (Lauran Neergaard, "Budget Crisis Imperils Research on Aging," Associated Press, May 17, 2011). In May 2012, the Obama administration created a Health and Human Services website for comprehensive information on AD—www.alzheimers.gov.

3. An outstanding essay that combines analysis with personal experience is Margaret Gullette's chapter on dementia in *Agewise*, "Overcoming the Terror of Forgetfulness." bell hooks writes movingly of her mother's dementia in "A Community of Care," in *Belonging: A Culture of Place* (Routledge, 2009).

4. The common belief that half of Americans over 65 suffer from Alzheimer's came from a seriously flawed study. For details, see Christiane Northrup, p. 565. *New York Times* Health columnist Jane Brody reported an Australian study that found that patients with memory problems showed cognitive function improvement after brisk walking for 150 minutes a week (September 5, 2011, D7).

5. For an excellent critique of claims made for dementia drugs, see Janice E. Graham, "The Science, Politics, and Everyday Life of Recognizing Effective Treatments for Dementia," in *Contesting Aging and Loss*, ed. Janice E. Graham and Peter H. Stephenson (Toronto: University of Toronto Press, 2010). See also Margaret Lock, "Alzheimer's Disease: A Tangled Concept," in *Complexities: Beyond Nature and Nurture*, eds. Susan McKinnon and Sydel Silverman (Chicago: University of Chicago Press), 2005.

6. Basting's recommendations in *Forget Memory* include advocate for better options; "embrace the gray"; understand the complexity of dementia stories; and "value listening, silence, and the present moment" (155–65).

7. For the benefits of volunteering in later life see *Aging News*, Institute on Aging, University of Wisconsin–Madison (Fall–Winter 2011).

8. Linda Gannon, *Women and Aging: Beyond the Myths* (New York: Routledge, 1999), 46. This excellent work, cited in the *Healthy Aging* chapters, interprets a large body of research on older women's health.

9. David Gutmann, *Reclaimed Powers: Toward a New Psychology of Men and Women in Later Life* (New York: Basic, 1987), 152–53. Chapters 3 and 4 of Gutmann's book consider late-life androgyny. The author cites numerous anthropological studies to support his claim that this role shift is cross-cultural. Toni P. Calasanti and Kathleen F. Slevin consider the idea "dubious," however (12).

10. In his original formulation of life review, Butler wrote that it may cause depression, not serenity, a caution overlooked in current discussions of the concept. "The Life Review: An Interpretation of Reminiscence in the Aged," *Psychiatry* 26 (1963): 65–76.

11. For life review and reminiscence see Ruth Ray, *Beyond Nostalgia* (Charlottesville: University Press of Virginia, 2000); Anne Wyatt-Brown, "The Future of Literary Gerontology," in *Handbook of Aging and the Humanities*, 2nd ed., ed. Thomas R. Cole, Robert Kastenbaum, and Ruth Ray (New York: Springer, 2000); Kathleen Woodward, "Reminiscence and the Life Review," in *What Does It Mean to Grow Old*, ed. Thomas R. Cole and Sally Gadow (Durham, NC: Duke University Press, 1986); Juliette Shellman, Everol Ennis, and Karen Bailey-Addison, "A Contextual Examination of Reminiscence Functions in Older African Americans," *Journal of Aging Studies* 25, no. 4 (2011): 348–54; Mary O'Brien Tyrrell and Anita Hecht, "Life Stories as Heirlooms: The Personal History Industry," in *Transformational Reminiscence: Life Story Work*, ed. John A. Kunz and Florence Gray Soltys (New York: Springer, 2007); Mary O'Brien Tyrrell, *Become a Memoirist for Elders* (St. Paul: Memoirs, Inc., 2012); William L. Randall, Suzanne M. Prior, and Marianne Skarborn, "How Listeners Shape What Tellers Tell: Patterns of Interaction in Life Story Interviews and Their Impact on Reminiscence by Elderly Interviewees," *Journal of Aging Studies* 20, no. 4 (2006): 381–96; Dale Dannefer and Richard A. Settersten, "The Study of the Life Course: Implications for Social Gerontology," in *The SAGE Handbook of Social Gerontology*, eds. Dale Dannefer and Chris Phillipson; and *Storying Later Life: Issues, Investigations, and Interventions in Narrative Gerontology*, eds. Gary Kenyon, Ernst Bohlmeijer, and William Randall (Oxford: Oxford University Press, 2011). According to Margaret Urban Walker, "The drive for coherence within a single linear story may be distinctive of Western culture" (*Moral Contexts*, 195). For narrative gerontology, see Chapter 10.

4 OVERMEDICATING OLD AMERICANS

1. Brody cites the Beers Criteria guidelines that identify 53 potentially inappropriate medications or classes of medications for elderly people. The list was updated in 2012 by the American Geriatrics Society. The Geriatric Society Foundation for Health in Aging has a one-page drug and supplement diary to help patients keep track of drugs and dosages. http://www.healthinaging.org/resources/resource:my-medication-diary/.

2. Katherine Sherif, M.D., Medical College of Pennsylvania, quoted in "Drugs and Older Women," 6. Wyeth-Ayerst Global Pharmaceuticals has a research unit on women's health, and Pfizer observes women's reactions to its drugs for diabetes and lung cancer.

3. In 1986, for example, Peter Lamy wrote that 25 percent of drugs prescribed for the elderly were unnecessary or ineffective ("Geriatric Drug Therapy," *American Family Physician* 34, no. 6); the percentage must be much higher now because of the great increase in the number of drugs and demand increased by television advertising. Although this article is dated, I cite it because of Lamy's eminence in the field of geriatric pharmacology.

4. "A Drumbeat on Profit Takers" profiles two former editors of the *New England Journal of Medicine*, Marcia Angell and Arnold S. Reiman, who oppose "the commercial exploitation of Medicine" (Abigail Zugar, *New York Times*, March 20, 2012, D1). Both Marcia Angell's *The Truth about the Drug Companies: How They Deceive*

Us and What to Do about It (New York: Random House, 2004) and Hugh Brody's *Hooked: Ethics, the Medical Profession, and the Pharmaceutical Industry* (Lanham, MD: Rowman & Littlefield, 2007) carefully document widespread fraud in the drug industry and its insidious influence upon doctors and medical journals. Melody Petersen examines marketing practices such as exaggerating minor symptoms and even inventing new diseases in *Our Daily Meds* (New York: Farrar Straus Giroux, 2008). See also Shannon Brownlee's review, "Big Pharma's Golden Eggs: Marketing, Not Research, Is Now the Core of the Drug Industry," *Washington Post*, April 6, 2008, BW03. Former industry workers who have become whistleblowers exposing corrupt practices include Cynthia Fitzgerald (*New York Times Sunday Magazine*, November 18, 2007); Christopher Lee, "Drugmakers, Doctors Get Cozier," *Washington Post*, April 29, 2007, A3; Patricia Barry, "Doctors Still Chummy with Drug Sales Reps," *AARP Bulletin* 48, no. 6 (2007): 4; Stephanie Saul, "Merck Wrote Drug Studies for Doctors," *New York Times*, April 16, 2008, C1; and Emily Ramshaw and Ryan Murphy, "Payments to Doctors by Pharmaceutical Companies Raise Issues of Conflict of Interest," *New York Times*, November 24, 2011). See also G. Allen Power, "The Pill Paradigm," chapter 2 of *Dementia beyond Drugs*, 21–30.

5. A series of articles in major newspapers in 2001 called attention to the dangers of new drugs, suppressed competition by colluding companies, payment of doctors with free trips, the unnecessary proliferation of new drugs, and inadequate FDA regulation. A drug company that bribed doctors to prescribe its products was fined $875 million (*Boston Globe*, October 7, 2001, B1). That large fraud case was dwarfed by the $3 billion settlement the Justice Department won against GlaxoSmithKline in July of 2012 for failure to report safety problems with a diabetes drug, Avandia, including increased risk of heart attack, and for unapproved uses of depression drugs (*Philadelphia Inquirer*, July 2, 2012; *Boston Globe*, July 4, 2012).

6. I thank Matile Rothschild for this point.

7. Problems with drug trials, including the failure of Merck to report dangers of Vioxx, are discussed by Nortin Hadler, *Rethinking Aging*, 27–43. For an analysis of problems with the dementia drug Aricept, British researchers' skepticism about it based on sound science, and the unwise approval by the FDA, see Ira Rosofsky, *Nasty, Brutish, and Long*, 143–54.

8. Information from Paul Seligman, M.D., Director, Office of Pharmaco-epidemiology and Statistical Science, Center for Drug Evaluation and Research, FDA.

9. Personal communication with Tami Kurashimo.

5 HEALTHY PHYSICAL AGING

1. For analyses of ACA see *The Affordable Care Act: A Way toward Aging with Dignity in America*, an issue of *Generations* 35, no. 1 (Spring 2011) and Jeff Madrick, "Obama & Health Care: The Straight Story," *New York Review of Books* 59 (June 21, 2012): 45–47.

2. For an excellent discussion of exercise and aging that interprets research findings, see Linda Gannon, *Women and Aging* (New York: Routledge, 1999), 55–67; 140–41; 159–62.

3. For tai chi see Gary Kenyon, "On Suffering Loss, and the Journey to Life: Tai Chi as Narrative," in *Storying Later Life*, eds. Gary Kenyon, Ernst Bohlmeijer, and William L. Randall.

4. In *Healthy Aging*, Andrew Weil recommends that we consciously breathe more slowly, deeply, and quietly and focus on our breathing when we can (209). Weil's two CDs, "Breathing: The Master Key to Self Healing" were produced by Shambhala, 1999. For clinical evidence of the benefits of breathwork, see Richard P. Brown and Patricia L. Gerbag, "Yoga, Breathing, Meditation, and Longevity," *Annals of the New York Academy of Sciences* 1172 (2009): 54–62.

5. Anna Morgan, "Just Keep Breathing," in *Fierce with Reality: An Anthology of Literature on Aging*, ed. Margaret Cruikshank (Topsham, ME: Just Write Books, 2007), 95.

6. For more on free radicals, see Gary Null, *Power Aging* (New York: New American Library, 2003), 45–46, 157–60; Andrew Weil, *Healthy Aging* (New York: Knopf, 2005), 73–76; and "Free Radicals and Oxidative Stress in Aging" by Reshma Shringapure and Kelvin J. A. Davies in *Handbook of Theories of Aging*, 2nd ed., ed. Vern L. Bengtson et al.

7. For an analysis of vitamins and dietary supplements in relation to aging see David Haber, *Health Promotion and Aging*, 4th ed. (New York: Springer, 2007).

8. Research on herbs by Purdue professor emeritus Varro E. Tyler is widely respected because he has no financial ties to herb manufacturers. With Steven Foster he wrote *Tyler's Honest Herbals: A Sensible Guide to the Use of Herbs and Related Products* (New York: Haworth, 1999).

9. Kathleen DesMaisons wrote *The Sugar Addict's Total Recovery Program* (New York: Ballantine, 2000). For a detailed discussion of sugar addiction see William Manahan, M.D., Eat for Health (Tiburon, CA: H. J. Kramer, 1988), chapters 6–9.

10. For depression, see Peter D. Kramer, *Against Depression* (New York: Viking, 2005) and Linda K. George's article on depression and aging in *Handbook of Aging and the Social Sciences*, ed. Binstock and George.

11. Natural and non-toxic treatments are seen as inferior to the "big guns of drugs, chemotherapy and radiation. Drug-free natural methods of treatment with well-studied, well-documented benefits are ignored. Treatments that offer complementary care are denigrated. Studies that demonstrate their worth are ignored as well" (Christiane Northrup, *Women's Bodies*, 8).

12. Information from Vicki Cohn Pollard, acupuncturist, Blue Hill, Maine.

13. Information from Annie Wyman, certified Rolfer, Walpole, Maine.

14. Nancy Werth, discussion of Feldenkrais with Bella Johnson, host of "Alternative Currents," WERU radio, Blue Hill, Maine, April 7, 2000.

15. Jane Burdick, presentation on Feldenkrais, Downeast School of Massage, Waldoboro, Maine, April 17, 2000.

16. These include Trager, Lomi, Rosen Method, and Alexander Technique. A comprehensive survey of these and other systems can be found in Thomas Claire's *Bodywork* (New York: William Morrow, 1995). Although she left behind no method named for her, Magda Proskauer was an important figure in the development of bodywork healing and teaching, in the early days of Esalen and

later. A Jungian analyst and physical therapist, she taught breathing classes for many years in San Francisco. She believed that the breath is a bridge between the conscious and unconscious and that exhaling fully is extremely important. Proskauer wrote an essay about her work in *Ways of Growth*, ed. Herbert Otto (New York: Viking, 1968).

17. See "Telomeres and the Arithmetic of Human Longevity" by Abraham Aviv and John D. Bogden," in *The Future of Aging: Pathways to Human Life Extension*, edited by Gregory M. Fahy et al. (New York: Springer, 2010). For an online video of Elizabeth Blackburn's lecture on telomeres, see www.bioseminars .org/.

18. In a ranking by state for healthy aging, Connecticut is number one and Minnesota number two. Charles Lockhart and Jean Giles-Sims, *Aging across the United States* (University Park: Pennsylvania State University Press, 2010), 173.

6 THE POLITICS OF HEALTHY AGING

1. Resource Centers for Minority Aging Research locations include the University of Michigan; the University of North Carolina; the University of California, San Francisco; and the University of North Dakota, Grand Forks. Minority aging is the focus of the National Resource Center on Native American Aging, National Caucus and Center on Black Aged, National Hispanic Council on Aging, National Indian Council on Aging, and the Pacific Asian Resource Center on Aging. *Closing the Gap* is a newsletter published by the Office of Minority Health, Public Health Service, U.S. Department of Health and Human Services. The American Society on Aging publishes *Diversity Currents*, the quarterly newsletter of its Multicultural Aging Network.

2. The authors believe that "ethnicity" as a category reproduces "othering" practices that create distinctions between "us" and "them."

3. The Health and Retirement Study, sponsored by the National Institute on Aging, is a national, longitudinal study of 20,000 individuals over 50 in which Hispanics and African-Americans are overrepresented (HRS, *Data on Aging in America*, NIA and the University of Michigan, February 2011).

4. See Valentine M. Villa et al., "Hispanic Baby Boomers: Health Inequities Likely to Persist in Old Age." *Gerontologist* 52, no. 2 (2012): 166–76.

5. Statements about anthropology and about American Indians' attitudes toward aging come from Robert John, professor and chair of Health Promotion Sciences, University of Oklahoma Health Sciences Center, personal communication, March 18, 2008.

6. For a feminist interpretation of menopause, see Margaret Morganroth Gullette, "Hormone Nostalgia: Estrogen, Not Menopause, Is the Public Health Menace," in *Agewise* (Chicago: University of Chicago Press, 2011).

7. See Jessica Kelley-Moore, "Disability and Ageing: The Social Construction of Causality," in *The SAGE Handbook of Social Gerontology*, eds. Dannefer and Phillipson; and S. M. Greco and C. Vincent, "Disability and Aging: An Evolutionary Concept Analysis," *Journal of Gerontological Nursing* 37, no. 8 (2011): 18–27.

7 CLASS, ETHNICITY, SEXUAL ORIENTATION, AND GENDER

1. Sana Loue explores the complexities and confusions surrounding the terms "race" and "ethnicity" in *Assessing Race, Ethnicity, and Gender Health* (New York: Springer, 2006). Researchers must explain what they mean by these terms and why they have used them to describe the populations they study (Loue, 108).

2. For other studies of ethnicity and aging see Jacqueline L. Angel and Ronald J. Angel, "Minority Group Status and Healthful Aging: Social Structure Still Matters," *American Journal of Public Health* 96, no. 7 (2006): 1152–59; K. Whitfield, "Minority Populations and Cognitive Aging," in *Handbook of Cognitive Aging*, ed. Scott M. Hofer and Duane Francis Alwin (Thousand Oaks, CA: SAGE, 2008); R. W. Schrauf, "Intracultural Variation in Cross-Cultural Gerontology," *Journal of Cross-Cultural Gerontology* 24, no. 2 (2009); Nancy Chu and A. Renee Leasure, "Aging in America: Quality of Life among Older Vietnamese Women Immigrants," *Journal of Cultural Diversity* 17, no. 3 (2010): 105–9; Judith Treas and Daisy Carreon, "Diversity and Our Common Future: Race, Ethnicity and the Older American," *Generations* 34, no. 3 (2010): 38–44; Tingjian Yan, Meril Silverstein, and Kathleen H. Wilber, "Does Race/Ethnicity Affect Aging Anxiety in American Baby Boomers?" *Research on Aging* 33, no. 4 (2011): 361–78; Lynn McDonald, "Theorizing about Ageing, Family, and Immigration," *Ageing and Society* 31, no. 7 (2011): 1180–1201; Liz Lloyd, Kate Wite, and Eileen Sutton, "Researching the End of Life in Old Age: Cultural, Ethical and Methodological Issues," *Ageing and Society* 31, no. 3 (2011); 386–407; May L. Wykle, "'Age Old' Health Disparities: Daunting Challenges in the New Millennium," in *Aging Well: Gerontological Education for Nurses and other Healthcare Professionals*, ed. May L.Wykle and Sarah Hall Gueldner (Burlington, MA: Jones & Bartlett Learning, 2011); and Susan W. Hinze, Jielu Lin, and Tanetta E. Andersson, "Can We Capture the Intersections? Older Black Women, Education, and Health," *Women's Health Issues* 22, no. 1 (2012): 91–98. For studies of particular issues for Arab American elders, American Indians, Hmong, and Japanese elders see E. Percil Stanford and Gerard Koskovich, eds., *Diversity and Aging in the 21st Century* (Washington, DC: AARP, 2010).

3. For gender issues see Madonna Harrington Meyer and Pamela Herd, *Market Friendly or Family Friendly? The State and Gender Inequality in Old Age* (New York: Russell Sage, 2007); Linda R. Gannon, *Women and Aging: Transcending the Myths* (London: Routledge, 1999); Toni M. Calasanti and Kathleen F. Slevin, eds., *Age Matters: Realigning Feminist Thinking* (New York: Routledge, 2006); the feminist gerontology issue of the *Journal of Aging Studies* 18, no. 1 (2004), edited by Calasanti; and Leni Marshall, ed. Aging and Ageism issue of the *National Women's Studies Association Journal* 18, no. 1 (2006).

4. Peggy McIntosh's influential essay "White Privilege: Unpacking the Invisible Knapsack," (in *Women: Images and Realities*, 3rd ed., ed. Amy Kesselman, Lily D. McNair, and Nancy Schniedewind [New York: McGraw-Hill, 2003]) helped me think about middle-class privilege.

5. In the social gerontology text *Worlds of Difference: Inequality in the Aging Experience*, edited by Eleanor Palo Stoller and Rose Campbell Gibson (Thousand Oaks,

CA: Pine Forge Press, 1994), working-class elders and people of color are central figures. The editors juxtapose literary texts and analytical essays.

6. Some of the earliest work on old lesbians was done by Sharon Raphael and Mina Robinson (Meyer). See "The Older Lesbian: Love Relationships and Friendship Patterns," *Alternative Lifestyles* 3, no. 2 (1980): 207–29. See also Marcy Adelman, *Long Time Passing: Lives of Older Lesbians* (Boston: Alyson, 1987). For other work on sexual orientation and aging see G. H. Herdt and Brian de Vries, eds., *Gay and Lesbian Aging: Research and Future Directions* (New York: Springer, 2004); Douglas Kimmel, Tara Rose, and Steven David, eds., *Gay, Lesbian, Bisexual, Transgender Aging: Research and Clinical Perspectives* (New York: Columbia University Press, 2006); Nancy J. Knauer, *Gay and Lesbian Elders: History, Law, and Identity Politics in the U.S.* (London: Ashgate, 2010); Dana Rosenfeld, "Lesbian, Gay, Bisexual and Transgender Ageing: Shattering Myths, Capturing Lives," in *The SAGE Handbook of Social Gerontology*, eds. Dale Dannefer and Chris Phillipson; Loree Cook-Daniels, "Transgender Elders: What Providers Need to Know and Don't Need to Know," *Diversity and Aging*, ed. E. Percil Stanford and Gerard Koskovich (Washington, DC: AARP, 2010); Paige Averett, Intae Yoon, and Carol L. Jenkins, "Older Lesbians: Experiences of Aging, Discrimination and Resilience," *Journal of Woman and Aging* 23, no. 3 (2011): 216–32; Stephanie A. Jacobson, "HIV/AIDS Interventions in an Aging U.S. Population," *Heath and Social Work* 36, no.1 (2011): 149–56; James Masten, *Aging with Aids: A Gay Man's Guide* (Oxford: Oxford University Press, 2011); Steven P. Wallace et al., "The Health of Aging Lesbian, Gay, and Bisexual Adults in California," UCLA Center for Health Policy Research (March, 2011):1–7; Daniel Redman, "Can Intergenerational Connection Battle Ageism within the Gay Community?" *Aging Today* (March–April 2012): 4; Amber Hollibaugh, "Sex, Senior Living and LGBTQ Elders: Willful Ignorance Is no Longer an Option," *Aging Today* (July–August 2011): 1; 12; and Elizabeth Price, "Gay and Lesbian Carers Ageing in the Shadow of Dementia," *Ageing and Society* 32 (2012): 516–32. MetLife published "Still Out, Still Aging: the Study of LGBT Baby Boomers" in 2010.

7. Works by Barbara Macdonald and Cynthia Rich and by Baba Copper are cited in chapters 9 and 10. "Golden Threads," a video produced by Lucy Weiner and Karen Eaton for the Point of View series on PBS, features Christine Burton, 93, founder of a group for older lesbians. "Living with Pride: Ruth Ellis at 100," a film by Yvonne Welbon, features a Detroit lesbian.

8. National Alliance for Caregivers/AARP, March 2009. This most recent study will be updated in 2014. A safe guess is that value of caregiving has risen substantially since 2009.

9. The observation on driving comes from Phyllis McGee in a conversation at the University of Victoria's Centre on Aging, October 12, 2007.

10. For caregiving, see Emily K. Abel, *Hearts of Wisdom: Caring for Kin 1850–1940* (Cambridge, MA: Harvard University Press, 2001); Martha Holstein and Phyllis Mitzen, eds., *Ethics in Community-Based Elder Care* (New York: Springer, 2001); Laura Katz Olson, *The Not-So-Golden Years: Caregiving, the Frail Elderly, and the Long-Term Care Establishment* (Lanham, MD: Rowman & Littlefield, 2003); and Agneta Stark, "Warm Hands in Cold Age: On the Need of a New World Order of Care," in *Warm Hands in Cold Age*, ed. Nancy Folbre, Lois B. Shaw, and Agneta

Stark (New York: Routledge, 2007); Anna Zajicek et al., "Intersectionality and Age Relations: Unpaid Care Work and Chicanas," in *Age Matters*, ed. Toni M. Calasanti and Kathleen F. Slevin (New York: Routledge, 2006); Neena L. Chappell and Karen Kusch, "The Gendered Nature of Filial Piety: A Study of Chinese Canadians," *Journal of Cross Cultural Gerontology* 22 (2007): 29–45; Jane Gross, *A Bittersweet Season: Caring for Our Aging Parents—and Ourselves* (New York: Knopf, 2011). Paula Spencer Scott, "Ways to Avoid Stress in Eldercare: What at Risk Groups Should Know," *Bay State Banner*, March 15, 2012, 1; 14; Ira Rosofsky, *Nasty, Brutish, and Long: Adventures in Eldercare* (New York: Avery Penguin, 2009); Clare L. Stacey, *The Caring Self: The Work Experiences of Home Care Aides* (Ithaca: Cornell University Press, 2011); and Sandra S. Butler, Sara Wardamasky, and Mark Brennan, "Older Women Caring for Older Women: The Rewards and Challenges of the Home Care Aide," *Journal of Women and Aging* 24, no. 3 (2012): 194–215.

For old people as caregivers, see Loe, *Aging Our Way*, 162–76. For a description of a campaign to organize home care workers, see Laura Flanders, "Can 'Caring across Generations' Change the World?" *The Nation*, April 30, 2012, 21–25.

11. For other work on women's retirement see Vanessa Wilson-Ford, "Poverty among Elderly Black Women," *Journal of Women and Aging* 2, no. 4 (1990): 5–20; Madonna Harrington Meyer and Pamela Herd, *Market Friendly or Family Friendly? The State and Gender Equality in Old Age* (New York: Russell Sage Foundation, 2007); Jeffrey A. Burr and Jan E. Mutchler, "Employment in Later Life: A Focus on Race/Ethnicity and Gender," *Generations* 31, no. 1 (2007); the retirement chapter of *Ageing Societies* by Sarah Harper (London: Hodder Arnold, 2006); Kanika Kapur and Jeannette Rogowski, "How Does Health Insurance Affect the Retirement Behavior of Women?" *Inquiry* 48, no.1 (2011): 51–67; Heidi Hartmann and Ashley English, "Older Women's Retirement Security: A Primer," *Journal of Women, Politics, and Policy* 30, nos. 2/3 (2009). Kerry Hannon, "Can Boomer Women Afford to Retire?" (Forbes, February 8, 2012); and Barbara A. Rutrica and Karen E. Smith, "Racial and Ethnic Differences in the Retirement Prospects of Divorced Women in the Baby Boomer and Generation X Cohorts," *Social Security Bulletin* 72, no.1 (2012): 23–36.

For retirement in general, see Ben Lenox Kail, Jill Quadagno, and Jennifer Reid Keene, "The Political Economy Perspective on Aging," in *Handbook of Theories of Aging*, 2nd ed., ed. Vern L. Bengtson et al. (New York: Springer, 2009); S. E. Rix, "Recovering from the Great Recession: Long Struggle Ahead for Older Americans" (Washington, DC: AARP Public Policy Institute, 2011); M. Heidcamp, Nicole Corre, and Carol E. Van Horn, "The 'New Unemployables': Older Job Seekers Struggle to Find Work during the Great Recession" (Boston College Sloan Center on Aging and Work, November 2010); Martha Burk, "Take off the Cap," *Ms.* 21, no. 1 (2011): 46–48; and Larry Polivka, "The Growing Neoliberal Threat to the Economic Security of Workers and Retirees," *Gerontologist* 52, no.1 (2012): 133–43.

A good resource is the WiserWoman newsletter from the Women's Institute for a Secure Retirement. www.wiserwoman.org.

12. Barbara Cabral, dissertation proposal, "The Transition of Single, Childfree Professional Women Involved in Social Activism and Creative Praxis in Retirement," California Institute of Integral Studies, San Francisco, April 2010.

8 AGEISM

1. The Anti-Ageism Task Force of the International Longevity Center published a 122-page online report, *Ageism in America* (2011). The ILC is affiliated with the Mailman School of Public Health, Columbia University.

2. Originally published in 1983, *Look Me in the Eye* was reissued in an expanded version in 1991. Both editions consist of alternating chapters by Macdonald and Rich. To make text references clear, I cite Macdonald when the quotation is from one of her chapters and Rich when quoting or paraphrasing a statement in one of her chapters.

3. According to the *Compact Oxford English Dictionary*, "geezer" is a derisive term for a man, not necessarily an old man. *Merriam-Webster's Collegiate Dictionary* traces geezer to the Scottish term "guiser," one in disguise, an odd or eccentric person, especially an elderly man. D. H. Lawrence used "guiser" to mean a mummer, according to the *Oxford English Dictionary*. Thus "guiser" once had a positive meaning: a disguised merrymaker. The *Scientific American* article appears in vol. 11, no. 2 (2000): 22–25.

4. In the Hurricane Katrina disaster, race and class bias were evident, as was the age bias revealed in death statistics: Seventy-eight percent of the dead were over fifty-one, and 39 percent were over seventy-five. Rescuers paid too little attention to the most vulnerable, according to Margaret Morganroth Gullette, "The Oldest Have Borne the Most: Katrina and the Politics of Later Life," chapter three of *Agewise*.

5. The abandonment or killing of elders in some societies may appear to be parallel cases, but typically the reason was extreme food shortage. The well-known example of the Inuit putting their old on ice floes is misleading because the custom was practiced only by some Inuit and because elders themselves determined when their lives were to end. The Japanese folktale "Oyasuteyama," or "The Mountain of the Old," describes the custom of taking aged parents far into the mountains and abandoning them. First a ritual farewell ceremony takes place and then the family grieves.

6. Trollope satirized imperial England in *The Fixed Period* by showing how easily it could use military power to impose its will.

7. Barbara Lane and Grace Lebow, *Coping with Your Difficult Older Parent* (New York: Avon, 1999). Gloria M. Davenport, *Working with Toxic Older Adults* (New York: Springer, 1999).

8. A study of women's use of anti-aging products found paradoxes: Women wanted to keep a youthful appearance but adopt a positive view of aging; they questioned the high cost and effectiveness of anti-aging products but still used them; and they wanted to control their appearance and at the same time age naturally. Amy Muise and Serge Demarais, "Women's Perceptions and Use of 'Anti-Aging' Products," *Sex Roles* 63 (2010): 126–37. Botox is a neurotoxin, meaning that it kills nerve cells, but in small doses it blocks muscles. It was originally used to treat people with crossed eyes, excessive blinking, and neck muscle disorders.

9. One precedent disregarded was the Court's 2008 decision that employers must prove that layoffs disproportionately affecting older workers are not based on age but on some other "reasonable factor." For analysis by Linda Greenhouse see "Justices, in Bias Case, Rule for Older Workers" (*New York Times*, June 20, 2008, A5). To call discrimination based on age unconstitutional "boggles my mind," wrote Justice Scalia (*New York Times*, October 14, 1999, A2). Workplace discrimination and many other aspects of ageism are examined in Todd D. Nelson, ed., *Ageism: Stereotyping and Prejudice against Older Persons* (Cambridge, MA: MIT Press, 2002) and Malcolm Sargeant, ed., *Age Discrimination and Diversity* (Cambridge: Cambridge University Press, 2011). See also the March–April 2012 issue of *Aging Today*, which focuses on ageism.

10. See Julia Twigg, "Fashion and Age: The Role of Women's Magazines in the Constitution of Aged Identities," in *Representing Ageing: Image and Identity*, ed Virpi Ylanne (Houndsmills, Basingtoke, Hampshire: Palgrave Macmillan, 2012).

11. Susan Sontag, "The Double Standard of Aging," in *The Other Within: Feminist Explorations of Women and Aging*, ed. Marilyn Pearsall (Boulder, CO: Westview, 1997). Originally published in 1972, Sontag's essay expresses outdated views of women and aging. Sontag calls old age an "ordeal," for example, and a "shipwreck." She was far ahead of her time, however, in recognizing that "aging is much more a social judgment than a biological eventuality" (21).

12. Anne Noggle, *Silver Lining* (Albuquerque: University of New Mexico Press, 1983). One face-lift photograph from this collection is reprinted in *Women and Aging*, ed. Jo Alexander et al. (Corvallis, OR: Calyx Books, 1986).

13. For another view see Margaret Morganroth Gullette's "Plastic Wrap: Turning against Cosmetic Surgery," chapter 5 of *Agewise*.

14. A conversation with San Francisco writer Judy MacLean clarified this point for me.

15. Research by Ellen Langer has demonstrated that ageist stereotypes can affect physical performance.

16. The interview with M. F. K. Fisher is one of many in Connie Goldman's *The Ageless Spirit*, 2nd ed. (Minneapolis, MN: Fairview Press, 2004). Fisher wrote one of the best portraits of late life in *Sister Age* (1984).

17. Maggie Kuhn (1905–1995) founded the Gray Panthers in 1970 after being forced to retire from a job with the Presbyterian Church. A dynamic speaker and leader, she inspired many Americans to recognize ageism. Kuhn is profiled by Jeanne E. Bader in *Contemporary Gerontology* 6, no. 4 (2000): 104–8, and is the subject of a delightful film, *Maggie Growls*, which combines interviews with Kuhn and animation (Barbara Attie and Janet Goldwater, 2002).

For an excellent appraisal of Kuhn's work, see Carroll Estes and Elena Portacolone, "Maggie Kuhn: Social Theorist of Radical Gerontology," *International Journal of Sociology and Social Policy* 29, nos. 1/2 (2009): 15–26. Among the concerns of the Gray Panthers are jobs, housing, the environment, health care, and military spending. See Sally Brown and Brooke Hollister, "Aging, Outrage and the Occupy Movement: Gray Panthers Join in, Speak out about Putting Profits over People," *Aging Today* 33, no. 2 (2012): 8 and www.graypanthers.org.

9 COUNTERCULTURAL GERONTOLOGY

1. Ruth Ray's *Endnotes* (2008) beautifully depicts erotic power in old age.

2. The depiction of old people as alcoholics reverts to a stereotype in Greek and Roman drama. Why contemporary writers rely on it is a question worth investigating. Drunken characters are supposed to be funny and they have an identifying tag.

3. Connie Goldman Productions, 1985. This excellent series broadcast on Wisconsin Public Radio includes interviews with M. F. K. Fisher, Josephine Miles, John Huston, Louise Nevelson, Burl Ives, John Cage, Hume Cronyn, and Jessica Tandy, reprinted in Goldman's *The Ageless Spirit: Reflections on Living Life to the Fullest in Midlife and the Years Beyond*, 2nd ed. (Minneapolis, MN: Fairview Press, 2004). See also Goldman's *Who Am I Now That I'm Not Who I Was? Conversations with Women in Mid-Life and Beyond* (Minneapolis: Nodin Press, 2009).

4. For creativity and aging see Robert Kastenbaum, "Creativity and the Arts," in *Handbook of the Humanities and Aging*, 2nd ed., ed. Thomas R. Cole, Robert Kastenbaum, and Ruth E. Ray (New York: Springer, 2000); Gene D. Cohen, "Creativity and Aging: Psychological Growth, Health, and Well-Being," in *A Guide to Humanistic Studies in Aging*, eds. Cole, Ray, and Kastenbaum; and Anne Wyatt-Brown's introduction to *Aging and Gender in Literature*, ed. Anne Wyatt-Brown and Janice Rossen (Charlottesville: University Press of Virginia, 1993). This collection includes Margaret Morganroth Gullette's excellent essay "Creativity, Aging, Gender: A Study of Their Intersections 1910–1935." See also "Arts and Aging," the Spring 2006 issue of *Generations* (vol. 30, no. 1); "Creative Uncertainty," chapter 6 of Ellen Langer's *Mindfulness* (Reading, PA: Addison-Wesley, 1989). The Gerontology Institute at Ithaca College has a Center for Creativity and Aging. For good examples of creativity in old age, see Meika Loe, *Aging Our Way*, 98–101.

5. Granny Edith extols the Raging Grannies' "blatant disregard for everything other people think is normal. . . . We sound so defiant" (Caissie, 138).

6. For summaries of research on religion and aging, see chapter 11 of Robert Atchley's *Social Forces and Aging* (Belmont, CA: Wadsworth, 2000). Several essays in *Aging and the Meaning of Time*, ed. Robert Atchley and Susan H. McFadden (New York: Springer, 2001) consider aging and spirituality. For an excellent brief discussion of the subject, see the last section of Margaret Urban Walker's essay "Getting Out of Line: Alternatives to Life as a Career" in *Mother Time: Women, Aging, and Ethics*, ed. Margaret Urban Walker (Lanham, MD: Rowman & Littlefield, 1999). See also Atchley's essay "Spirituality," in the *Handbook of the Humanities and Aging*, 2nd ed. (New York: Springer, 2000); Mel Kimble and Susan H. McFadden, eds., *Aging, Spirituality, and Religion* (Minneapolis: Augsburg Fortress Press, 2003); Susan H. McFadden and Janet L. Ramsey, "Encountering the Numinous: Relationality, the Arts, and Religion in Later Life," in *A Guide to Humanistic Studies in Aging*, eds. Thomas Cole, Ruth Ray, and Robert Kastenbaum; and Lydia K. Manning, "An Exploration of Paganism: Aging Women Embracing the Divine Feminine," *Journal of Religion, Spirituality and Aging* 22, no. 3 (2010): 196–210.

7. David Van Tassel edited *Aging and the Completion of Being* (Philadelphia: University of Pennsylvania Press, 1989). See also Christine Overall, *Aging, Death, and Human Longevity: A Philosophical Inquiry* (Berkeley: University of California Press,

2003). *Aging Today*, published by the American Society on Aging, features articles on the humanities and aging. "Aging and Human Values" is an online newsletter edited by Harry R. Moody at aarpnews@news.aarp.org.

8. See Zalman Schachter-Shalomi and R. S. Miller, *From Age-ing to Sage-ing* (New York: Warner Books, 1997). The website is www.sage-ingguild.org.

9. Matthew Fox, *Illuminations of Hildegard of Bingen* (Santa Fe, NM: Bear Books, 1985).

10. Lars Tornstam reports in his book *Gerotranscendance* that he used mail surveys to gather the information on which his theory is based (78). Since he was dealing with highly subjective questions about meanings and values, findings from in-person interviews would have strengthened his conclusions.

11. For an original and stimulating exploration of time, see Peter H. Stephenson, "Age and Time: Contesting the Paradigm of Loss in the Age of Novelty," in *Contesting Aging and Loss*, edited by Janice E Graham and Peter H. Stephenson.

12. A number of the sources cited in previous chapters are examples of critical gerontology. Others include Stephen Katz, "Thinking of Age: Personal Reflections on Critical Gerontology," *Journal of Aging Studies* 22, no. 2 (2008: 140–46; J. Brandon McKelvey, "Globalization and Ageing Workers: Constructing a Global Life Course," *International Journal of Sociology and Social Policy* 29, nos. 1–2 (2009): 49–59; Diane Sedgley, Annette Pritchard, and Nigel Morgan, "Tourism and Ageing: A Transformative Research Agenda," *Annals of Tourism* 38, no. 2 (2011): 422–36; and Pamela Gravagne, "The Becoming of Age: How Discourses of Aging and Old Age in Contemporary Popular Film both Reinforce and Reimagine the Narrative of Aging as Decline," doctoral dissertation, American Studies, University of New Mexico, 2012.

10 A FEMINIST'S VIEW OF GERONTOLOGY AND WOMEN'S AGING

1. Marilyn Pearsall's anthology *The Other within Us* (Boulder, CO: Westview, 1997) reprints some of the notable early feminist work, including Pauline Bart's essay on older Jewish women, Jacqueline Johnson Jackson's essay on older black women, Emily Abel's study of caregivers, and an essay on older women in the city by Elizabeth W. Markson and Beth B. Hess.

2. Kristen Hawkes, "Grandmothers and the Evolution of Human Longevity," *American Journal of Biology* 15, no. 3 (2000): 380–400. See also Whitehouse and George, 293–94 and Carstensen, *A Long Bright Future*, 129–30.

3. See also the other essays in the "Living Arrangements" section of *Mother Time*: Anita Silvers on reciprocity and interdependence, Martha Holstein on home care, and Joan C. Tronto on age-segregated housing.

4. See Barbara Walker, *The Crone* (San Francisco: Harper and Row, 1985), and Ursula LeGuin, "The Space Crone" in *The Other within Us*, ed. Marilyn Pearsall.

5. I thank Mirtha Quintanales for this connection.

6. Isabelle Maynard (1929–2007), a retired social worker in San Francisco, an oral historian and playwright, published much work beginning in her fifties, including *China Dreams: Growing Up Jewish in Tientsin* (Iowa City: University of

Iowa, 1996). In her seventies, Maynard learned to paint and compose music. "The House on Fell Street" is published in *Fierce with Reality*, my anthology of literature on aging.

7. See *Storying Later Life: Issues, Investigations, and Interventions in Narrative Gerontology*, eds. Gary Kenyon, Ernst Bohlmeijer, and William Randall.

8. See also Briony Dow and Melanie Joosten, "Understanding Elder Abuse: a Social Rights Perspective," *International Psychogeriatrics* 24, no. 6 (2012): 853–55.

9. Several essays on globalization and aging are included in *The SAGE Handbook of Social Gerontology*, eds. Dannefer and Phillipson, e.g. on inequality by Angela O'Rand, Katelin Isaacs, and Leslie Roth; on families by Ariela Lowenstein and Ruth Katz; on migration by Tony Warnes; and on sub-Saharan Africa by Isabella Abordin.

CONCLUSION: THE PARADOXES OF AGING

1. Satyam Barakoti told me about the palanquin rides in Nepal.

References

Abel, Emily K. "Family Care of the Frail Elderly: Framing an Agenda for Change." *Women's Studies Quarterly* 17, nos. 1–2 (1989): 75–85.

———. *Who Cares for the Elderly? Public Policy and the Experiences of Adult Daughters.* Philadelphia: Temple University Press, 1991.

Achenbaum, W. Andrew. "Afterword." In *Handbook of the Humanities and Aging.* 2nd ed. Edited by Thomas R. Cole, Robert Kastenbaum, and Ruth E. Ray. New York: Springer, 2000.

Ackerman, Felicia. "The More the Merrier." *Dialogue: Canadian Philosophical Review* 45, no. 3 (July 2006): 549–58.

Adams, Chris. "FDA Scrambles to Police Drug Ads' Truthfulness." *Wall Street Journal*, January 2, 2000, A24.

Agronin, Marc E. "The New Frontier in Geriatric Psychiatry: Nursing Homes and Other Long-Term Care Settings." *Gerontologist* 38, no. 3 (1998): 388–91.

Alcon, Arnaa, and Judith Apt Bernstein. *Women of Labor Speak Out on Retirement, Finances, Health Care, and Caregiving.* Waltham, MA: National Policy and Resource Center on Women and Aging, Brandeis, n.d.

Alex, Lena, and Berit Lundman. "Lack of Resilience among Very Old Men and Women: A Qualitative Gender Analysis." *Research and Theory for Nursing Practice* 25, no. 4 (2011): 302–16.

Allen, Jessie. "Caring Work and Gender Equity in an Aging Society." In *Women on the Front Lines*, edited by Jessie Allen and Alan Piper. Washington, DC: Urban Institute, 1993.

Allen, Paula Gunn. "Indian Summer." In *Long Time Passing: Lives of Older Lesbians*, edited by Marcy Adelman. Boston: Alyson, 1986.

———. *Off the Reservation.* Boston: Beacon, 1998.

American Association of Retired Persons (AARP). Minority Affairs. *A Portrait of Older Minorities.* Washington, DC: AARP, 1995.

Andrews, Molly. "The Narrative Complexity of Successful Ageing." *International Journal of Sociology and Social Policy* 29, nos. 1–2 (2009): 73–83.

——. "The Seductiveness of Agelessness." *Ageing and Society* 19 (1999): 301–18.

Angel, Jacqueline L. "Coming of Age: Minority Elders in the United States." *Gerontologist* 40, no. 4 (2000): 502–7.

Angel, Jacqueline L., and Ronald J. Angel. "Minority Group Status and Healthful Aging: Social Structure Still Matters." *American Journal of Public Health* 96, no. 7 (2006): 1152–59.

Angell, Marcia. *The Truth about the Drug Companies: How They Deceive Us and What to Do about It*. New York: Random House, 2005.

Angier, Natalie. *Women: An Intimate Geography*. New York: Anchor Books, 1999.

Angus, Jocelyn, and Patricia Reeve. "Ageism: A Threat to 'Aging Well' in the 21st Century." *Journal of Applied Gerontology* 25, no. 2 (2006): 137–52.

Annan, Kofi. Address at Ceremony Launching the International Year of Older Persons (1999). *Journal of Gerontology: Psychological Sciences* 54B, no. 1 (1999): P5–P6.

Anzaldúa, Gloria. "Introduction" to *Making Face, Making Soul: Haciendo Caras*, edited by Gloria Anzaldúa. San Francisco: Aunt Lute Books, 1990.

Anzick, Michael A., and David A. Weaver. "Reducing Poverty among Elderly Women." ORES Working Paper Series, no. 87, Office of Research, Evaluation, and Statistics, Social Security Administration, 2001, 1–25.

Applebome, Peter. "Second Acts and Beyond." *New York Times*, November 22, 1998, sec. 4, 1.

Arber, Sara. "Gender and Later Life: Change, Choice, and Constraints." In *The Futures of Old Age*, edited by John A. Vincent, Chris R. Phillipson, and Murna Downs. London: Sage, 2006.

Arber, Sara, and Jay Ginn, eds. *Connecting Gender and Ageing*: A Sociological Approach. Buckingham: Open University Press, 1995.

——. *Gender and Later Life*. London: Sage, 1991.

Archbold, Patricia A. "The Impact of Parent Caring on Women." *Family Relations* 32, no. 1 (1983): 39–45.

Arluke, Arnold, and John Peterson. "Accidental Medicalization of Old Age and Its Social Control Implications." In *Dimensions: Aging, Culture, and Health*, edited by Christine L. Fry. New York: Praeger, 1981.

Atchley, Robert C. *Social Forces and Aging*. 9th ed. Belmont, CA: Wadsworth, 2000.

——. *Spirituality and Aging*. Baltimore: Johns Hopkins University Press, 2009.

——. "Spirituality and Aging." *Religious Studies Review* 37, no. 3 (2011): 188.

Avallone, Charlene. "The Red Roots of White Feminism." In *Teaching and Research in the Academy*, edited by Mary Anderson et al. East Lansing: Michigan State University Women's Studies Program, 1997.

Baars, Jan. "Chronological Time and Chronological Age: Problems of Temporal Diversity." In *Aging and Time: Multidisciplinary Perspectives*, edited by Jan Baars and Henk Visser. Amityville, NY: Baywood, 2007.

Baltes, Margret M. *The Many Faces of Dependency in Old Age*. Cambridge: Cambridge University Press, 1996.

Barker, Judith C. "Lesbian Aging: An Agenda for Social Research." In *Lesbian and Gay Aging: Research and Future Directions*, edited by Gilbert Herdt and Brian de Vries. New York: Springer, 2004.

Barker, Pat. "Alice Bell." *Union Street*. New York: Putnam, 1983.

Barnes, Kate. *Where the Deer Were: Poems*. Boston: David R. Godine, 1994.

Barusch, Amanda S. "Narrative Gerontology Comes into Its Own." *Journal of Gerontological Social Work* 55, no. 1 (January 2012): 1–3.

———. *Older Women in Poverty*. New York: Springer, 1994.

Basting, Anne Davis. "Dolly Descending a Staircase: Stardom, Age, and Gender in Times Square." In *Figuring Age: Women, Bodies, Generations*, edited by Kathleen Woodward. Bloomington: Indiana University Press, 1999.

———. *Forget Memory. Creating Better Lives for People with Dementia*. Baltimore: Johns Hopkins University Press, 2009.

Bateson, Mary Catherine. *Composing a Further Life*. New York: Knopf, 2010.

Bayne-Smith, M. "Health and Women of Color: A Contextual Overview." In *Race, Gender, and Health*, edited by M. Bayne-Smith. Thousand Oaks, CA: Sage, 1996.

Bazzini, Doris G. "The Aging Woman in Popular Films: Underrepresented, Unattractive, Unfriendly, and Unintelligent." *Sex Roles* 36, nos. 7–8 (1997): 531–44.

Behuniak, Susan M. "The Living Dead? The Construction of People with Alzheimer's Disease as Zombies." *Ageing and Society* 31, no. 1 (2011): 70–92.

Beizer, Judith. "Medications and the Aging Body: Alteration as a Function of Age." *Generations* 8, no. 2 (1994): 13–17.

Bellow, Saul. "Leaving the Yellow House." In *Literature and Aging: An Anthology*, edited by Martin Kohn, Carol Donley, and Delese Wear. Kent, OH: Kent State University Press, 1992.

Bennett, James. "Hidden Malnutrition Worsens Health of Elderly." *New York Times*, October 10, 1992, sec. 1, 10.

Berdes, Celia, and Mary Erdmans. "Aging in Polonia: Polish and Polish American Elderly." In *Age through Ethnic Lenses: Caring for the Elderly in a Multicultural Society*, edited by Laura Katz Olson. Lanham, MD: Rowman & Littlefield, 2001.

Berg, Geri, and Sally Gadow. "Toward More Human Meanings of Aging." In *Fierce with Reality: An Anthology of Literature about Aging*, edited by Margaret Cruikshank. Topsham, ME: Just Write Books, 2007.

Bergman, Barbara R., and Jim Bush. *Is Social Security Broke? A Cartoon Guide to the Issues*. Ann Arbor: University of Michigan, 2000.

Bernard, Miriam. "Backs to the Future? Reflections on Women, Ageing, and Nursing." *Journal of Advanced Nursing* 27 (1998): 633–40.

Biggs, Simon, Ariela Lowenstein, and Jon Hendricks, eds. *The Need for Theory: Critical Approaches to Social Gerontology*. Amityville, NY: Baywood, 2003.

Binstock, Robert H. "Is Responsibility across Generations Politically Feasible?" In *Challenges of an Aging Society: Ethical Dilemmas, Political Issues*, edited by Rachel A. Pruchno and Michael A. Smyer. Baltimore: Johns Hopkins University Press, 2007.

———. "Public Policy and Minority Elders." In *Serving Minority Elders in the 21st Century*, edited by May L. Wykle and Amasa B. Ford. New York: Springer, 1999.

Birren, James. "Theories of Aging: Personal Perspective." In *Handbook of Theories of Aging*, edited by Vern Bengtson and K. Warner Schaie. New York: Springer, 1999.

Bishop, Christine E. "Prescription Drugs and Elders in the 21st Century." In *Challenges of an Aging Society*, edited by Rachel Pruchno and Michael A. Smyer. Baltimore: Johns Hopkins University Press, 2007.

Black, Helen K., and Robert L. Rubinstein. *Old Souls: Aged Women, Poverty, and the Experience of God*. New York: Aldine De Gruyter, 2000.

Blakeslee, Sandra. "A Decade of Discovery Yields a Shock about the Brain." *New York Times*, January 4, 2000, D1.

Blythe, Ronald. *The View in Winter*. New York: Harcourt Brace, 1979.

Bodily, Christopher. "'I Have No Opinions. I'm 73 Years Old!' Rethinking Ageism." *Journal of Aging Studies* 5, no. 3 (1991): 245–64.

Bonner, Joseph, and William Harris. *Healthy Aging*. Claremont, CA: Hunter House, 1988.

Bonnesen, Jaye L., and Elizabeth O. Burger. "Senior Moment: The Acceptability of an Ageist Phrase." *Journal of Aging Studies* 18, no. 2 (2004): 123–42.

Boorstein, Sylvia. Foreword to *Aging as a Spiritual Practice* by Lewis Richmond. New York: Gotham Books Penguin, 2012.

Bortz, Walter. "Aging and Activity." In *The Practical Guide to Aging*, edited by Christine Cassel. New York: New York University Press, 1999.

———. *We Live Too Short and Die Too Long*. New York: Bantam, 1991.

Bowling, Ann. "Aspirations for Older Age in the 21st Century: What Is Successful Aging?" *International Journal of Aging and Human Development* 64, no. 3 (2007): 263–97.

Bowron, Craig. "Our Unreliable Attitudes about Death through a Doctor's Eyes." February 17, 2012. www.washingtonpost.com/opinions/our-unrealistic-views-of-death-through-a-doctors-eyes/2012/01/31/gIQAeaHpJR_story.html.

Brandler, Sondra M. "Aged Mothers, Aging Daughters." *NWSA Journal* 10, no. 1 (1998): 43–56.

Brant, Beth. "Anodynes and Amulets. In *Writing as Witness: Essay and Talk*. Toronto: Women's Press, 1994.

Brody, Hugh. *Hooked: How Medicine's Dependence on the Pharmaceutical Industry Undermines Professional Ethics*. Lanham, MD: Rowman & Littlefield, 2007.

Brody, Jacob A. "Postponement as Prevention in Aging." In *Delaying the Onset of Late-Life Dysfunction*, edited by Robert N. Butler and Jacob A. Brody. New York: Springer, 1995.

Brody, Jane. "Americans Gamble on Herbs as Medicine." *New York Times*, February 9, 1999, D1.

———. "Changing Nutritional Needs Put the Elderly at Risk because of Inadequate Diets." *New York Times*, February 8, 1990, B7.

———. "Drunk on Liquid Candy: U.S. Overdoses on Sugar." *New York Times*, November 24, 1998, D7.

———. "Too Much Medicine, and Too Few Checks." *New York Times*, April 17, 2012, D7.

Brooks, Abigail. "Growing Older in a Surgical Age: An Analysis of Women's Lived Experiences and Interpretations of Aging in an Era of Cosmetic Surgery." Doctoral dissertation, Graduate School of Arts and Sciences, Boston College, 2008.

Brown, David. "Life Expectancy Drops for Some U.S. Women." *Washington Post,* April 22, 2008, A1.

Buell, John. "Drug Prices That Fuel Monopolies." *Bangor Daily News,* October 12, 2000, A11.

Burkhauser, Richard V., and Timothy M. Smeeding. *Social Security Reform: A Budget Neutral Approach to Reducing Older Women's Disproportionate Risk of Poverty.* Syracuse, NY: Maxwell School of Citizenship and Public Affairs/Center for Public Policy Research, 1994.

Burton, Linda M., Peggye Dilworth-Anderson, and Vern L. Bengtson. "Creating Culturally Relevant Ways of Thinking about Diversity and Aging: Theoretical Challenges for the Twenty-First Century." In *Diversity: New Approaches to Ethnic Minority Aging,* edited by E. Percil Stanford and Fernando M. Torres-Gil. Amityville, NY: Baywood, 1992.

Burwell, Elinor J. "Sexism in Social Science Research on Aging." In *Taking Sex into Account: The Policy Consequences of Sexist Research,* edited by Jill McCalla Vickers. Ottawa: Carleton University, 1984.

Butler, Robert. "Ageism: Another Form of Bigotry." *Gerontologist* 9 (1969): 243–46.

———. "Butler Reviews Life Review." *Aging Today* (July–August 2000): 9.

———. "New World of Longevity: 12 Ideas for Vital Aging." September 1999. www.ncoa/news.

———. "Revolution in Longevity." In *Delaying the Onset of Late-Life Dysfunction,* edited by Robert Butler and Jacob A. Brody. New York: Springer, 1995.

———. *Why Survive? Being Old in America.* New York: Harper and Row, 1975.

Butler, Robert, and Myrna I. Lewis, eds. *Aging and Mental Health.* 3rd ed. Columbus: Charles E. Merrill, 1986.

Butler, Sandra S., and Barbara Hope. "Relying on Themselves and Their Communities: Healthcare Experience of Older Rural Lesbians." *Outward* 5, no. 1 (1998): 2.

Bytheway, Bill. "Age-Identities and the Celebration of Birthdays." *Ageing and Society* 25 (2005): 463–77.

———. *Ageism.* Bristol, PA: Open University Press, 1995.

———. *Unmasking Age: The Significance of Age for Social Research.* Bristol: The Policy Press, 2011.

Caissie, Linda. "The Raging Grannies: Narrative Construction of Gender and Aging." In *Storying Later Life,* edited by Gary Kenyon, Ernst Bohnmeijer, and William L. Randall. Oxford: Oxford University Press, 2011.

Calasanti, Toni. "Ageism, Gravity, and Gender: Experiences of Aging Bodies." *Generations* (Fall 2005): 8–12.

———. "Bringing in Diversity: Toward an Inclusive Theory of Retirement." *Journal of Aging Studies* 7, no. 2 (1993): 133–50.

———. "A Feminist Confronts Ageism." *Journal of Aging Studies* 22, no. 2 (2008): 152–57.

———. "Gender and Ageing in the Context of Globalization" in *Social Gerontology,* edited by Dale Dannefer and Chris Phillipson. Los Angeles: SAGE, 2010

———. "Gender Relations and Applied Research on Aging." *Gerontologist* 50, no. 6 (2010): 720–34.

———. "Incorporating Diversity: Meaning, Levels of Research, and Implications for Theory." *Gerontologist* 36, no. 2 (1996): 147–56.

———. "Is Feminist Gerontology Marginal?" *Contemporary Gerontology* 11, no. 3 (2005): 107–11.

———. "Theorizing Age Relations." In *The Need for Theory*, edited by Simon Biggs, Ariela Lowenstein, and Jon Hendricks. Amityville, NY: Baywood, 2003.

———. "Theorizing Feminist Gerontology, Sexuality, and Beyond: An Intersectional Approach." In *Handbook of Theories of Aging*, 2nd ed., edited by Vern L. Bengtson et al. New York: Springer, 2009.

Calasanti, Toni M., and Kathleen F. Slevin, eds. *Age Matters*. New York: Routledge, 2006.

Calasanti, Toni M., and Anna M. Zajicek. "A Socialist-Feminist Approach to Aging: Embracing Diversity." *Journal of Aging Studies* 7, no. 2 (1993): 117–31.

Calbom, Cherie, and Maureen Keene. *Juicing for Life*. Garden City, NY: Avery, 1992.

Callahan, Daniel. "Age, Sex, and Resource Allocation." In *Mother Time: Women, Aging, and Ethics*, edited by Margaret Urban Walker. Lanham, MD: Rowman & Littlefield, 1999.

Callahan, James J. "Imagination: A Resource Policy." *Gerontologist* 38, no. 3 (1999): 388.

Cameron, Kathleen A. "Drug Risk Should Not Be Ignored." *Aging Today* (November–December 1999): 10.

Campbell, A. L. *How Policies Make Citizens: Senior Political Activism and the American Welfare State*. Princeton, NJ: Princeton University Press, 2003.

Campbell, Steve. "Allen Stirs Up Drug Industry with Senior Discount Bill." *Maine Sunday Telegram*, June 30, 1999, 1A.

Cappeliez, Philippe, and Jeffrey Dean Webster. "Mneme and Anamnesis: The Contribution of Involuntary Reminiscences to the Construction of a Narrative Self in Older Age." In *Storying Later Life*, edited by Gary Kenyon, Ernst Bohlmeijer, and William L. Randall. Oxford: Oxford University Press, 2011.

Carp, Frances M. "Living Arrangements for Midlife and Older Women." In *Handbook on Women and Aging*, edited by Jean M. Coyle. Westport, CT: Greenwood, 1997.

Carstensen, Laura L. "Growing Old or Living Long: Take Your Pick." *Issues in Science and Technology* 23, no. 2 (2007): 41–50.

———. *A Long Bright Future: Happiness, Health, and Financial Security in an Age of Increased Longevity*. New York: Public Affairs, 2011.

Caselli, Graziella. "Future Longevity among the Elderly." In *Health and Morality among Elderly Populations*, edited by Graziella Caselli and Alan D. Lopez. Oxford: Clarendon Press, 1996.

Cassel, Christine K. "Ethics and the Future of Aging Research." *Generations* 16, no. 4 (1992): 61–65.

———, ed. *The Practical Guide to Aging*. New York: New York University Press, 1999.

Cathcart, Mary, and Joanne D'Arcangelo. "A Leap Ahead for Women's Health Care." *Bangor Daily News*, August 23, 2011.

Chappell, Neena, Lynn McDonald, and Michael Stones. *Aging in Contemporary Canada*. 2nd ed. Toronto: Pearson Education Canada, 2008.

Chase, Karen. *Old Age and the Victorians*. Oxford: Oxford University Press, 2009.

Chaufan, Claudia, et al. "Medical Ideology as a Double-Edged Sword: The Politics of Cure and Care in the Making of Alzheimer's Disease." *Social Science and Medicine* 74, no. 5 (March 2012): 788–95.

Chen, Feinian, Guangya Liu, and Christine A. Mair. "Intergenerational Ties in Context: Caring for Grandchildren in China." *Social Forces* 90, no. 2 (2011): 571–94.

Chinen, Allan B. *In the Ever After: Fairy Tales and the Second Half of Life*. Wilmette, IL: Chiron, 1989.

Chivers, Sally. *From Old Woman to Older Women: Contemporary Culture and Women's Narratives*. Columbus: Ohio State University Press, 2003.

Christian, Barbara. "The Race for Theory." In *Making Face, Making Soul: Haciendo Caras*, edited by Gloria Anzaldúa. San Francisco: Aunt Lute Books, 1990.

Chu, Nancy, and Renee A. Leasure. "Aging in America: Quality of Life among Older Vietnamese Women Immigrants." *Journal of Cultural Diversity* 17, no. 3 (Fall 2010): 105–9.

Claire, Thomas. *Bodywork*. New York: William Morrow, 1995.

Clark, Margaret. "Contributions of Cultural Anthropology to the Study of the Aged." In *Cultural Illness and Health*, edited by Laura Nader and Thomas Maretzki. Washington, DC: American Anthropological Society, 1973.

———. "Cultural Values and Dependency in Later Life." In *Aging and Modernization*, edited by Donald O. Cowgill and Lowell D. Holmes. New York: Appleton-Century-Crofts, 1972.

Clark, Margaret, and Barbara Anderson. *Culture and Aging: An Anthropological Study of Older Americans*. Springfield, IL: Charles C. Thomas, 1967.

Clark, Thomas. "The Role of Medications in the Lives of Older Adults: An Overview." *Generations* 35, no. 4 (Winter 2011): 6–11.

Clifton, Lucille. "The Things Themselves." In *What We Know So Far: Wisdom among Women*, edited by Beth Benatovich. New York: St. Martin's, 1995.

Cohen, Gene D. "Creativity and Aging: Psychological Growth, Health, and Well-Being." In *A Guide to Humanistic Studies in Aging*, edited by Thomas R. Cole, Ruth E. Ray, and Robert Kastenbaum. Baltimore: Johns Hopkins University Press, 2010.

———. *The Mature Mind: The Positive Power of the Aging Brain*. New York: Basic, 2005.

Cohen, Lawrence. *No Aging in India: Alzheimer's, the Bad Family, and Other Modern Things*. Berkeley: University of California Press, 1998.

———. "No Aging in India: The Uses of Gerontology." *Culture, Medicine, and Psychiatry* 16 (1992): 123–61.

Cole, Thomas R. *The Journey of Life: A Cultural History of Aging in America*. Cambridge: Cambridge University Press, 1992.

Cole, Thomas R., et al., eds. *Voices and Visions of Aging: Toward a Critical Gerontology*. New York: Springer, 1993.

Cole, Thomas R., Ruth Ray, and Robert Kastenbaum, eds. *A Guide to Humanistic Studies in Aging*. Baltimore: Johns Hopkins University Press, 2010.

Coleman, Peter G. "Religious Belonging and Spiritual Questioning: a Western European Perspective on Ageing and Religion. In *Valuing Older People*, edited by Ricca Edmondson and Hans-Joachim von Kondratowitz. Bristol: The Policy Press, 2009.

Coleman, Peter G., Marie A. Mills, and Peter Speck. "Ageing and Belief: Between Tradition and Change." In *The Futures of Old Age*, edited by John A. Vincent, Chris R. Phillipson, and Murna Downs. London: Sage, 2006.

Colette. *The Blue Lantern*, tr. Roger Senhouse. New York: Farrar, Straus, Giroux, 1963.

Collins, Patricia Hill. "Defining Black Feminist Thought." In *The Woman That I Am*, edited by D. Soyini Madison. New York: St. Martin's, 1997.

———. "Toward a New Vision: Race, Class, and Gender as Categories of Analysis and Connection." In *Women's Voices, Feminist Visions*, edited by Susan M. Shaw and Janet Lee. Mountain View, CA: Mayfield, 2001.

Colman, Hila. "Just Desserts." *New York Times Magazine*, May 3, 1998, 84.

Comfort, Alexander. "Age Prejudice in America." *Social Policy* 7, no. 3 (1976): 3–8.

———. *A Good Age*. New York: Crown, 1976.

Connell, C. M., and G. D. Gibson. "Racial, Ethnic, and Cultural Differences in Dementia Caregiving: Review and Analysis." *Gerontologist* 37 (1997): 355–64.

Conway-Turner, Katherine. "Inclusion of Black Studies in Gerontology Courses." *Journal of Black Studies* 25, no. 5 (1995): 577–88.

Cook-Daniel, Loree. *Transgender Elders and Significant Others, Friends, Families, and Allies (SOFFAs): A Primer for Service Providers and Advocates*. Milwaukee, WI: Transgender Aging Network, 2007.

Cool, Linda E. "The Effects of Social Class and Ethnicity on the Aging Process." In *The Elderly as Modern Pioneers*, edited by Philip Silverman. Bloomington: Indiana University Press, 1987.

———. "Ethnicity: Its Significance and Measurement." In *New Methods for Old-Age Research*, edited by Jennie Keith and Christine L. Fry. South Hadley, MA: Bergin & Garvey, 1986.

Cool, Linda E., and Justine McCabe. "The 'Scheming Hag' and the 'Dear Old Thing': The Anthropology of Aging Women." In *Growing Old in America*. 3rd ed. Edited by Beth B. Hess and Elizabeth W. Markson. New Brunswick, NJ: Transaction, 1986.

Cool, Lisa Collier. "Forgotten Women: How Minorities Are Underserved by Our Healthcare System." In *Women's Health Annual Editions 98/99*, edited by Maureen Edwards and Nora L. Howley. Guilford, CT: Dushkin McGraw-Hill, 1998.

Coontz, Stephanie. *The Way We Never Were: American Families and the Nostalgia Trap*. New York: Basic, 1992.

Copper, Baba. *Over the Hill: Reflections on Ageism between Women*. Freedom, CA: Crossing Press, 1988.

Coupland, Justine. "Time, the Body and the Reversibility of Aging: Commodify the Decade." *Ageing and Society* 29, no. 6 (August 2009): 953–76.

Coyle, Jean M., ed. *Handbook on Women and Aging*. Westport, CT: Greenwood, 2001.

Crawford, Mary, and Ellen Kimmel. "Promoting Methodological Diversity in Feminist Research." *Psychology of Women Quarterly* 23 (1999): 1–6.

Crimmins, Eileen M. "Defining Disability and Examining Trends." *Critical Issues in Aging*, no. 2 (1998): 10–11.

Cross, Suzanne L, Angelique G. Day, and Lisa G. Byers. "American Indian Grand Families: A Qualitative Study Conducted with Grandmothers and Grandfathers Who Provide Sole Care for Their Grandchildren." *Journal of Cross-Cultural Gerontology* 25 (2010): 371–83.

Cruikshank, Margaret, ed. *Fierce with Reality: An Anthology of Literature on Aging.* Topsham, ME: Just Write Books, 2007.

Currey, Richard. "Ageism in Health Care: Time for a Change." *Aging Well* 1, no. 1 (2008): 16–21.

Dailey, Nancy. *When Baby Boom Women Retire.* Westport, CT: Praeger, 1998.

D'Alton, Simon, and Daniel R. George. "Changing Perspectives on Alzheimer's Disease: Thinking outside the Amyloid Box." *Journal of Alzheimer's Disease* 25, no. 4 (2011): 571–81.

Dannefer, Dale, and Chris Phillipson, eds. *The SAGE Handbook of Social Gerontology.* Los Angeles: SAGE, 2010.

Dannefer, Dale, et al. "On the Shoulders of a Giant: The Legacy of Matilda White Riley for Gerontology." *Journal of Gerontology: Social Sciences* 60B, no. 6 (2005): S296–S304.

Dass, Ram. *Still Here: Embracing Aging, Changing, and Dying.* New York: Riverhead, 2000.

Datan, Nancy. "The Lost Cause: Aging Women in American Feminism." In *Toward the Second Decade,* edited by Betty Justice and Renate Pore. Westport, CT: Greenwood, 1981.

Davidson, Patricia M., Michelle DiGiacomo, and Sarah J. McGrath. "The Feminization of Aging: How Will This Impact on Health Outcomes and Services?" *Health Care for Women International* 32, no. 12 (2011): 1031–45.

Davidson, Warren. "Metaphors of Health and Aging: Geriatrics as Metaphor." In *Metaphors of Aging in Science and the Humanities,* edited by Gary Kenyon, James E. Birren, and Johannes J. F. Schroot. New York: Springer, 1991.

Davis, Karen, Paula Grant, and Diane Rowland. "Alone and Poor: The Plight of Elderly Women." In *Gender and Aging,* edited by Lou Glasse and Jon Hendricks. Amityville, NY: Baywood, 1992.

Deaton, Gail, et al. "The Eden Alternative: An Evolving Paradigm for Long-Term Care." In *Annual Editions Aging, 02/03,* edited by Harold Cox. Guilford, CT: Dushkin McGraw-Hill, 2002.

de Beauvoir, Simone. *The Coming of Age.* Translated by Patrick O'Brian. New York: Norton, 1996. Paris: Editions Gallimard, 1970.

Degnen, Cathrine. "Minding the Gap: The Construction of Old Age and Oldness amongst Peers." *Journal of Aging Studies* 21, no. 1 (2007): 69–80.

Delany, Sarah Louise, and Annie Elizabeth Delany. *Having Our Say: The Delany Sisters' First 100 Years.* New York: Kodansha International, 1993.

Dembner, Alice. "Hip Fractures a Mortal Test for Elders and for Medicare." *Boston Globe,* December 10, 2006, A1.

———. "Research Integrity Declines." *Boston Globe,* August 22, 2000, E1.

de Medeiros, Kate. "The Complementary Self: Multiple Perspectives in the Aging Person." *Journal of Aging Studies* 19, no. 1 (2005): 1–13.

DeParle, Jason. "Early Sex Abuse Hinders Many Women on Welfare." *New York Times,* November 28, 1999, 1.

Diller, Vivian, and Jill Muir-Sukenick. *Face It: What Women Really Feel as Their Looks Change*. Carlsbad, CA: Hay House, 2010.

Dillon, Michele. "Integrating the Sacred in Creative Ageing." In *Valuing Older People*, edited by Ricca Edmondson and Hans-Joachim von Kondratowitz. Bristol: The Policy Press, 2009.

Dilworth-Anderson, Peggye, and Monique D. Cohen. "Theorizing across Cultures." In *Handbook of Theories of Aging*, edited by Vern L. Bengtson et al. New York: Springer, 2009.

Donohue, Julie. "A History of Drug Advertising: The Evolving Roles of Consumers and Consumer Protection." *Milbank Quarterly* 84, no. 4 (2006): 659–99.

Donovan, Josephine, and Carol J. Adams, eds. *Beyond Animal Rights: A Feminist Caring Ethic for the Treatment of Animals*. New York: Continuum, 1996.

Doress-Worters, Paula B., and Diana Lasker Siegal, eds. *The New Ourselves Growing Older*. New York: Simon & Schuster, 1994.

Downes, Peggy, ed. *The New Older Woman*. Berkeley: Celestial Arts, 1996.

Dressel, Paula. "Gender, Race, and Class: Beyond the Feminization of Poverty in Later Life." In *The Other Within: Feminist Explorations of Women and Aging*, edited by Marilyn Pearsall. Boulder, CO: Westview, 1997.

Dressel, Paula, Meredith Minkler, and Irene Yen. "Gender, Race, Class, and Aging: Advances and Opportunities." In *Critical Gerontology: Perspectives from Political and Moral Economy*, edited by Meredith Minkler and Carroll L. Estes. Amityville, NY: Baywood, 1999.

"Drugs and Older Women: How to Protect Yourself." *Women's Health Advocate* (September 1997): 4–6.

"Drugs Fuel Health Costs." *AARP Bulletin* 41, no. 1 (2000): 8.

Eastman, Peggy. "Drugs That Fight Can Hurt You." *Modern Maturity* 40, no. 3 (1999): 14–16.

Eaton, Susan C. "Eldercare in the United States: Inadequate, Inequitable, but Not a Lost Cause." *Feminist Economics* 11, no. 2 (2005): 37–51.

Ebersole, Priscilla, and Patricia Hess. *Toward Healthy Aging*. 5th ed. St. Louis: Mosby, 1998.

Edmonds, Mary McKinney. "The Health of the Black Aged Female." In *Black Aged*, edited by Zev Harel, Edward A. McKinney, and Michael Williams. Newbury Park, CA: Sage, 1990.

Eichenwald, Kurt, and Gina Kolata. "A Doctor's Drug Studies Turn into Fraud." *New York Times*, May 17, 2000, A1.

Ekerdt, David. "The Busy Ethic: Moral Continuity between Work and Retirement." In *Annual Editions: Aging*. 13th ed. Edited by Harold Cox. Guilford, CT: Dushkin McGraw-Hill, 2000.

Emerman, Jim. "Futurecare: The Web, Virtual Services, and Even 'Carebots.'" *Aging Today* 22, no. 1 (2001): 11–12.

Emerson, Ralph Waldo. "Self-Reliance." 1841; 1847. *The Heath Anthology of American Literature*. 3rd ed. Vol. 1. Edited by Paul Lauter. Boston: Houghton Mifflin, 1998.

Epstein, Helen. "Flu Warning: Beware the Drug Companies." *New York Review of Books* 58, no. 8 (May 12, 2011): 57–61.

Erikson, Joan. *The Life Cycle Completed*. Extended Version. New York: Norton, 1997.

Estes, Carroll L. *The Aging Enterprise*. San Francisco: Jossey-Bass, 1979.

———. "The Aging Enterprise Revisited." In *Critical Gerontology: Perspectives from Political and Moral Economy*, edited by Meredith Minkler and Carroll L. Estes. Amityville, NY: Baywood, 1999.

———. "Critical Gerontology and the New Political Economy of Aging." In *Critical Gerontology*, edited by Meredith Minkler and Carroll L. Estes. Amityville, NY: Baywood, 1999.

———. "A Feminist Perspective on the Privatization of Social Security." Paper presented at the annual meeting of the Gerontological Society of America, Chicago, November 17, 2001.

———. "The New Political Economy of Aging." In *Critical Perspectives on Aging*, edited by Meredith Minkler and Carroll L. Estes. Amityville, NY: Baywood, 1991.

———. "Social Security Privatization and Older Women: A Feminist Political Economy Perspective." *Journal of Aging Studies* 18 (2004): 9–26.

———. "Theoretical Perspectives on Old Age Policy: A Critique and a Proposal." In *The Need for Theory: Critical Approaches to Social Gerontology*. Amityville, NY: Baywood, 2003.

Estes, Carroll L., Simon Biggs, and Chris Phillipson. *Social Theory, Social Policy, and Ageing: A Critical Introduction*. Maidenhead, Berkshire: Open University Press, 2003.

Estes, Carroll L., Elizabeth Binney, and Richard Culbertson. "The Gerontological Imagination: Social Influences on the Development of Gerontology, 1945–Present." *International Journal of Aging and Human Development* 35, no. 1 (1992): 49–65.

Estes, Carroll L., and Liz Close. "Public Policy and Long-Term Care." In *Aging and Quality of Life*, edited by Ronald P. Abeles et al. New York: Springer, 1994.

Estes, Carroll L., and Karen W. Linkins. "Decentralization, Devolution, and the Deficit: The Changing Role of the State and the Community." In *Resecuring Social Security and Medicare: Understanding Privatization and Risk*, edited by Judith Gonyea. Washington, DC: Gerontological Society of America, 1998.

Estes, Carroll L., and Steven P. Wallace. "Globalization, Social Policy, and Ageing: A North American Perspective." In *The SAGE Handbook of Social Gerontology*, edited by Dale Dannefer and Chris Phillipson. Los Angeles: SAGE, 2010.

Evans, W. and D. Cyr-Campbell. "Nutrition, Exercise, and Healthy Aging." *Journal of the American Dietetic Association* 97, no. 6 (1997): 632–38.

Facio, Elisa. "Chicanas and Aging: Toward Definitions of Womanhood." In *Handbook on Women and Aging*, edited by Jean M. Coyle. Westport, CT: Greenwood, 1997.

Fahs, Marianne C. "Preventative Medical Care: Targeting Elderly Women in an Aging Society." In *Women on the Front Lines*, edited by Jessie Allen and Alan Pifer. Washington, DC: Urban Institute, 1993.

Family Caregiving in the U.S.: Findings from a National Survey. Washington, DC: National Alliance for Caregiving and AARP, 1997.

Farris, Martha, and John W. Gibson. "The Older Woman Sexually Abused as a Child: Untold Stories and Unanswered Questions." *Journal of Woman and Aging* 4, no. 3 (1992): 31–44.

Fealy, Gerald, et al. "Constructing Ageing and Age Identities: A Case Study of Newspaper Discourses. *Ageing and Society* 32, no. 1 (Jan. 2012): 85–102.

Featherstone, Mike, and Andrew Wernick, eds. *Images of Aging: Cultural Represen-tations of Later Life*. New York: Routledge, 1995.

Feinson, Margorie Chary. "Where Are the Women in the History of Aging?" *Social Science History* 9, no. 4 (1985): 429–52.

Felsteiner, Mary Lowenthal. "Casing My Joints: A Private and Public Story of Arthritis." *Feminist Studies* 26, no. 2 (2000): 273–85.

Fiore, Robin N. "Caring for Ourselves: Peer Care in Autonomous Aging." In *Mother Time: Women, Aging, and Ethics*, edited by Margaret Urban Walker. Lanham, MD: Rowman & Littlefield, 1999.

Fishman, Ted. *Shock of Gray*. New York: Scribner, 2010.

Fiske, Amy, and Randi S. Jones. "Depression." In *The Cambridge Handbook of Age and Ageing*, edited by Malcolm L. Johnson et al. Cambridge: Cambridge University Press, 2006.

Flaherty, Julie. "Preaching the Merits of a Multistep Program." *New York Times*, June 13, 1999, p. 3.

Flanders, Laura. "A Campaign about Caring." *The Nation*, April 30, 2012, 21–25.

Fleming, Juanita. "Ensuring Racial and Ethnic Diversity in the Health Professions." *Healthcare Trends and Transitions* 6, no. 4 (1995): 24–32.

Foner, Nancy. "Caring for the Elderly: A Cross-Cultural View." In *Growing Old in America*. 3rd ed. Edited by Beth B. Hess and Elizabeth W. Markson. New Brunswick, NJ: Transaction Books, 1986.

Foster, Susan E., and Jack A. Brizius. "Caring Too Much? American Women and the Nation's Caregiving Crisis." In *Women on the Front Lines*, edited by Jessie Allen and Alan Pifer. Washington, DC: Urban Institute, 1993.

Fraser, Joy, and Janet Ross Kerr. "Psychophysiological Effects of Back Massage on Elderly Institutionalized Patients." *Journal of Advanced Nursing* 18 (1993): 238–45.

Freedman, Marc. *Prime Time*. New York: Public Affairs, 1999.

———. "Senior Citizens: A New Force in Community Service." In *Annual Editions: Aging*, edited by Harold Cox. Guilford, CT: Dushkin McGraw-Hill, 2000.

Freeman, Mary E. Wilkins. "A Mistaken Charity." In *A Humble Romance and Other Stories*. New York: Harper and Brothers, 1887.

———. "A Village Singer." In *A New England Nun and Other Stories*. New York: Harper and Brothers, 1891.

Freixas, A., B. Luque, and A. Reina. "Critical Feminist Gerontology in the Back Room of Research." *Journal of Women and Aging* 24, no. 1 (2012): 44–58.

Freund, Katherine. "Surviving without Driving: Creating Sustainable Transportation for Seniors." Speech to the Muskie Forum, Muskie School of Public Service, University of Southern Maine. Maine Public Radio, January 11, 2002.

Frey, William F. "Mapping the Growth of Older America: Seniors and Boomers." Washington, DC: Brookings Institution, June 2007.

Friedan, Betty. *The Fountain of Age*. New York: Simon & Schuster, 1993.

Friedman, Leonore. "Aging as a Russian Doll." In *Being Bodies: Buddhist Women on the Paradox of Embodiment*. Boston: Shambhala, 1997.

Fry, Christine L. "Out of the Armchair and Off the Veranda: Anthropological Theories and the Experiences of Aging." In *Handbook of Theories of Aging*. 2nd ed. Edited by Vern L. Bengtson et al. New York: Springer, 2009.

Fry, Prem S., and Corey L. M. Keyes, eds. *New Frontiers in Resilient Aging: Life Strengths and Wellness in Late Life*. Cambridge: Cambridge University Press, 2010.

Fullmer, Elise M, Dena Shenk, and Lynette J. Eastland. "Negative Identity: A Feminist Analysis of the Social Invisibility of Older Lesbians." *Journal of Women and Aging* 11, nos. 2–3 (1999): 131–48.

Fulmer, Terry, et al. "The Complexity of Medication Compliance in the Elderly: What the Literature Tells Us." *Generations* 24, no. 4 (2000–2001): 43–48.

Furman, Frida Kerner. *Facing the Mirror: Older Women and Beauty Shop Culture*. New York: Routledge, 1997.

Fyhrquist, F., and O. Saijonmaa. "Telomere Length and Cardiovascular Aging." *Annals of Medicine* 44, supplement 1 (2012): S138–42.

Gabbay, Sarah G., and James J. Wahler. "Lesbian Aging: Review of a Growing Literature." *Journal of Gay and Lesbian Social Sciences* 14, no. 3 (2002): 1–21.

Gadow, Sally. "Covenant without Care: Letting Go and Holding On to Chronic Illness." In *The Ethics of Care and the Ethics of Cure*, edited by Jean Watson and Marilyn Ann Ray. New York: National League for Nursing, 1988.

———. "Frailty and Strength: The Dialectic in Aging," *Gerontologist* 23, no. 2 (1983): 144–47.

———. "Whose Body, Whose Story? The Question about Narratives in Women's Health Care." *Soundings* 77, nos. 3–4 (1994): 295–307.

Gagnier, Regenia. "Feminist Postmodernism: The End of Feminism or the End of Theory?" In *Theoretical Perspectives on Sexual Difference*, edited by Deborah Rhode. New Haven, CT: Yale University Press, 1990.

Gamliel, Tova, and Haim Hazan. "The Meaning of Stigma: Identity Construction in Two Old-Age Institutions." *Ageing and Society* 26, no. 3 (2006): 355–71.

Gannon, Linda R. *Women and Aging: Transcending the Myths*. New York: Routledge, 1999.

Garner, J. Dianne. "From the Editor." *Journal of Women and Aging* 23, no. 4 (2011): 281–82.

Gawande, Atul. "The Way We Age Now." *New Yorker*, April 30, 2007: 50–59.

Gaylord, Susan. "Women and Aging: A Psychological Perspective." In *Women as They Age*. 2nd ed. Edited by J. Dianne Garner and Susan O. Mercer. New York: Haworth, 2001.

Gee, Ellen M. "Voodoo Demography, Population Aging, and Canadian Social Policy." In *The Overselling of Population Aging*, edited by Ellen M. Gee and Gloria Gutman. Oxford: Oxford University Press, 2000.

Gee, Ellen M., and Gloria Gutman, eds. *The Overselling of Population Aging*. Oxford: Oxford University Press, 2000.

George, Linda K. "Social Factors, Depression, and Aging." In *Handbook of Aging and the Social Sciences*, edited by Robert H. Binstock and Linda K. George. Amsterdam: Elsevier, 2011.

Geronimus, Arline T., et al. "Do U.S. Black Women Experience Stress-Related Accelerated Biological Aging?" *Human Nature* 21 (2010): 19–38.

Gerth, Jeff, and Sheryl Gay Stolberg. "Drug Firms Reap Profits on Tax-Backed Research." *New York Times*, April 23, 2000, 1.

Ghilarducci, Teresa. "Our Ridiculous Approach to Retirement." *New York Times* Sunday Review, July 22, 2012, 5.

Gibson, Diane. "Broken Down by Age and Gender: The 'Problem of Older Women' Redefined." *Gender and Society* 10, no. 4 (1996): 433–48.

Gibson, Rose Campbell. "Reconceptualizing Retirement for Black Americans." In *Worlds of Difference: Inequality in the Aging Experience*, edited by Eleanor Palo Stoller and Rose Campbell Gibson. Thousand Oaks, CA: Pine Forge, 1994.

Glaeser, Edward P. "Goodbye Golden Years." *New York Times*, November 20, 2011.

Goldberg, Carey. "New Life inside the Depressed Brain." *Boston Globe*, November 19, 2007, D1.

Gomberg, Edith S. "Alcohol and Drugs." In *Encyclopedia of Gerontology*, edited by James E. Birren. Vol. 1. New York: Academic Press, 1996.

Goodman, Catherine Chase. "The Caregiving Roles of Asian American Women." *Journal of Women and Aging* 2, no. 1 (1990): 109–20.

Gould, Jean, ed. *Dutiful Daughters: Caring for Our Parents As They Grow Old*. Seattle: Seal Press, 1999.

Gould, Ketayun. "A Minority-Feminist Perspective on Women and Aging." *Journal of Women and Aging* 1 (1989): 195–216.

Gould, Mary-Louise. "Overcoming Blindness: Facing the Effects of Trauma and Interpersonal Violence; What One Holotropic Breathwork Practitioner Has Learned." *The Inner Door. Association for Holotropic Breathwork International* 11, no. 4 (1999): 1, 6.

Grady, Denise. "In Heart Disease, the Focus Shifts to Women." *New York Times*, April 18, 2006, D1.

———. "Scientists Say Herbs Need More Regulation." *New York Times*, March 7, 2000, D1.

Graham, Janice E., and Peter H. Stephenson, eds. *Contesting Aging and Loss*. Toronto: University of Toronto Press, 2010.

Grant, Diane. "Older Women, Work and the Impact of Discrimination." In *Age Discrimination and Diversity*, edited by Malcolm Sargeant. Cambridge: Cambridge University Press, 2011.

Gravagne, Pamela. "The Becoming of Age: How Discourses of Aging and Old Age in Contemporary Popular Film Both Reinforce and Reimagine the Narrative of Aging as Decline." Doctoral dissertation, American Studies, University of New Mexico, 2012.

Green, Brent. "Internal Colonialism vs. the Elderly," *Berkeley Journal of Sociology* (1979): 129–49.

Grimshaw, Jean. *Philosophy and Feminist Thinking*. Minneapolis: University of Minnesota, 1986.

Gross, Jane. *A Bittersweet Season: Caring for Our Aging Parents—and Ourselves*. New York: Knopf, 2011.

———. "How Medicare Fails the Elderly." *New York Times*, October 16, 2011.

Grumbach, Doris. *Coming into the End Zone: A Memoir*. New York: Norton, 1991.

———. *Extra Innings: A Memoir*. New York: Norton, 1993.

Gubrium, Jaber F., and James Holstein. "Constructionist Perspectives on Aging." In *Handbook of Theories of Aging*, edited by Vern L. Bengtson and K. Warner Schaie. New York: Springer, 1999.

Gubrium, Jaber F., and Robert J. Lynott. "Rethinking Life Satisfaction." *Human Organization* 42, no. 1 (1983): 30–38.

Gullette, Margaret Morganroth. "Age, Aging." In *Encyclopedia of Feminist Literary Theory*. New York: Garland, 1997.

———. *Aged by Culture*. Chicago: University of Chicago Press, 2004.

———. "Age Studies as Cultural Studies." In *Handbook of the Humanities and Aging*. 2nd ed. Edited by Thomas R. Cole, Robert Kastenbaum, and Ruth E. Ray. New York: Springer, 2000.

———. *Agewise: Fighting the New Ageism in America*. Chicago: Chicago University Press, 2011.

———. *Declining to Decline: Cultural Combat and the Politics of Midlife*. Charlottesville: University Press of Virginia, 1997.

Haber, David. *Health Promotion and Aging*. 4th ed. New York: Springer, 2007.

———. "Life Review: Implementation, Theory, Research, and Therapy." *International Journal of Aging and Human Development* 63, no. 2 (2006): 153–70.

Hadler, Nortin M. *Rethinking Aging: Growing Old and Living Well in an Overtreated Society*. Chapel Hill: University of North Carolina Press, 2011.

Hall, Stephen S. "The Older and Wiser Hypothesis." *New York Times Magazine*, May 6, 2007, 58–66.

———. "Prescription for Profit." *New York Times Magazine*, March 11, 2001, 40–45.

Haney, Mitchell R. "Social Media, Speed, and Listening to Oneself." *Listening* 46, no. 1 (Winter 2011): 37–50.

Harding, Sandra. "Conclusion: Epistemological Questions." In *Feminist Methodologies*, edited by Sandra Harding. Bloomington: Indiana University Press, 1987.

Harper, Mary S. "Aging Minorities." *Healthcare Trends and Transition* 6, no. 4 (1995): 9–20.

Harper, Sarah. *Ageing Societies: Myth, Challenges, and Opportunities*. London: Hodder and Arnold, 2006.

Harrington Meyer, Madonna. "Declining Marital Rates and Changing Eligibility for Social Security." Paper presented at the annual meeting of the Gerontological Society of America, Chicago, November 17, 2001.

———. "Family Status and Poverty among Older Women: The Gendered Distribution of Retirement Income in the United States." In *Aging for the 21st Century*, edited by Jill Quadagno and Debra Street. New York: St. Martin's, 1996.

Harrington Meyer, Madonna, and Pamela Herd. *Market Friendly or Family Friendly? The State and Gender Inequality in Old Age*. New York: Russell Sage, 2007.

Harrington Meyer, Madonna, and Wendy M. Parker. "Gender, Aging, and Social Policy." In *Handbook of Aging and the Social Sciences*, edited by Robert H. Binstock and Linda K. George. Amsterdam: Elsevier, 2011.

Hartmann, Heidi, and Ashley English. "Older Women's Retirement Security: A Primer." *Journal of Women, Politics, and Policy* 30, nos. 2–3 (2009): 109–40.

Hartzband, Pamela, and Jerome Groopman. "Rise of the Medical Expertocracy." *Wall Street Journal*, March 31–April 1, 2012, C3.

Harwood, Jake. "What We Watch: An Alternate—and Ageist Reality with Dubious Health Effects." *Aging Today* 33, no. 2 (March–April 2012): 9, 13.

Hatch, Laurie Russell. "Women's and Men's Retirement: Plural Pathways, Diverse Destinations." In *Social Gerontology*, edited by David E. Redburn and Robert P. McNamara. Westport, CT: Auburn House, 1998.

Hausdorff, Jeffrey M., Becca R. Levy, and Jeanne Y. Wei. "The Power of Ageism on Physical Function of Older Persons: Reversibility of Age-Related Gait Changes." *Journal of the American Geriatric Society* 47 (1999): 1346–49.

Hayflick, Leonard. "From Here to Immortality." *Public Policy and Aging Report* 14, no. 2 (2004): 1–7.

Hazan, Haim. *Old Age: Constructions and Deconstructions*. Cambridge: Cambridge University Press, 1994.

Healey, Shevy. "Calling the Question: Confronting Ageism." Paper presented at the National Women's Studies Association, Akron, Ohio, June 1990.

———. "Confronting Ageism: A Must for Mental Health." In *Faces of Women and Aging*, edited by Nancy D. Davis, Ellen Cole, and Esther D. Rothblum. New York: Haworth, 1993.

———. "Diversity with a Difference: On Being Old and Lesbian." *Journal of Gay and Lesbian Social Services* 1, no. 1 (1994): 109–17.

———. "Growing to Be an Old Woman." In *Women and Aging*, edited by Jo Alexander et al. Corvallis, OR: Calyx Books, 1986.

Healy, Tara. "Women's Ethic of Care in Its Social and Economic Context: Implications for Practice." Paper presented at the Women and Aging Conference of Mabel Wadsworth Women's Health Center, Husson College, Bangor, Maine, November 20, 1999.

Heilbrun, Carolyn. Letter to the Editor. *Women's Review of Books* 17, no. 5 (February 2000).

Hekman, Susan. "Truth and Method: Feminist Standpoint Theory Revisited." In *Provoking Feminisms*, edited by Carolyn Allen and Judith A. Howard. Chicago: University of Chicago Press, 2000.

Hendricks, Jon. "Creativity over the Life Course: A Call for a Relational Perspective." *International Journal of Aging and Human Development* 48, no. 2 (1999): 85–111.

———. "Generations and the Generation of Theory in Social Gerontology." *International Journal of Aging and Human Development* 35, no. 1 (1992): 31–47.

———. "Practical Consciousness, Social Class, and Self-Concept: A View from Sociology," in *The Self and Society in Aging Processes*, edited by Carol D. Ryff and Victor W. Marshall. New York: Springer, 1999.

Hendricks, Jon, and W. Andrew Achenbaum. "Historical Development of Theories of Aging." In *Handbook of Theories of Aging*, edited by Vern Bengtson and K. Warner Schaie. New York: Springer, 1999.

Hendricks, Jon, and Laurie Russell Hatch. "Theorizing Lifestyle: Exploring Agency and Structure in the Life Course." In *Handbook of Theories of Aging*. 2nd ed. Edited by Vern L. Bengtson et al. New York: Springer, 2009.

Hepworth, Mike. "Images of Old Age." In *Handbook of Communication and Aging Research*, edited by Jon F. Nussbaum and Justine Coupland. Mahwah, NJ: Lawrence Erlbaum, 1995.

Herd, Pamela, Stephanie A. Robert, and James S. House. "Health Disparities Among Older Adults: Life Course Influences and Policy Solutions." In *Handbook of Aging and Social Sciences*, edited by Robert H. Binstock and Linda K. George. Amsterdam: Elsevier, 2011.

Herzog, A. Regula. "Methodological Issues in Research on Older Women." In *Health and Economic Status of Older Women*, edited by A. Regula Herzog, Karen C. Holden, and Mildred M. Seltzer. Amityville, NY: Baywood, 1989.

Hewitt, Rich. "New Aged." *U Maine Today* (Spring 2012): 2–5.

Hillyer, Barbara. "The Embodiment of Old Women: Silences." *Frontiers* 19, no. 1 (1998): 48–60.

Himmelstein, David U., and Steffie Woolhandler. "I Am Not a Health Reform." *New York Times*, December 15, 2007, A35.

Hine, Rochelle. "In the Margins: The Impact of Sexualised Images on the Mental Health of Ageing Women." *Sex Roles* 65 (2011): 632–46.

Hirschmann, Nancy J. *Rethinking Obligation: A Feminist Method for Political Theory.* Ithaca, NY: Cornell, 1992.

Hoare, Carol Wren. *Erikson on Development in Adulthood: New Insights from Unpublished Papers.* Oxford: Oxford University Press, 2002.

Hoblitzelle, Olivia Ames. "Touch of Grey." *Shambhala Sun*, March 2011, 27–29.

Hogan, Paul. "It's Not Just Your Father's Longevity Anymore! Aging Is Not the Problem." Speech delivered at the Metropolitan Club, New York, February 28, 2011. *Vital Speeches of the Day* (May 2011): 184–87.

Hollibaugh, Amber, Jim Campbell, and Ana Olivera. "Aging Gay Men and Lesbians: Challenges, Resources, and Community Responses." AARP Conference, Diversity in the 21st Century, Los Angeles, June 20, 2007.

Holstein, Martha. "Ethics and Aging: Retrospectively and Prospectively." In *A Guide to Humanistic Research on Aging*, edited by Thomas R. Cole, Ruth E. Ray, and Robert Kastenbaum. Baltimore: Johns Hopkins University Press, 2010.

———. "Ethics and Old Age: The Second Generation." In *Social Gerontology*, edited by Dale Dannefer and Chris Phillipson. Los Angeles: SAGE, 2010.

———. "A Feminist Perspective on Anti-Aging Medicine." *Generations* 25, no. 2 (2001): 38–43.

———. "Home Care, Women, and Aging: A Case Study of Injustice." In *Mother Time: Women, Aging, and Ethics*, edited by Margaret Urban Walker. Lanham, MD: Rowman & Littlefield, 1999.

———. "Long-Term Care, Feminism, and an Ethics of Solidarity." In *Challenges of an Aging Society*, edited by Rachel A. Pruchno and Michael A. Smyer. Baltimore: Johns Hopkins University Press, 2007.

———. "The 'New Aging': Imagining Alternative Futures." In *Evolution of the Aging Self*, edited by K. Warner Schaie and Jon Hendricks. New York: Springer, 2000.

———. "Productive Aging: A Feminist Critique." *Journal of Aging and Social Policy* 4, nos. 3–4 (1992): 17–34.

———. "What Is Home Care?" *Park Ridge Center Bulletin* (September–October 1999): 3–4.

———. "Women and Productive Aging: Troubling Implications." In *Critical Gerontology*, edited by Meredith Minkler and Carroll L. Estes. Amityville, NY: Baywood, 1999.

———. "Women's Lives, Women's Work: Productivity, Gender, and Aging." In *Achieving a Productive Aging Society*, edited by Scott A. Bass, Francis G. Caro, and Yung-Ping Chen. Westport, CT: Auburn House, 1993.

Holstein, Martha, and Meredith Minkler. "Self, Society, and the 'New Gerontology.'" *Gerontologist* 43, no. 6 (2003): 787–96.

Holstein, Martha, Jennifer A. Parks, and Mark H. Waymack. *Ethics, Aging, and Society: The Critical Turn.* New York: Springer, 2011.

Holstein, Martha, and Mark Waymack. "The Contributions of Philosophy and Ethics in the Study of Age." In *Enduring Questions in Gerontology*, edited by Debra J. Sheets, Dana Burr Bradley, and Jon Hendricks. New York: Springer, 2006.

Honore, Carl. *In Praise of Slowness: Challenging the Cult of Speed*. New York: HarperCollins, 2004.

hooks, bell. *Where We Stand: Class Matters*. New York: Routledge, 2000.

Hooyman, Nancy. "Research on Older Women: Where Is Feminism?" *Gerontologist* 39, no. 1 (1999): 115–18.

———. "Women as Caregivers of the Elderly: Implications for Social Welfare Policy and Practice." In *Aging and Caregiving: Theory, Research, and Policy*, edited by David C. Biegel and Arthur Blum. Newbury Park, CA: Sage, 1990.

Hooyman, Nancy, Collette V. Browne, Ruth Ray, and Virginia Richardson. "Feminist Gerontology and the Life Course: Policy, Research and Teaching Issues." *Gerontology and Geriatric Education* 22, no. 4 (2002): 3–26.

Hooyman, Nancy, and Judith Gonyea. "A Feminist Model of Family Care: Practice and Policy Directions." In *Fundamentals of Feminist Gerontology*, edited by J. Dianne Garner. New York: Haworth, 1999.

———. *Feminist Perspectives on Family Care*. Thousand Oaks, CA: Sage, 1995.

Hounsell, Cindy, and Alma Morales Riojas. "Older Women Face Tarnished 'Golden Years.'" *Aging Today* (March–April 2006): 7, 9.

Hsu, Caroline. "The Greening of Aging." *U.S. News and World Report*, June 11, 2006.

Hudson, Robert B. "Privatizing Old-Age Benefits: Re-emergent Ideology Encounters Organized Interests." In *Resecuring Social Security and Medicare: Understanding Privatization and Risk*, edited by Judith Gonyea. Washington, DC: Gerontological Society of America, 1998.

Hudson, Robert B., and Judith Gonyea. "Baby Boomers and the Shifting Political Construction of Old Age." *Gerontologist* 52, no. 2 (2012): 272–82.

———. "The Evolving Role of Public Policy in Promoting Work and Retirement." *Generations* 31, no. 1 (2007): 68–75.

Hulko, Wendy, et al. "Views of First Nation Elders on Memory Loss and Memory Care in Later Life." *Journal of Cross Cultural Gerontology* 25 (2010): 317–42.

Hummert, Mary Lee. "Stereotypes of the Elderly and Patronizing Speech." In *Interpersonal Communication in Older Adulthood*, edited by Mary Lee Hummert et al. Thousand Oaks, CA: Sage, 1994.

Hurd, Laura C. "'We're Not Old!': Older Women's Negotiations of Aging and Oldness." *Journal of Aging Studies* 13, no. 4 (1999): 419–39.

Hurd Clarke, Laura. *Facing Age: Women Growing Older in an Anti-Aging Culture*. Lanham, MD: Rowman & Littlefield, 2010.

Hurd Clarke, Laura, and Meredith Griffin. "The Body Natural and the Body Unnatural: Beauty Work and Aging." *Journal of Aging Studies* 21 (2007): 187–201.

Hurley, Ben, and Iris Reuter. "Aging, Physical Activity, and Disease Prevention." *Journal of Aging Research* 2011. http://www.ncbi.nlm.nih.gov/pmc/articles/PMC3124955. Accessed April 17, 2012.

Hurtado, Aida. "Strategic Suspensions: Feminists of Color Theorize the Production of Knowledge." In *Knowledge, Difference, and Power*, edited by Nancy Goldberger et al. New York: Basic, 1996.

Hynes, Denise M. "The Quality of Breast Cancer Care in Local Communities: Implications for Health Care Reform." *Medical Care* 32 (1994): 328–40.

Innes, J. Bruce, et al. "Beyond the Myths of Aging." *Critical Issues in Aging*, no. 1 (1997): 42–45.

"In Search of the Secrets of Aging." NIH Publication no. 93-2756. Bethesda, MD: National Institutes of Health, National Institute on Aging, 1996.

International Longevity Center (ILC-USA). Anti-Ageism Task Force. *Ageism in America*. New York: ILC, 2006.

Jackson, Jacquelyne Johnson. "Aging Black Women and Public Policies." *Black Scholar*, May–June 1988, 31–43.

Jackson, Jacquelyne Johnson, and Charlotte Perry. "Physical Health Conditions of Middle-Aged and Aged Blacks." In *Aging and Health: Perspectives on Gender, Race, Ethnicity, and Class*, edited by Kyriakos S. Markides. Newbury Park, CA: Sage, 1989.

Jackson, James S., Ishtar O. Govia, and Sherrill L. Sellers. "Racial and Ethnic Influences over the Life Course." In *Handbook of Aging and Social Sciences*, edited by Robert H. Binstock and Linda K. George. Amsterdam: Elsevier, 2011.

Jackson, Pamela Brayboy, and David R. Williams. "The Intersection of Race, Gender, and SES." In *Gender, Race, Class, and Health: Intersectional Approaches*, edited by Amy J. Schulz and Leith Mullings. San Francisco: Jossey-Bass, 2006.

Jacobs, Ruth Harriet. *Be an Outrageous Older Woman*. New York: HarperCollins, 1997.

———. "Friendships among Old Women." In *Women, Aging, and Ageism*, edited by Evelyn R. Rosenthal. New York: Harrington Park Press, 1990.

Jacoby, Susan. *Never Say Die: The Myth and Marketing of Old Age*. New York: Pantheon, 2011.

Jervis, Lori L. "Aging, Health, and the Indigenous People of North America." *Journal of Cross-Cultural Gerontology* 25 (2010): 299–301.

Jervis, Lori L., Mathew E. Boland, and Alexandra Fickenscher. "American Indian Family Care-Givers' Experiences with Helping Elders." *Journal of Cross-Cultural Gerontology* 25 (2010): 355–69.

Jewett, Sarah Orne. "The Flight of Betsey Lane." In *A Native of Winby and Other Stories*. Boston: Houghton Mifflin, 1893.

John, Robert. "Aging among American Indians: Income Security, Health, and Social Support Networks." In *Full-Color Aging*, edited by Toni P. Miles. Washington, DC: Gerontological Society of America, 1999.

———. "Native Americans and Alaska Natives." In *Encyclopedia of Health and Aging*, edited by Kyriakos S. Markides et al. Los Angeles: Sage, 2007.

John, Robert, Patrice Blanchard, and Catherine Hagan Hennessy. "Hidden Lives: Aging and Contemporary American Indian Women." In *Handbook on Women and Aging*, edited by Jean M. Coyle. Westport, CT: Greenwood, 1997.

John, Robert, Catherine Hagan Hennessy, and Clark H. Denny. "Preventing Chronic Illness and Disability among Native American Elders." In *Serving Minority Elders in the 21st Century*, edited by May L. Wykle and Amasa B. Ford. New York: Springer, 1999.

Johns, Elizabeth. "Redefining Retirement: Women Who Continue to Work after Age 65." Master's thesis, University of Maine, 2002.

Johnson, Colleen L. "Cultural Diversity in the Late-Life Family." In *Handbook of Aging and the Family*, edited by Rosemary Blieszner and Victoria Hilkevitch Bedford. Westport, CT: Greenwood, 1995.

Johnson, Colleen L., and Barbara Barer. *Life beyond 85 Years: The Aura of Survivorship*. New York: Springer, 1997.

Johnson, Don Hanlon. *Body, Spirit, and Democracy*. Berkeley: North Atlantic Books Somatic Resources, 1994.

Jolanki, Outi. "Talk about Old Age, Health, and Morality." In *Valuing Older People: A Humanistic Approach to Ageing*. Edited by Ricca Edmondson and Hans-Joachim von Kondratowitz. Bristol: The Policy Press, 2009.

Jones, Helen. "Visibility and Consent: The Sexual Abuse of Elderly Women." In *Foucault and Aging*, edited by Jason L. Powell and Azrini Wahidin. New York: Nova Science, 2006.

Joyce, Kelly, and Laura Mamo. "Graying the Cyborg: New Directions in Feminist Analyses of Aging, Science, and Technology." In *Age Matters*, edited by Toni M. Calasanti and Kathleen F. Slevin. New York: Routledge, 2006.

Kalache, A., S. M. Barreto, and J. Keller. "Global Aging." In *Cambridge Handbook of Age and Ageing*, edited by Malcolm L. Johnson. Cambridge: Cambridge University Press, 2005.

Kalish, Richard. "The New Ageism and the Failure Models." In *Aging and the Human Spirit*, edited by Carol LeFevre and Perry LeFevre. Chicago: Exploration Press, 1985.

Kane, Robert L. "What Havoc Will the Baby Boomers Wreak?" In *Social Structures: Demographic Changes and the Well-Being of Older Persons*, edited by K. Warner Schaie and Peter Uhlenberg. New York: Springer, 2007.

Kane, Robert L., and Rosalie A. Kane. "HCBS: the Next Thirty Years." *Generations* 36, no. 1 (2012): 131–34.

Kane, Rosalie A. "Thirty Years of Home- and-Community Based Services: Getting Closer and Closer to Home." *Generations* 36, no. 1 (2012): 6–13.

Kaplan, George A. "Behavioral, Social, and Socioenvironmental Factors Adding Years to Life and Life to Years." In *Public Health and Aging*, edited by Tom Hickey, Marjorie A. Speers, and Thomas R. Prohaska. Baltimore: Johns Hopkins University Press, 1998.

Kaplan, George A., and William J. Strawbridge. "Behavioral and Social Factors in Healthy Aging." In *Aging and Quality of Life*, edited by Ronald Abeles et al. New York: Springer, 1994.

Kaplan, Sheila. "The New Generation Gap: The Politics of Generational Justice." *Common Cause* 13, no. 2 (1987): 13–15.

Kastenbaum, Robert. "Encrusted Elders: Arizona and the Political Spirit of Postmodern Aging." In *Voices and Visions of Aging: Toward a Critical Gerontology*, edited by Thomas R. Cole et al. New York: Springer, 1993.

Katz, Ira R. "Late-Life Suicide and the Euthanasia Debate: What Should We Do about Suffering in Terminal Illness and Chronic Disease?" *Gerontologist* 34, no. 5 (1997): 269–71.

Katz, Stephen. "Critical Gerontology Discourse: Nomadic Thinking or Postmodern Sociology?" *Discourse of Sociological Practice* (Spring 2000): 7–11.

——. *Cultural Aging: Life Course, Lifestyle, and Senior Worlds*. Peterborough, ON: Broadview Press, 2005.

——. *Disciplining Old Age: The Formation of Gerontological Knowledge*. Charlottesville: University of Virginia Press, 1996.

Katz, Stephen, and Kevin McHugh. "Age, Meaning, and Place: Cultural Narratives and Retirement Communities." In *A Guide to Humanistic Studies in Aging*, edited by Thomas R. Cole, Ruth Ray, and Robert Kastenbaum. Baltimore: Johns Hopkins University Press, 2010.

Kaufman, Sharon. "The Age of Reflexive Longevity: How the Clinic and Changing Expectations of the Life Course Are Reshaping Old Age." In *A Guide to Humanistic Studies in Aging*, edited by Thomas R. Cole, Ruth E. Ray, and Robert Kastenbaum. Baltimore: Johns Hopkins University Press, 2010.

Kaye, Lenard, with Keith Shortall. "Maine Voices." Maine Public Radio, June 5, 2012.

Kelchner, Elizabeth. "Ageism's Impact and Effect on Society: Not Just a Concern for the Old." *Journal of Gerontological Social Work* 32, no. 4 (1999): 85–100.

Kelley-Moore, Jessica. "Disability and Ageing: The Social Construction of Causality." In *Social Gerontology*, edited by Dale Dannefer and Chris Phillipson. Los Angeles: SAGE, 2010.

Kemper, Susan, and Tamara Harden. "Experimentally Disentangling What's Beneficial about Elderspeak from What's Not." *Psychology and Aging* 14, no. 4 (1999): 656–70.

Kennedy, Jae, and Meredith Minkler. "Disability Theory and Public Policy: Implications for Critical Gerontology." In *Critical Gerontology: Perspectives from Political and Moral Economy*, edited by Meredith Minkler and Carroll L. Estes. Amityville, NY: Baywood, 1999.

Kenyon, Gary, Ernst Bohlmeijer, and William L. Randall, eds. *Storying Later Life: Issues, Investigations, and Interventions in Narrative Gerontology*. Oxford: Oxford University Press, 2011.

Kimmel, Douglas, Tara Rose, and Steven David, eds. *Lesbian, Gay, Bisexual, and Transgender Aging: Research and Clinic Perspectives*. New York: Columbia University Press, 2006.

King, Neil, and Toni Calasanti. "Empowering the Old: Critical Gerontology and Anti-Aging in a Global Context." In *Aging, Globalization, and Inequality: The New Critical Gerontology*, edited by Jan Baars et al. Amityville, NY: Baywood, 2006.

Kingson, Eric. "Perspectives on the Economic Implications of the Aging of Baby Boomers." In *Social Structures: Demographic Changes and the Well-Being of Older Persons*, edited by K. Warner Schaie and Peter Uhlenberg. New York: Springer, 2007.

Kingson, Eric, and Jill Quadagno. "Social Security: Marketing Radical Reform." In *Critical Gerontology: Perspectives from Political and Moral Economy*, edited by Meredith Minkler and Carroll L. Estes. Amityville, NY: Baywood, 1999.

Kingston, Maxine Hong. *I Love a Broad Margin to My Life*. New York: Vintage, 2011.

Kirkman, Allison. "Caring from 'Duty and the Heart': Gendered Caring and Alzheimer's." *Women's Studies Journal* 25, no. 1 (2011): 2–16.

Kivett, Vira. "Rural Old Women." In *Handbook on Women and Aging*, edited by Jean M. Coyle. Westport, CT: Greenwood, 1997.

Kivnick, Helen Q., and Rachel Pruchno. "Bridges and Boundaries: Humanities and Arts Enhance Gerontology." *Gerontologist* 51, no. 2 (2011): 142–44.

Kiyak, H. Asuman, and Nancy R. Hooyman. "Minority and Socioeconomic Status: Impact on Quality of Life in Aging." In *Aging and Quality of Life*, edited by Ronald Abeles et al. New York: Springer, 1994.

Kleyman, Paul. "The Economic Crisis Facing Seniors of Color." New American Media. http://greenlining.org/publications/pdf/613/613.pdf. Accessed July 16, 2012.

Knight, Eric L., and Jerry Avorn. "Use and Abuse of Drugs in Older Persons." *Gerontologist* 39, no. 1 (1999): 109–11.

Knox, Richard. "Living Longer Is the Best Revenge." *Boston Globe Magazine*, May 23, 1999, 40.

Koehn, Sharon, and Karen Kobayashi. "Age and Ethnicity." In *Age Discrimination and Diversity*, edited by Malcolm Sargeant. Cambridge: Cambridge University Press, 2011.

Koenig, Harold, et al. "Mental Health Care for Older Adults in the Year 2020: A Dangerous and Avoided Topic." *Gerontologist* 34, no. 5 (1994): 674–79.

Kolata, Gina. "Estrogen Use Tied to Slight Increase in Risks to Heart." *New York Times*, April 5, 2000, A1.

Kontos, Pia C. "Embodied Selfhood: Ethnographic Reflections, Performing Ethnography, and Humanizing Dementia Care." In *Contesting Aging and Loss*, edited by Janice E. Graham and Peter H. Stephenson. Toronto: University of Toronto Press, 2010.

Kotlikoff, Laurence J., and Scott Burns. *The Coming Generational Storm: What You Need to Know about America's Economic Future*. Cambridge, MA: MIT Press, 2004.

Kreager, Philip, and Elisabeth Schroeder-Butterfill. *Ageing without Children: European and Asian Perspectives*. New York: Berghahn, 2005.

Krekula, Clary. "The Intersection of Age and Gender: Reworking Gender Theory and Social Gerontology." *Current Sociology* 55 (2007): 155–71.

Kryspin-Exner, Ilse, Elisabeth Lamplmayr, and Anna Feinhofer. "Geropsychology: The Gender Gap in Human Aging—a Mini-Review." *Gerontology* 57 (2011): 539–48.

Kunow, Rudiger. "Old Age and Globalization." In *A Guide to Humanistic Studies in Aging*, edited by Thomas R. Cole, Ruth E. Ray, and Robert Kastenbaum. Baltimore: Johns Hopkins, 2010.

Kunz, John, and Florence Gray Soltys, eds. *Transformational Reminiscence: Life Story Work*. New York: Springer, 2007.

Kunzmann, Ute. "Wisdom." In *The Encyclopedia of Aging*. 4th ed. Vol. 2. Edited by Richard Schulz. New York: Springer, 2006.

Labouvie-Vief, Gisela. "Dynamic Integration Theory: Emotion, Cognition, and Equilibrium in Later Life." In *Handbook of Theories of Aging*. 2nd ed. Edited by Vern L. Bengtson et al. New York: Springer, 2009.

———. "Women's Creativity and Images of Gender." In *Women Growing Older: Psychological Perspectives*, edited by Barbara F. Turner and Lillian E. Troll. Thousand Oaks, CA: Sage, 1994.

Labowitz, Shoni. *God, Sex, and Women of the Bible*. New York: Simon & Schuster, 1998.

Lamphere-Thorpe, Jo-Ann, and Robert J. Blendon. "Years Gained and Opportunities Lost: Women and Healthcare in an Aging America." In *Women on the Front Lines*, edited by Jessie Allen and Alan Pifer. Washington, DC: Urban Institute, 1993.

Lamy, Peter. "Actions of Alcohol and Drugs in Older People." *Generations* 12, no. 4 (1988): 9–13.

———. "Geriatric Drug Therapy." *American Family Physician* 34, no. 6 (1986): 118–24.

Langellier, K. M., and Eric E. Peterson. *Story Telling in Daily Life*: Performing Narrative. Philadelphia: Temple University Press, 2004.

Langer, Ellen J. *Mindfulness*. Reading, MA: Addison-Wesley, 1989.

———. *The Power of Mindful Learning*. Reading, MA: Addison-Wesley, 1997.

Langford, Jean M. *Fluent Bodies: Ayurvedic Remedies for Postcolonial Imbalance*. Durham, NC: Duke University Press, 2002.

Lassiter, Judith. *Relax and Renew: Restful Yoga for Stressful Times*. Berkeley: Rodmell Press, 1995.

Laws, Glenda. "Understanding Ageism: Lessons from Feminism and Postmodernism." *Gerontologist* 35, no. 1 (1995): 112–18.

Laz, Cheryl. "Age Embodied." *Journal of Aging Studies* 17 (2003): 503–19.

le Carré, John. "In Place of Nations." *The Nation*, April 9, 2001, 11–13.

Lessing, Doris. *Walking in the Shade*. Vol.2. 1949–1962. New York: Harper Perennial, 1998.

LeVande, Diane I. "Growth and Development in Older Women: A Critique and Proposal." In *Doing Feminism: Teaching and Research in the Academy*, edited by Mary Anderson et al. Lansing: Michigan State Women's Studies Program, 1997.

Levin, Jack, and William Levin. *Ageism*. Belmont, CA: Wadsworth, 1980.

Levy, Becca R. "Eradication of Ageism Requires Addressing the Enemy Within." *Gerontologist* 41, no. 5 (2001): 578–79.

———. "The Inner Self of the Japanese Elderly: A Defense against Negative Stereotypes of Aging." *International Journal of Aging and Human Development* 48, no. 2 (1999): 131–44.

———. "Unconscious Ageism." In *Encyclopedia of Ageism*, edited by Erdman Palmore, Laurence G. Branch, and Diana K. Harris. New York: Haworth Pastoral Press, 2005.

Levy, Becca R., and Mahzarin R. Banaji. "Implicit Ageism." In *Ageism*, edited by Todd D. Nelson. Cambridge, MA: MIT Press, 2002.

Lieberman, Trudy. "How the Media Has Shaped the Social Security Debate." *Columbia Journalism Review* Campaign Desk. April 18, 2012.

Lock, Margaret. "Alzheimer's Disease: A Tangled Concept." In *Complexities: Beyond Nature and Nurture*, edited by Susan McKinnon and Sydel Silverman. Chicago: University of Chicago Press, 2005.

Loe, Meika. *Aging Our Way: Lessons for Living from 85 and Beyond*. New York: Oxford, 2011.

———. "Doing It My Way: Old Women, Technology and Wellbeing." *Sociology of Health and Illness* 32, no. 2 (February 2010): 319–34.

Longino, Charles F. "The Gray Peril Mentality and the Impact of Retirement Migration." *Journal of Applied Gerontology* 7, no. 4 (1988): 448–55.

Longman, Philip J. "The World Turns Gray." *U.S. News and World Report*, March 1, 1999, 30–39.

Lopata, Helen Znaniecka. "Feminist Perspectives on Social Gerontology." In *Handbook of Aging and the Family*, edited by Rosemary Blieszner and Victoria Hilkevitch Bedford. Westport, CT: Greenwood, 1995.

Lopes, Alexandra. "Aging and Social Class." In *Age Discrimination and Diversity*, edited by Malcolm Sargeant. Cambridge: Cambridge University Press, 2011.

Lorber, Judith. *Gender and the Social Construction of Illness*. Walnut Creek, CA: Alta Mira, 2000.

Loue, Sana. *Assessing Race, Ethnicity, and Gender in Health*. New York: Springer, 2006.

Louie, Kem B. "Status of Mental Health Needs of Asian Elderly." In *Serving Minority Elders in the 21st Century*, edited by May L. Wykle and Amasa B. Ford. New York: Springer, 1999.

Lugones, Maria. "Playfulness, 'World' Travelling, and Loving." In *The Woman That I Am: The Literature and Culture of Contemporary Women of Color*, edited by D. Soyini Madison. New York: St. Martin's, 1994.

Lyder, Courtney H., et al. "Appropriate Prescribing for Elders: Disease Management Alone Is Not Enough." *Generations* 24, no. 4 (2000–2001): 55–59.

Lynott, Robert J., and Patricia Passath Lynott. "Critical Gerontology." *Encyclopedia of Aging*. Vol. 1. Edited by David J. Ekerdt. New York: Thomson Gale, 2002.

Macdonald, Barbara, with Cynthia Rich. *Look Me in the Eye: Old Women, Aging, and Ageism*. 2nd ed. Minneapolis: Spinsters Ink, 1991.

Macy, Joanna. "Gratitude: Where Healing the Earth Begins." *Shambhala Sun*, November 2007, 48–51.

Malveaux, Julianne. "Gender Differences and Beyond: An Economic Perspective on Diversity and Commonality among Women." In *Theoretical Perspectives on Sexual Difference*, edited by Deborah L. Rhode. New Haven, CT: Yale University Press, 1990.

——. "Race, Poverty, and Women's Aging." In *Women on the Front Lines*, edited by Jessie Allen and Alan Pifer. Washington, DC: Urban Institute, 1993.

Manahan, William. *Eat for Health*. Tiburon, CA: H. J. Kramer, 1988.

Manheimer, Ronald J. Review of *Handbook of Emotion, Adult Development, and Aging*. *Gerontologist* 38, no. 2 (1998): 262–67.

——. "Wisdom and Method: Philosophical Contributions to Gerontology." In *Handbook of the Humanities and Aging*, edited by Thomas R. Cole, David D. Van Tassel, and Robert Kastenbaum. New York: Springer, 1992.

Mann, Charles C. "Swallowing Hard: Review of *Bitter Pills: Inside the Hazardous World of Legal Drugs* by Stephen Fried." *New York Times Review of Books*, June 13, 1998.

Manning, Lydia K. "Experiences from Pagan Women: A Closer Look at Croning Rituals." *Journal of Aging Studies* 26, no. 1 (January 2012): 102–8.

Margolies, Luisa. *My Mother's Hip: Lessons from the World of Eldercare*. Philadelphia: Temple University Press, 2004.

Markides, Kyriakos S. "Aging, Gender, Race, Ethnicity, Class, and Health: A Conceptual Overview." In *Aging and Health*, edited by Kyriakos S. Markides. Newbury Park, CA: Sage, 1989.

———. "Minorities and Aging." In *The Encyclopedia of Aging*. Vol. 2. Edited by Richard Schulz. New York: Springer, 2006.

Markides, Kyriakos S., Jeannine Coreil, and Linda Perkowski Rogers. "Aging and Health among Southwestern Hispanics." In *Aging and Health*, edited by Kyriakos S. Markides. Newbury Park, CA: Sage, 1989.

Markson, Elizabeth. "Communities of Resistance: Older Women in a Gendered World." *Gerontologist* 39, no. 4 (1999): 495–502.

———. "Gender Roles and Memory Loss in Old Age: An Exploration of Linkages." In *Growing Old in America*. 3rd ed. Edited by Beth B. Hess and Elizabeth Markson. New Brunswick, NJ: Transaction Books, 1986.

Markson, Elizabeth W., and Carol A. Taylor. "The Mirror Has Two Faces." *Ageing and Society* 20 (2000): 137–60.

Marshall, Leni, ed. Aging and Ageism issue. *National Women's Studies Association Journal* 18, no. 1 (2006).

———. "The Kiss of the Spider Woman: Native American Storytellers and Cultural Transmission." *Journal of Aging, Humanities, and the Arts* 1, no. 1 (2007): 35–52.

Marshall, Peter, et al. "Personality and Longevity: Findings from the Georgia Centenarian Study." *Age* 28 (2006): 343–52.

Martin, Linda. "Demography and Aging." In *Handbook of Aging and the Social Sciences*, 7th ed. Edited by Robert H. Binstock and Linda K. George. Amsterdam: Elsevier, 2011.

Martin-Matthews, Anne. "Revisiting Widowhood in Later Life." *Canadian Journal on Aging/La Revue Canadienne du Vieillissement* 30, no. 3 (2011): 339–54.

Martinez, Iveris L., et al. "Invisible Civic Engagement among Older Adults: Valuing the Contributions of Informal Volunteering." *Journal of Cross-Cultural Gerontology* 26, no. 1 (March 2011): 23–37.

Matthews, Anne Martin, and Lori D. Campbell. "Gender Roles, Employment, and Informal Care." In *Connecting Gender and Age*, edited by Sara Arber and Jay Ginn. Buckingham: Open University Press, 1995.

Maynard, Isabelle. "The House on Fell Street." In *Fierce with Reality*, edited by Margaret Cruikshank. Topsham, ME: Just Write Books, 2007.

McDaniel, Susan. "A Sociological Perspective on Women and Aging as the Millennium Turns." In *Women As They Age*. 2nd ed. Edited by J. Dianne Garner and Susan O. Mercer. New York: Haworth, 2001.

———. "Women and Aging: A Sociological Perspective." In *Women As They Age*, edited by J. Dianne Garner and Susan O. Mercer. New York: Haworth, 1989.

McDonald, Kim. "Sport Scientists Gain New Respect as They Shift Focus to the Elderly." *Chronicle of Higher Education*, September 25, 1998, A15–A16.

McDowell, Linda. *Gender, Identity, and Place: Understanding Feminist Geographies*. Minneapolis: University of Minnesota Press, 1999.

McFadden, Susan. "Feminist Scholarship as a Meeting Ground for Age and Disability Studies." *Gerontologist* 41, no. 1 (2001): 133–37.

McGeehan, Patrick. "Health Care Drives Job Growth in Region, but with Many Jobs That Pay Poorly." *New York Times*, May 25, 2007, C13.

McLendon, Amber N., and Penny S. Shelton. "New Symptoms in Older Adults: Disease or Drug?" *Generations* 35, no. 4 (Winter 2011–2012): 25–29.

McLeod, Beth Witrogen, and Theodore Roszak. "Tomorrow's Caregivers: New Opportunities, New Challenges." *Aging Today* 22, no. 1 (2001): 9–10.

McQueen, Anjetta. "Prescriptions Reportedly Claim Growing Share of Health Costs." *Boston Globe*, March 12, 2001, A3.

Megret, Frederic. "The Human Rights of Older Persons: A Growing Challenge." *Human Rights Law Review* 11, no. 1 (2011): 37–66.

Meigs, Mary. *Beyond Recall*. Edited by Lise Weil. Vancouver, BC: Talonbooks, 2005.

———. *In the Company of Strangers*. Vancouver, BC: Talonbooks, 1991.

Meilaender, Gilbert. "Thinking about Aging." *First Things* (April 2011): 37–43.

Mellencamp, Patricia. "From Anxiety to Equanimity: Crisis and Generational Continuity on TV, at the Movies, in Life, in Death." In *Figuring Age: Women, Bodies, Generations*, edited by Kathleen Woodward. Bloomington: Indiana University Press, 1999.

Meyers, Diana Tietjens. "Miroir, Memoire, Mirage: Appearance, Aging, and Women." In *Mother Time: Women, Aging, and Ethics*, edited by Margaret Urban Walker. Lanham, MD: Rowman & Littlefield, 1999.

Michocki, K. J., et al. "Drug Prescribing for the Elderly." *Archives of Family Medicine* 2, no. 4 (1993): 441–44.

Miles, Steven H. "Sexuality in the Nursing Home: Iatrogenic Loneliness." *Generations* 23, no. 1 (1999): 36–44.

Miles, Toni P. "Aging and the New Multicultural Reality." *Gerontologist* 39, no. 1 (1999): 118–20.

———. "Living with Chronic Illness and the Policies That Bind." In *Full-Color Aging*, edited by Toni P. Miles. Washington, DC: Gerontological Society of America, 1999.

Minkler, Meredith. "Scapegoating the Elderly: New Voices, Old Theme." *Journal of Health Care Policy* 18 (1997): 6–12.

Minkler, Meredith, and Carroll L. Estes, eds. *Critical Gerontology: Perspectives from Political and Moral Economy*. Amityville, NY: Baywood, 1999.

Mitchell, Margaretta. "Imogene through Her Camera." Introduction to *After 90*. Seattle: University of Washington Press, 1977.

Mitchell, Valory, and Cindy M. Bruns. "Writing One's Own Story: Women, Aging, and the Social Narrative." *Women and Therapy* 34 (2011): 114–28.

Mollenkott, Virginia Ramey. "Ageism." *Dictionary of Feminist Theologies*, edited by Letty Russell and J. Shannon Clarkson. Louisville, KY: Westminster John Knox Press, 1996.

Montgomery, Sy. "A Return to Native Foods." *Boston Globe*, March 7, 2000, A1.

Moody, Harry R. *Abundance of Life*. New York: Columbia University Press, 1988.

———. "Age, Productivity, and Transcendence." In *Achieving a Productive Aging Society*, edited by Scott Bass et al. Westport, CT: Auburn House, 1993.

———. "Bioethics and Aging." *In Handbook of Aging and the Humanities*, edited by Thomas R. Cole et al. New York: Springer, 2000.

———. "The Humanities and Aging: A Millennial Perspective." *Gerontologist* 41, no. 3 (2001): 411–15.

———. "Overview: What Is Critical Gerontology and Why Is It Important?" In *Voices and Visions of Aging*, edited by Thomas R. Cole et al. New York: Springer, 1993.

Moody, Harry R., and Jennifer R. Sasser. *Aging: Concepts and Controversies*. 7th ed. Los Angeles: SAGE, 2011; 6th ed. Los Angeles: SAGE, 2010.

Moore, Thomas J. "FDA Math Needs Warning Label." *Boston Globe*, December 3, 2000, D1.

———. *Prescription for Disaster: The Hidden Dangers in Your Medicine Cabinet*. New York: Simon & Schuster, 1998.

———. "Why Estrogen's Promise Fell Short." *Boston Globe*, April 9, 2000, A1.

Morell, Carolyn. "Empowerment Theory and Long-Living Women: A Feminist and Disability Perspective." *Journal of Human Behavior in the Social Environment* 7, nos. 3–4 (2003): 225–36.

Morgan, Anna. "Just Keep Breathing." In *Fierce with Reality: An Anthology of Literature on Aging*, edited by Margaret Cruikshank. Topsham, ME: Just Write Books, 2007.

Mosteller, Sue. Preface to *Finding My Way Home* by Henri Nouwen. New York: Crossroad Publishing, 2001.

Mulnard, Ruth, et al. "Estrogen Replacement Therapy for Treatment of Mild to Moderate Alzheimer's Disease: A Randomized Controlled Trial." *Journal of the American Medical Association* 238, no. 8 (February 23, 2000): 1007–15.

Munro, Alice. Interview in *The Paris Review Interviews II*, edited by Philip Gorevitch. New York: Picador, 2006.

———. "Spelling." In *The Beggar Maid*. New York: Knopf, 1978.

Murnen, Sarah K., and Linda Smolak. "Are Feminist Women Protected from Body Image Problems? A Meta-analytic Review of Relevant Research." *Sex Roles* (2009): 186–97.

Myerhoff, Barbara. "Aging and the Aged in Other Cultures: An Anthropological Perspective." In *Remembered Lives: The Work of Ritual, Storytelling, and Growing Older*, edited by Marc Kaminsky. Ann Arbor: University of Michigan, 1992.

———. *Number Our Days*. New York: Simon & Schuster, 1980.

———. "Rites and Signs of Ripening: The Intertwining of Ritual, Time, and Growing Older." In *Age and Anthropological Theory*, edited by David Kertzer and Jennie Keith. Ithaca, NY: Cornell University Press, 1984.

Myerhoff, Barbara, and Virginia Tufte. "Life History as Integration: Personal Myth and Aging." In *Remembered Lives*: The Work of Ritual, Storytelling, and Growing Older, edited by Marc Kaminsky. Ann Arbor: University of Michigan, 1995.

Napoleon, Val. "My Grandmother's Skin." In *I Feel Great about My Hands and the Unexpected Joys of Aging*, edited by Shari Graydon. Vancouver: Douglas & McIntyre, 2011.

Naughton, Corina, et al. "Elder Abuse and Neglect in Ireland: Results from a National Prevalence Survey." *Age and Ageing* 41, no. 1 (2012): 98–103.

Nelson, Hilde Lindemann. "Stories of My Old Age." In *Mother Time: Women, Aging, and Ethics*, edited by Margaret Urban Walker. Lanham, MD: Rowman & Littlefield, 1999.

Ness, Jose, et al. "Use of Complementary Medicine in Older Americans: Results from the Health and Retirement Study." *Gerontologist* 45, no. 4 (2005): 516–24.

Nesteruk, Olena, and Christine A. Price. "Retired Women and Volunteering: the Good, the Bad, and the Unrecognized. *Journal of Women and Aging* 23, no. 2 (2011): 99–112.

Netting, F. Ellen. "Bridging Critical Feminist Gerontology and Social Work to Interrogate the Narrative of Civic Engagement." *Affilia: Journal of Women and Social Work* 26, no. 3 (2011): 239–49.

Neuhaus, Ruby, and Robert Neuhaus. *Successful Aging*. Lanham, MD: University Press of America, 1992.

Newberg, Andrew B. "Spirituality and the Aging Brain." *Generations* 35, no. 2 (2011): 83–89.

"New Report Shows Inequity in Women's Earnings Continues with Social Security." *Aging Today* 33, no. 4 (July–August 2012): 10.

Neysmith, Sheila. "Feminist Methodologies: A Consideration of Principles and Practice for Research in Gerontology." *Canadian Journal on Aging/La Revue Canadienne Du Vieillissment* 14, supplement 1 (1995): 100–118.

Nikola, R. J. *Creatures of Water*. Salt Lake City, UT: Europa Therapeutic, 1997.

Northrup, Christiane. *Women's Bodies, Women's Wisdom*. New York: Bantam, 1998.

Nussbaum, Paul D. "Brain Health: Bridging Neuroscience to Consumer Application." *Generations* 35, no. 2 (2011): 6–12.

Nydegger, Corinne N. "Family Ties of the Aged in Cross-Cultural Perspective." In *Growing Old in America*. 3rd ed. Edited by Beth B. Hess and Elizabeth Markson. New Brunswick, NJ: Transaction Books, 1986.

Oakley, Robin. "Empowering Knowledge and Practices of Namaqualand Elders." In *Contesting Aging and Loss*, edited by Janice E. Graham and Peter H. Stephenson. Toronto: University of Toronto Press, 2010.

O'Brien, Sharon J., and Patricia Vertinsky. "Elderly Women, Exercise, and Healthy Aging." *Journal of Women and Aging* 3 (1990): 41–65.

Older Women's League. "The Path to Poverty: An Analysis of Women's Retirement Income." In *Critical Gerontology*, edited by Meredith Minkler and Carroll L. Estes. Amityville, NY: Baywood, 1999.

Oldman, Christine. "Later Life and the Social Model of Disability: A Comfortable Partnership?" *Ageing and Society* 22 (2002): 791–806.

Ollenburger, Jane C., and Helen A. Moore. *A Sociology of Women*. 2nd ed. Upper Saddle River, NJ: Prentice Hall, 1998.

Olshansky, S. Jay, et al. "Potential Decline in Life Expectancy in the 21st Century." *New England Journal of Medicine* 352, no. 11 (March 17, 2005): 1138–45.

Olson, Laura Katz, ed. *Age through Ethnic Lenses: Caring for the Elderly in a Multicultural Society*. Lanham, MD: Rowman & Littlefield, 2001.

———. *The Not-So-Golden Years: Caregiving, the Frail Elderly, and the Long-Term Care Establishment*. Lanham, MD: Rowman & Littlefield, 2003.

———. "Women and Old Age Income Security in the United States." In *Aging in a Gendered World*. Santo Domingo: INSTRAW, 1999.

Onyx, Jenny, and Pam Benton. "What Does Retirement Mean for Women?" In *Revisioning Aging: Empowerment of Older Women*, edited by Jenny Onyx, Rosemary Leonard, and Rosslyn Reed. New York: Peter Lang, 1999.

Onyx, Jenny, Rosemary Leonard, and Rosslyn Reed, eds. *Revisioning Aging: Empowerment of Older Women*. New York: Peter Lang, 1999.

O'Rand, Angela M., and John C. Henretta. *Age and Inequality*. Boulder, CO: Westview, 1999.

Ory, Marcia G., and Huber R. Warner, eds. *Gender, Health and Longevity: Multidisciplinary Perspectives.* New York: Springer, 1990.

"Our Mothers, Ourselves: Older Women's Health Care." In *Annual Editions: Women's Health 98/99.* Guilford, CT: Dushkin McGraw-Hill, 1998.

Overall, Christine. *Aging, Death, and Human Longevity: A Philosophical Inquiry.* Berkeley: University of California Press, 2003.

———. "Old Age and Ageism, Impairment and Ableism: Exploring the Conceptual and Material Connections." *National Women's Studies Association Journal* 18, no. 1 (2006): 126–37.

Ovrebo, Beverly, and Meredith Minkler. "The Lives of Older Women: Perspectives from Political Economy and the Humanities." In *Voices and Visions of Aging,* edited by Thomas R. Cole et al. New York: Springer, 1993.

Palmore, Erdman B. *Ageism.* 2nd ed. New York: Springer, 1999.

Pan, Cynthia, Emily Chai, and Jeff Farber. *Myths of the High Medical Cost of Old Age and Dying.* New York: International Longevity Center USA, 2007.

"Part D Disaster." *The Alliance* [Maine People's Alliance] (Summer 2006): 12.

Patterson, Michael C. and Susan Perlstein. "Good for the Heart, Good for the Soul: The Creative Arts and Brain Health in Later Life." *Generations* 35, no. 2 (Summer 2011): 27–36.

Pear, Robert. "Gap in Life Expectancy Widens for the Nation." *New York Times,* March 23, 2008, 14.

———. "In a Shift, Medicare Pushes Bids." *New York Times,* April 12, 2012, B1.

———. "Medicare Spending for Care at Home Plunges by 45%." *New York Times,* April 21, 2000, A1, A18.

Peck, Richard A., and Iva Lim Peck. "Tai Chi Chuan for Pain Management." *Pain Practitioner* 9, no. 4 (1999): 1–2.

Peron, Emily P., and Christine M. Ruby. "A Primer on Medication Use in Older Adults for the Non-Clinician." *Generations* 35, no. 4 (Winter 2011–12): 12–18.

Perry, Daniel. "Entrenched Ageism in Healthcare Isolates, Ignores and Imperils Elders." *Aging Today* 33, no. 2 (2012): 1, 10.

Perry, Merry G. "Animated Gerontophobia: Ageism, Sexism, and the Disney Villainess." In *Aging and Identity: A Humanities Perspective,* edited by Sara Munson Deats and Lagretta Tallent Lenker. Westport, CT: Praeger, 1999.

Phelan, Amanda. "Socially Constructing Older People: Examining Discourses which Can Shape Nurses' Understanding and Practice." *Journal of Advanced Nursing* 67, no. 4 (2011): 893–903.

Phillipson, Chris. "Ageing and Globalization." In *Social Theory, Social Policy: A Critical Introduction,* edited by Simon Biggs, Carroll L. Estes, and Chris Phillipson. Maidenhead, Berkshire: Open University Press, 2003.

———. "The Dynamic Nature of Societal Aging in a Global Perspective." In *Enduring Questions in Gerontology,* edited by Debra J. Sheets, Dana Burr Bradley, and Jon Hendricks. New York: Springer, 2006.

———. *Reconstructing Old Age: New Agendas in Social Theory and Practice.* London: Sage, 1998.

Polivka, Larry. "The Growing Neoliberal Threat to the Economic Security of Workers and Retirees." *Gerontologist* 52, no. 1 (2012): 133–43.

Polivka, Larry, and Charles F. Longino Jr. "The Emerging Postmodern Culture of Aging and Retirement Security." In *Aging, Globalization and Inequality: The New Critical Gerontology*, edited by Jan Baars et al. Amityville, NY: Baywood, 2006.

Poor, Susan, Candace Baldwin, and Judy Willett. "The Village Movement Empowers Older Adults to Stay Connected to Home and Community." *Generations* 36, no. 1 (2012): 112–17.

Porcino, Jane. "Psychological Aspects of Aging in Women." In *Health Needs of Women as They Age*, edited by Sharon Golub and Rita Jackaway Freedman. New York: Haworth, 1985.

Posner, Richard. *Aging and Old Age*. Chicago: University of Chicago Press, 1995.

Pousada, Lidia. "Hip Fractures." *The Encyclopedia of Aging*. 2nd ed. Edited by George L. Maddox. New York: Springer, 1995.

Powell, Jason L. "Social Theory, Aging, and Health and Welfare Professionals: A Foucauldian 'Toolkit.'" *Journal of Applied Gerontology* 28, no. 6 (2009): 669–82.

Power, G. Allen. *Dementia beyond Drugs: Changing the Culture of Care*. Baltimore: Health Professions Press, 2010.

Price, Christine Ann. *Women and Retirement: The Unexplored Tradition*. New York: Garland, 1998.

Price, Elizabeth. "Gay and Lesbian Carers: Ageing in the Shadow of Dementia." *Ageing and Society* 32 (2012): 516–32.

Pruchno, Rachel. "Not Your Mother's Old Age: Baby Boomers at Age 65." *Gerontologist* 52, no. 2 (2012): 149–52.

Pruchno, Rachel A., and Michael A. Smyer. *Challenges of an Aging Society: Ethical Dilemmas, Political Issues*. Baltimore: Johns Hopkins University Press, 2007.

Quadagno, Jill. *Aging and the Life Course*. Boston: McGraw-Hill, 1999.

———. *One Nation Uninsured: Why the U.S. Has No National Health Insurance*. Oxford: Oxford University Press, 2005.

———. "Social Security and the Myth of the Entitlement 'Crisis.'" *Gerontologist* 36, no. 3 (1996): 391–99.

Quinn-Musgrove, Sandra L. "Extended Caregiving: The Experience of Surviving Spouses." In *Women, Aging, and Ageism*, edited by Evelyn R. Rosenthal. New York: Harrington Park, 1990.

Randall, William L. "Memory, Metaphor, and Meaning: Reading for Wisdom in the Stories of Our Lives." In *Storying Later Life*, edited by Gary Kenyon, Ernst Bohlmeijer, and William Randall. Oxford: Oxford University Press, 2011.

Rao, Shoba S. "Prevention of Falls in Older Patients." *American Family Physician* 72, no. 1 (2005): 81–88.

Ray, Ruth E. *Beyond Nostalgia: Aging and Life-Story Writing*. Charlottesville: University Press of Virginia, 2000.

———. "Coming of Age in Critical Gerontology." *Journal of Aging Studies* 22, no. 2 (2008): 1–4.

———. *Endnotes: An Intimate Look at the End of Life*. New York: Columbia University Press, 2008.

———. "Feminist Readings of Older Women's Life Stories." *Journal of Aging Studies* 12, no. 2 (1998): 117–27.

——. "A Postmodern Perspective on Feminist Gerontology." *Gerontologist* 36, no. 5 (1996): 674–80.

——. "Researching to Transgress: The Need for Critical Feminism in Gerontology." *Journal of Women and Aging* 11, nos. 2–3 (1999): 171–84.

——. "Social Influences on the Older Woman's Life Story." *Generations* (Winter 1999–2000): 56–62.

Red Horse, John G. "American Indian Elders: Unifiers of Families." *Social Casework* 61 (1980): 490–93.

Reed, Alyson. "Health Care Special: Women, Disparities, and Discrimination." *Civil Rights Journal* 4, no. 1 (1999): 42–48.

Reich, Robert B. "Broken Faith: Why We Need to Renew the Social Contract." *Generations* 22, no. 4 (1998–1999): 19–24.

Reinhardt, Uwe E. "How to Lower the Cost of Drugs." *New York Times*, January 3, 2000, A19.

Reinharz, Shulamit. "Friends or Foes? Gerontological and Feminist Theory." In *The Other Within: Feminist Explorations of Aging*, edited by Marilyn Pearsall. Boulder, CO: Westview, 1997.

Rendell, Jane, Barbara Penner, and Iain Borden, eds. *Gender, Space, Architecture*. London: Routledge, 2000.

Rentsch, Thomas. "Aging as Becoming Oneself: A Philosophical Ethics of Late Life." *Journal of Aging Studies* 11, no. 4 (1997): 263–72.

"Report Calls Substance Abuse, Addiction by Older Women 'Epidemic.'" *Women's Health Weekly*, June 15, 1998, 2–4.

"Researchers Warn of Drug Price Crisis." *Portland Press Herald*, July 27, 1999, 8A.

Riley, Matilda White, and John W. Riley Jr. "Structural Lag: Past and Future." In *Age and Structural Lag*, edited by Matilda White Riley, Robert L. Kahn, and Anne Foner. New York: Wiley, 1994.

Rimer, Sara. "Caring for Elderly Kin Is Costly, Study Finds." *New York Times*, November 27, 1999, A8.

Rizza, Carolyn C. "Caregiving: A Deeply Felt Human Need." In *Social Gerontology*, edited by David E. Redburn and Robert P. McNamara. Westport, CT: Auburn House, 1998.

Robert, Stephanie A., and James S. House. "Socioeconomic Status and Health over the Life Course." In *Aging and Quality of Life*, edited by Ronald P. Abeles et al. New York: Springer, 1994.

Roberto, Karen. "The Study of Chronic Pain in Later Life: Where Are the Women?" *Journal of Women and Aging* 6, no. 4 (1994): 1–7.

Robertson, Ann. "Beyond Apocalyptic Demography: Toward a Moral Economy of Interdependence." In *Critical Gerontology*, edited by Meredith Minkler and Carroll L. Estes. Amityville, NY: Baywood, 1999.

Rodeheaver, Dean. "When Old Age Became a Social Problem, Women Were Left Behind." *Gerontologist* 27, no. 6 (1987): 741–46.

Rodeheaver, Dean, and Nancy Datan. "The Challenge of Double Jeopardy: Toward a Mental Health Agenda for Aging Women." *American Psychologist* 43, no. 8 (1988): 648–54.

Rose, Michael. *The Long Tomorrow: How Advances in Evolutionary Biology Can Help Us Postpone Aging*. Oxford: Oxford University Press, 2005.

Roseberry, Lynn. "Beyond Intersectionality: Toward a Post-Structuralist Approach to Multiple Discrimination." Online Social Science Research Network, Sept. 1, 2010. ssrn.com/abstract=1686774.

Rosenfeld, Dana. "Lesbian, Gay, Bisexual and Transgender Ageing: Shattering Myths, Capturing Lives." In *The SAGE Handbook of Social Gerontology*, edited by Dale Dannefer and Chris Phillipson. Los Angeles: SAGE, 2010.

Rosenthal, Evelyn R. "Women and Varieties of Ageism." In *Women, Aging, and Ageism*, edited by Evelyn R. Rosenthal. New York: Harrington Park, 1990.

Rosofsky, Ira. *Nasty, Brutish, and Long: Adventures in Eldercare*. New York: Avery Penguin, 2009.

Rossi, Alice. "Sex and Gender in the Aging Society." In *Our Aging Society*, edited by Alan Pifer and Lydia Bronte. New York: Norton, 1986.

Roszak, Theodore. *America the Wise*. Boston: Houghton Mifflin, 1998.

Roush, Wade. "Live Longer and Prosper." *Science* 273 (July 5, 1996): 42.

Rowe, John W., and Robert L. Kahn. *Successful Aging*. New York: Pantheon, 1998.

Rozanova, Julia. "Discourse of Successful Aging in *The Globe & Mail*: Insights from Critical Gerontology." *Journal of Aging Studies* 24 (2010): 213–22.

Rozanova, Julia, Norah Keating, and Jacquie Eales. "Unequal Social Engagement for Older Adults." *Canadian Journal of Aging* 31, no. 1 (2012).

Rubin, Lillian B. *60 on Up: The Truth about Aging in America*. Boston: Beacon Press, 2007.

Ruddick, Sara. "Virtues and Age." In *Mother Time: Women, Aging, and Ethics*, edited by Margaret Urban Walker. Lanham, MD: Rowman & Littlefield, 1999.

Russo, Mary. "Aging and the Scandal of Anachronism." In *Figuring Age*, edited by Kathleen Woodward. Bloomington: Indiana University Press, 1999.

Sager, Alan, and Deborah Socolar. "Let's Seek a Drug Price Peace Treaty." *AARP Bulletin* 42, no. 6 (2001): 29.

Said, Edward. *Out of Place: A Memoir*. New York: Vintage Random, 1999.

Sankar, Andrea. "'It's Just Old Age': Old Age as a Diagnosis in American and Chinese Medicine." In *Age and Anthropological Theory*, edited by David Kertzer and Jenny Keith. Ithaca, NY: Cornell University Press, 1984.

Sapiro, Virginia. *Women in American Society: An Introduction to Women's Studies*. 4th ed. Mountain View, CA: Mayfield, 1999.

Sarton, May. *As We Are Now*. New York: Norton, 1973.

Scannell, Kate. "An Aging Un-American." *New England Journal of Medicine* 355, no. 14 (October 5, 2006): 1415–17.

Sceriha, Madge. "Women and Ageing: The Dreaded Older Woman Fights Back." In *Women's Health*. 3rd ed. Edited by Nancy Worcester and Marianne H. Whatley. Dubuque, IA: Kendall Hunt, 2000.

Schaie, K. Warner. "Intellectual Development in Adulthood." In *Handbook of the Psychology of Aging*. 4th ed. Edited by James E. Birren. San Diego: Academic Press, 1996.

Scharlach, Andrew E. "Caregiving and Employment: Competing or Complementary Roles?" *Gerontologist* 34, no. 3 (1994): 378–85.

——. "Creating Age-Friendly Cities." *Ageing International* 37, no. 1 (2012): 25–38.

Schmidt, Robert M. "Preventative Healthcare for Older Adults: Societal and Individual Services." *Generations* (Spring 1994): 33–38.

Scholl, Jane M., and Steven R. Sabat. "Stereotypes, Stereotype Threat and Ageing: Implications for the Understanding and Treatment of People with Alzheimer's Disease." *Ageing and Society* 28 (2008): 103–30.

Schor, Juliet. "The New Politics of Consumption." *Boston Review* (Summer 1999): 4–9.

Schulz, James H., and Robert H. Binstock. *Aging Nation: The Economics and Politics of Growing Older in America*. Westport, CT: Praeger, 2006.

Scott-Maxwell, Florida. *The Measure of My Days*. New York: Alfred Knopf, 1968.

Seltzer, Mildred. Review of *Women Growing Older: Psychological Perspectives*, by Barbara Turner and Lillian E. Troll. *Contemporary Gerontology* 1, no. 3 (1994): 101–3.

Sharpe, Patricia A. "Older Women and Health Services: Moving from Ageism toward Empowerment." *Women and Health* 22, no. 3 (1995): 9–23.

Sherman, David. "Geriatric Psychopharmacotherapy: Issues and Concerns." *Generations* 18, no. 2 (1994): 34–39.

Sinnott, Jan. "Developmental Models of Midlife and Aging in Women: Metaphors for Transcendence and for Individuality in Community." In *Handbook on Women and Aging*, edited by Jean M. Coyle. Westport, CT: Greenwood, 1997.

Sison, Alan. "Mental Functioning May Predict Mortality in Elderly." *Medical Tribune*, January 29, 2000. www.metrib.com.

Skinner, John H. "Aging in Place: The Experience of African American and Other Minority Elders." *Generations* 16, no. 2 (1992): 49–51.

Slevin, Kathleen. "If I Had Lots of Money I'd Have a Body Makeover: Managing the Aging Body." *Social Forces* 88, no. 3 (2010): 1003–20.

Small, Gary. "Predicting Alzheimer's 20 Years in Advance of Symptoms." *Aging News*. Newsletter of the Institute on Aging, University of Wisconsin–Madison (Fall–Winter 2010): 1.

Small, Helen. *The Long Life*. Oxford: Oxford University Press, 2010.

Smith, Glenna. *Old Maine Woman*. Yarmouth, ME: Islandport Press, 2011.

Smith, James. "New Directions in Socioeconomic Research in Aging." In *Aging and Quality of Life*, edited by Ronald P. Abeles et al. New York: Springer, 1994.

Sorgman, Margo I., and Marilou Sorensen. "Ageism: A Course of Study." *Theory into Practice* 23, no. 2 (1984): 119–23.

Spector-Mercel, G. "Never-Ending Stories: Western Hegemonic Masculinity Scripts." *Journal of Gender Studies* 15, no. 1 (2006): 67–82.

Stanford, E. Percil. "Diverse Black Aged." In *Aging and Inequality*, edited by Robynne Neugebauer-Visano. Toronto: Canadian Scholars Press, 1995.

———. "Mental Health, Aging, and Americans of African Descent." In *Serving Minority Elders in the 21st Century*, edited by May L. Wykle and Amasa B. Ford. New York: Springer, 1999.

Stanford, E. Percil, and Gerard Koskovich. *Diversity and Aging in the 21st Century. The Power of Inclusion*. Washington DC: AARP, 2010.

Stanford, E. Percil, and Donna L. Yee. "Gerontology and the Relevance of Diversity." In *Diversity: New Approaches to Ethnic Minority Aging*, edited by E. Percil Stanford and Fernando M. Torres-Gil. Amityville, NY: Baywood, 1992.

Stanley, Liz. "The Impact of Feminism on Sociology in the Last Twenty Years." In *The Knowledge Explosion: Generations of Feminist Scholarship*, edited by Cheris Kramarae and Dale Spender. New York: Teachers College Press, 1992.

Stannard, David. "Dilemmas of Aging in a Bureaucratic Society." In *Aging and the Elderly: Perspectives from the Humanities*, edited by Stuart Spicker, Kathleen Woodward, and David Van Tassel. Atlantic Highlands, NJ: Humanities Press, 1978.

Stavig, G. R., et al. "Hypertension among Asians and Pacific Islanders in California." *American Journal of Epidemiology* 119, no. 5 (1984): 677–91.

Steckenrider, Janie. "Aging as a Female Phenomenon." In *New Directions in Old Age Policies*, edited by Janie Steckenrider and Tonya M. Parrott. Albany: SUNY Press, 1998.

Steinman, Michael. "Handle with Caution." Letter to the Editor, *New York Times*, April 23, 2012.

Sternberg, Robert J. "Older but Not Wiser: The Relationship between Age and Wisdom." *Ageing International* 30, no. 1 (2005): 5–26.

Stolberg, Sheryl Gay. "Alternative Medical Care Gains a Foothold." *New York Times*, January 31, 2000, A1, A6.

———. "The Boom in Medications Brings Rise in Fatal Risks." *New York Times*, June 3, 1999, A1.

———. "Drug Switching Saves Money, but There Is a Cost." *New York Times*, June 13, 1999, sec. 4, 3.

———. "FDA Pushes for Prescription Drug Guides." *New York Times*, June 4, 1999, A23.

———. "Gasping for Breath." Two-part series. *New York Times*, October 18–19, 1999.

Stolberg, Sheryl Gay, and Jeff Gerth. "How Companies Stall Generics and Keep Themselves Healthy." *New York Times*, July 23, 2000, 1.

Stoller, Nancy. "Innovative Models of Chronic Care: Lessons for Aging from Grassroots Movements." *Critical Issues in Aging* no. 2 (1998): 15–17.

Svetkey, L. P., et al. "Black/White Differences in Hypertension in the Elderly." *American Journal of Epidemiology* 137, no. 1 (1993): 64–73.

Swift, Jonathan. *Gulliver's Travels*, edited by Robert A. Greenberg. New York: Norton, 1961.

Tagliabue, John. "Taking on Dementia with the Experiences of Normal Life." *New York Times*, April 25, 2012, A12.

Talbot, Margaret. "The Placebo Prescription." *New York Times Magazine*, January 9, 2000, 34–39.

Tappan, Frances M., and Patricia J. Benjamin. *Tappan's Handbook of Healing Massage Techniques*. Stamford, CT: Appleton and Lange, 1998.

Taylor, Anne L. "Coronary Heart Disease in Women." In *Serving Minority Elders in the 21st Century*, edited by May L. Wykle and Amasa B. Ford. New York: Springer, 1999.

Teaster, Pamela B., Karen A. Roberto, and Tyler A. Dugar. "Intimate Partner Violence of Rural Aging Women." *Family Relations* 55 (2006): 636–48.

Temin, Christine. "The Faces of Alice Neel." *Boston Globe*, October 13, 2000, C1.

Tesh, Sylvia Noble. *Hidden Arguments: Political Ideology and Disease Prevention Policy*. New Brunswick, NJ: Rutgers University Press, 1988.

Thomas, Vicki. "Overdosing on Drug Ads." *Aging Today* 20, no. 5 (1999): 7–8.

Thompson, April. "Inside the Brain: New Research Prescribes Mental Exercise." *Aging Today* 20, no. 4 (1999): 8.

Thompson, Neil. Review of *Ageism, the Aged, and Aging*, by Ursala Adler Falk and Gerhard Falk. *Ageing and Society* 18 (1998): 379–80.

Toner, Robin. "Mother: Free, Equal, and Not at Home." Review of *Care and Equality* by Mona Harrington. *New York Times Book Review*, August 29, 1999, 29.

Tornstam, Lars. *Gerotranscendance*. New York: Springer, 2005.

Torres, Sara. "Barriers to Mental-Health-Care Access Faced by Hispanic Elderly." In *Serving Minority Elders in the 21st Century*, edited by May L. Wykle and Amasa B. Ford. New York: Springer, 1999.

Torres-Gil, Fernando M. "Immigrants Aging in America." Presentation at the American Society on Aging/National Council on Aging annual meeting, Washington, DC, March 28, 2008.

Tournier, Paul. *Learn to Grow Old*. Translated by Edwin Hudson. New York: Harper and Row, 1972.

Townsend, Peter. "Ageism and Social Policy." In *Aging and Social Policy: A Critical Assessment*, edited by Chris Phillipson and Alan Walker. London: Gower, 1986.

Trager, Ellen Lutch. "Cheaper RXs for Seniors." *Boston Globe*, January 4, 1999, A13.

Trawinski, Lori. "The Foreclosure Crisis: Ending the Nightmare for Older Americans." AARP/Public Policy Institute presentation, July 23, 2012.

Trease, Judy. "Immigrants Aging in America." Presentation at the American Society on Aging/National Council on Aging annual meeting, Washington, DC, March 28, 2008.

Tripp-Reimer, Toni. "Culturally Competent Care." In *Serving Minority Elders in the 21st Century*, edited by May L. Wykle and Amasa B. Ford. New York: Springer, 1999.

Trollope, Anthony. *The Fixed Period*. Edited by R. H. Super. Ann Arbor: University of Michigan Press, 1990 [1882].

Tronto, Joan. "Age-Segregated Housing as a Moral Problem: An Exercise in Rethinking Ethics." In *Mother Time: Women, Aging, and Ethics*, edited by Margaret Urban Walker. Lanham, MD: Rowman & Littlefield, 1999.

Tulle, Emmanuelle. "Rethinking Agency in Later Life." In *Old Age and Agency*, edited by Emmanuelle Tulle. New York: Nova Science, 2004.

Tuokko, Holly, and Fiona Hunter. "Using Age as a Fitness-to-Drive Criterion for Older Adults." Report prepared for the Law Commission of Canada, 2002.

Turkle, Sherry. "Technology and Conversation." *New York Times*, April 22, 2012.

Twigg, Julia. "The Body, Gender, and Age: Feminist Insights in Social Gerontology." *Journal of Aging Studies* 18, no. 1 (2004): 59–73.

———. "Clothing, Age, and the Body: A Critical Review." *Ageing and Society* 27 (2007): 285–305.

———. "Fashion and Age: The Role of Women's Magazines in the Constitution of Aged Identities." In *Representing Ageing: Image and Identity*, edited by Virpi Ylanne. Houndmills, Basingstoke, Hampshire: Palgrave Macmillan, 2012.

"Two MetLife Studies Reveal the High Cost of Caregiving." *Aging Today* (November–December 2006): 4.

Tyrrell, Mary O'Brien. *Become a Memoirist for Elders*. St. Paul: Memoirs, Inc., 2012.

Tyson, Ann Scott. "Old Women and Retirement: A Luxury They Can't Afford." *Christian Science Monitor*, July 17, 1998, 8.

Verbrugge, Lois M. "Disability in Late Life." In *Aging and Quality of Life*, edited by Ronald P. Abeles et al. New York: Springer, 1994.

———. "Gender, Aging, and Health." In *Aging and Health: Perspectives on Gender, Race, Ethnicity, and Class*, edited by Kyriakos S. Markides. Newbury Park, CA: Sage, 1989.

———. "The Twain Meet: Empirical Evidence of Sex Differences in Health and Mortality." In *Gender, Health, and Longevity*, edited by Marcia G. Ory and Huber R. Warner. New York: Springer, 1990.

Verbrugge, Lois M., and Deborah L. Wingard. "Sex Differentials in Health and Mortality." *Women and Health* 12, no. 2 (1987): 103–43.

Villa, Valentine M. "Aging Policy and the Experience of Older Minorities." In *New Directions in Old Age*, edited by Janie S. Steckenrider and Tonya M. Parrott. Albany: SUNY Press, 1998.

Villa, Valentine M., et al. "Hispanic Baby Boomers: Health Inequities Likely to Persist in Old Age." *Gerontologist* 52, no. 2 (2012): 166–76.

Vincent, John A. "Globalization and Critical Theory: Political Economy of World Population Issues." In *Aging, Globalization and Inequality: The New Critical Gerontology*, edited by Jan Baars, Dale Dannefer, Chris Phillipson, and Alan Walker. Amityville, NY: Baywood, 2006.

———. *Inequality and Old Age*. New York: St. Martin's, 1995.

———. "Science and Imagery in the 'War on Old Age.'" *Ageing and Society* 27 (2007): 941–61.

Vinton, Linda. "Working with Abused Older Women from a Feminist Perspective." *Journal of Women and Aging* 11, nos. 3–4 (1999): 85–100.

"Vitamin D Deficiency Is a Major Factor in Half of Women's Falls." *Aging News Alert*, May 4, 1999, 10.

Wade-Gayles, Gloria. "Who Says an Older Woman Can't/Shouldn't Dance?" In *Body Politics and the Fictional Double*, edited by Debra Walker King. Bloomington: Indiana University Press, 2000. Reprinted in *Fierce with Reality: An Anthology of Literature on Aging*, edited by Margaret Cruikshank. Topsham, ME: Just Write Books, 2007.

Wadsworth, Nancy S., and Stephanie J. FallCreek. "Culturally Competent Care Teams." In *Serving Minority Elders in the 21st Century*, edited by Amasa B. Ford and May L. Wykle. New York: Springer, 1999.

Walford, Roy. *Maximum Life Span*. New York: Norton, 1983.

Walker, Alan. "Re-examining the Political Economy of Aging: Understanding the Structure/Agency Tension." In *Aging, Globalization, and Inequality: The New Gerontology*, edited by Jan Baars et al. Amityville, NY: Bayview, 2006.

Walker, Alice. "In Search of Our Mothers' Gardens." In *In Search of Our Mothers' Gardens: Womanist Prose*. New York: Harcourt Brace, 1983.

Walker, Barbara. *The Crone: Women of Age, Wisdom, and Power*. San Francisco: Harper and Row, 1985.

Walker, Margaret Urban. "Getting Out of Line: Alternatives to Life as a Career." In *Mother Time: Women, Aging, and Ethics*, edited by Margaret Urban Walker. Lanham, MD: Rowman & Littlefield, 1999.

———. *Moral Contexts*. Lanham, MD: Rowman & Littlefield, 2003.

———. ed. *Mother Time: Women, Aging, and Ethics*. Lanham, MD: Rowman & Littlefield, 1999.

Wallace, Steven P. "The Political Economy of Health Care for Elderly Blacks." In *Critical Perspectives on Aging*, edited by Meredith Minkler and Carroll L. Estes. Amityville, NY: Baywood, 1991.

Wallace, Steven P., and Elisa Linda Facio. "Moving beyond Familism: Potential Contributions of Gerontological Theory to Studies of Chicano/Latino Aging." *Journal of Aging Studies* 1, no. 4 (1987): 337–54.

Wallace, Steven P., and V. M. Villa. "Caught in Hostile Crossfire: Public Policy and Minority Elderly in the United States." In *Minorities, Aging, and Health*, edited by K. S. Markides and M. R. Miranda. Thousand Oaks, CA: Sage, 1997.

Wallack, Lawrence. "Japan's Health Sacrifice." Letter to the Editor, *New York Times*, January 7, 2000, A22.

Wallis, Velma. *Two Old Women: An Alaskan Legend of Betrayal, Courage, and Survival*. Fairbanks, AK: Epicenter Press, 1993.

Ward-Griffin, Catherine, and Jenny Ploeg. "A Feminist Approach to Health Promotion for Older Women." *Canadian Journal of Aging* 17, no. 2 (1997): 279–96.

Warren, Lorna, and Amanda Clarke. "'Woo-hoo, What a Ride!' Older People, Life Stories and Active Ageing." In *Valuing Older People*, edited by Ricca Edmondson and Hans-Joachim von Kondratowitz. Bristol: The Policy Press, 2009.

Weg, Ruth. "Beyond Babies and Orgasm." In *Growing Old in America*. 3rd ed. Edited by Beth B. Hess and Elizabeth Markson. New Brunswick, NJ: Transaction Books, 1986.

Wei, Wenhui, et al. "Gender Differences in Out-of-Pocket Prescription Drug Expenditures among the Elderly." *Research on Aging* 28, no. 4 (2006): 427–53.

Weil, Andrew. *Healthy Aging*. New York: Knopf, 2005.

Weintraub, Arlene. "Selling the Fountain of Youth: How the Anti-Aging Industry Made a Disease out of Getting Old and Made Billions." In *Aging Concepts and Controversies*. 7th ed. Edited by Harry R. Moody and Jennifer R. Sasser. Los Angeles: SAGE, 2012.

Weiss, David, and Frieder R. Lang. "'They' Are Old but 'I' Feel Younger: Age-group Dissociation as Self-Protective Strategy in Old Age." *Psychology and Aging* 27, no. 1 (2012): 153–63.

Welch, H. Gilbert, Lisa Schwartz, and Steven Woloshin. "What's Making Us Sick Is an Epidemic of Diagnoses." *New York Times*, January 2, 2007.

Wendell, Susan. "Old Women out of Control: Some Thoughts on Aging, Ethics, and Psychosomatic Medicine." In *Mother Time: Women, Aging, and Ethics*, edited by Margaret Urban Walker. Lanham, MD: Rowman & Littlefield, 1999.

Wenger, G. Clare. "Dependence, Interdependence, and Reciprocity after Eighty." *Journal of Aging Studies* 1, no. 4 (1987): 355–77.

Wheeler, Helen Rippier. *Women and Aging: A Guide to the Literature*. Boulder, CO: Lynne Rienner, 1997.

Whitbourne, Susan Krauss. *The Aging Individual: Physical and Psychological Perspectives*. New York: Springer, 1996.

Whitehouse, Peter, and Daniel George. "The Aesthetics of Natural Elderhood." *Journal of Aging, Humanities and the Arts* 4 (2010): 292–301.

Whitfield, Keith E., and Tamara Baker-Thomas. "Individual Differences in Aging Minorities." *International Journal of Aging and Human Development* 48, no. 1 (1999): 73–79.

Whittaker, Terri. "Gender and Elder Abuse." In *Connecting Gender and Ageing*, edited by Sara Arber and Jay Ginn. Buckingham: Open University Press, 1995.

Wierenga, Christina E., and Mark W. Bondi. "Dementia and Alzheimer's Disease: What We Know Now." *Generations* 35, no. 2 (2011): 37–45.

Wilkinson, Jody A., and Kenneth F. Ferraro. "Thirty Years of Ageism Research." In *Ageism*, edited by Todd D. Nelson. Cambridge, MA: MIT Press, 2002.

Willett, Walter C., Graham Colditz, and Meir Stampfer. "Postmenopausal Estrogens: Opposed, Unopposed, or None of the Above." *Journal of the American Medical Association* 238, no. 4 (January 26, 2000): 534–35.

Williams, Angie, and Howard Giles. "Communication of Ageism." In *Communicating Prejudice*, edited by Michael L. Hecht. Thousand Oaks, CA: Sage, 1998.

Williamson, John B., and Sara E. Rix. "Social Security Reform: Implications for Women." *Journal of Aging and Social Policy* 11, no. 4 (2000): 41–68.

Winakur, Jerald. "'Frankenfolks and the Rise of Ageism." *Health Affairs* 30, no. 5 (May 2011): 995–97.

Winker, Margaret A. "Managing Medicine." In *The Practical Guide to Aging*, edited by Christine Cassel. New York: New York University Press, 1998.

Wohlrab-Sahr, Monika. "Atheist Convictions, Christian Beliefs, or 'Keeping Things Open.'" In *Valuing Older People*, edited by Ricca Edmondson and Hans-Joachim Kondratowitz. Bristol: The Policy Press, 2009.

"Women Face Challenges Ensuring Financial Security in Retirement." U.S. Government Accountability Office Report, October 2007.

Woo, Jean, Athena Hong, Edith Lau, and Henry Lynn. "Tai Chi and Resistance Exercise in the Elderly." *Age and Ageing* 36, no. 3 (2007): 262–68.

Wood, January. "'Productive Aging' Highlights Strengths." *National Association of Social Workers News* (February 2001): 12.

Woodward, Kathleen. "Against Wisdom: The Social Politics of Anger and Aging." *Cultural Critique* no. 51 (2002): 186–218. Reprinted in *Journal of Aging Studies* 17, no. 1 (2003): 55–67.

———, ed. *Figuring Age: Women, Bodies, Generations*. Bloomington: Indiana University Press, 1999.

———. "Telling Stories: Aging, Reminiscence, and the Life Review." *Journal of Aging and Identity* 2, no. 3 (1997): 149–63.

———. "Tribute to the Older Woman: Psychoanalysis, Feminism, and Ageism." In *Images of Aging: Cultural Representations of Later Life*, edited by Mike Featherstone and Andrew Wernick. London: Routledge, 1995.

Wray, L. A. "Health Policy and Ethnic Diversity in Older Americans: Dissonance or Harmony?" *Western Journal of Medicine* 157, no. 3 (1992): 357–61.

Wyatt-Brown, Anne, and Janice Rossen, eds. *Aging and Gender in Literature: Studies in Creativity*. Charlottesville: University of Virginia Press, 1993.

Wylie, Alison. "Afterword: On Waves." In *Feminist Anthropology*, edited by Pamela L. Geller and Miranda K. Stockett. Philadelphia: University of Pennsylvania Press, 2006.

Yee, Barbara W. K. "Gender and Family Issues in Minority Groups." In *Gender and Aging*, edited by Lou Glasse and Jon Hendricks. Amityville, NY: Baywood, 1992.

Yee, Barbara W. K., and Gayle D. Weaver. "Ethnic Minorities and Health Promotion: Developing a 'Culturally Competent' Agenda." *Generations* 18, no. 1 (1994): 39–44.

Yee, Donna L. "Preventing Chronic Iilness and Disability: Asian Americans." In *Serving Minority Elders in the 21st Century*, edited by May L. Wykle and Amasa B. Ford. New York: Springer, 1999.

Yeo, Gwen. "Ethnogeriatrics: Cross-Cultural Care of Older Adults." *Generations* 20, no. 4 (1996–1997): 72–77.

Yeo, Gwen, and Nancy Hikoyeda. "Asian and Pacific Islander American Elders." In *The Encyclopedia of Aging*. 3rd ed. Edited by George L. Maddox. New York: Springer, 2001.

Yeo, Gwen, and Melen McBride. "Cultural Diversity in Geriatrics and Gerontology Education." *Annual Review of Geriatrics and Gerontology Education* 28 (2008): 93–109.

Yorck von Wartenburg, Marion. *The Power of Solitude: My Life in the German Resistance*. Lincoln: University of Nebraska Press, 2000.

Zeilig, Hannah. "The Critical Use of Narratives and Literature in Gerontology." *International Journal of Aging and Later Life* 6, no. 2 (2011): 7–37.

Zuess, Jonathan. *The Wisdom of Depression*. New York: Harmony Books, 1998.

Index

About the Author

Margaret Cruikshank retired from the women's studies program and the graduate faculty of the University of Maine, where she continues as a faculty associate of the Center on Aging. For many years, Dr. Cruikshank taught English at City College of San Francisco.

Her book *Fierce with Reality: An Anthology of Literature on Aging* grew out of graduate study in gerontology at San Francisco State University. The first edition of *Learning to Be Old* received honorable mention on the best books of the year list of the Gustavus Myers Center for Human Rights in Boston. She has also written or edited books in history, literature, women's studies, and LGBT studies. Her numerous articles cover many subjects.

Cruikshank lives in a small coastal village in eastern Maine.